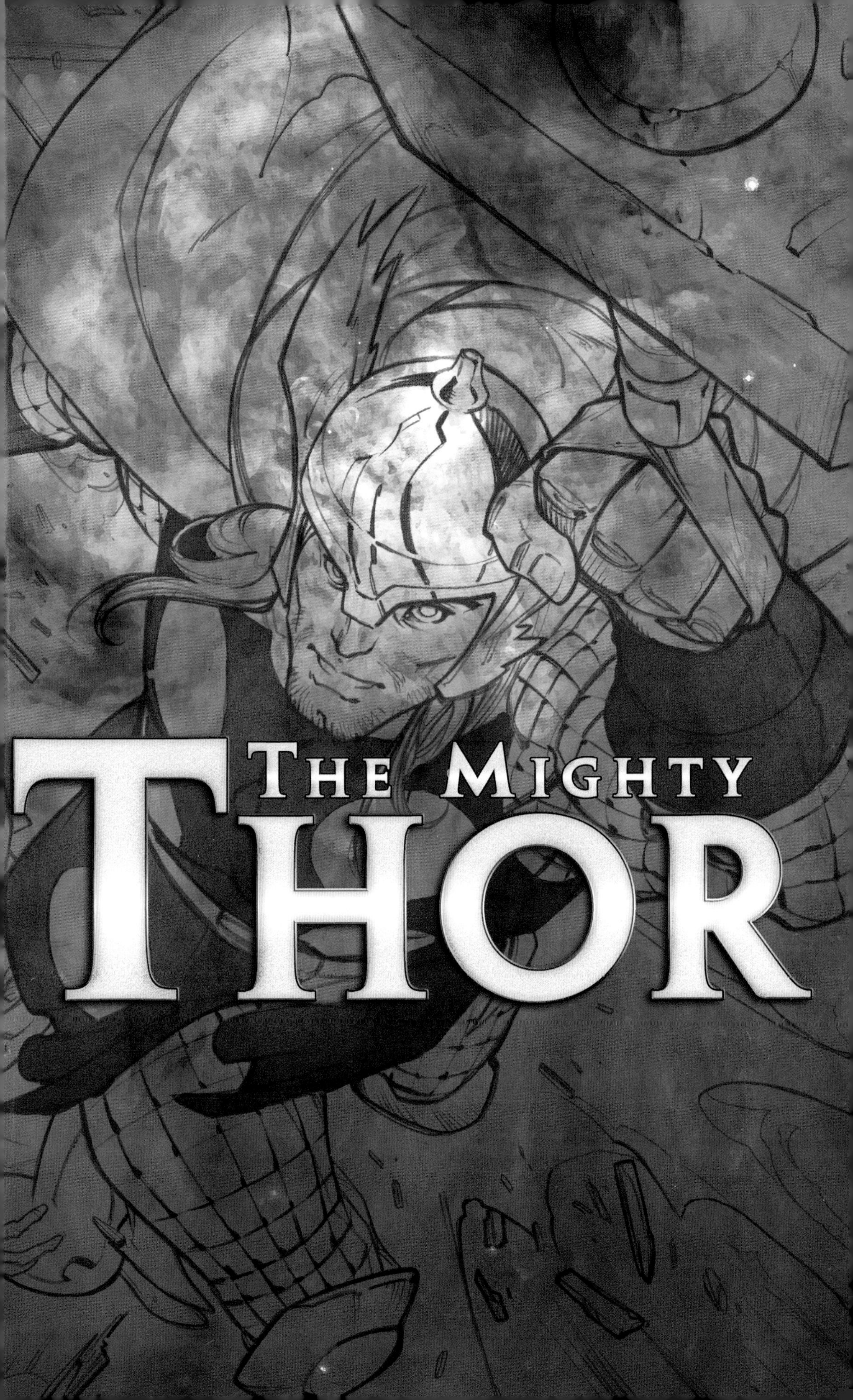
THE MIGHTY
THOR

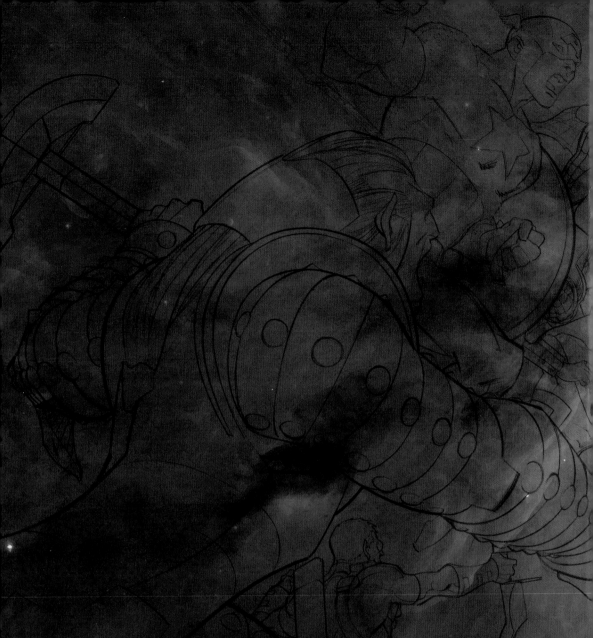

COLLECTION EDITOR: JENNIFER GRÜNWALD · ASSISTANT EDITORS: ALEX STARBUCK & NELSON RIBEIRO
EDITOR, SPECIAL PROJECTS: MARK D. BEAZLEY · SENIOR EDITOR, SPECIAL PROJECTS: JEFF YOUNGQUIST
SENIOR VICE PRESIDENT OF SALES: DAVID GABRIEL
SVP OF BRAND PLANNING & COMMUNICATIONS: MICHAEL PASCIULLO

EDITOR IN CHIEF: AXEL ALONSO · CHIEF CREATIVE OFFICER: JOE QUESADA
PUBLISHER: DAN BUCKLEY · EXECUTIVE PRODUCER: ALAN FINE

THE MIGHTY THOR BY MATT FRACTION VOL. 2. Contains material originally published in magazine form as THE MIGHTY THOR #7-12 and FEAR ITSELF: THOR #7.2. First printing 2012. Hardcover ISBN# 978-0-7851-6243-8. Softcover ISBN# 978-0-7851-5625-3. Published by MARVEL WORLDWIDE, INC., a subsidiary of MARVEL ENTERTAINMENT, LLC. OFFICE OF PUBLICATION: 135 West 50th Street, New York, N 10020. Copyright © 2011 and 2012 Marvel Characters, Inc. All rights reserved. Hardcover: $24.99 per copy in the U.S. and $27.99 in Canada (GST #R127032852). Softcover: $19.99 per copy in the U.S. an $21.99 in Canada (GST #R127032852). Canadian Agreement #40668537. All characters featured in this issue and the distinctive names and likenesses thereof, and all related indicia are trademarks of Marve Characters, Inc. No similarity between any of the names, characters, persons, and/or institutions in this magazine with those of any living or dead person or institution is intended, and any such similari which may exist is purely coincidental. **Printed in the U.S.A.** ALAN FINE, EVP - Office of the President, Marvel Worldwide, Inc. and EVP & CMO Marvel Characters B.V.; DAN BUCKLEY, Publisher & Preside - Print, Animation & Digital Divisions; JOE QUESADA, Chief Creative Officer; TOM BREVOORT, SVP of Publishing; DAVID BOGART, SVP of Operations & Procurement, Publishing; RUWAN JAYATILLEKE, SVP Associate Publisher, Publishing; C.B. CEBULSKI, SVP of Creator & Content Development; DAVID GABRIEL, SVP of Publishing Sales & Circulation; MICHAEL PASCIULLO, SVP of Brand Planning & Communication JIM O'KEEFE, VP of Operations & Logistics; DAN CARR, Executive Director of Publishing Technology; SUSAN CRESPI, Editorial Operations Manager; ALEX MORALES, Publishing Operations Manager; STA LEE, Chairman Emeritus. For information regarding advertising in Marvel Comics or on Marvel.com, please contact John Dokes, SVP Integrated Sales and Marketing, at jdokes@marvel.com. For Marv subscription inquiries, please call 800-217-9158. **Manufactured between 4/9/2012 and 11/14/2012 (hardcover), and 4/9/2012 and 11/12/2012 (softcover), by R.R. DONNELLEY, INC., SALEM, VA, USA**

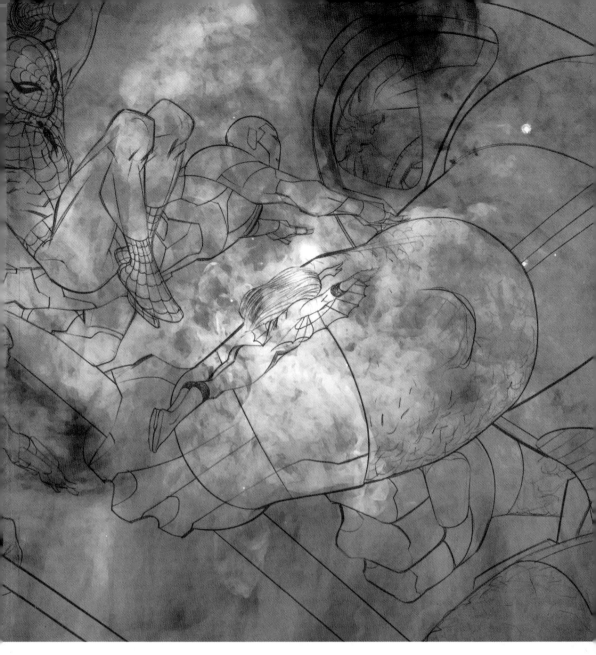

WRITER
MATT FRACTION

ARTISTS, #7-11 **PASQUAL FERRY** (#7 9 & #11) & **PEPE LARRAZ** (#9-11)
BREAKDOWNS, #12 **GIUSEPPE CAMUNCOLI** FINISHES, #12 **KLAUS JANSON**
COLOR ARTIST **FRANK D'ARMATA** LETTERER **VC'S JOE SABINO**
COVER ART **PASQUAL FERRY** & **FRANK D'ARMATA** (#7-10);
DALE KEOWN & **PETER STEIGERWALD** (#11); AND **GABRIELE DELL'OTTO** (#12)
ASSISTANT EDITORS **CHARLIE BECKERMAN** & **JOHN DENNING**
EDITORS **RALPH MACCHIO** & **LAUREN SANKOVITCH**

FEAR ITSELF: THOR #7.2
PENCILER **ADAM KUBERT**

INKER **MARK ROSLAN** COLORIST **LAURA MARTIN** LETTERER **CHRIS ELIOPOULOS**
COVER ART **ADAM KUBERT** & **FRANK D'ARMATA** ASSISTANT EDITOR **JOHN DENNING**
EDITOR **LAUREN SANKOVITCH** EXECUTIVE EDITOR **TOM BREVOORT**

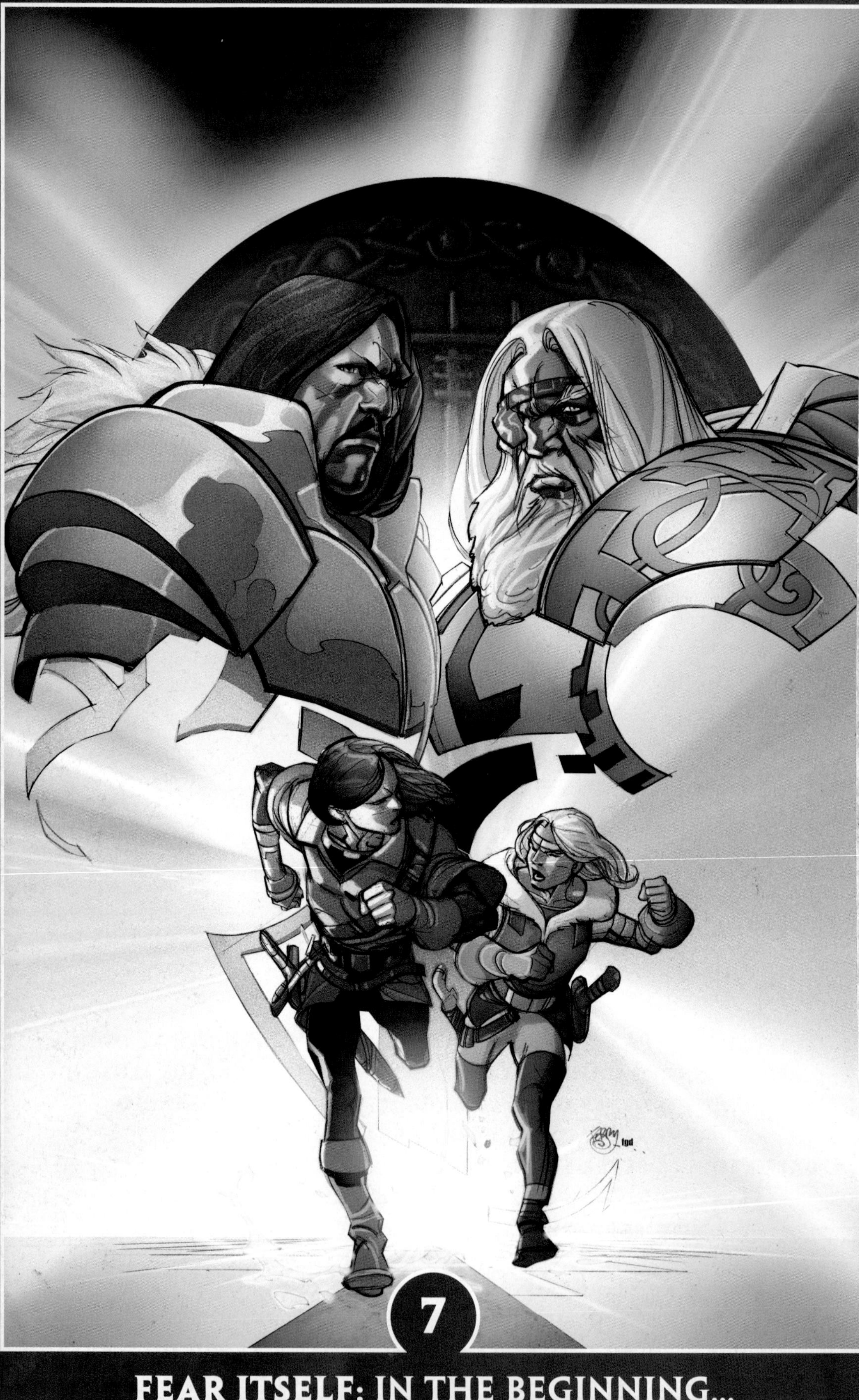

7

FEAR ITSELF: IN THE BEGINNING...

THE MIGHTY THOR
FEAR ITSELF: *IN THE BEGINNING...*

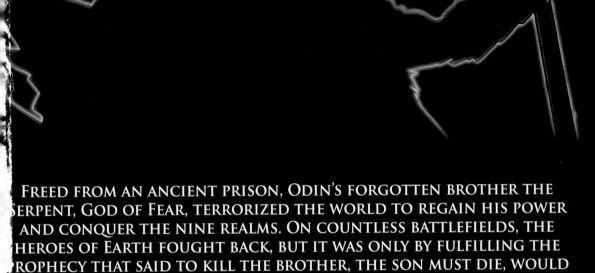

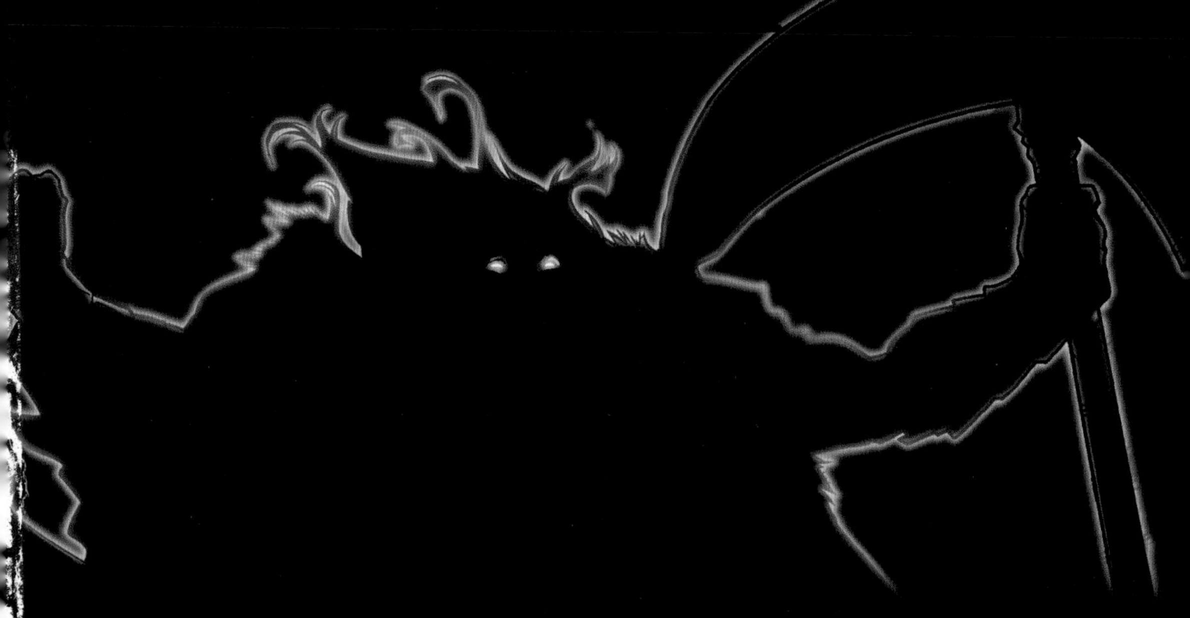

FREED FROM AN ANCIENT PRISON, ODIN'S FORGOTTEN BROTHER THE SERPENT, GOD OF FEAR, TERRORIZED THE WORLD TO REGAIN HIS POWER AND CONQUER THE NINE REALMS. ON COUNTLESS BATTLEFIELDS, THE HEROES OF EARTH FOUGHT BACK, BUT IT WAS ONLY BY FULFILLING THE PROPHECY THAT SAID TO KILL THE BROTHER, THE SON MUST DIE, WOULD EVERYONE BE SAVED FROM DARKNESS. SO IT WAS FORETOLD, WHEN THE SERPENT WAS DEAD, THOR TOOK NINE STEPS AND FELL.

THIS WAS THE SECOND WAR OF THE SERPENT. THE FIRST HAPPENED IN AESHEIM, WHICH WAS EARTH BEFORE THE DAWN OF OUR HISTORY, AND IT STARTED WITH TWO BROTHER GODS, THE SONS OF BOR...

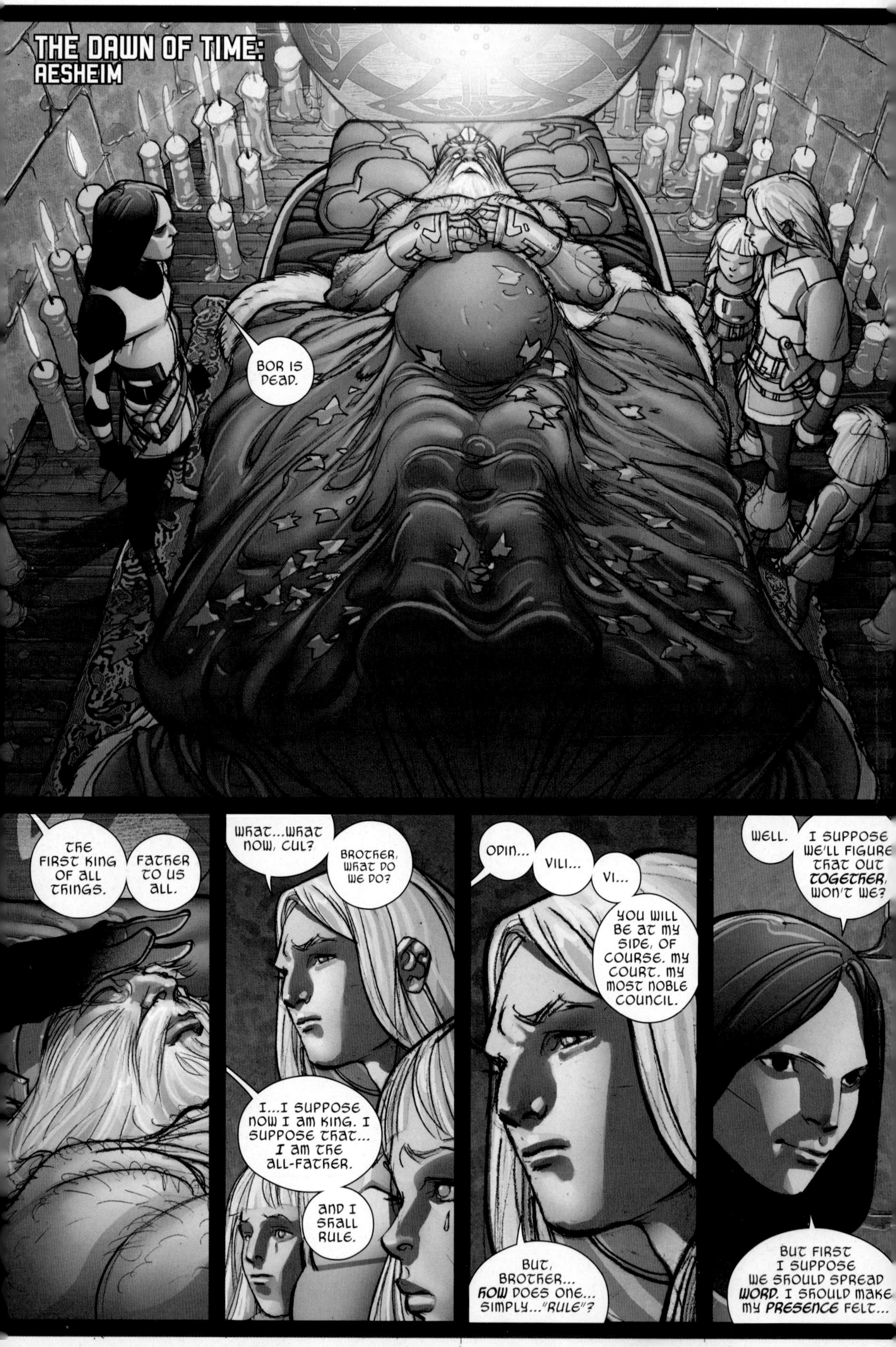
THE DAWN OF TIME:
AESHEIM
BOR IS DEAD.
THE FIRST KING OF ALL THINGS.
FATHER TO US ALL.
WHAT...WHAT NOW, CUL?
BROTHER, WHAT DO WE DO?
I...I SUPPOSE NOW I AM KING. I SUPPOSE THAT... I AM THE ALL-FATHER.
AND I SHALL RULE.
ODIN...
VILI...
VE...
YOU WILL BE AT MY SIDE, OF COURSE. MY COURT. MY MOST NOBLE COUNCIL.
BUT, BROTHER... HOW DOES ONE... SIMPLY..."RULE"?
WELL.
I SUPPOSE WE'LL FIGURE THAT OUT TOGETHER, WON'T WE?
BUT FIRST I SUPPOSE WE SHOULD SPREAD WORD. I SHOULD MAKE MY PRESENCE FELT...

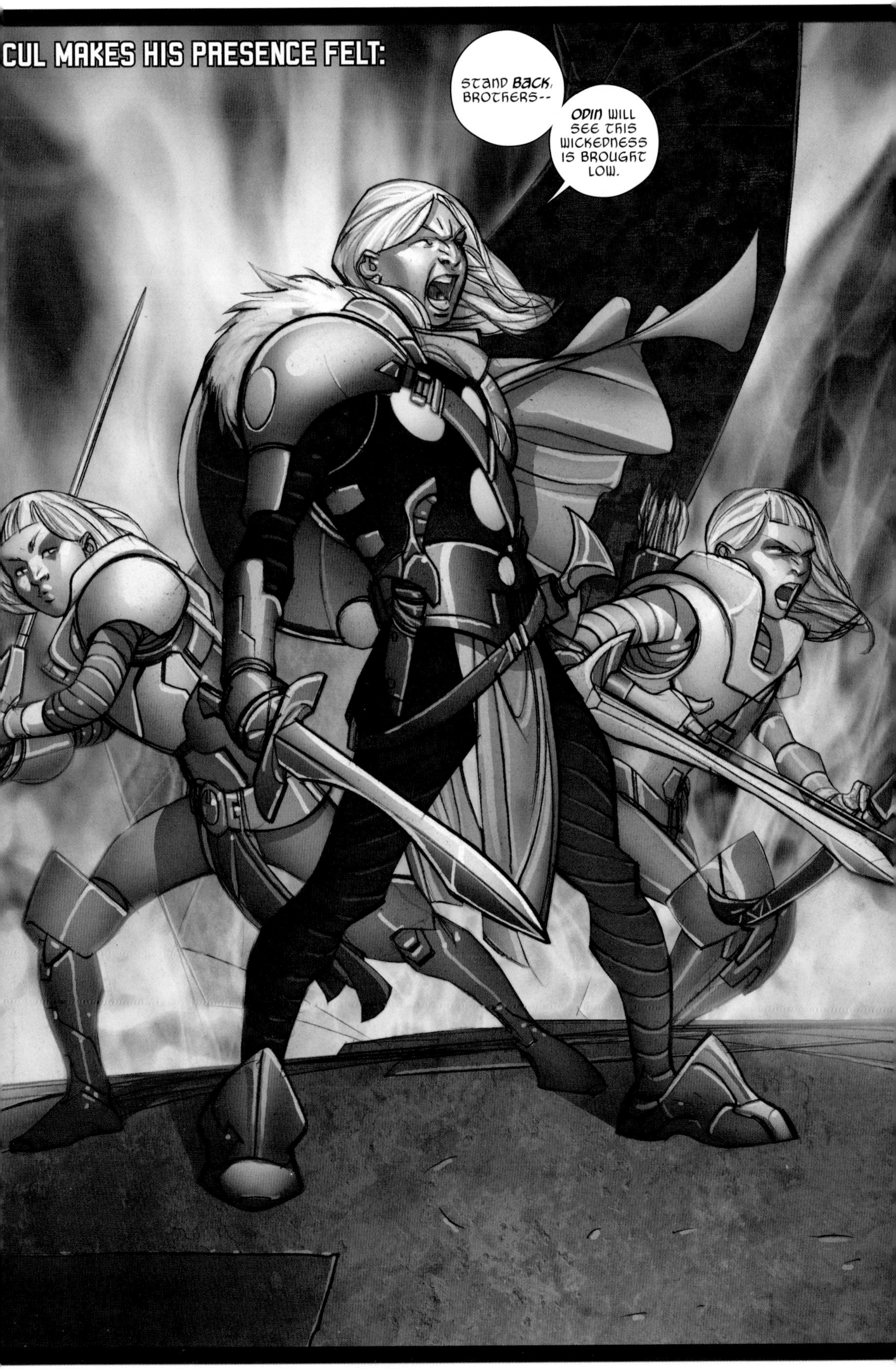
CUL MAKES HIS PRESENCE FELT:
STAND BACK, BROTHERS--
ODIN WILL SEE THIS WICKEDNESS IS BROUGHT LOW.

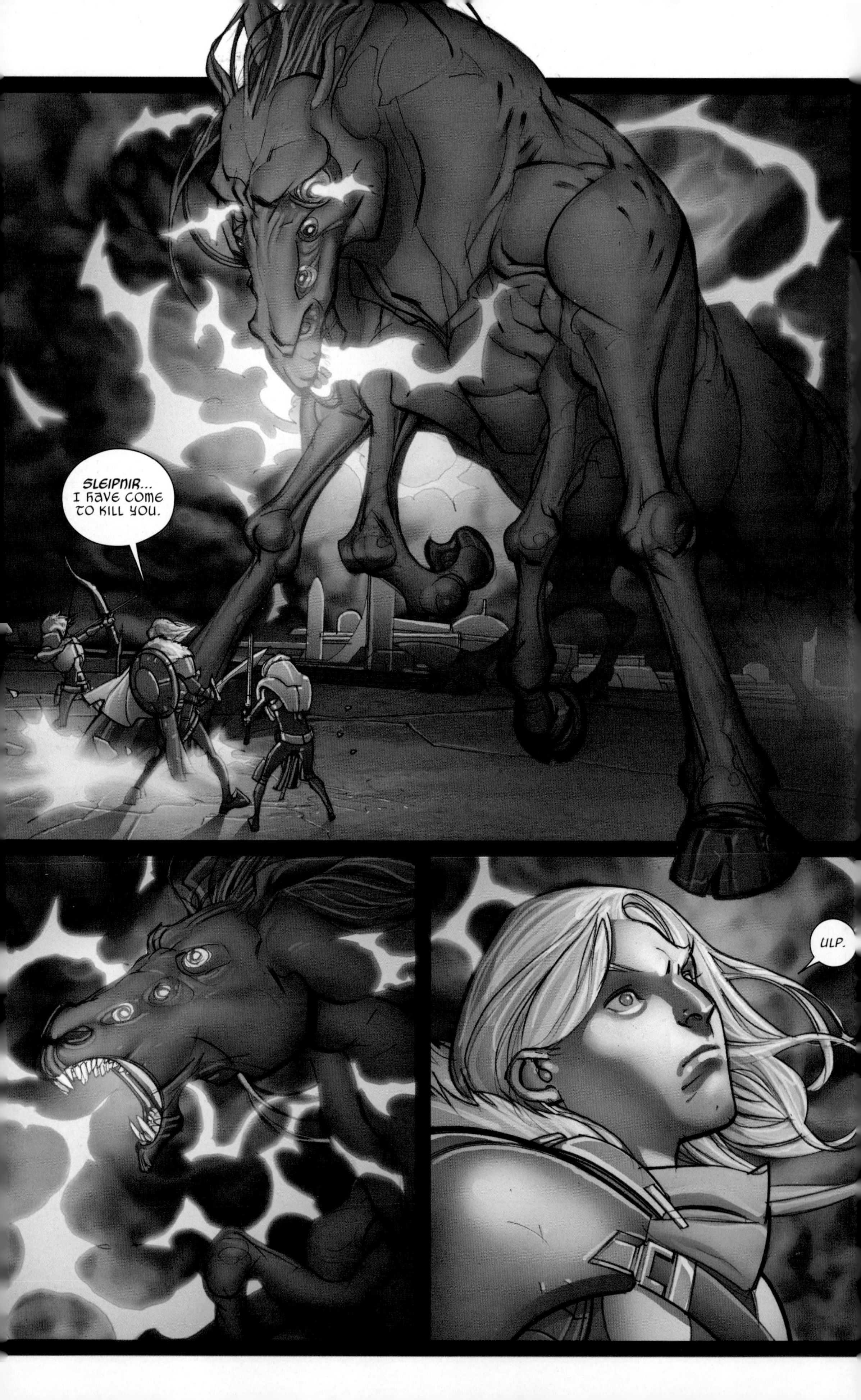
SLEIPNIR...
I HAVE COME TO KILL YOU.
ULP.

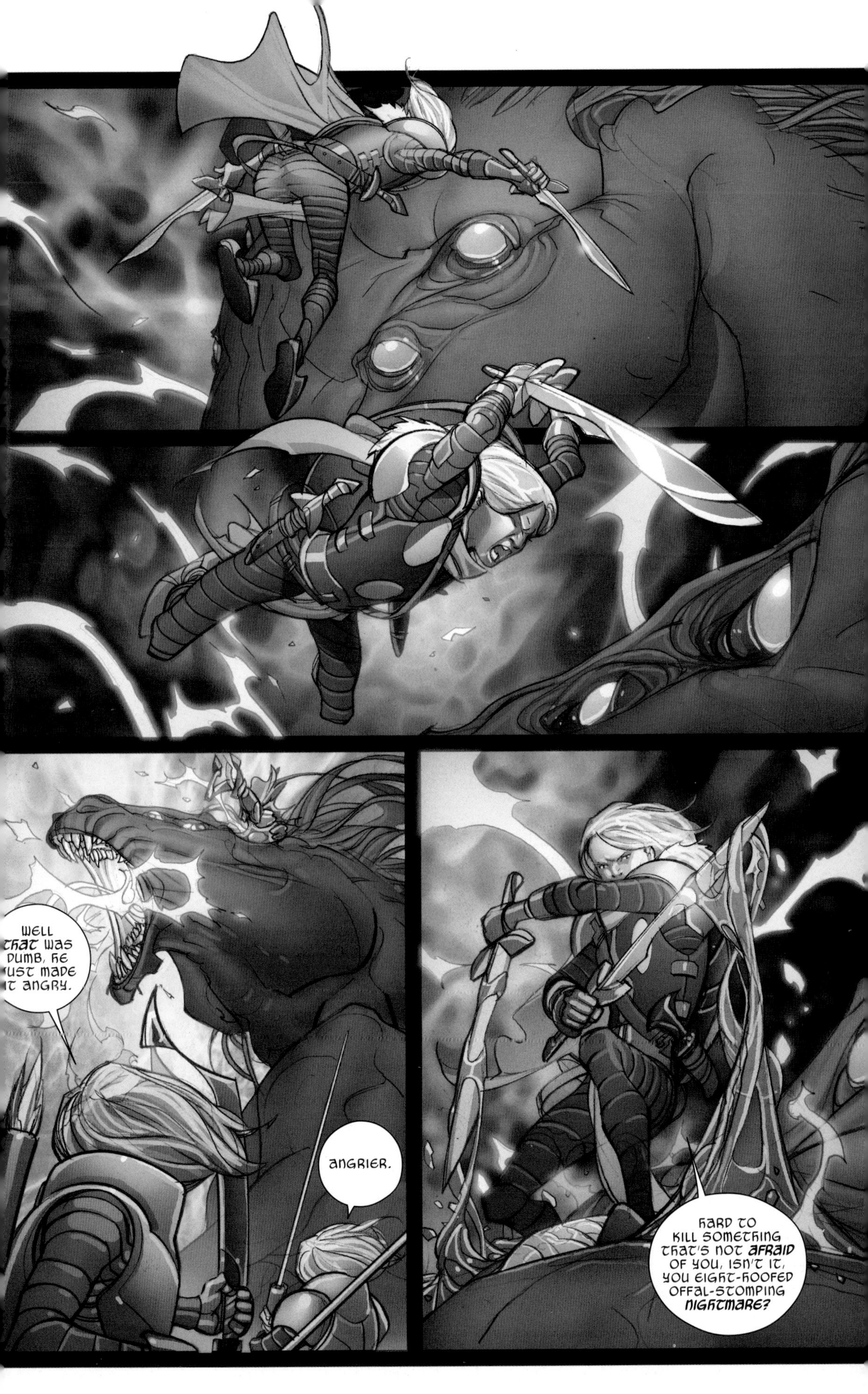

WELL THAT WAS DUMB, HE UST MADE IT ANGRY.
ANGRIER.
HARD TO KILL SOMETHING THAT'S NOT AFRAID OF YOU, ISN'T IT, YOU EIGHT-HOOFED OFFAL-STOMPING NIGHTMARE?

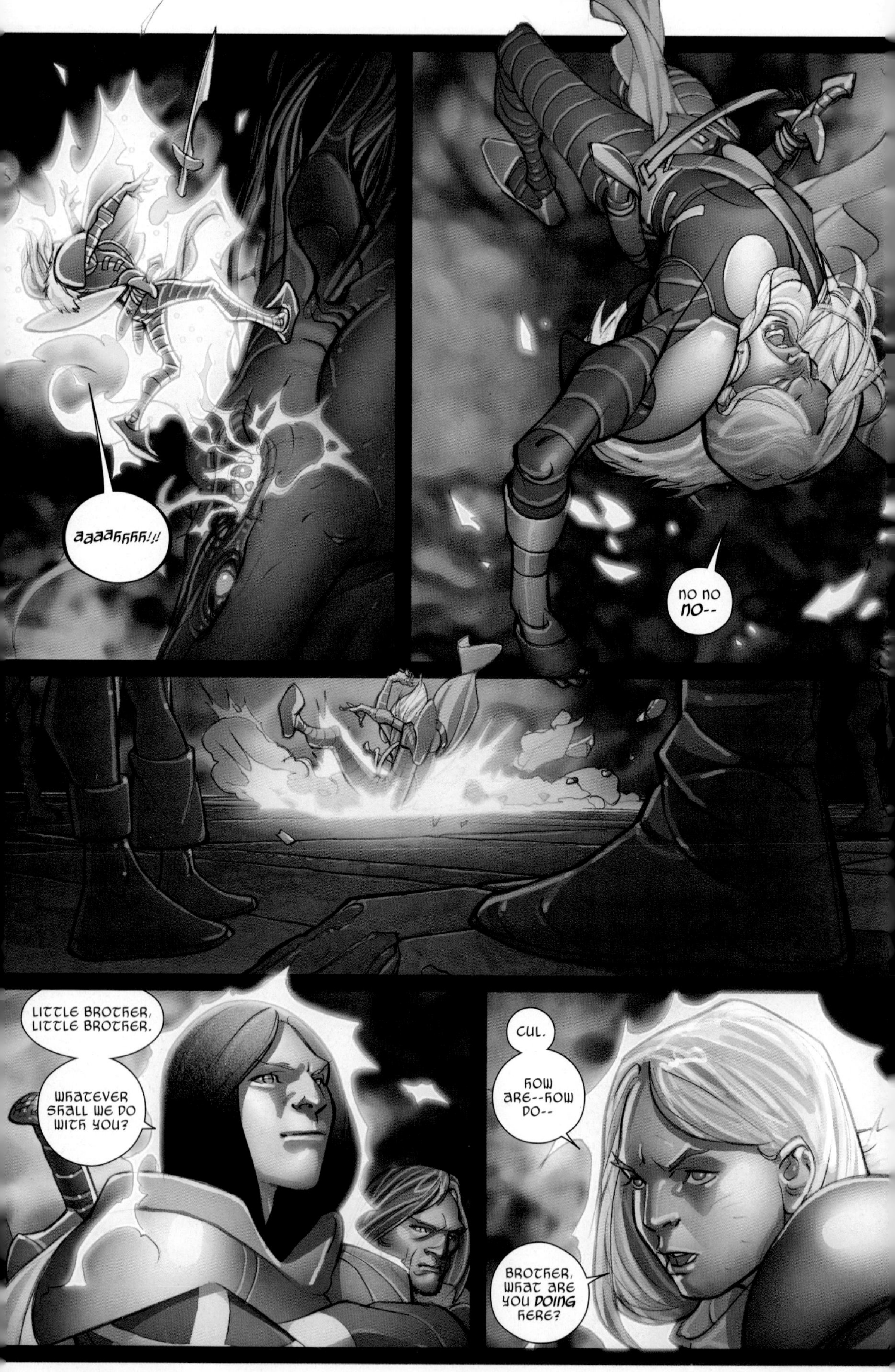
AAAAHHHH!!!
NO NO NO--
LITTLE BROTHER, LITTLE BROTHER.
WHATEVER SHALL WE DO WITH YOU?
CUL.
HOW ARE--HOW DO--
BROTHER, WHAT ARE YOU DOING HERE?

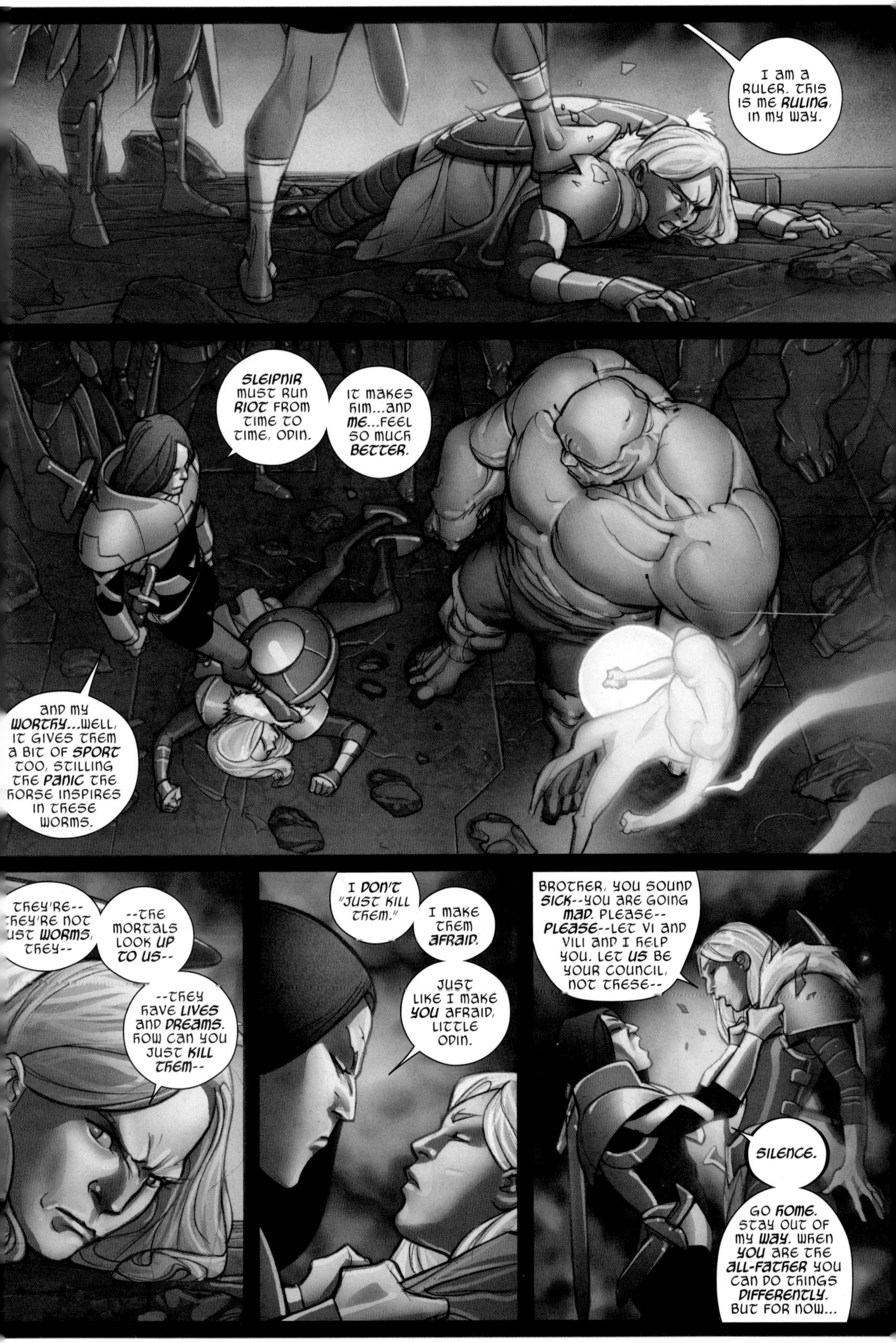
I am a RULER. THIS IS ME RULING, IN MY WAY.
SLEIPNIR MUST RUN RIOT FROM TIME TO TIME, ODIN.
IT MAKES HIM...AND ME...FEEL SO MUCH BETTER.
AND MY WORTHY...WELL, IT GIVES THEM A BIT OF SPORT TOO, STILLING THE PANIC THE HORSE INSPIRES IN THESE WORMS.
THEY'RE-- THEY'RE NOT JUST WORMS, THEY--
--THE MORTALS LOOK UP TO US--
--THEY HAVE LIVES AND DREAMS. HOW CAN YOU JUST KILL THEM--
I DON'T "JUST KILL THEM."
I MAKE THEM AFRAID.
JUST LIKE I MAKE YOU AFRAID, LITTLE ODIN.
BROTHER, YOU SOUND SICK--YOU ARE GOING MAD. PLEASE-- PLEASE--LET VI AND VILI AND I HELP YOU. LET US BE YOUR COUNCIL, NOT THESE--
SILENCE.
GO HOME. STAY OUT OF MY WAY. WHEN YOU ARE THE ALL-FATHER YOU CAN DO THINGS DIFFERENTLY. BUT FOR NOW...

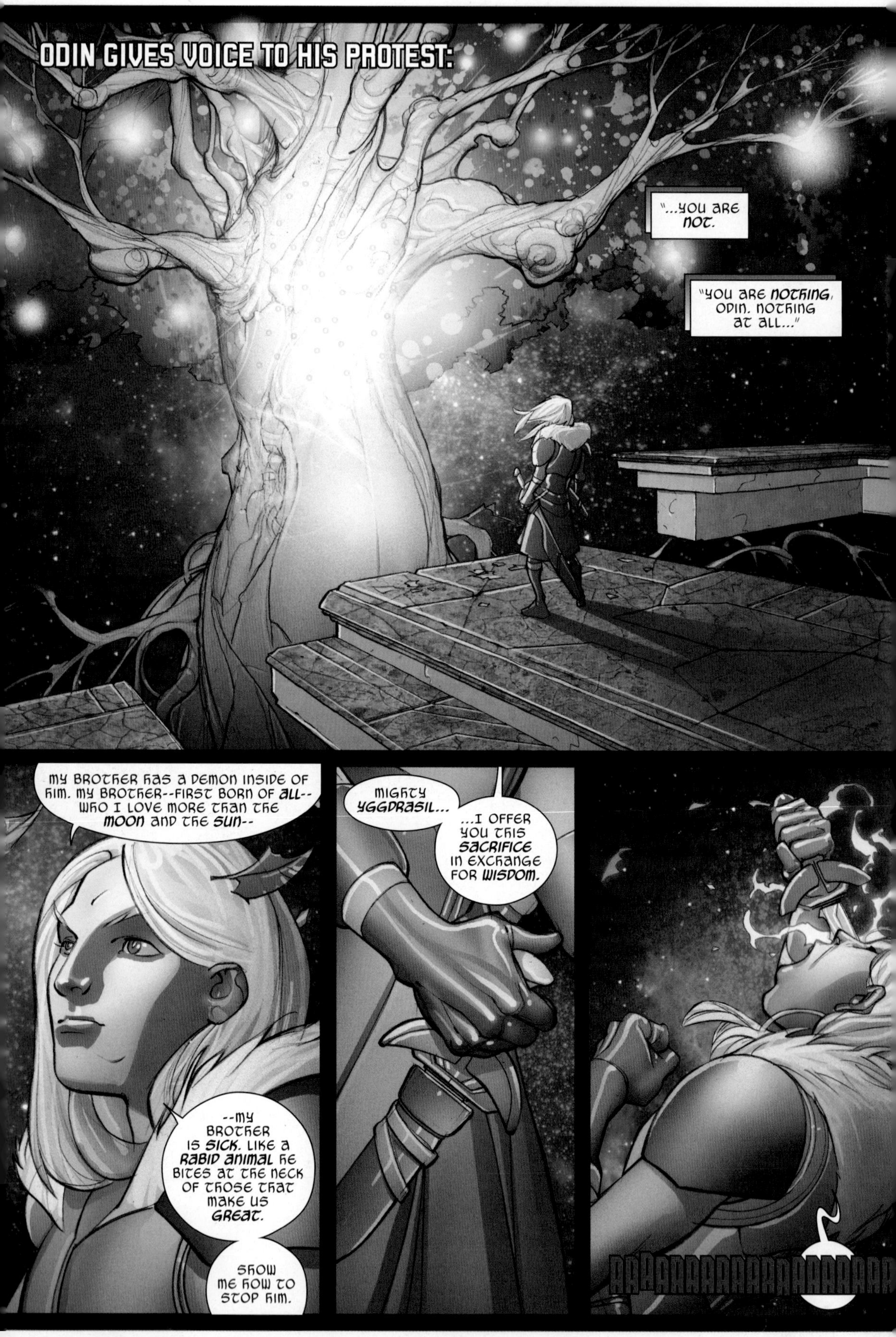
ODIN GIVES VOICE TO HIS PROTEST:
"...YOU ARE NOT.
"YOU ARE NOTHING, ODIN. NOTHING AT ALL..."
MY BROTHER HAS A DEMON INSIDE OF HIM. MY BROTHER--FIRST BORN OF ALL--WHO I LOVE MORE THAN THE MOON AND THE SUN--
--MY BROTHER IS SICK. LIKE A RABID ANIMAL HE BITES AT THE NECK OF THOSE THAT MAKE US GREAT.
SHOW ME HOW TO STOP HIM.
MIGHTY YGGDRASIL...
...I OFFER YOU THIS SACRIFICE IN EXCHANGE FOR WISDOM.
AAAAAAAAAAAAAAAAAA

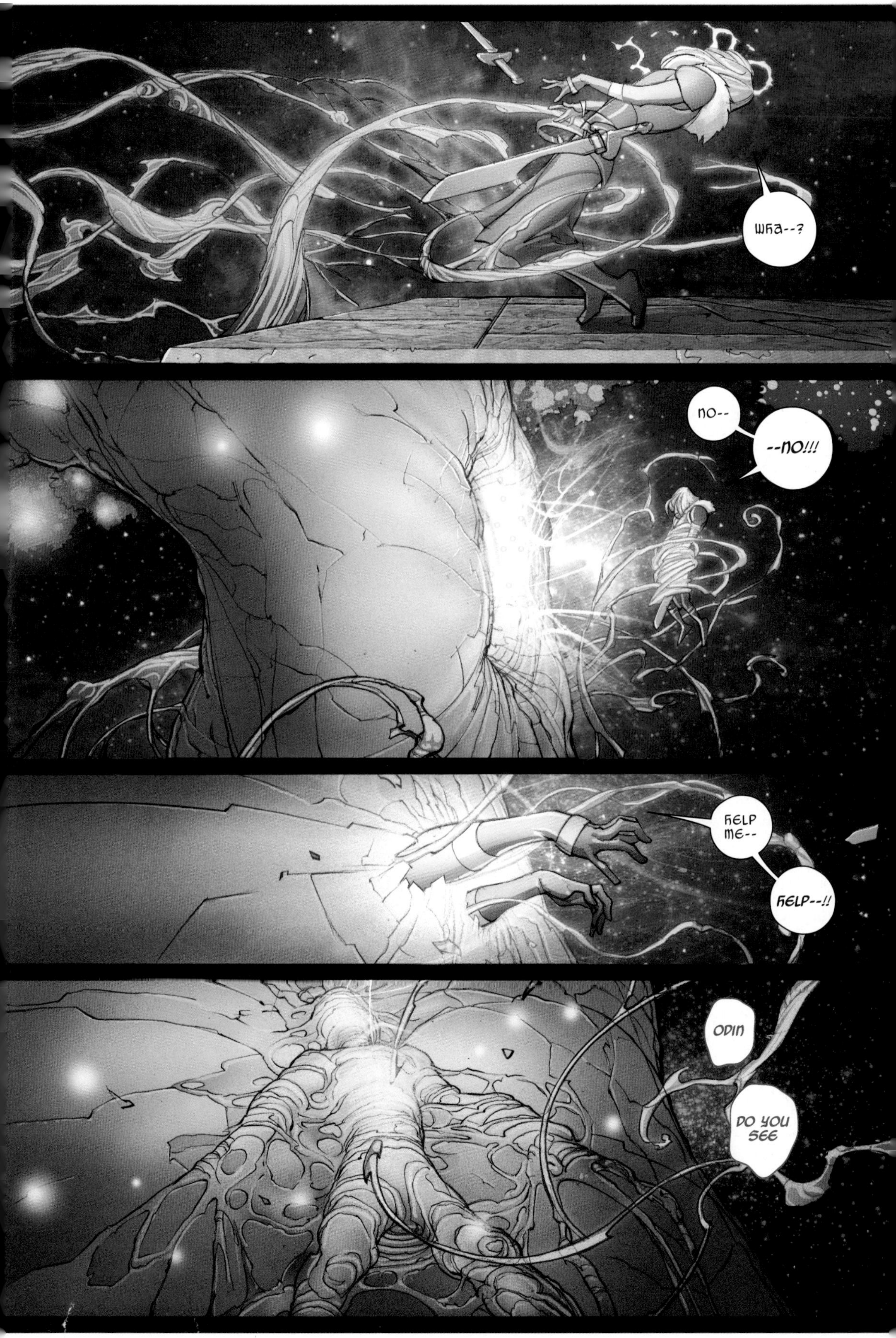
WHA--?
NO--
--NO!!!
HELP ME--
HELP--!!
ODIN
DO YOU SEE

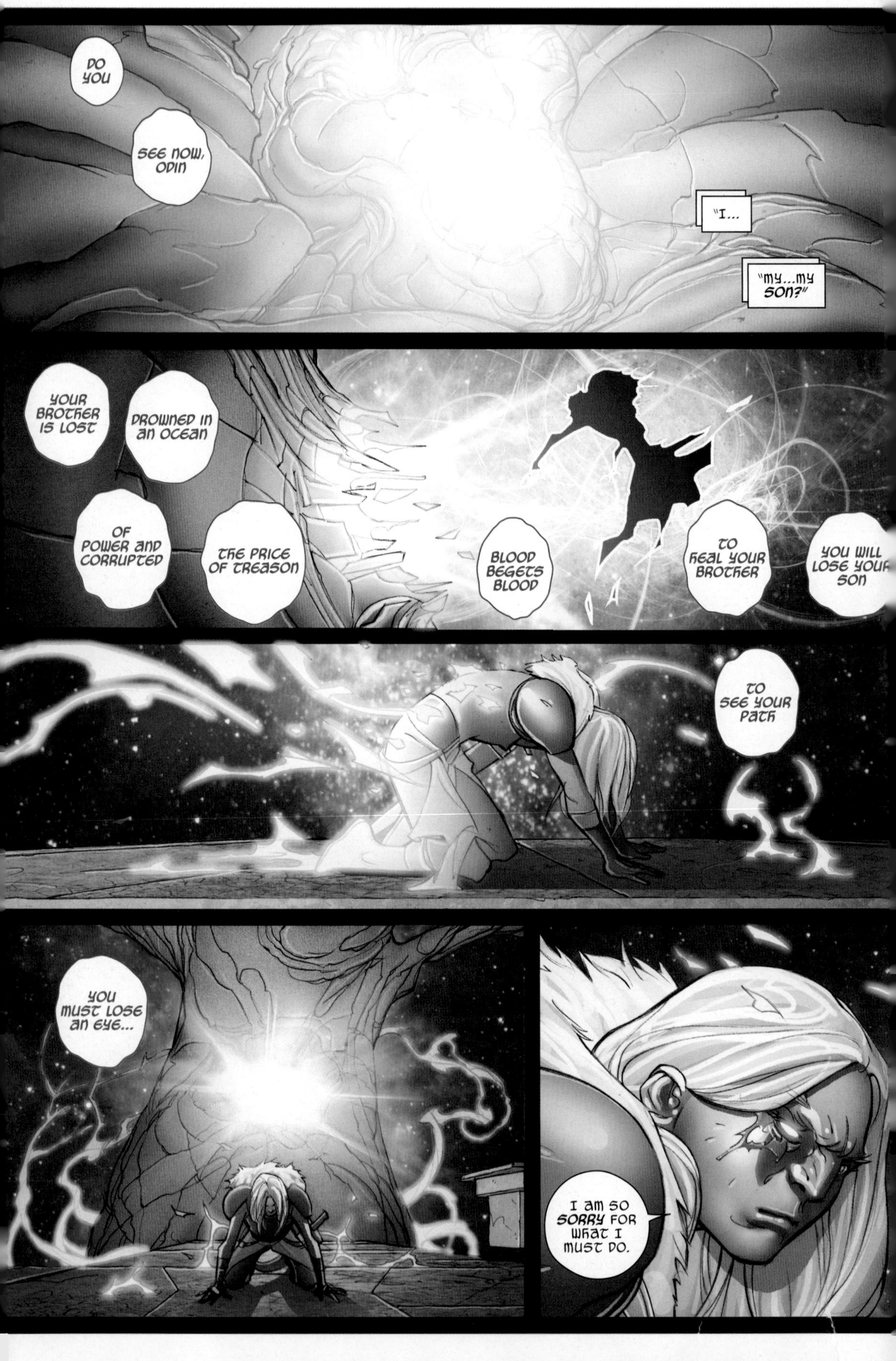
DO YOU
SEE NOW, ODIN
"I...
"MY...MY SON?"
YOUR BROTHER IS LOST
DROWNED IN AN OCEAN
OF POWER AND CORRUPTED
THE PRICE OF TREASON
BLOOD BEGETS BLOOD
TO HEAL YOUR BROTHER
YOU WILL LOSE YOUR SON
TO SEE YOUR PATH
YOU MUST LOSE AN EYE...
I AM SO SORRY FOR WHAT I MUST DO.

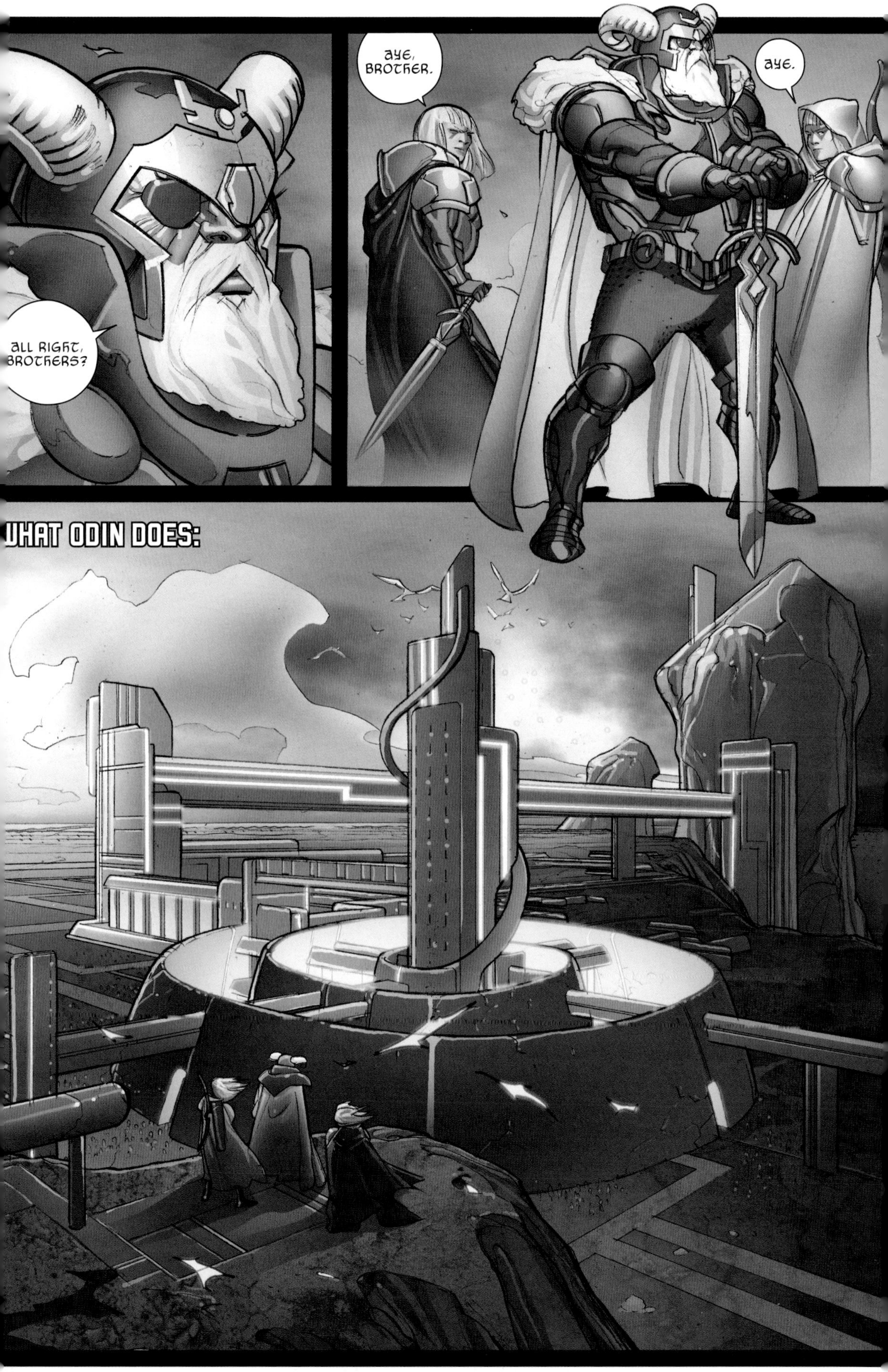
ALL RIGHT, BROTHERS?
AYE, BROTHER.
AYE.
WHAT ODIN DOES:

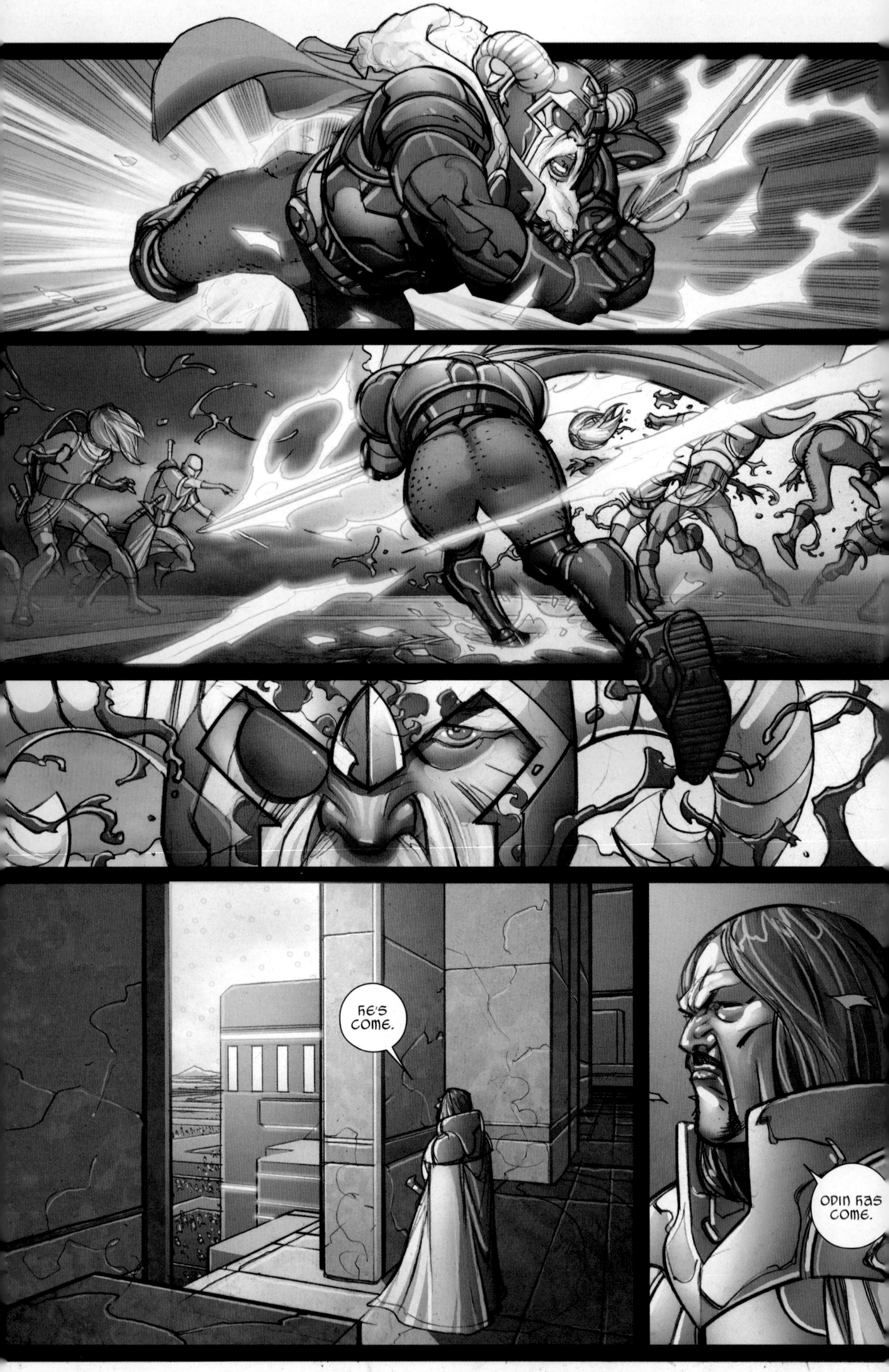
HE'S COME.
ODIN HAS COME.

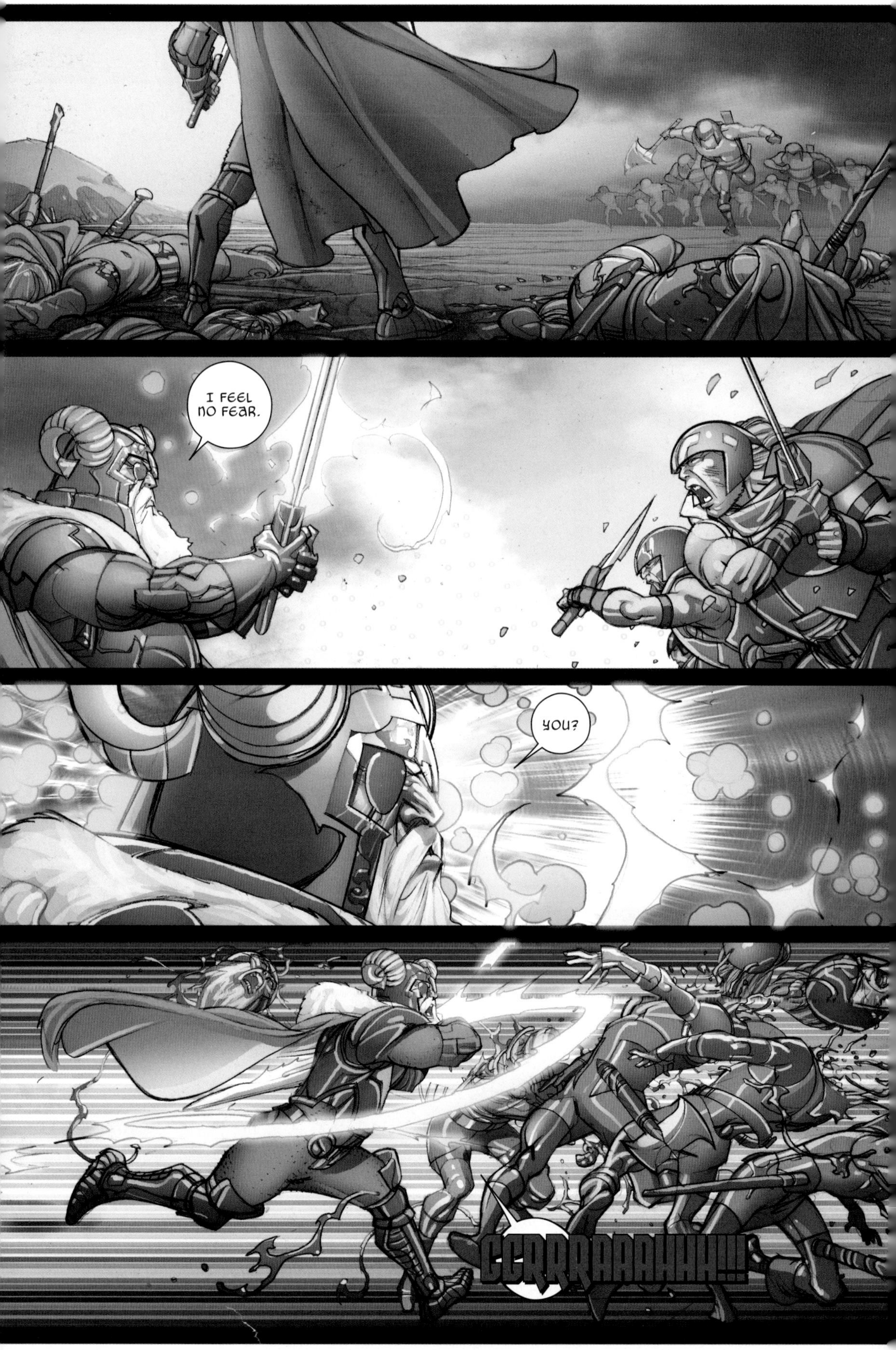
I FEEL NO FEAR.
YOU?
GGRRRAAAHHH!!!

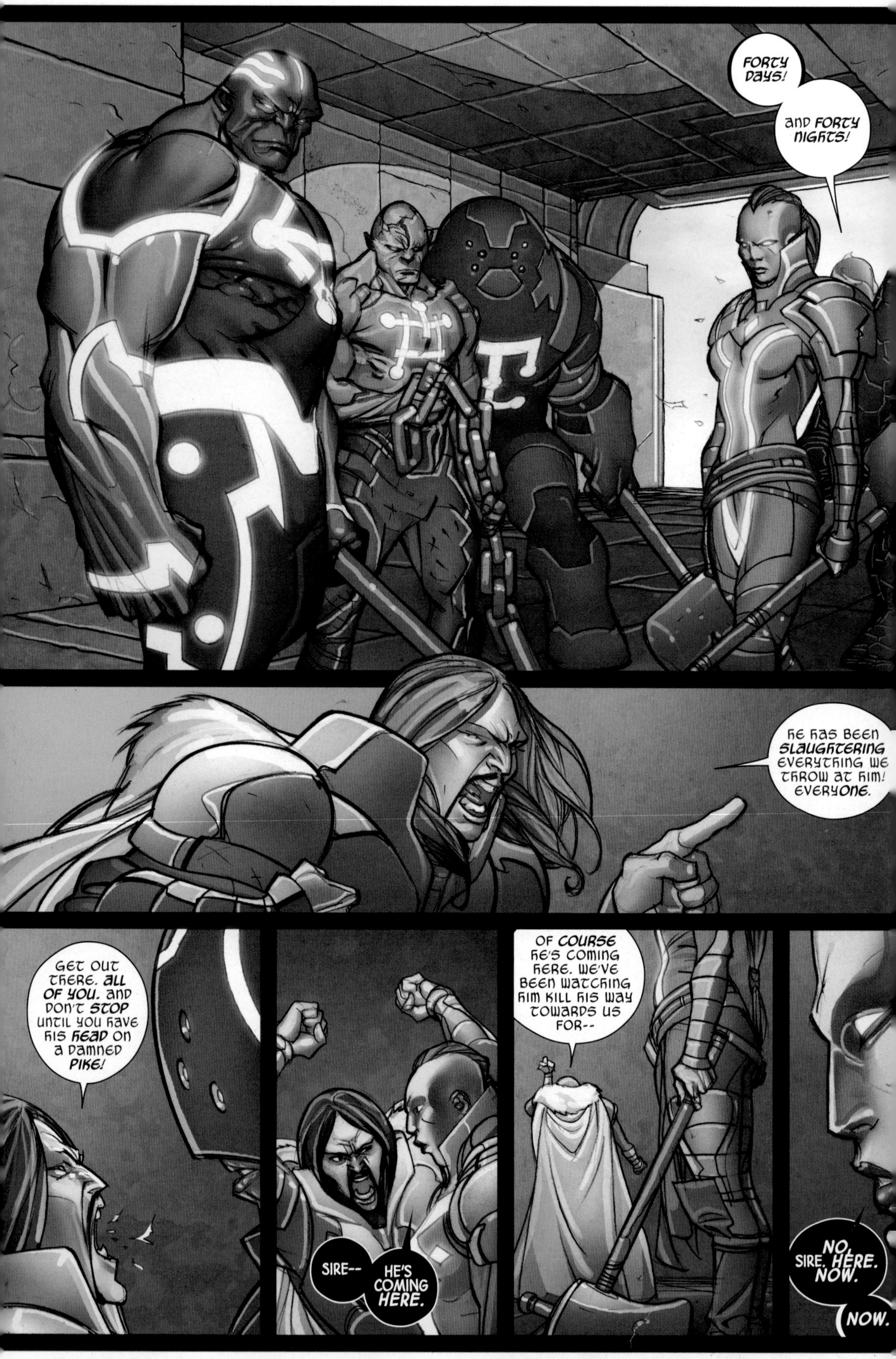
FORTY DAYS!
AND FORTY NIGHTS!
HE HAS BEEN SLAUGHTERING EVERYTHING WE THROW AT HIM! EVERYONE.
GET OUT THERE. ALL OF YOU. AND DON'T STOP UNTIL YOU HAVE HIS HEAD ON A DAMNED PIKE!
SIRE--
HE'S COMING HERE.
OF COURSE HE'S COMING HERE. WE'VE BEEN WATCHING HIM KILL HIS WAY TOWARDS US FOR--
NO, SIRE. HERE. NOW.
NOW.

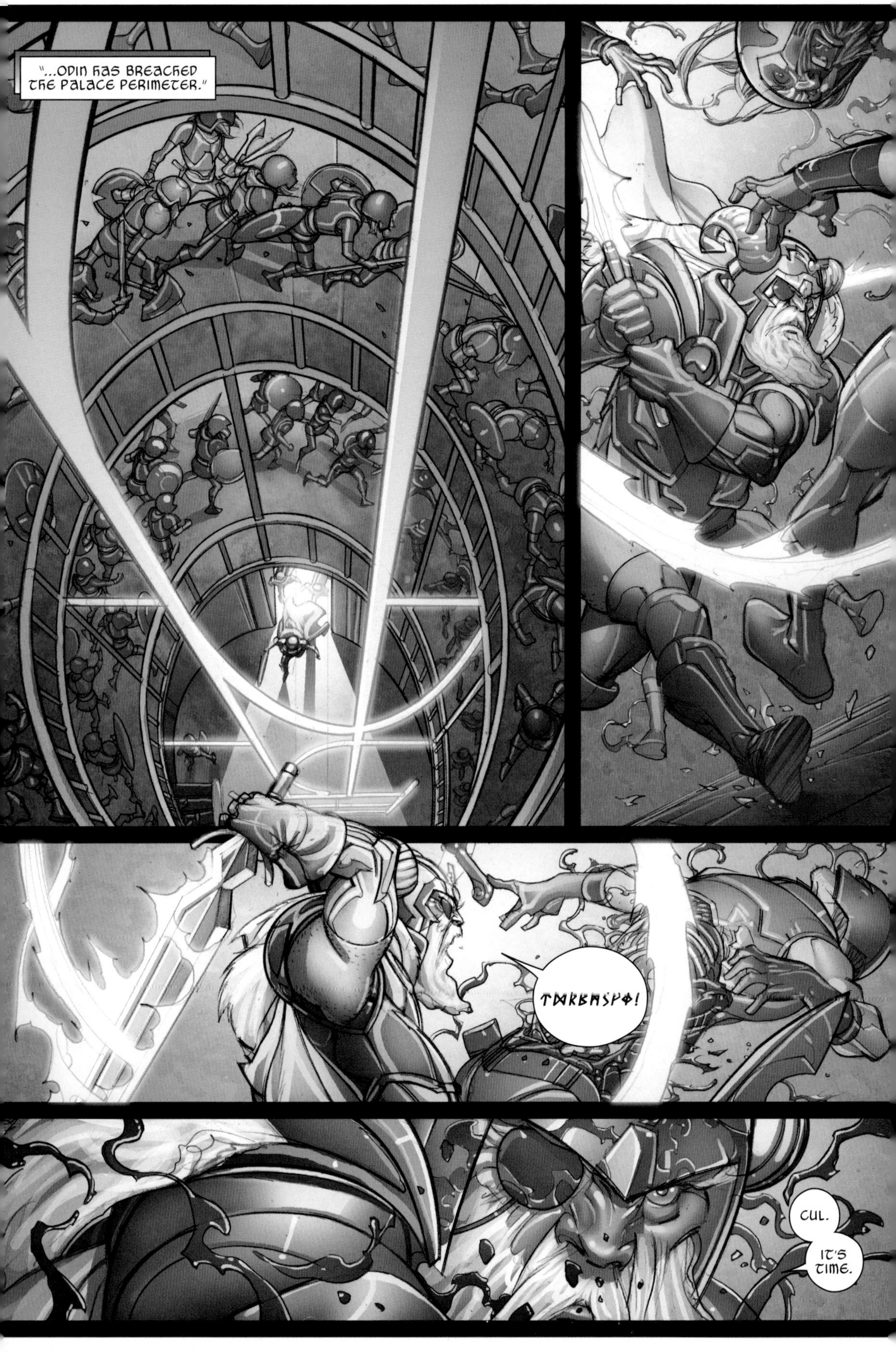
"...ODIN HAS BREACHED THE PALACE PERIMETER."
ᛏᛞᚱᛒᛗᛊᛈᛟ!
CUL.
IT'S TIME.

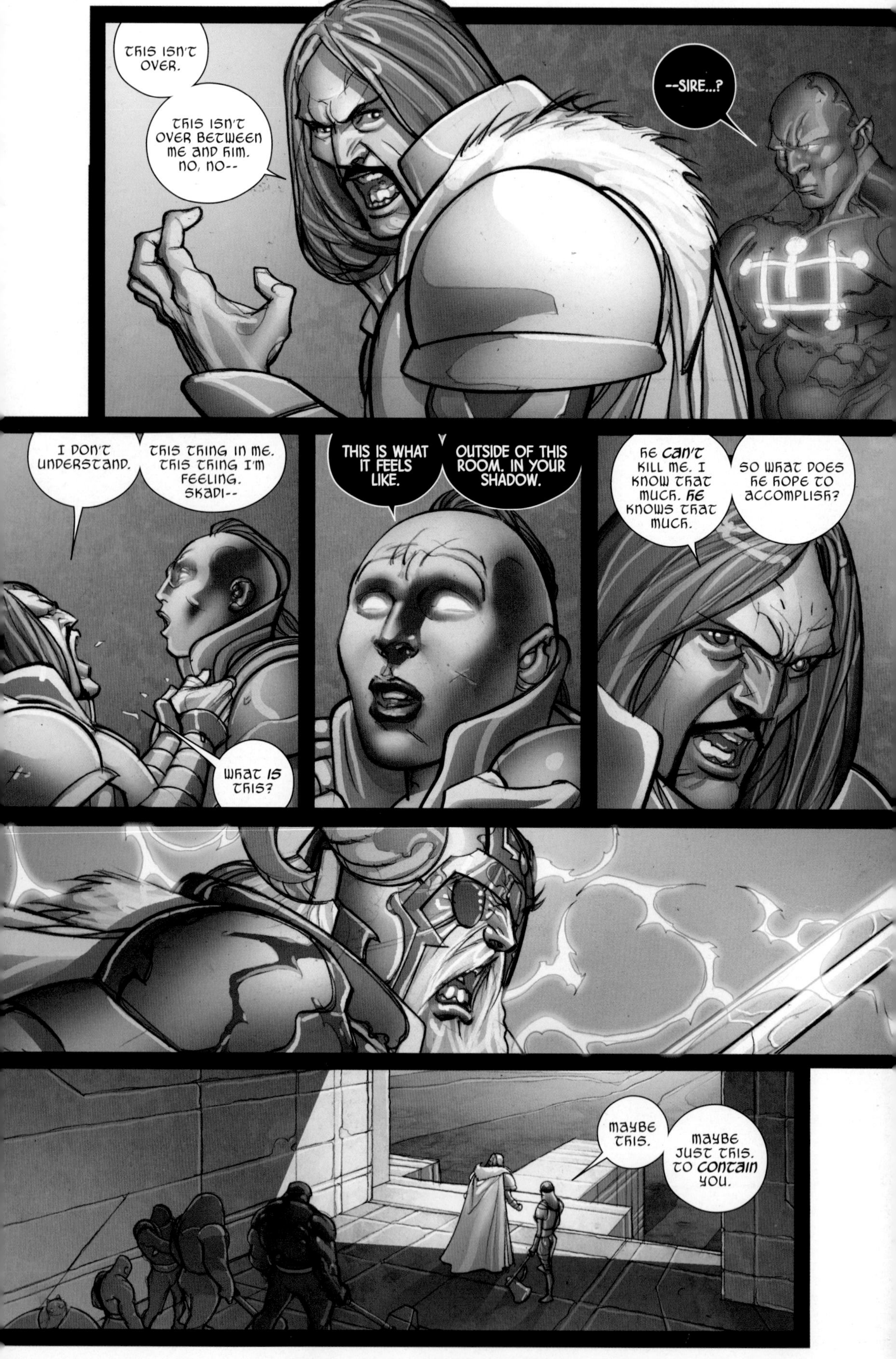

THIS ISN'T OVER.
THIS ISN'T OVER BETWEEN ME AND HIM. NO, NO--
--SIRE...?
I DON'T UNDERSTAND.
THIS THING IN ME. THIS THING I'M FEELING. SKADI--
WHAT IS THIS?
THIS IS WHAT IT FEELS LIKE.
OUTSIDE OF THIS ROOM. IN YOUR SHADOW.
HE CAN'T KILL ME. I KNOW THAT MUCH. HE KNOWS THAT MUCH.
SO WHAT DOES HE HOPE TO ACCOMPLISH?
MAYBE THIS.
MAYBE JUST THIS. TO CONTAIN YOU.

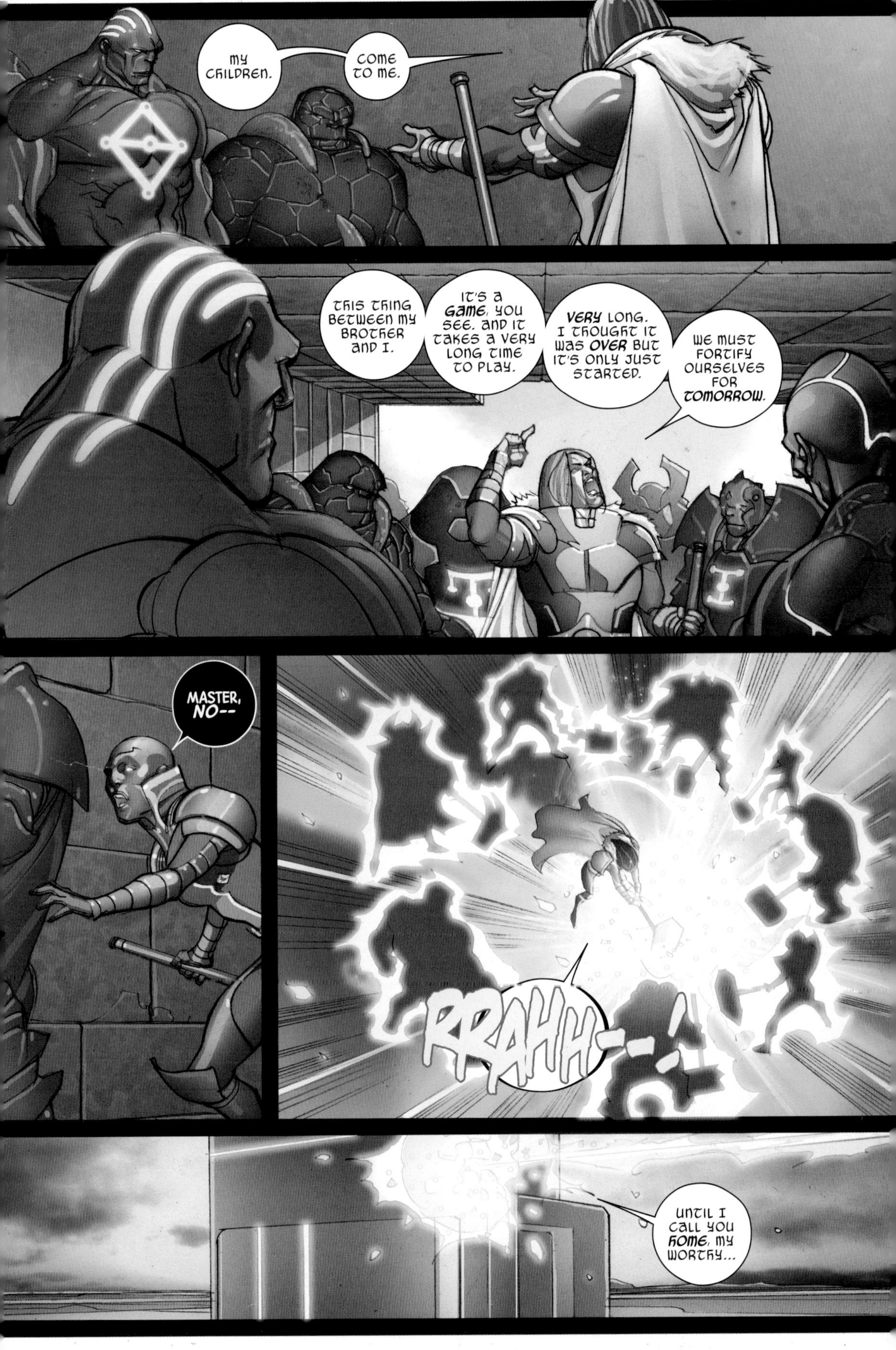
MY CHILDREN.
COME TO ME.
THIS THING BETWEEN MY BROTHER AND I.
IT'S A GAME, YOU SEE. AND IT TAKES A VERY LONG TIME TO PLAY.
VERY LONG. I THOUGHT IT WAS OVER BUT IT'S ONLY JUST STARTED.
WE MUST FORTIFY OURSELVES FOR TOMORROW.
MASTER, NO--
RRAHH--!
UNTIL I CALL YOU HOME, MY WORTHY...

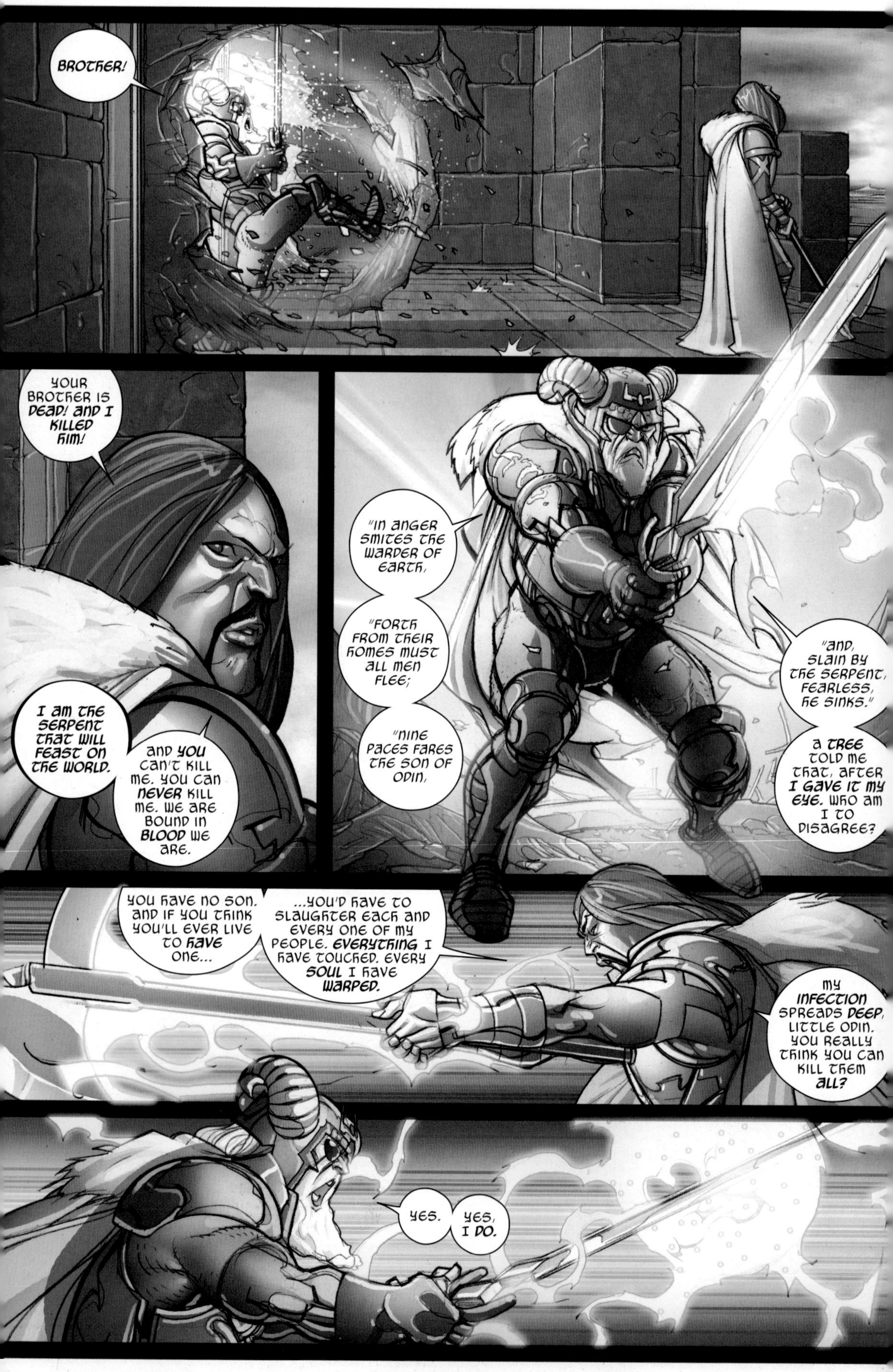
BROTHER!
YOUR BROTHER IS DEAD! AND I KILLED HIM!
I AM THE SERPENT THAT WILL FEAST ON THE WORLD.
AND YOU CAN'T KILL ME. YOU CAN NEVER KILL ME. WE ARE BOUND IN BLOOD WE ARE.
"IN ANGER SMITES THE WARDER OF EARTH,
"FORTH FROM THEIR HOMES MUST ALL MEN FLEE;
"NINE PACES FARES THE SON OF ODIN,
"AND, SLAIN BY THE SERPENT, FEARLESS, HE SINKS."
A TREE TOLD ME THAT, AFTER I GAVE IT MY EYE. WHO AM I TO DISAGREE?
YOU HAVE NO SON. AND IF YOU THINK YOU'LL EVER LIVE TO HAVE ONE...
...YOU'D HAVE TO SLAUGHTER EACH AND EVERY ONE OF MY PEOPLE. EVERYTHING I HAVE TOUCHED. EVERY SOUL I HAVE WARPED.
MY INFECTION SPREADS DEEP, LITTLE ODIN. YOU REALLY THINK YOU CAN KILL THEM ALL?
YES.
YES, I DO.

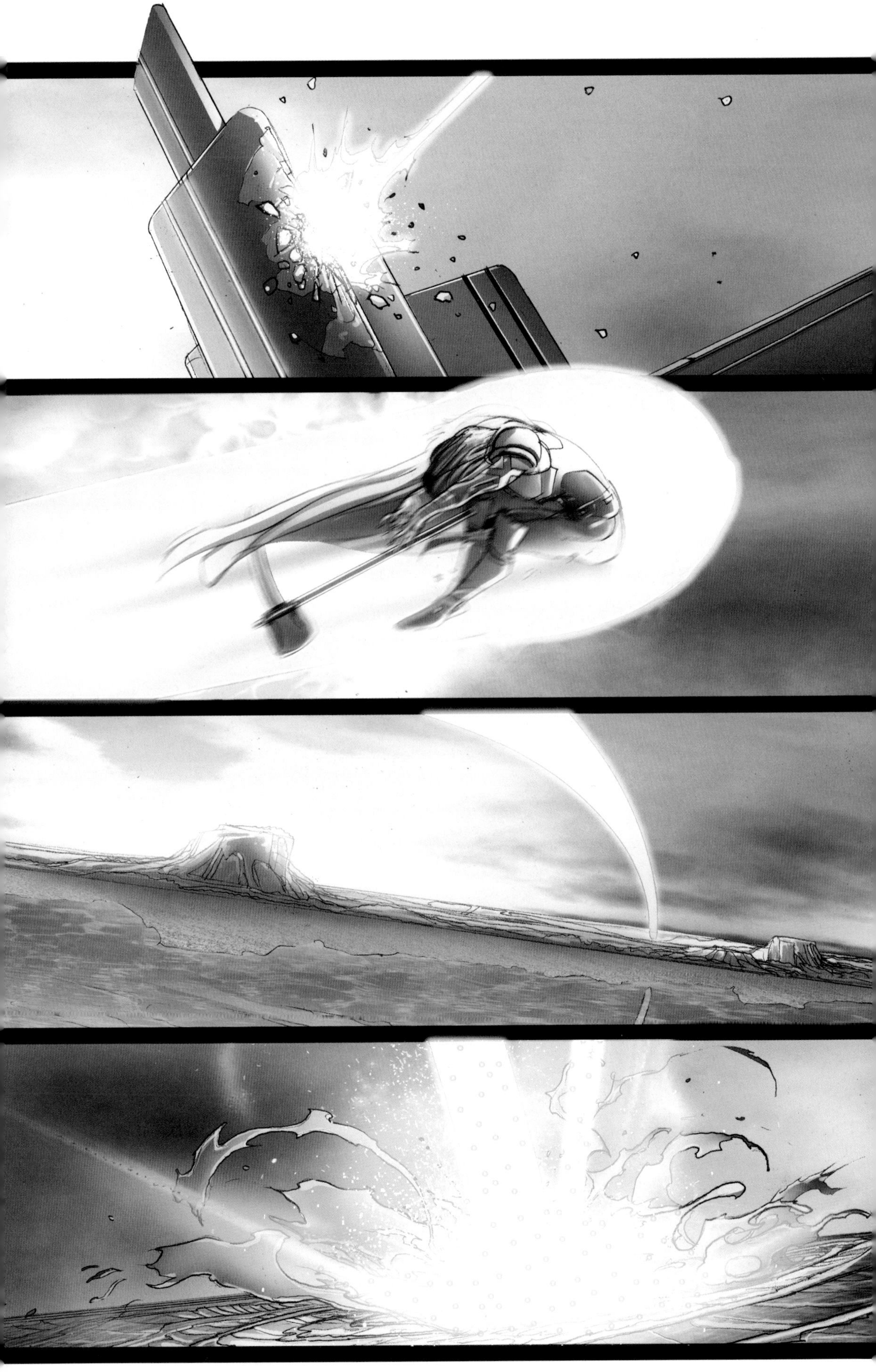

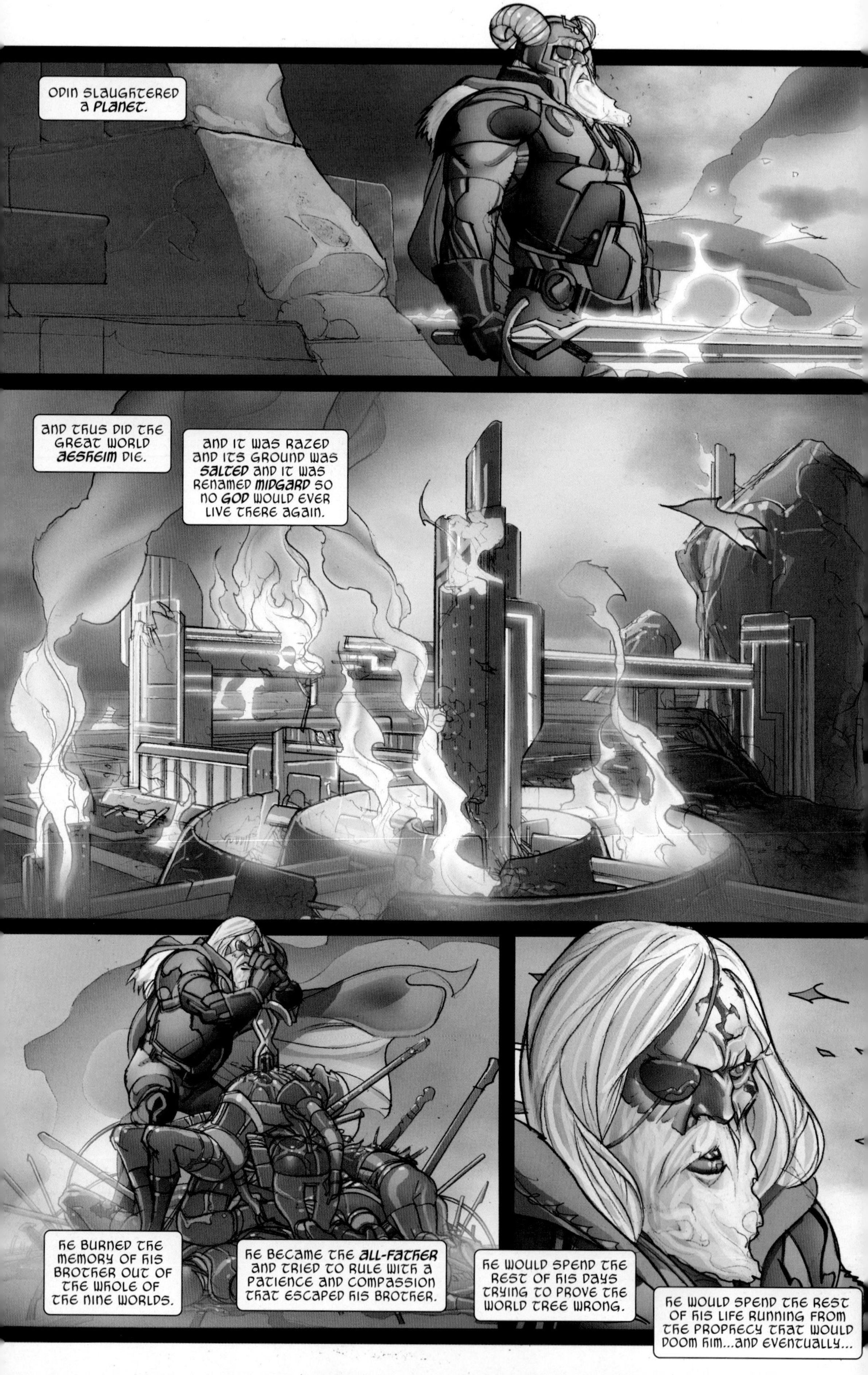
ODIN SLAUGHTERED A PLANET.
AND THUS DID THE GREAT WORLD AESHEIM DIE.
AND IT WAS RAZED AND ITS GROUND WAS SALTED AND IT WAS RENAMED MIDGARD SO NO GOD WOULD EVER LIVE THERE AGAIN.
HE BURNED THE MEMORY OF HIS BROTHER OUT OF THE WHOLE OF THE NINE WORLDS.
HE BECAME THE ALL-FATHER AND TRIED TO RULE WITH A PATIENCE AND COMPASSION THAT ESCAPED HIS BROTHER.
HE WOULD SPEND THE REST OF HIS DAYS TRYING TO PROVE THE WORLD TREE WRONG.
HE WOULD SPEND THE REST OF HIS LIFE RUNNING FROM THE PROPHECY THAT WOULD DOOM HIM...AND EVENTUALLY...

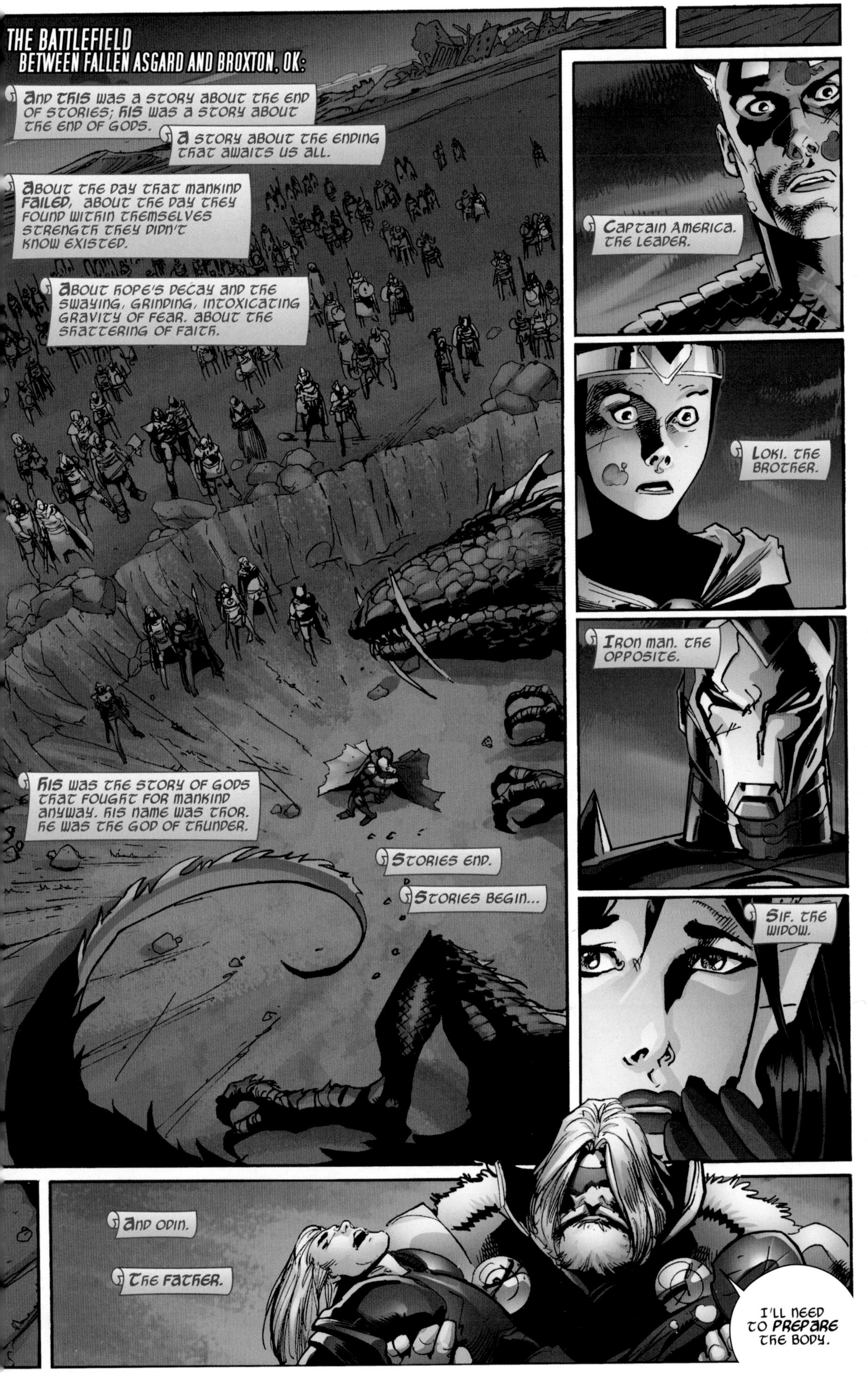

THE BATTLEFIELD
BETWEEN FALLEN ASGARD AND BROXTON, OK:
AND THIS WAS A STORY ABOUT THE END OF STORIES; HIS WAS A STORY ABOUT THE END OF GODS.
A STORY ABOUT THE ENDING THAT AWAITS US ALL.
ABOUT THE DAY THAT MANKIND FAILED, ABOUT THE DAY THEY FOUND WITHIN THEMSELVES STRENGTH THEY DIDN'T KNOW EXISTED.
ABOUT HOPE'S DECAY AND THE SWAYING, GRINDING, INTOXICATING GRAVITY OF FEAR. ABOUT THE SHATTERING OF FAITH.
HIS WAS THE STORY OF GODS THAT FOUGHT FOR MANKIND ANYWAY. HIS NAME WAS THOR. HE WAS THE GOD OF THUNDER.
STORIES END.
STORIES BEGIN...
CAPTAIN AMERICA. THE LEADER.
LOKI. THE BROTHER.
IRON MAN. THE OPPOSITE.
SIF. THE WIDOW.
AND ODIN.
THE FATHER.
I'LL NEED TO PREPARE THE BODY.

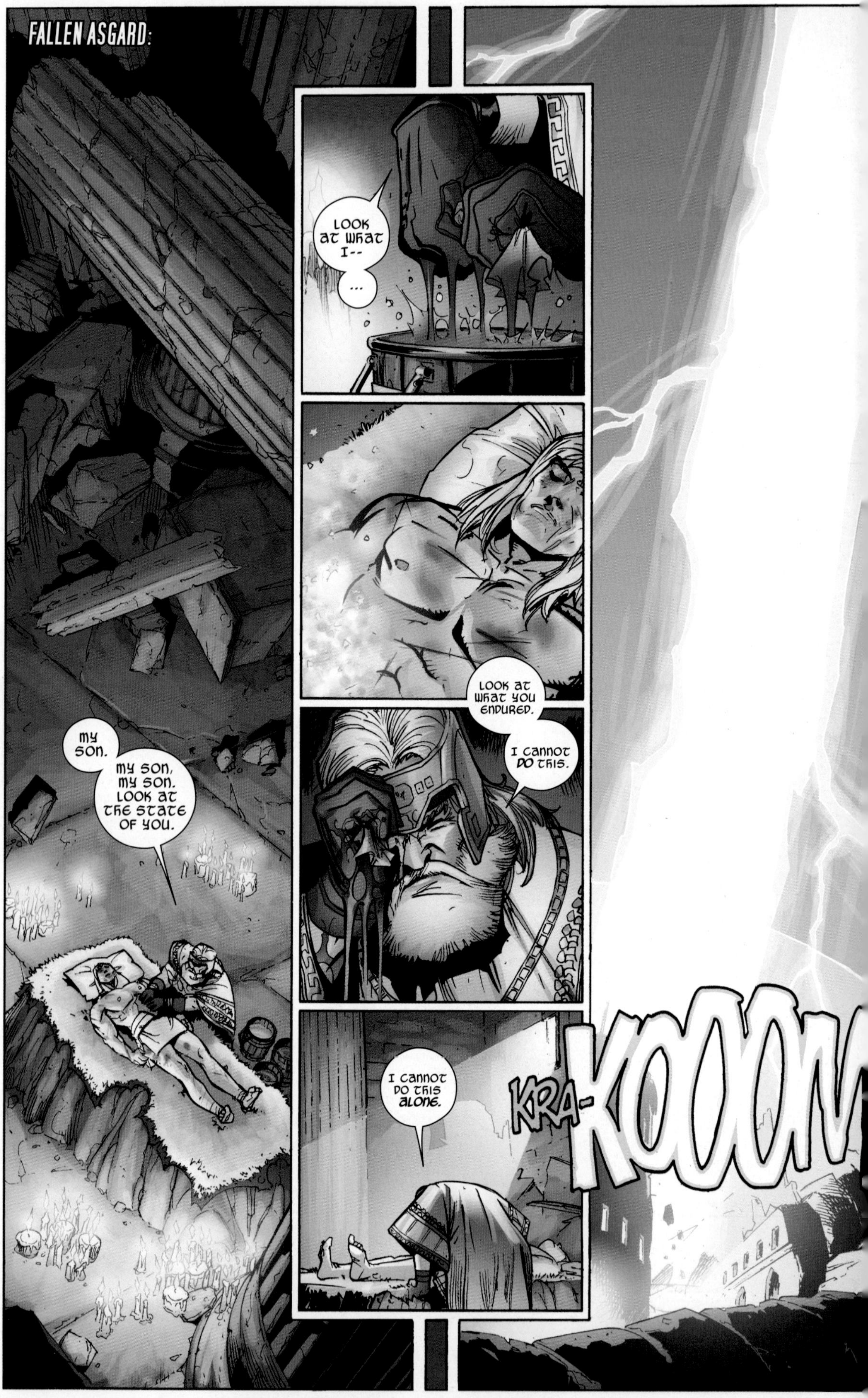

FALLEN ASGARD:
MY SON.
MY SON, MY SON. LOOK AT THE STATE OF YOU.
LOOK AT WHAT I--
...
LOOK AT WHAT YOU ENDURED.
I CANNOT DO THIS.
I CANNOT DO THIS ALONE.
KRA-KOOOM

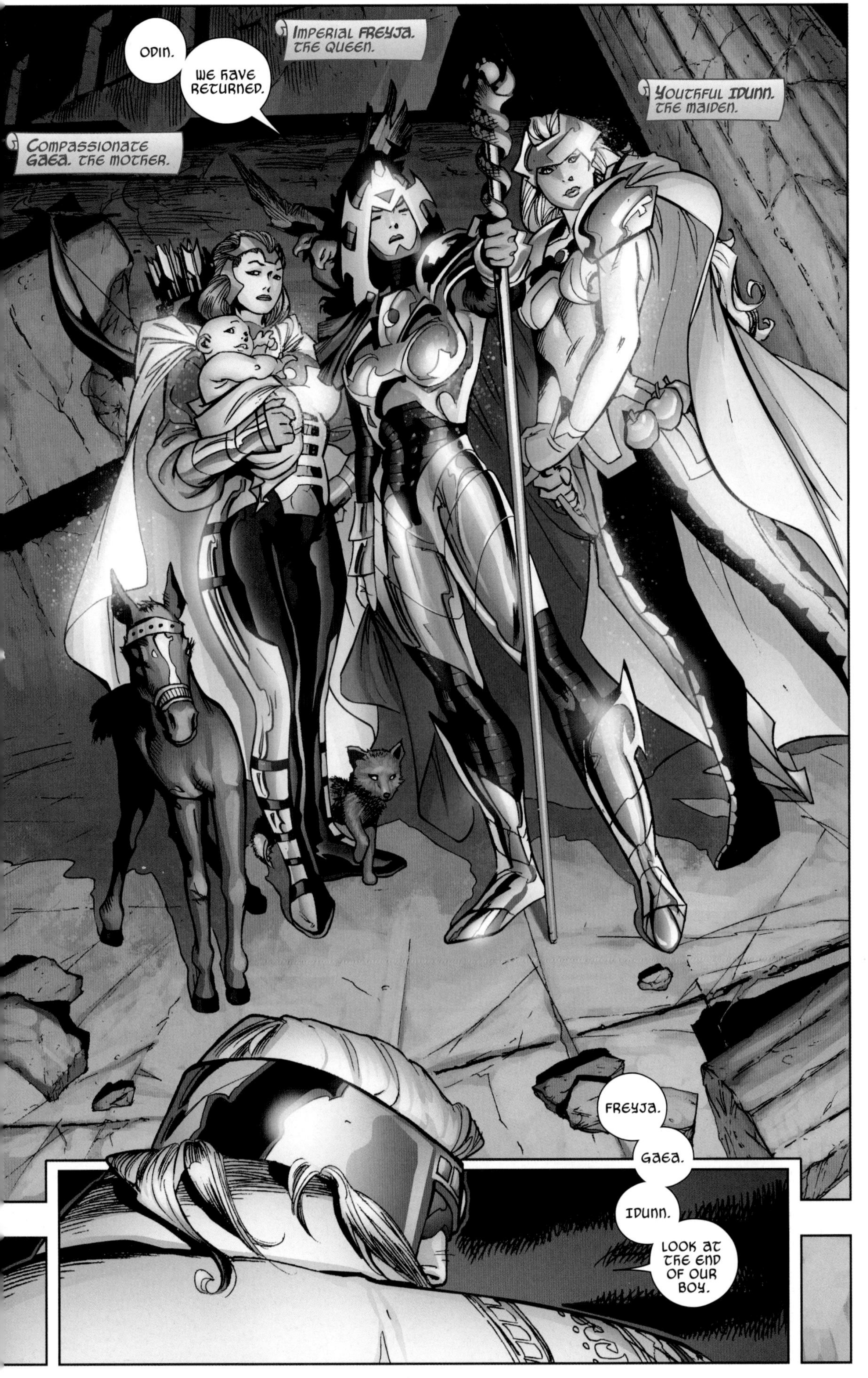
ODIN.
WE HAVE RETURNED.
IMPERIAL FREYJA. THE QUEEN.
YOUTHFUL IDUNN. THE MAIDEN.
COMPASSIONATE GAEA. THE MOTHER.
FREYJA.
GAEA.
IDUNN.
LOOK AT THE END OF OUR BOY.

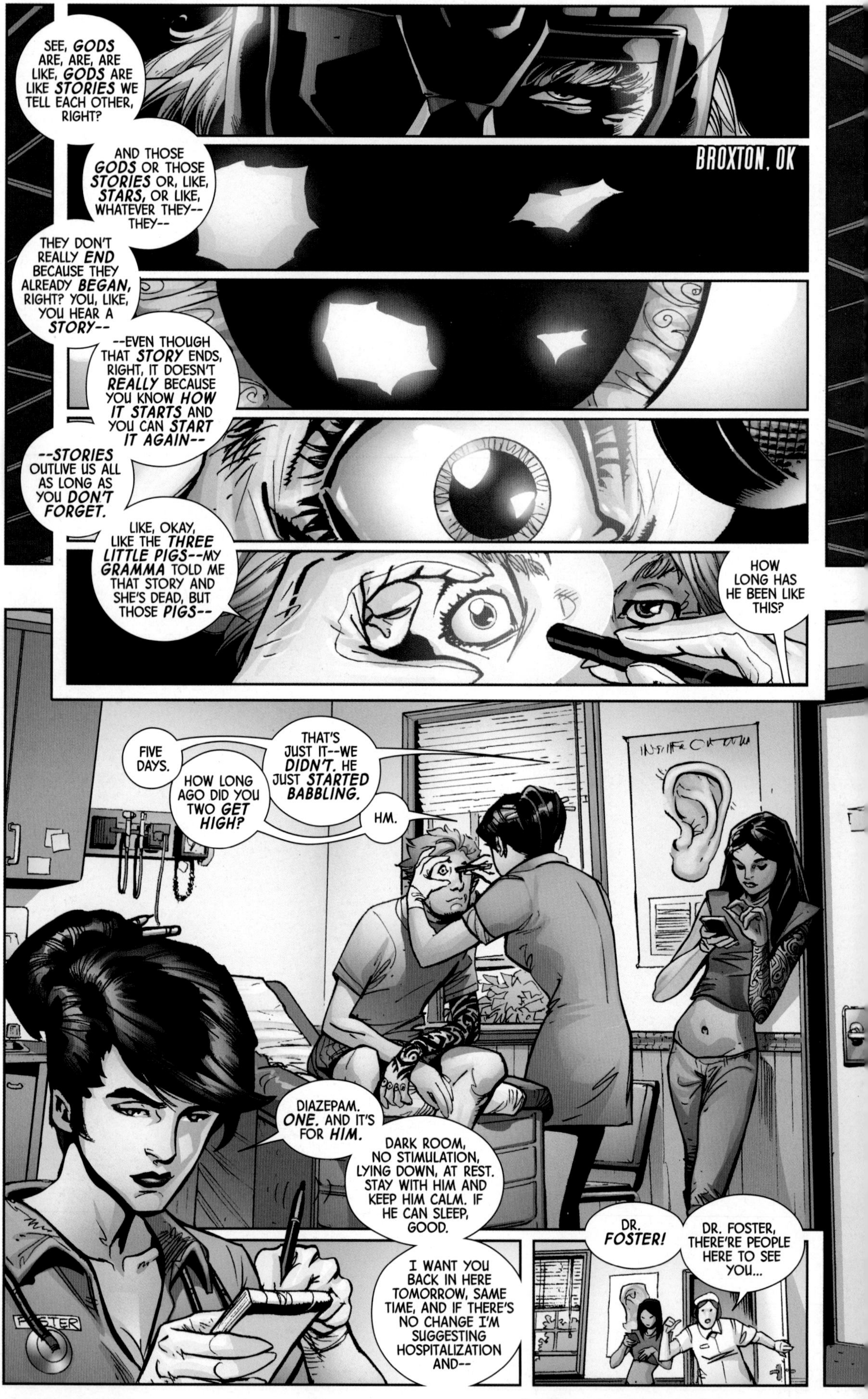
SEE, GODS ARE, ARE, ARE LIKE, GODS ARE LIKE STORIES WE TELL EACH OTHER, RIGHT?
BROXTON, OK
AND THOSE GODS OR THOSE STORIES OR, LIKE, STARS, OR LIKE, WHATEVER THEY-- THEY--
THEY DON'T REALLY END BECAUSE THEY ALREADY BEGAN, RIGHT? YOU, LIKE, YOU HEAR A STORY--
--EVEN THOUGH THAT STORY ENDS, RIGHT, IT DOESN'T REALLY BECAUSE YOU KNOW HOW IT STARTS AND YOU CAN START IT AGAIN--
--STORIES OUTLIVE US ALL AS LONG AS YOU DON'T FORGET.
LIKE, OKAY, LIKE THE THREE LITTLE PIGS--MY GRAMMA TOLD ME THAT STORY AND SHE'S DEAD, BUT THOSE PIGS--
HOW LONG HAS HE BEEN LIKE THIS?
FIVE DAYS.
HOW LONG AGO DID YOU TWO GET HIGH?
THAT'S JUST IT--WE DIDN'T. HE JUST STARTED BABBLING.
HM.
DIAZEPAM. ONE. AND IT'S FOR HIM.
DARK ROOM, NO STIMULATION, LYING DOWN, AT REST. STAY WITH HIM AND KEEP HIM CALM. IF HE CAN SLEEP, GOOD.
I WANT YOU BACK IN HERE TOMORROW, SAME TIME, AND IF THERE'S NO CHANGE I'M SUGGESTING HOSPITALIZATION AND--
FOSTER
DR. FOSTER!
DR. FOSTER, THERE'RE PEOPLE HERE TO SEE YOU...

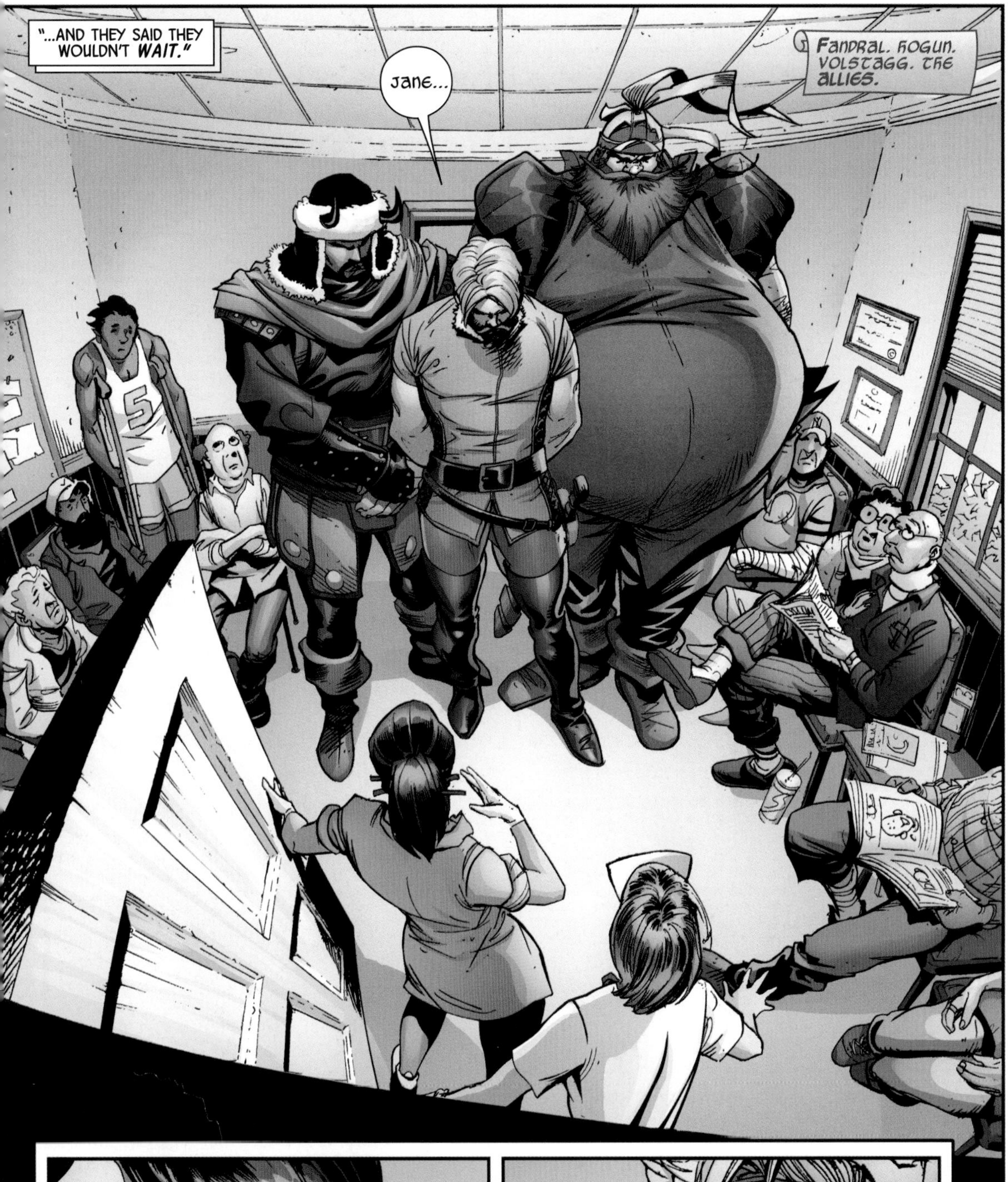
"...AND THEY SAID THEY WOULDN'T WAIT."
JANE...
FANDRAL. HOGUN. VOLSTAGG. THE ALLIES.

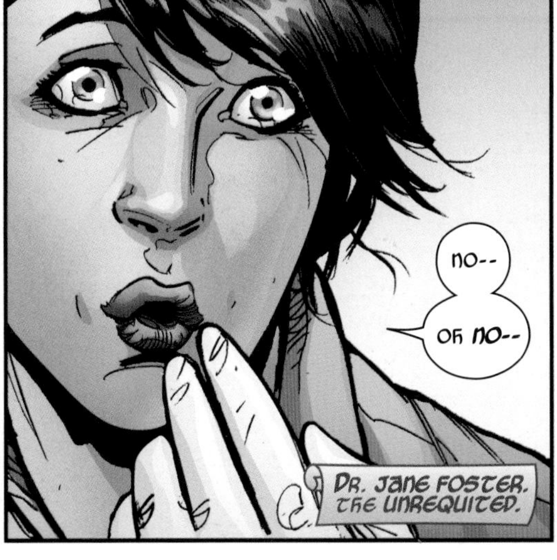
NO--
OH NO--
DR. JANE FOSTER. THE UNREQUITED.

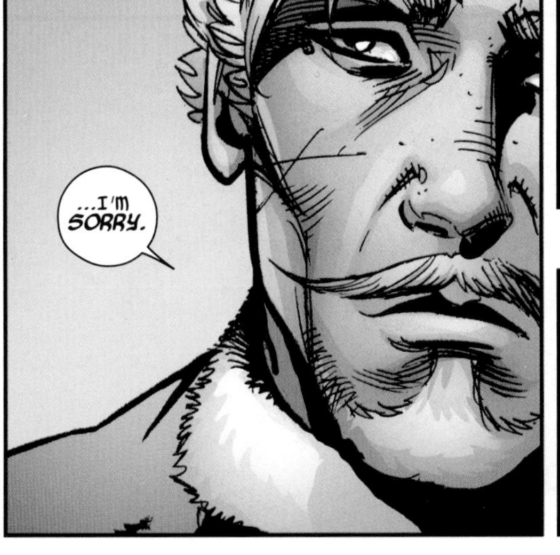
...I'M SORRY.

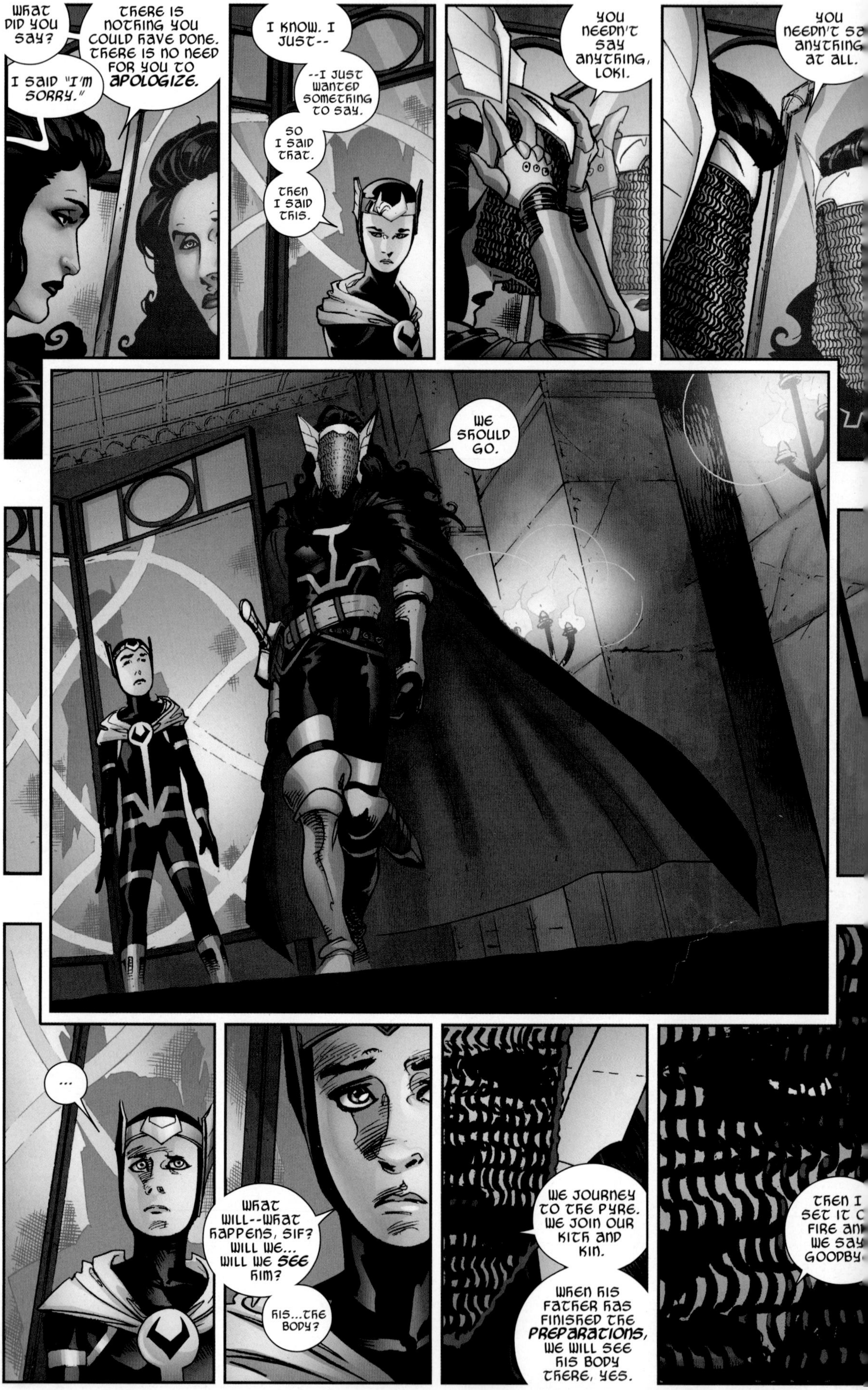
WHAT DID YOU SAY?
I SAID "I'M SORRY."
THERE IS NOTHING YOU COULD HAVE DONE. THERE IS NO NEED FOR YOU TO APOLOGIZE.
I KNOW. I JUST--
--I JUST WANTED SOMETHING TO SAY.
SO I SAID THAT.
THEN I SAID THIS.
YOU NEEDN'T SAY ANYTHING, LOKI.
YOU NEEDN'T SA ANYTHING AT ALL.
WE SHOULD GO.
...
WHAT WILL--WHAT HAPPENS, SIF? WILL WE... WILL WE SEE HIM?
HIS...THE BODY?
WE JOURNEY TO THE PYRE. WE JOIN OUR KITH AND KIN.
WHEN HIS FATHER HAS FINISHED THE PREPARATIONS, WE WILL SEE HIS BODY THERE, YES.
THEN I SET IT C FIRE AN WE SAY GOODBY

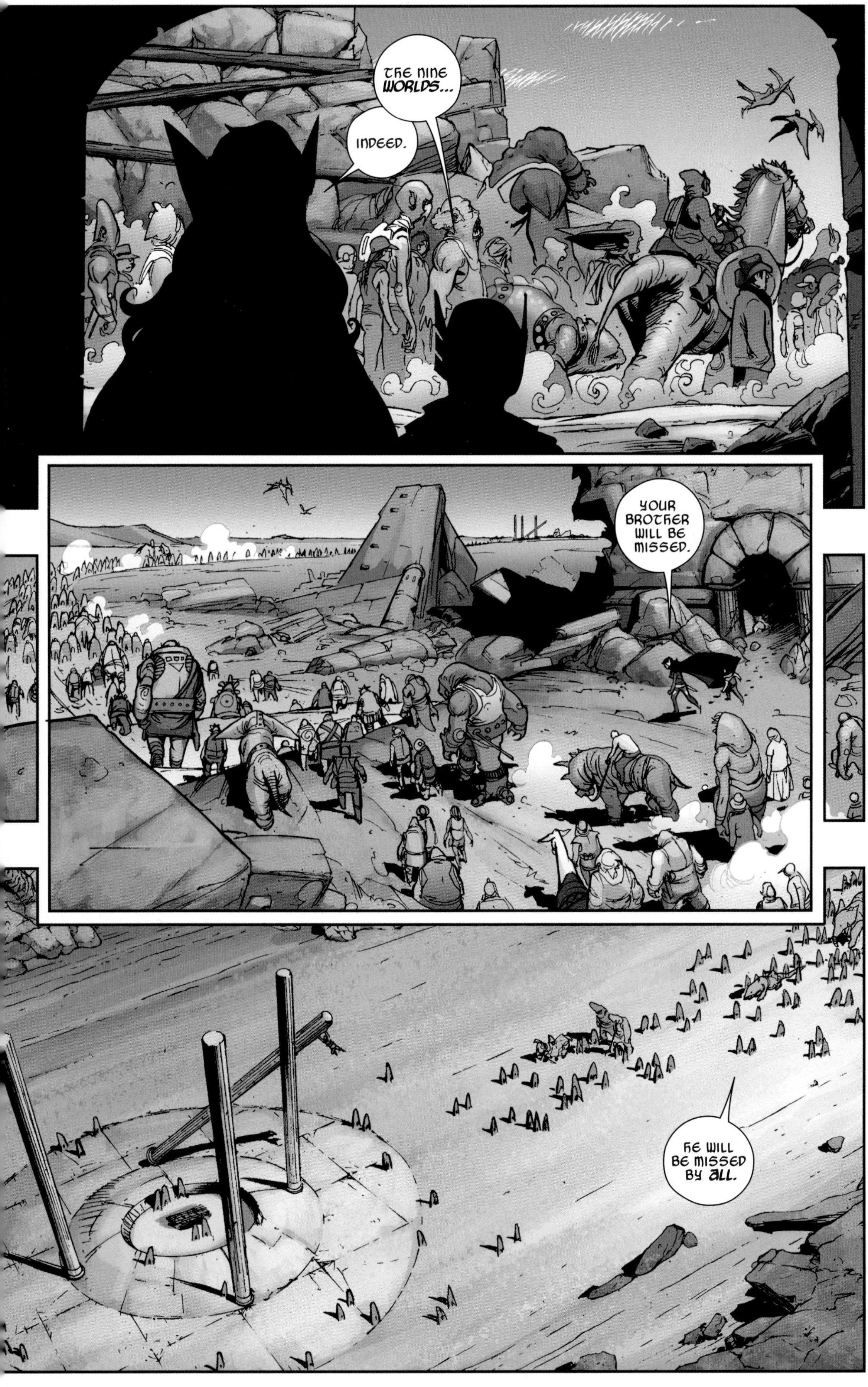
THE NINE WORLDS...
INDEED.
YOUR BROTHER WILL BE MISSED.
HE WILL BE MISSED BY ALL.

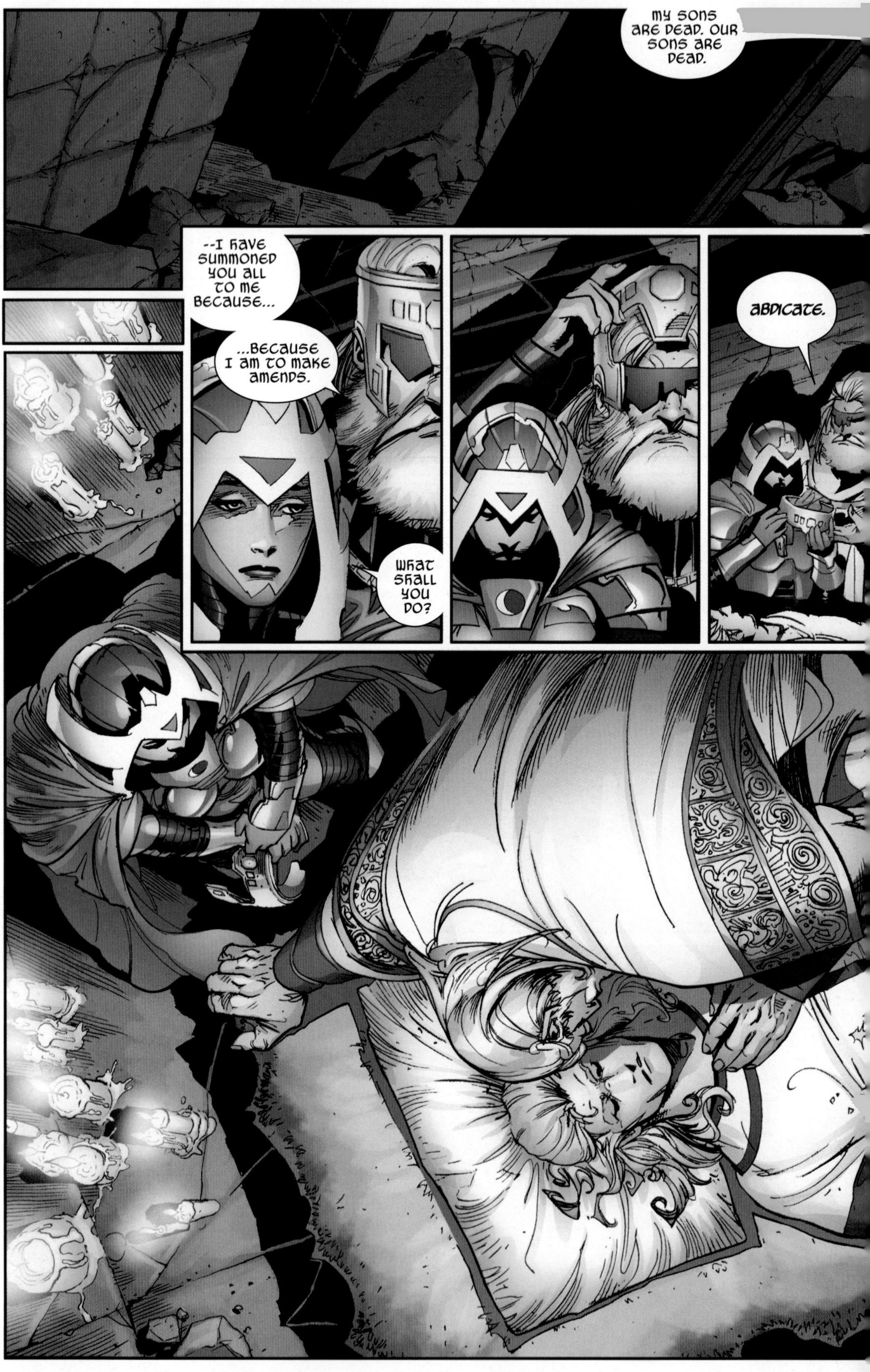

MY SONS ARE DEAD. OUR SONS ARE DEAD.
--I HAVE SUMMONED YOU ALL TO ME BECAUSE...
...BECAUSE I AM TO MAKE AMENDS.
WHAT SHALL YOU DO?
ABDICATE.

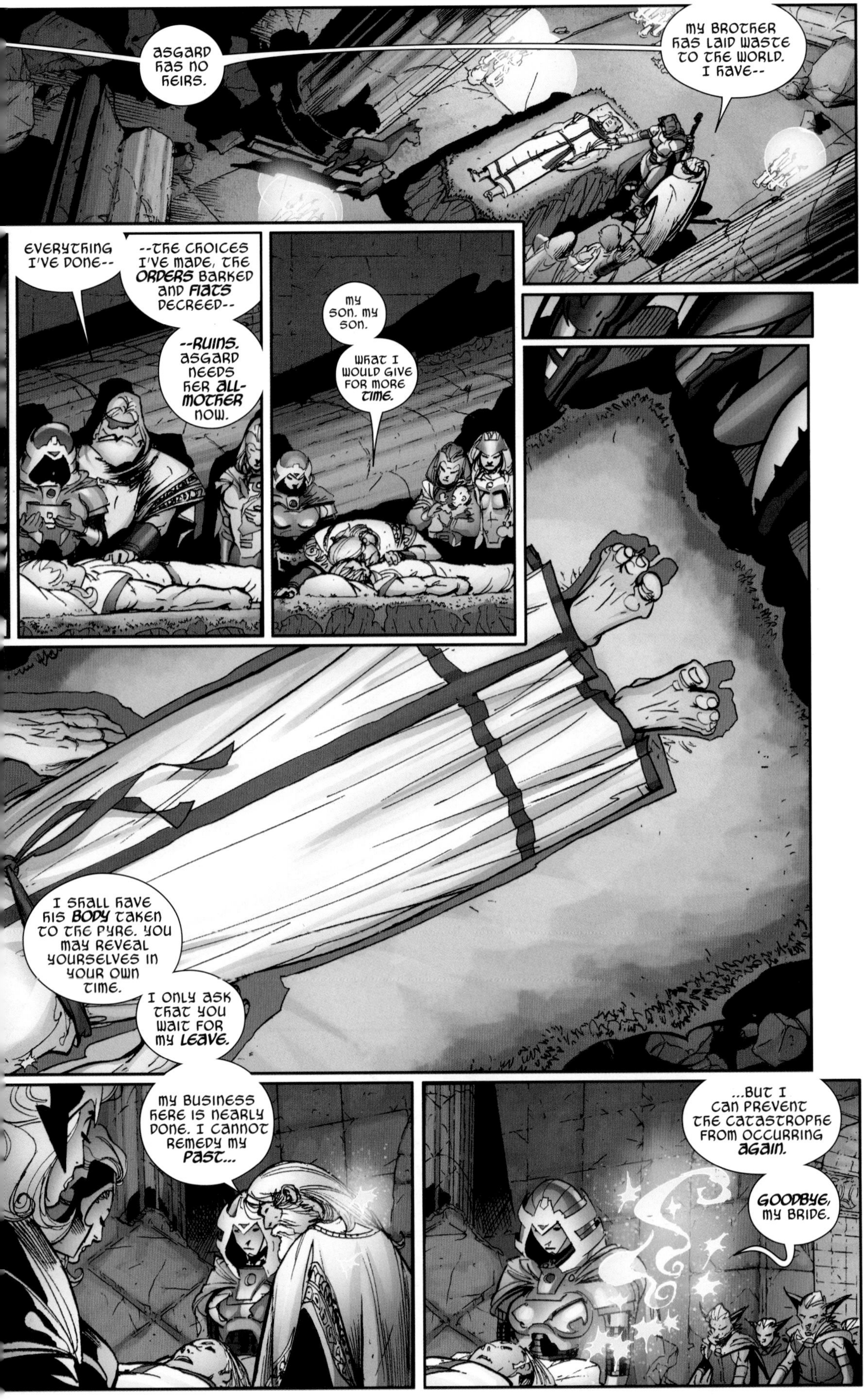
ASGARD HAS NO HEIRS.
MY BROTHER HAS LAID WASTE TO THE WORLD. I HAVE--
EVERYTHING I'VE DONE--
--THE CHOICES I'VE MADE, THE ORDERS BARKED AND FIATS DECREED--
--RUINS. ASGARD NEEDS HER ALL-MOTHER NOW.
MY SON. MY SON.
WHAT I WOULD GIVE FOR MORE TIME.
I SHALL HAVE HIS BODY TAKEN TO THE PYRE. YOU MAY REVEAL YOURSELVES IN YOUR OWN TIME.
I ONLY ASK THAT YOU WAIT FOR MY LEAVE.
MY BUSINESS HERE IS NEARLY DONE. I CANNOT REMEDY MY PAST...
...BUT I CAN PREVENT THE CATASTROPHE FROM OCCURRING AGAIN.
GOODBYE, MY BRIDE.

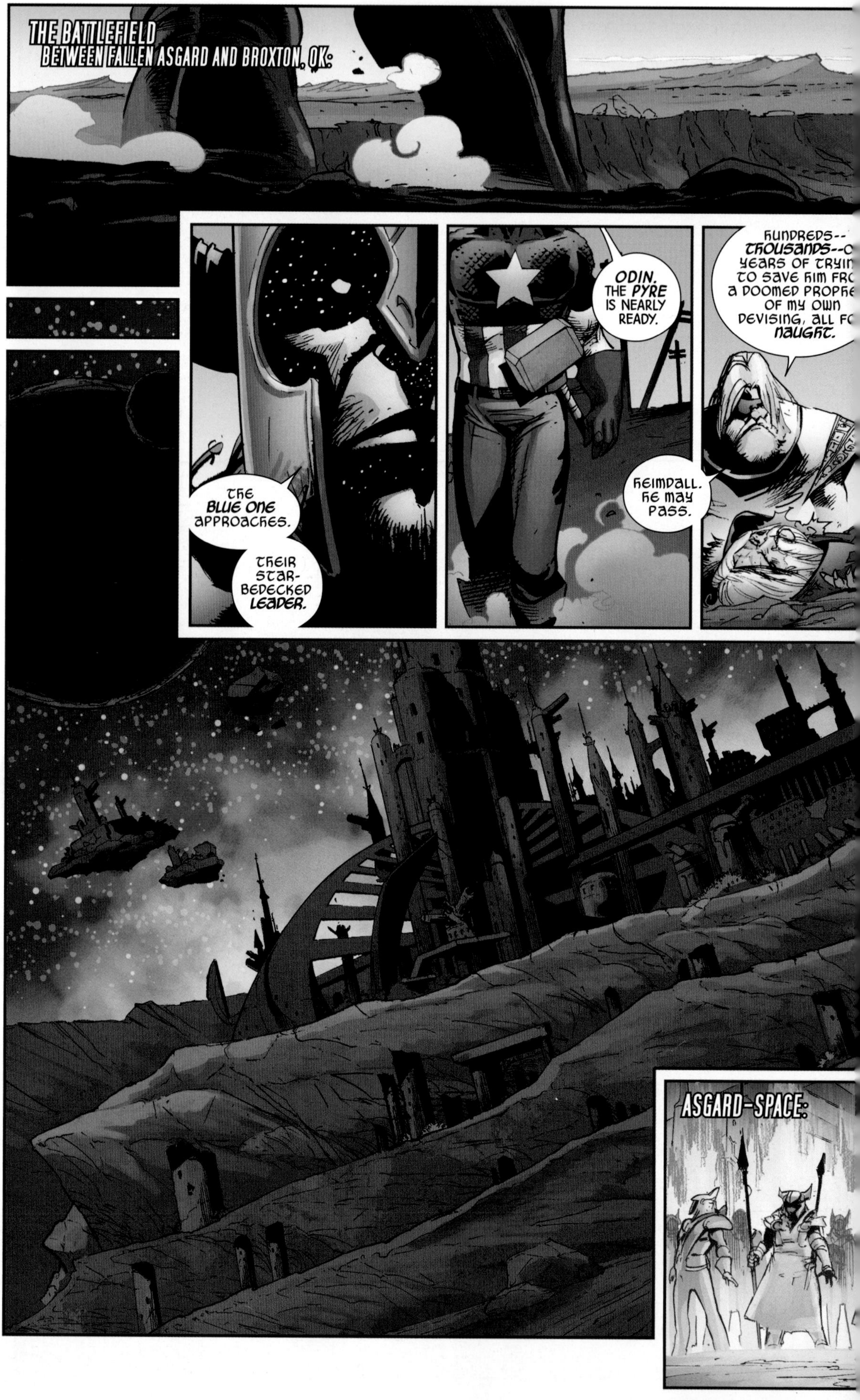
THE BATTLEFIELD
BETWEEN FALLEN ASGARD AND BROXTON, OK:
THE BLUE ONE APPROACHES.
THEIR STAR-BEDECKED LEADER.
ODIN. THE PYRE IS NEARLY READY.
HEIMDALL. HE MAY PASS.
HUNDREDS-- THOUSANDS--O YEARS OF TRYIN TO SAVE HIM FRO A DOOMED PROPHE OF MY OWN DEVISING, ALL FO NAUGHT.
ASGARD-SPACE:

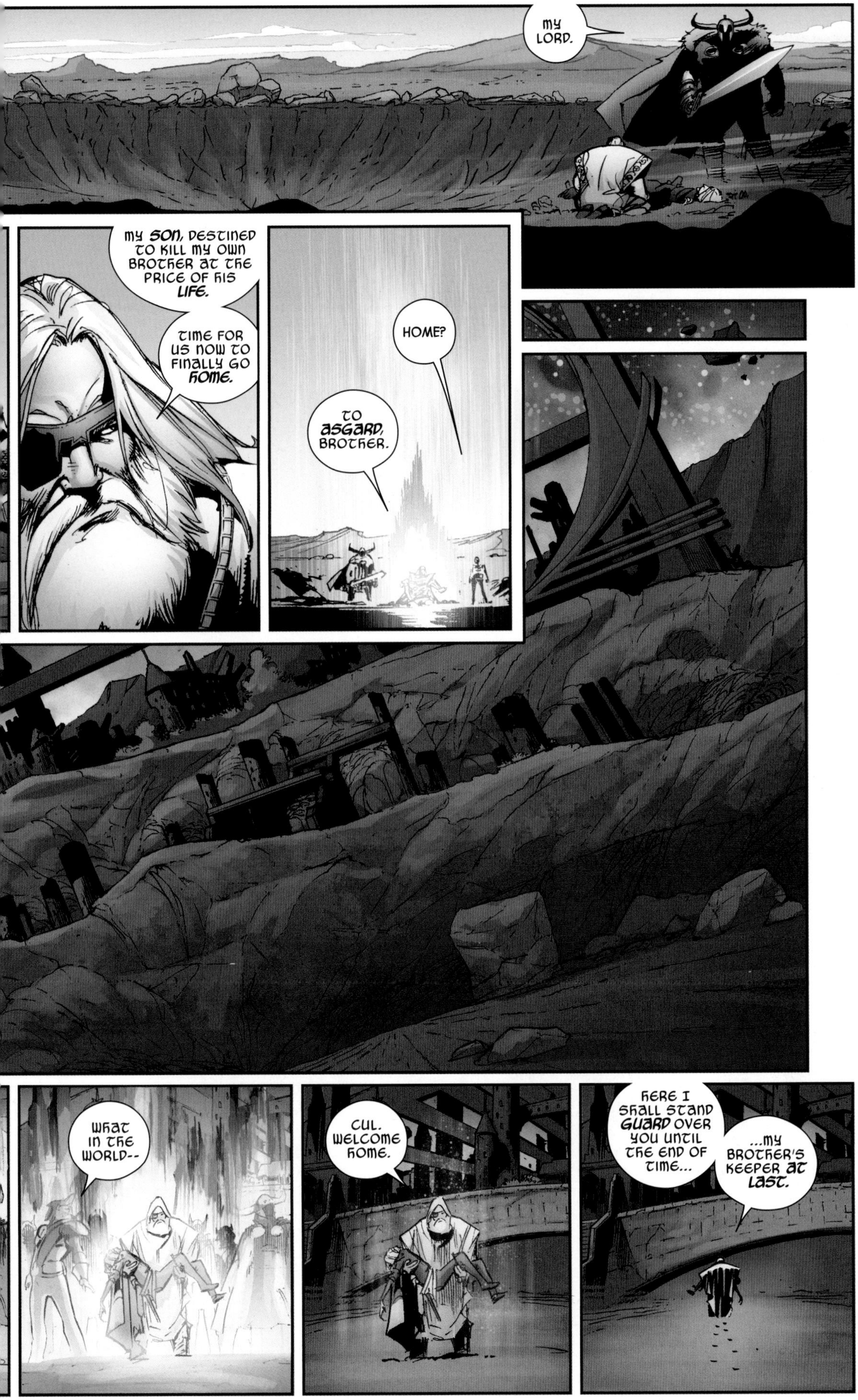
MY LORD.
MY SON, DESTINED TO KILL MY OWN BROTHER AT THE PRICE OF HIS LIFE.
TIME FOR US NOW TO FINALLY GO HOME.
HOME?
TO ASGARD, BROTHER.
WHAT IN THE WORLD--
CUL. WELCOME HOME.
HERE I SHALL STAND GUARD OVER YOU UNTIL THE END OF TIME...
...MY BROTHER'S KEEPER AT LAST.

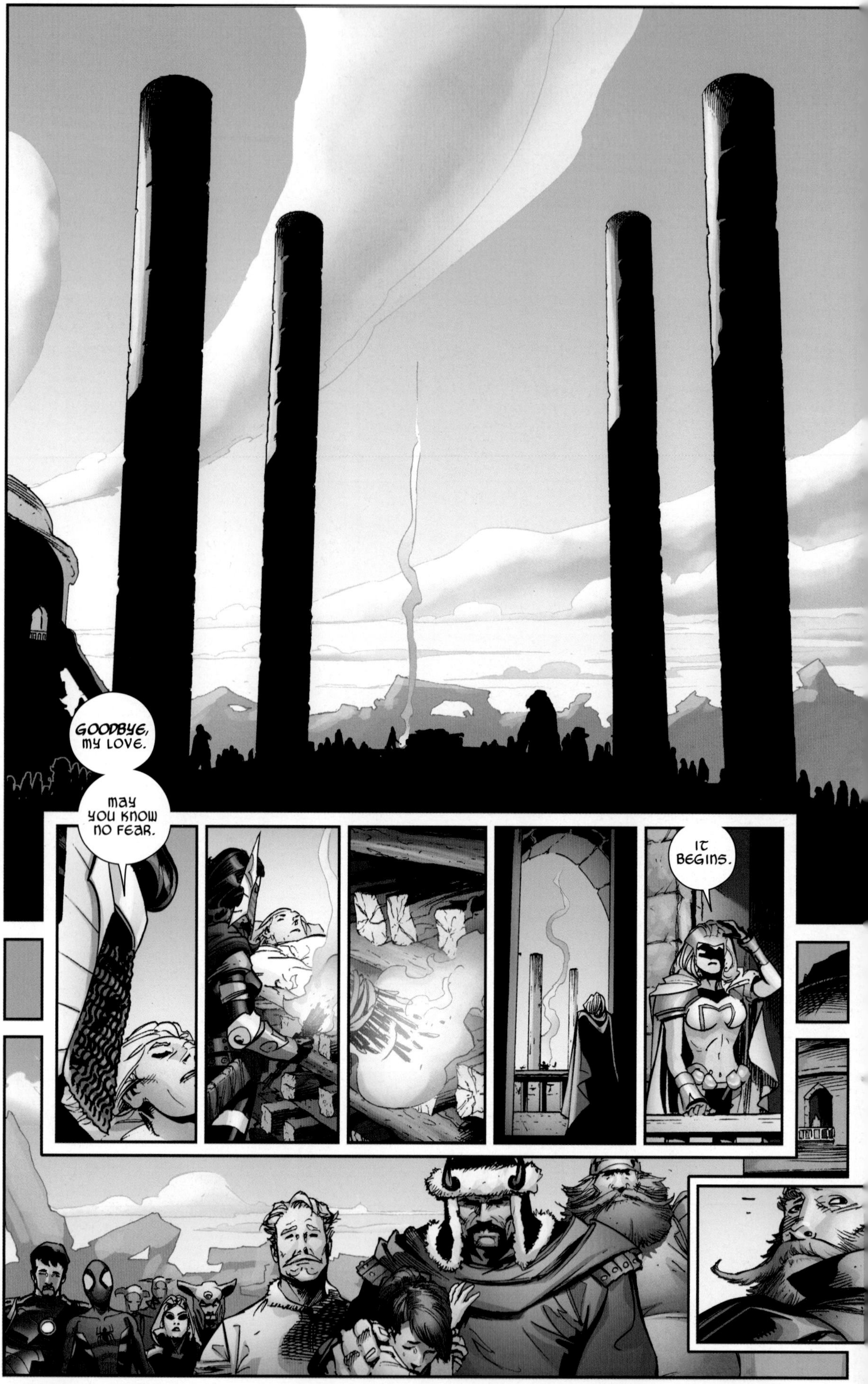
GOODBYE, MY LOVE.
MAY YOU KNOW NO FEAR.
IT BEGINS.

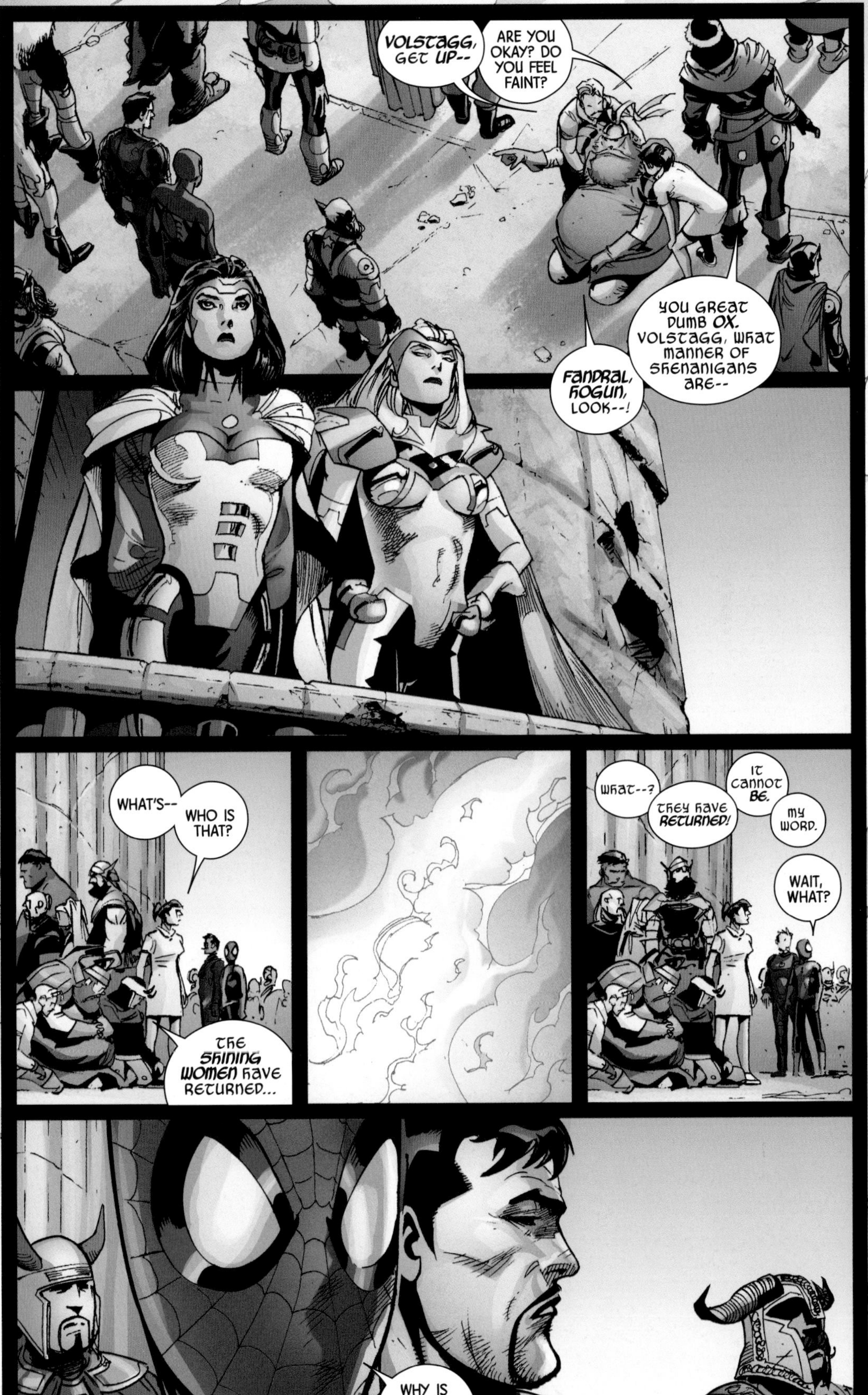
VOLSTAGG, GET UP--
ARE YOU OKAY? DO YOU FEEL FAINT?
YOU GREAT DUMB OX. VOLSTAGG, WHAT MANNER OF SHENANIGANS ARE--
FANDRAL, HOGUN, LOOK--!
WHAT'S--
WHO IS THAT?
THE SHINING WOMEN HAVE RETURNED...
WHAT--?
IT CANNOT BE.
THEY HAVE RETURNED!
MY WORD.
WAIT, WHAT?
WHY IS EVERYBODY SITTING DOWN?

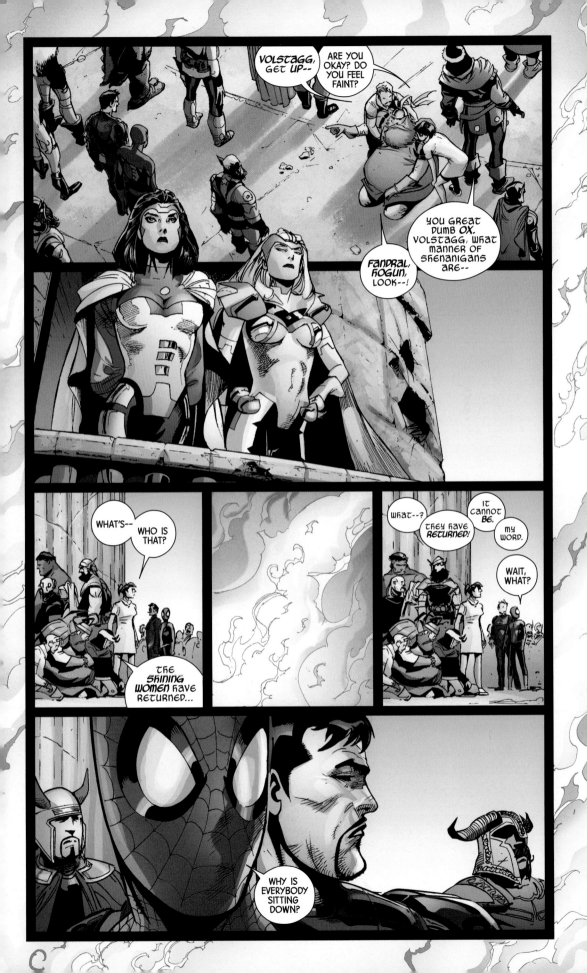

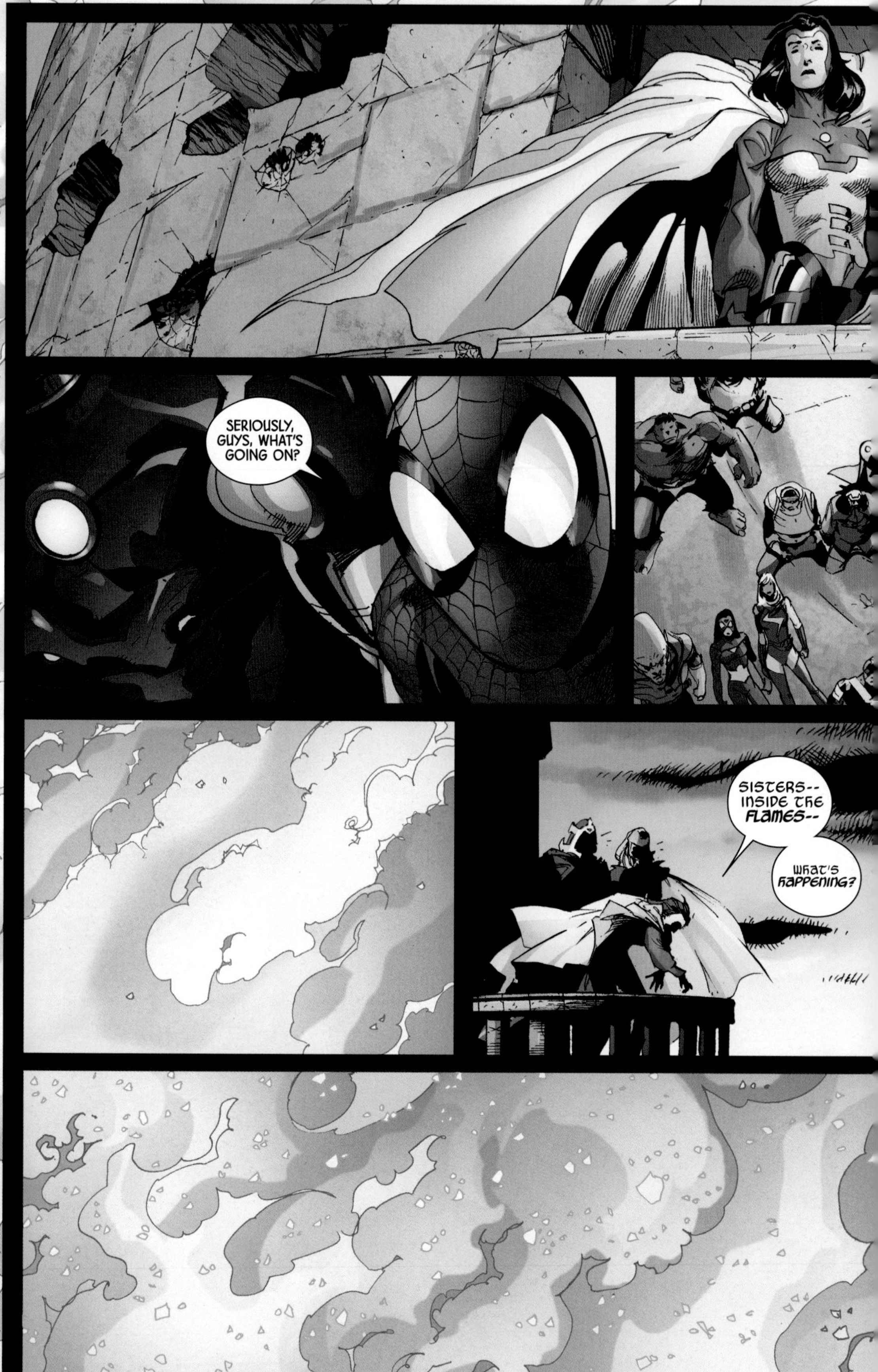
SERIOUSLY, GUYS, WHAT'S GOING ON?
SISTERS-- INSIDE THE FLAMES--
WHAT'S HAPPENING?

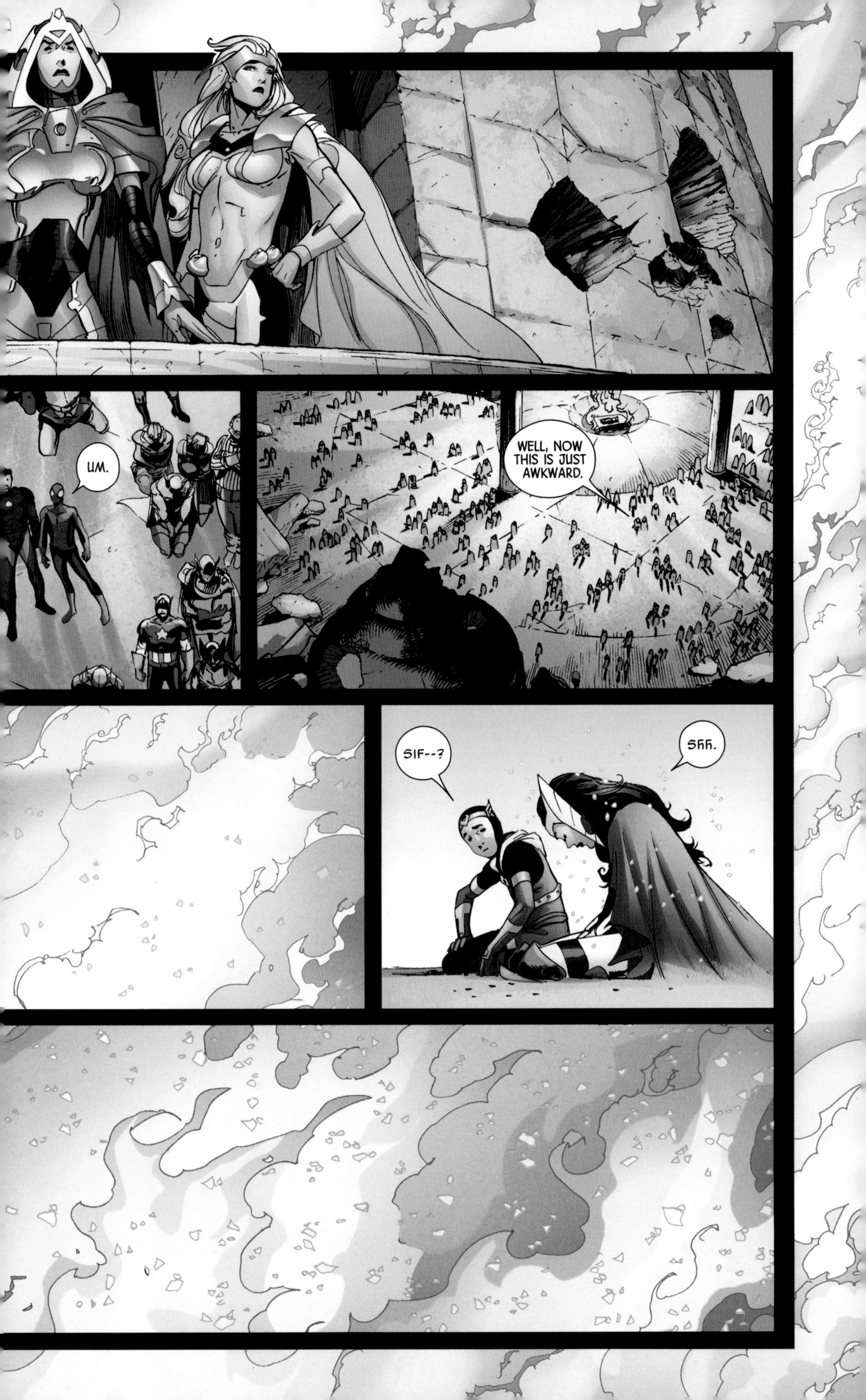
UM.
WELL, NOW THIS IS JUST AWKWARD.
SIF--?
SHH.

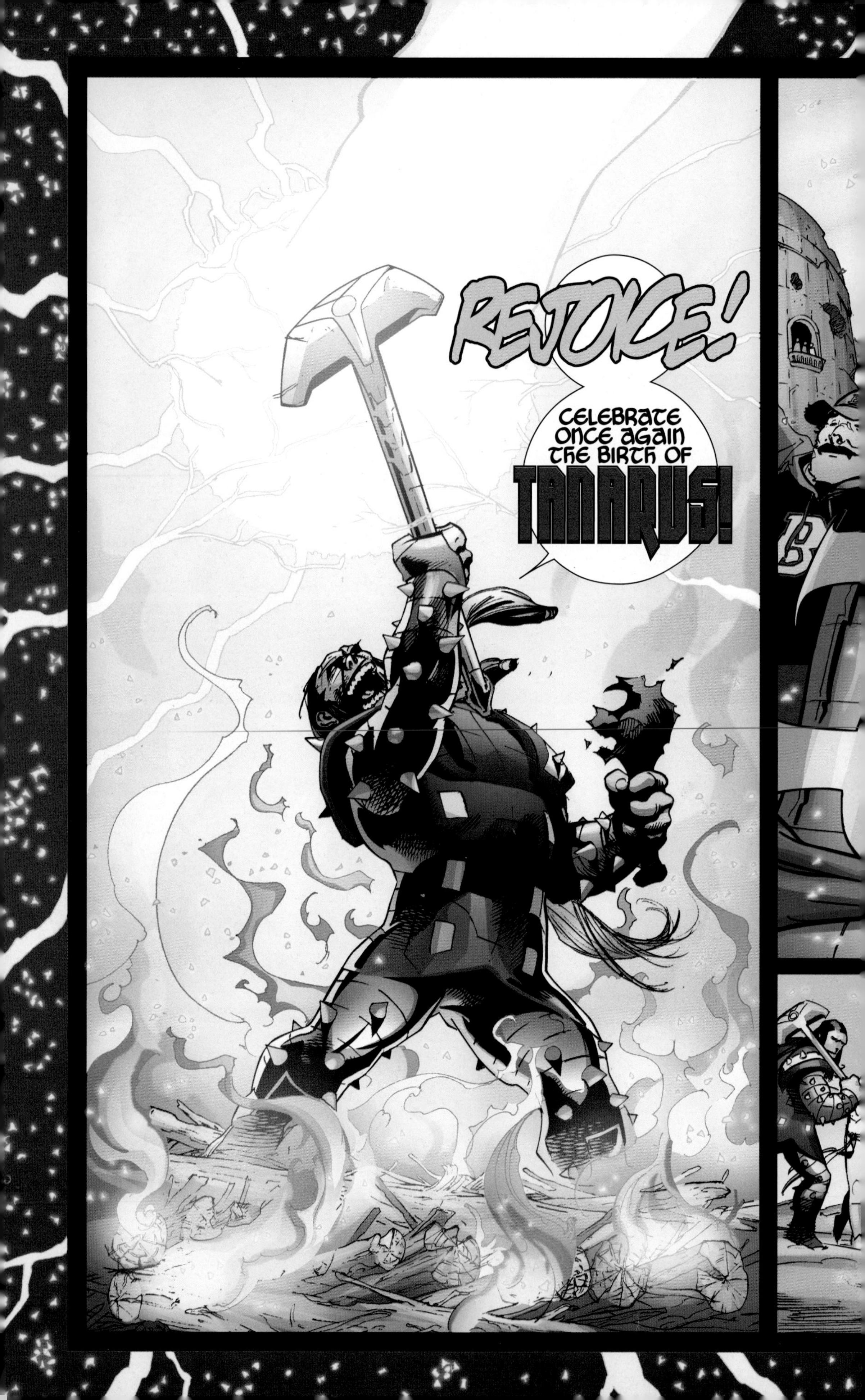
REJOICE!
CELEBRATE ONCE AGAIN THE BIRTH OF TANARUS!

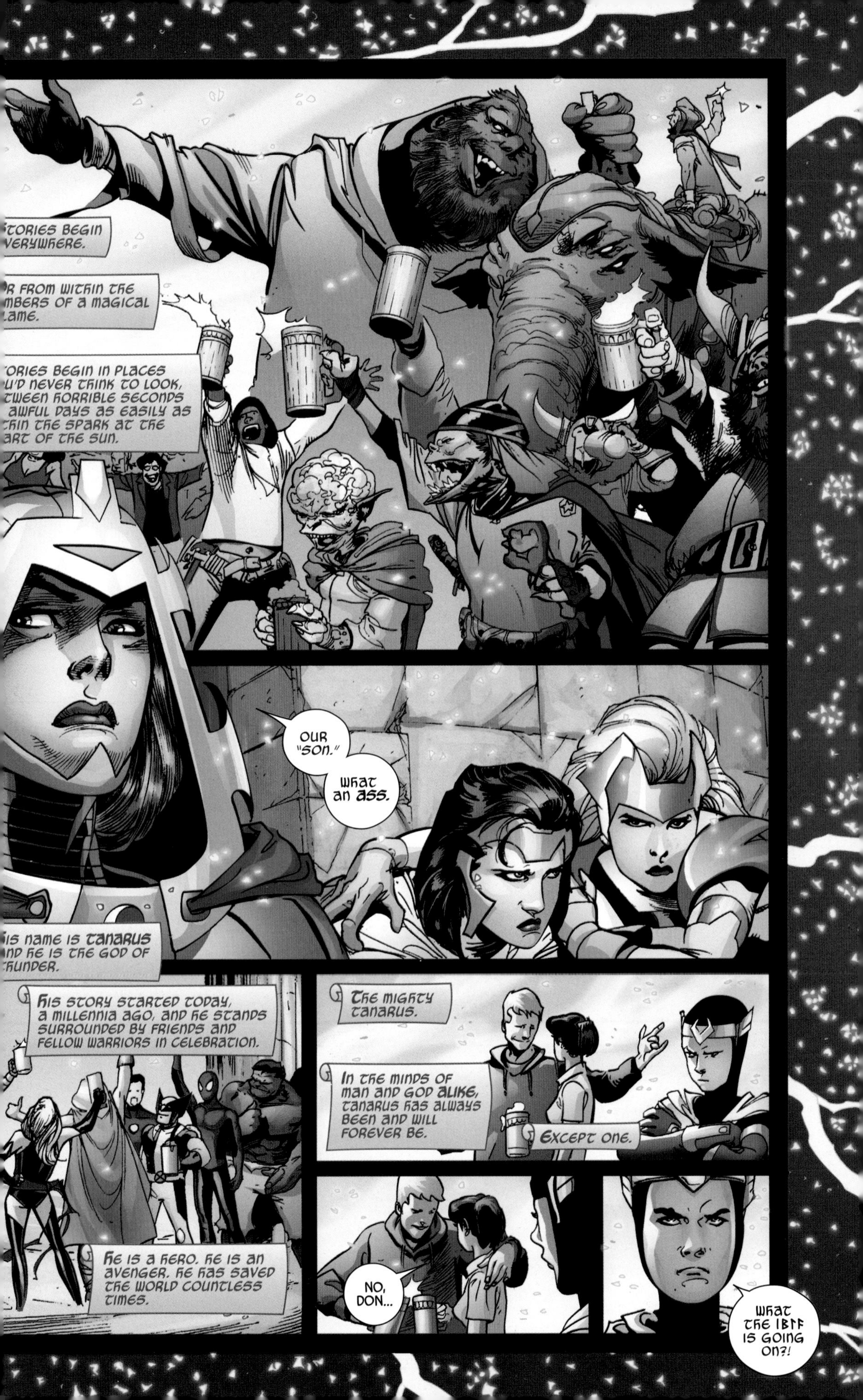
TORIES BEGIN
VERYWHERE.
R FROM WITHIN THE
MBERS OF A MAGICAL
LAME.
TORIES BEGIN IN PLACES
U'D NEVER THINK TO LOOK,
TWEEN HORRIBLE SECONDS
AWFUL DAYS AS EASILY AS
THIN THE SPARK AT THE
ART OF THE SUN.
OUR "SON."
WHAT AN ASS.
IS NAME IS TANARUS
ND HE IS THE GOD OF
THUNDER.
HIS STORY STARTED TODAY, A MILLENNIA AGO, AND HE STANDS SURROUNDED BY FRIENDS AND FELLOW WARRIORS IN CELEBRATION.
HE IS A HERO. HE IS AN AVENGER. HE HAS SAVED THE WORLD COUNTLESS TIMES.
THE MIGHTY TANARUS.
IN THE MINDS OF MAN AND GOD ALIKE, TANARUS HAS ALWAYS BEEN AND WILL FOREVER BE.
EXCEPT ONE.
NO, DON...
WHAT THE ᛁᛒᛚᚠ IS GOING ON?!

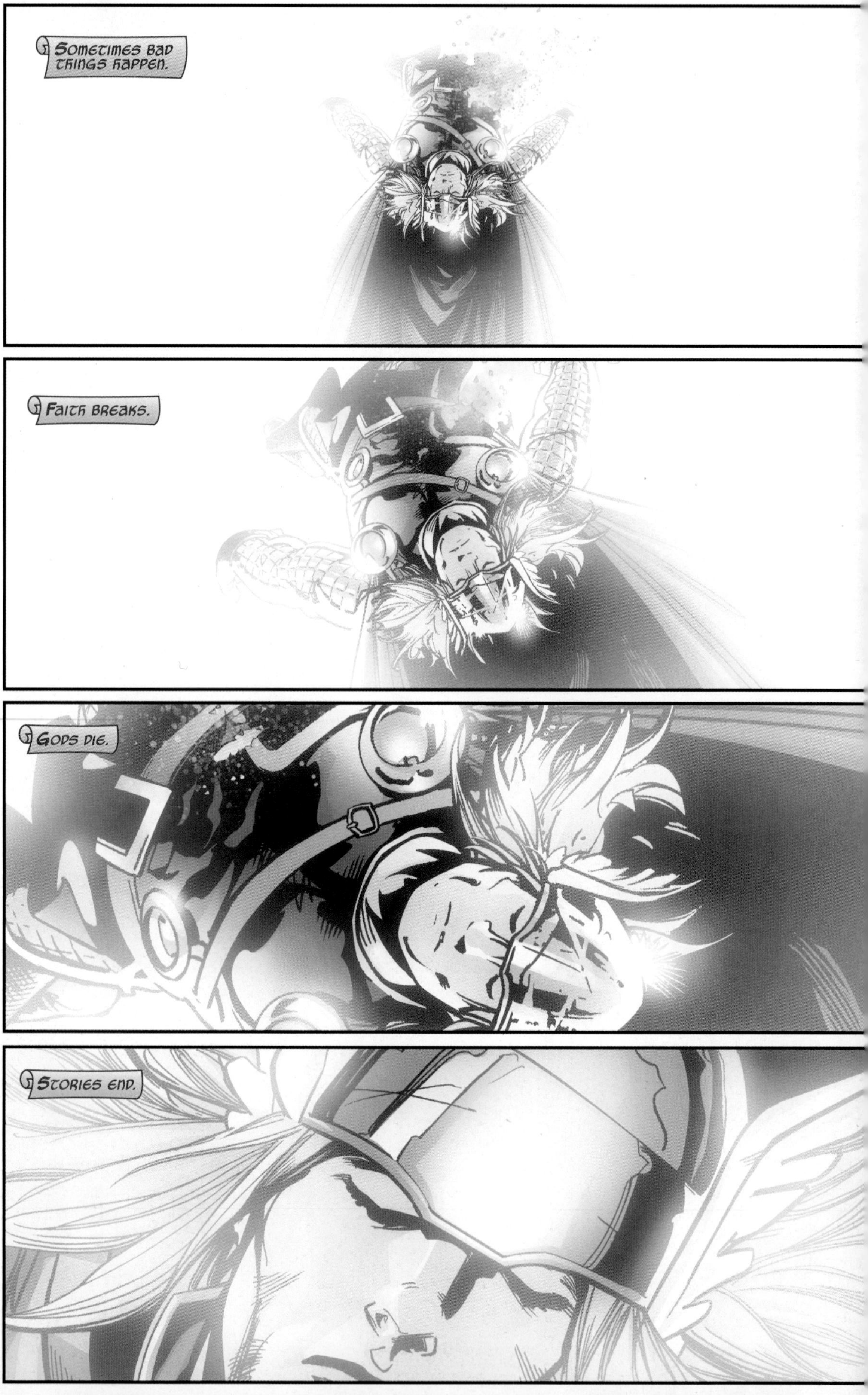
Sometimes bad things happen.
Faith breaks.
Gods die.
Stories end.

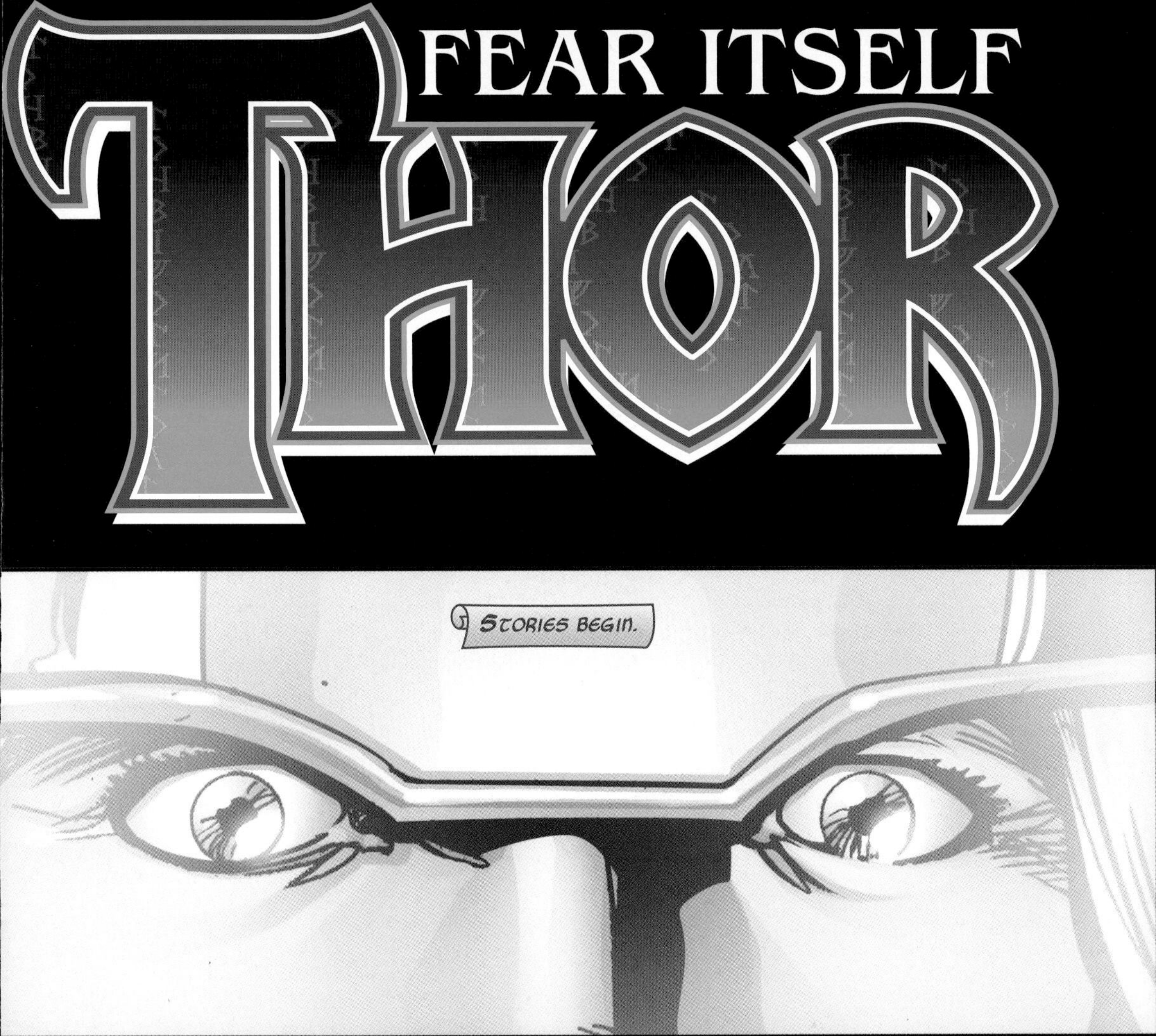
FEAR ITSELF
THOR
STORIES BEGIN.

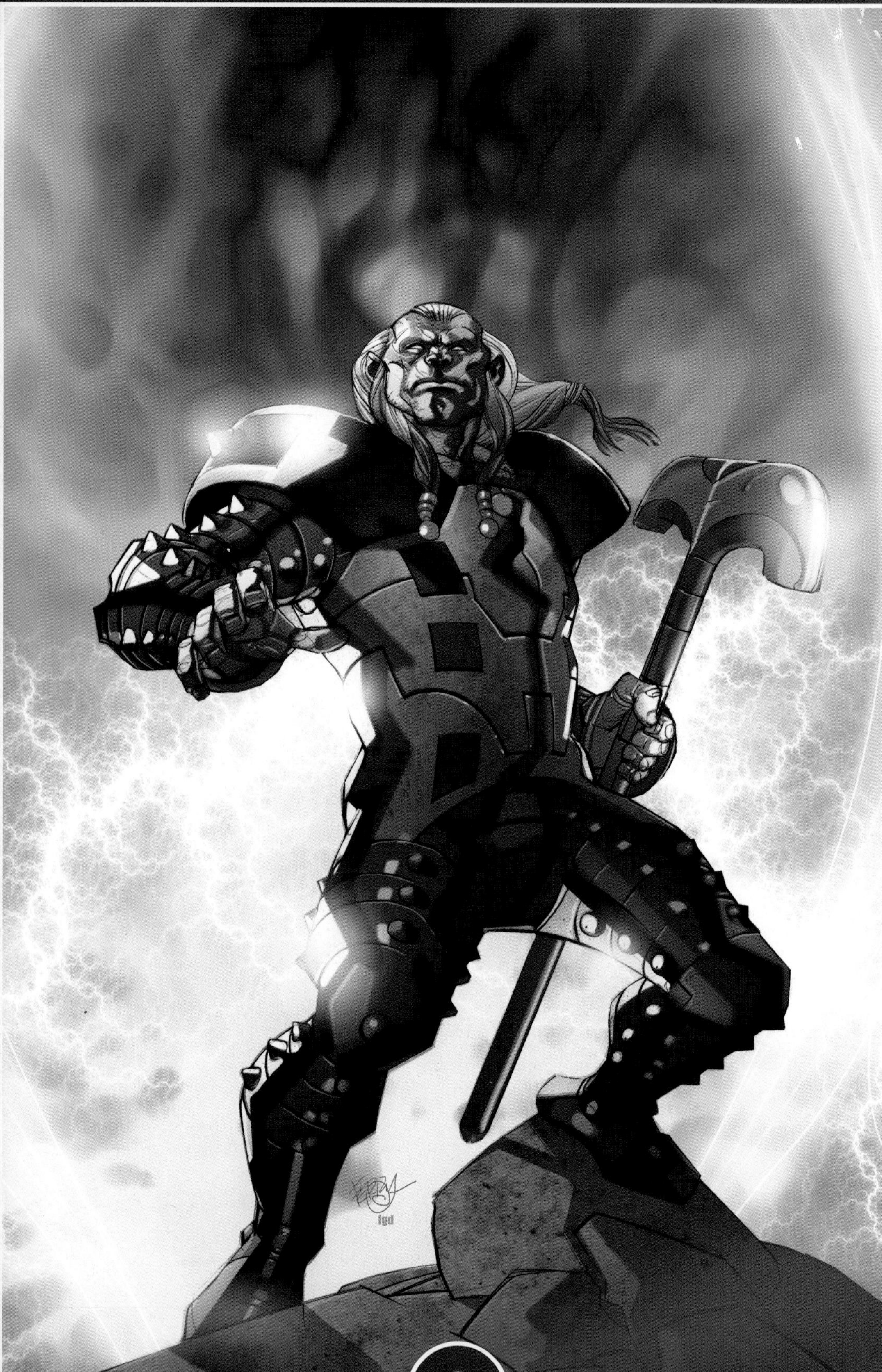

8

THE MIGHTY TANARUS 1: LOST

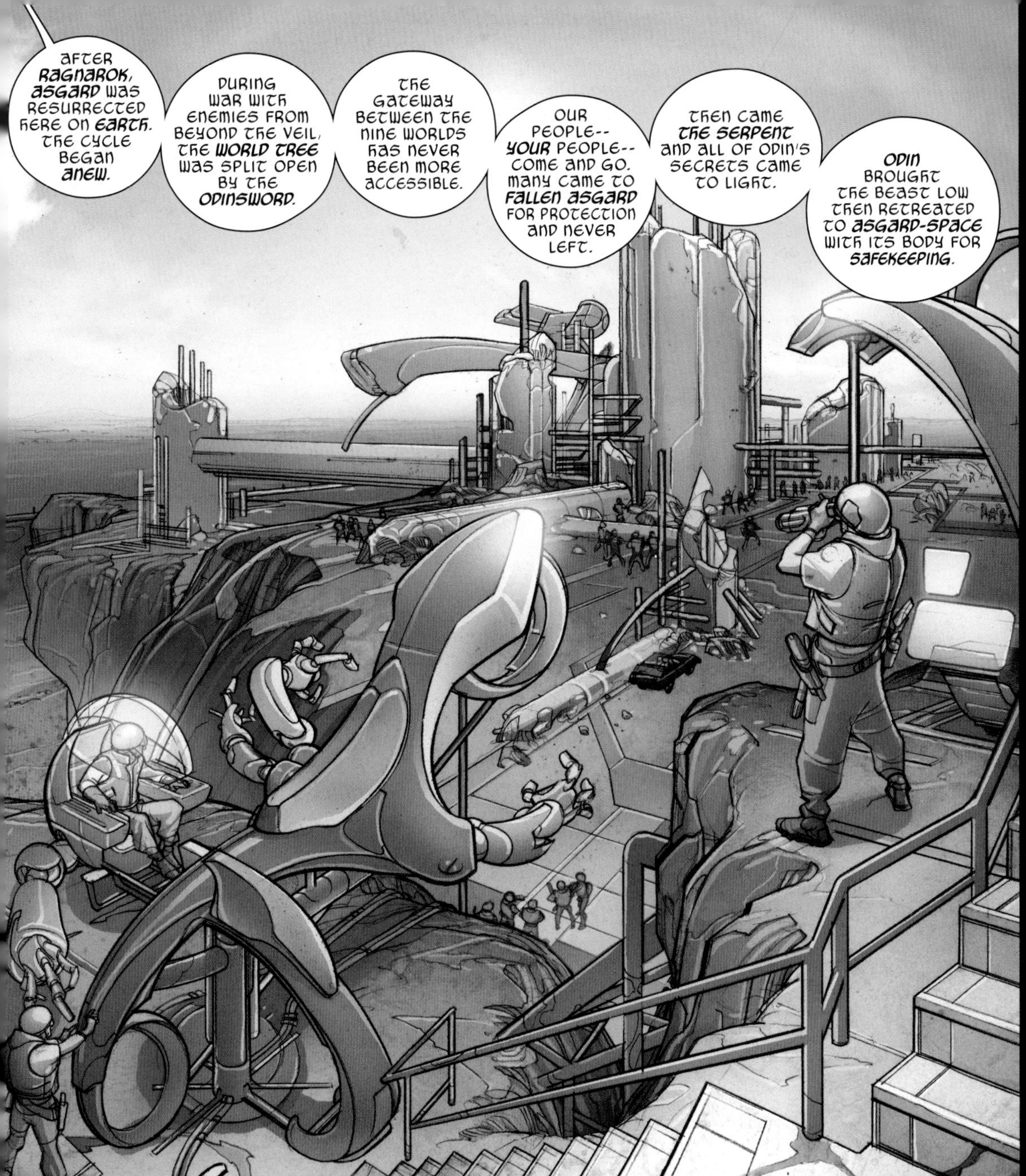
AFTER RAGNAROK, ASGARD WAS RESURRECTED HERE ON EARTH. THE CYCLE BEGAN ANEW.
DURING WAR WITH ENEMIES FROM BEYOND THE VEIL, THE WORLD TREE WAS SPLIT OPEN BY THE ODINSWORD.
THE GATEWAY BETWEEN THE NINE WORLDS HAS NEVER BEEN MORE ACCESSIBLE.
OUR PEOPLE-- YOUR PEOPLE-- COME AND GO. MANY CAME TO FALLEN ASGARD FOR PROTECTION AND NEVER LEFT.
THEN CAME THE SERPENT AND ALL OF ODIN'S SECRETS CAME TO LIGHT.
ODIN BROUGHT THE BEAST LOW THEN RETREATED TO ASGARD-SPACE WITH ITS BODY FOR SAFEKEEPING.

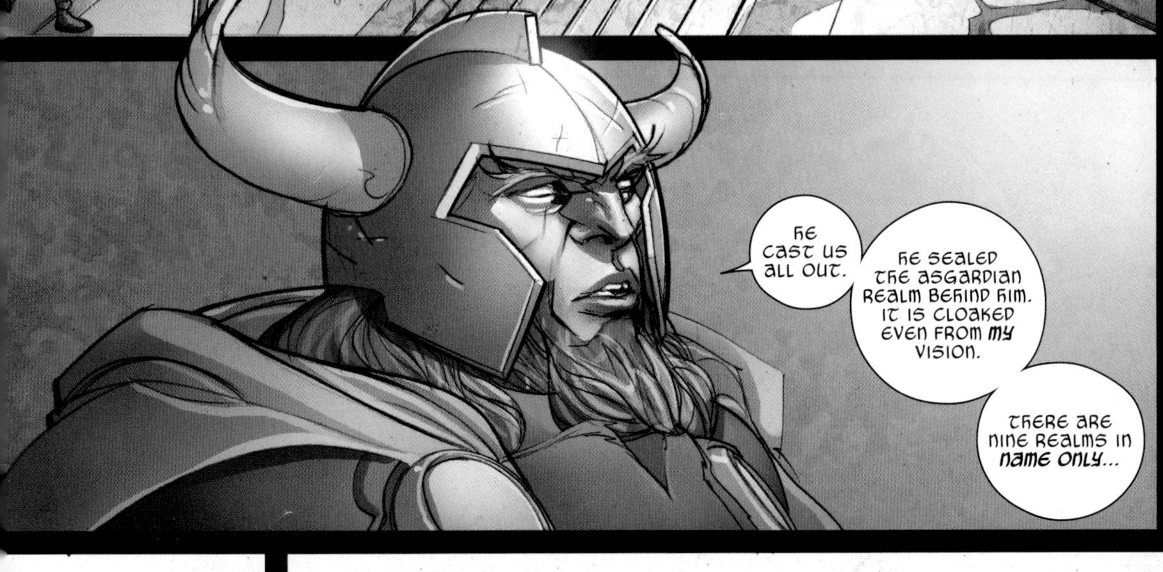
HE CAST US ALL OUT.
HE SEALED THE ASGARDIAN REALM BEHIND HIM. IT IS CLOAKED EVEN FROM MY VISION.
THERE ARE NINE REALMS IN NAME ONLY...

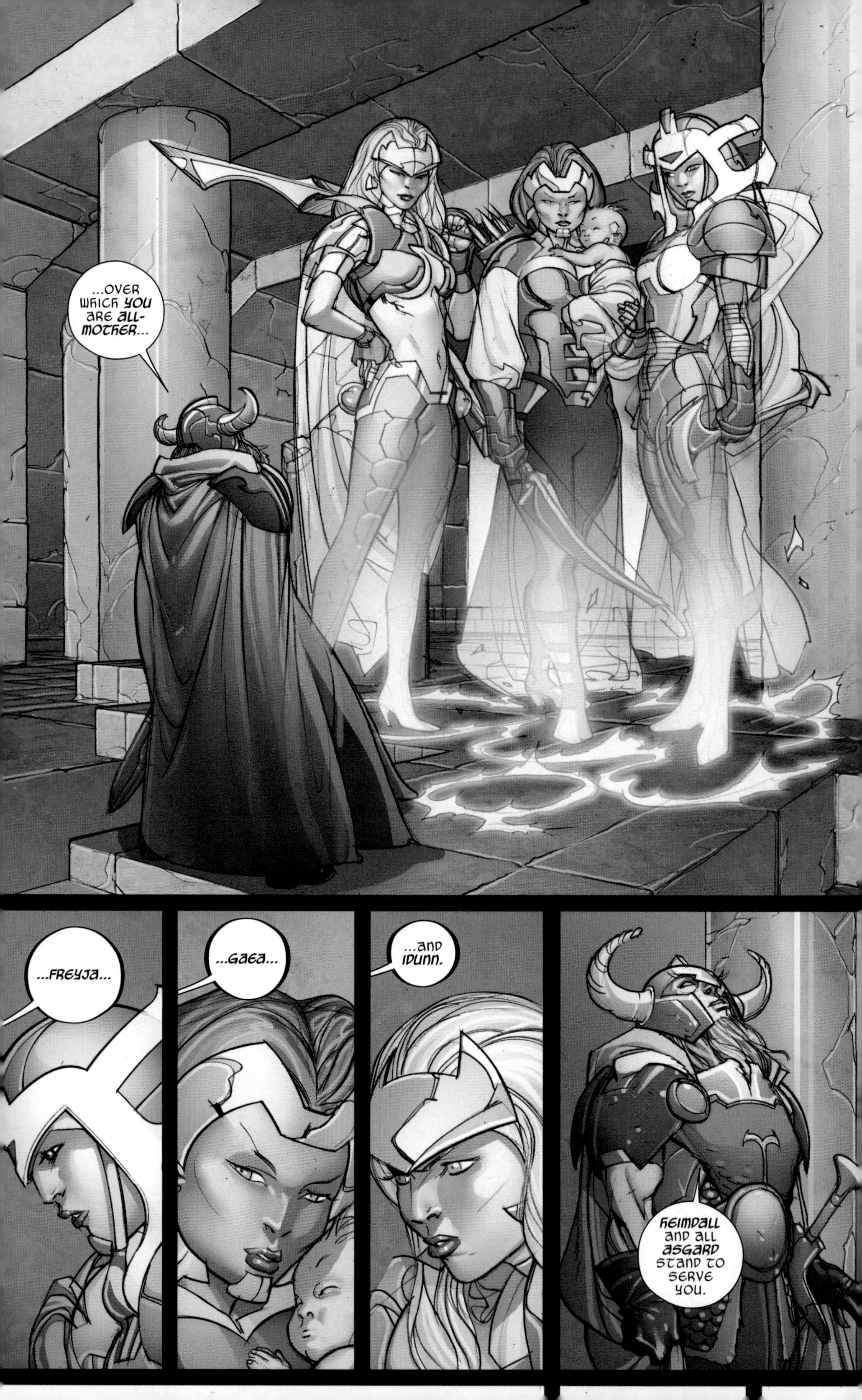
...OVER WHICH YOU ARE ALL-MOTHER...
...FREYJA...
...GAEA...
...AND IDUNN.
HEIMDALL AND ALL ASGARD STAND TO SERVE YOU.

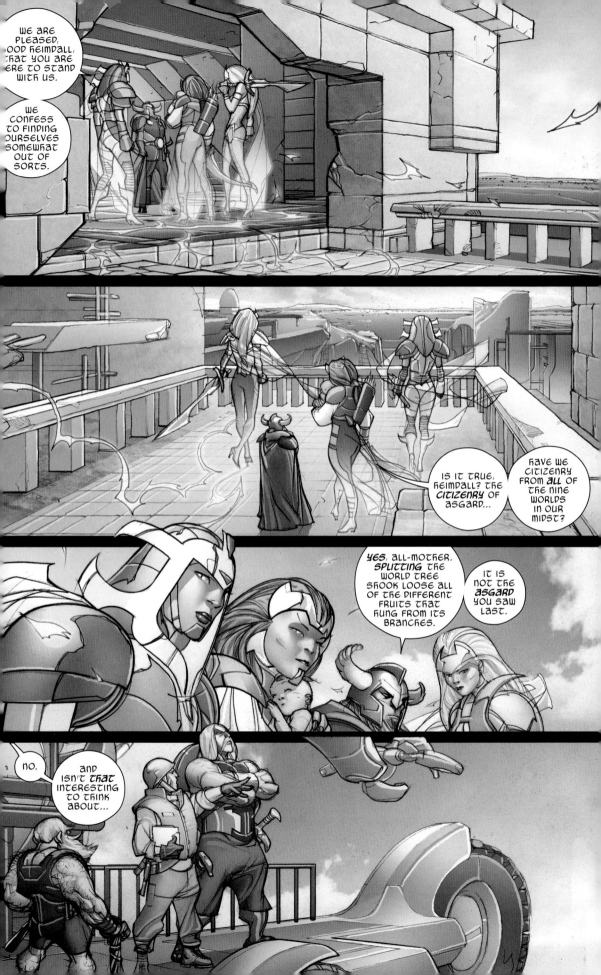

WE ARE PLEASED, GOOD HEIMDALL, THAT YOU ARE HERE TO STAND WITH US.

WE CONFESS TO FINDING OURSELVES SOMEWHAT OUT OF SORTS.

IS IT TRUE, HEIMDALL? THE *CITIZENRY* OF ASGARD...

HAVE WE CITIZENRY FROM *ALL* OF THE NINE WORLDS IN OUR MIDST?

YES, ALL-MOTHER. *SPLITTING* THE WORLD TREE SHOOK LOOSE ALL OF THE DIFFERENT FRUITS THAT HUNG FROM ITS BRANCHES.

IT IS NOT THE *ASGARD* YOU SAW LAST.

NO.

AND ISN'T *THAT* INTERESTING TO THINK ABOUT...

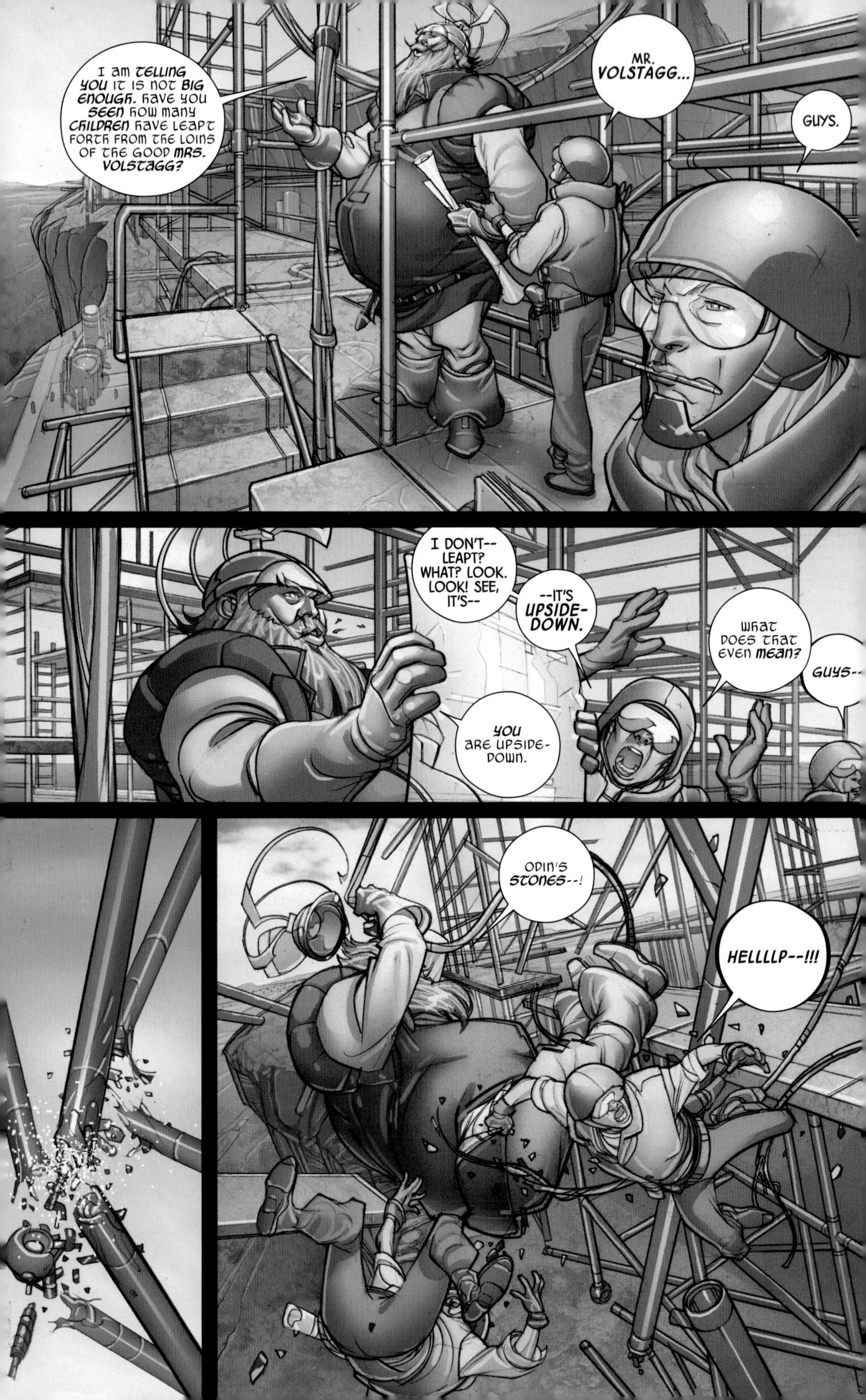
I am TELLING YOU it is not BIG ENOUGH. Have you SEEN how many CHILDREN have leapt forth from the loins of the good MRS. VOLSTAGG?
MR. VOLSTAGG...
GUYS.
I DON'T-- LEAPT? WHAT? LOOK. LOOK! SEE, IT'S--
--IT'S UPSIDE-DOWN.
YOU are upside-down.
What does that even MEAN?
GUYS--
Odin's STONES--!
HELLLLP--!!!

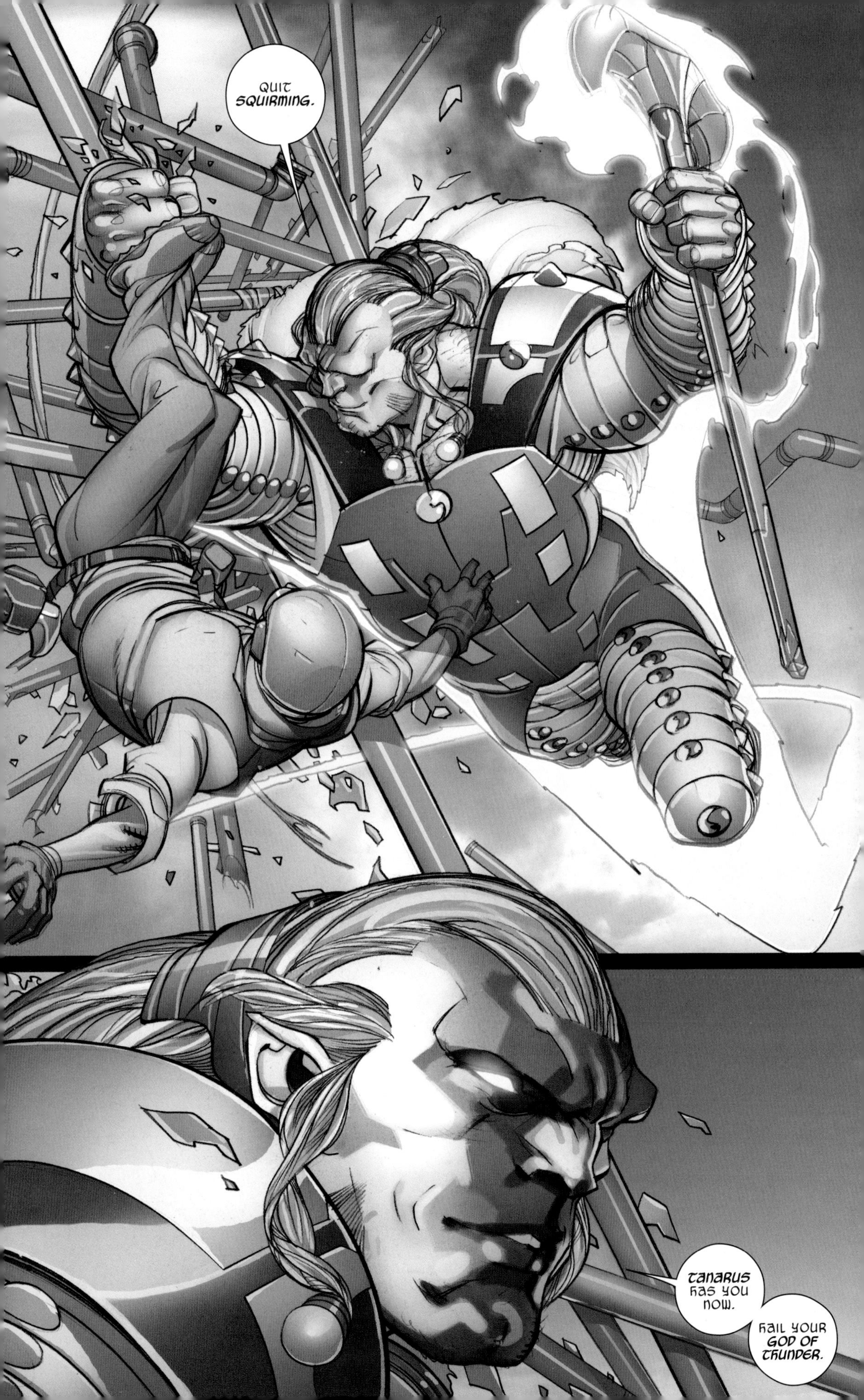
QUIT SQUIRMING.
TANARUS HAS YOU NOW.
HAIL YOUR GOD OF THUNDER.

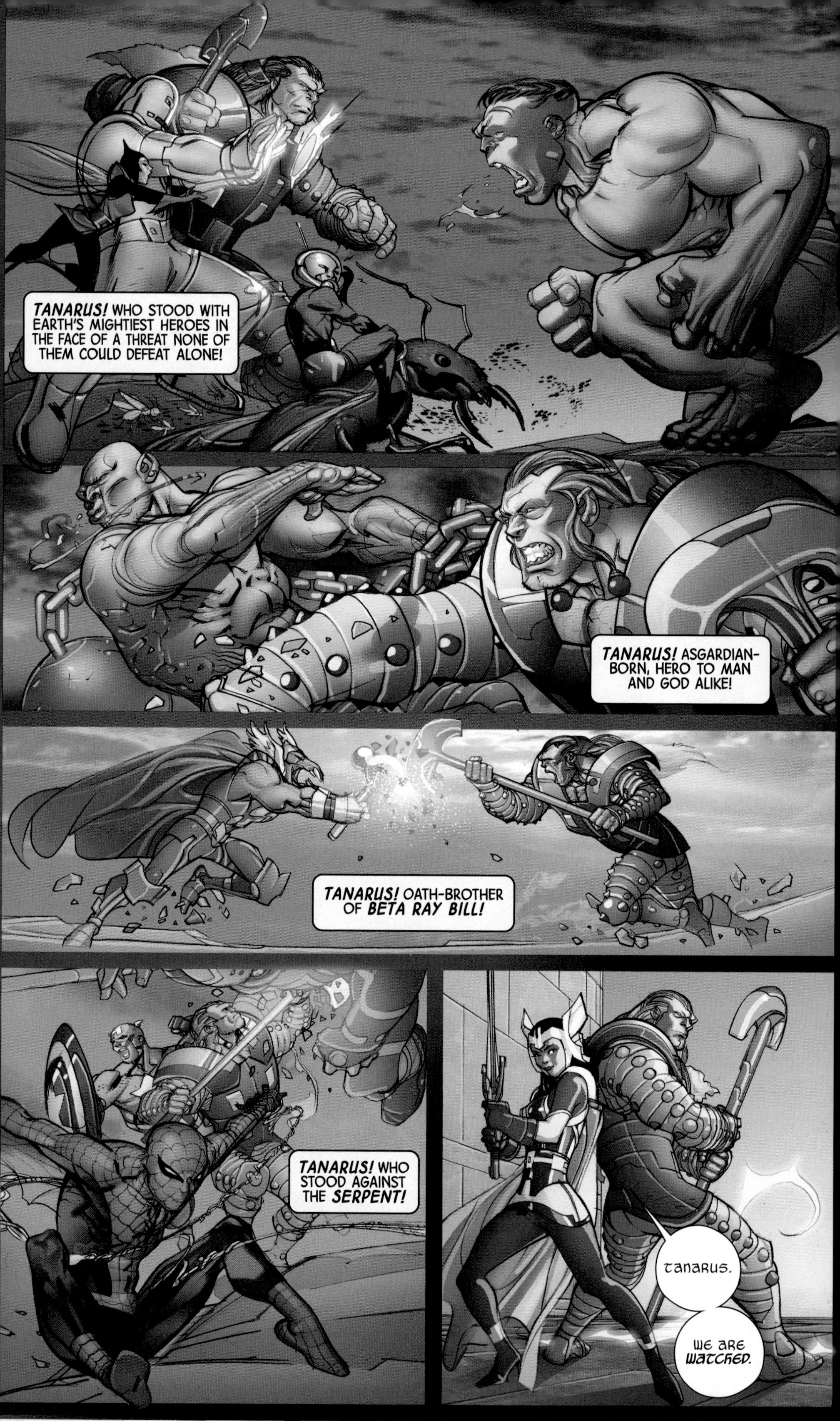
TANARUS! WHO STOOD WITH EARTH'S MIGHTIEST HEROES IN THE FACE OF A THREAT NONE OF THEM COULD DEFEAT ALONE!
TANARUS! ASGARDIAN-BORN, HERO TO MAN AND GOD ALIKE!
TANARUS! OATH-BROTHER OF BETA RAY BILL!
TANARUS! WHO STOOD AGAINST THE SERPENT!
TANARUS.
WE ARE WATCHED.

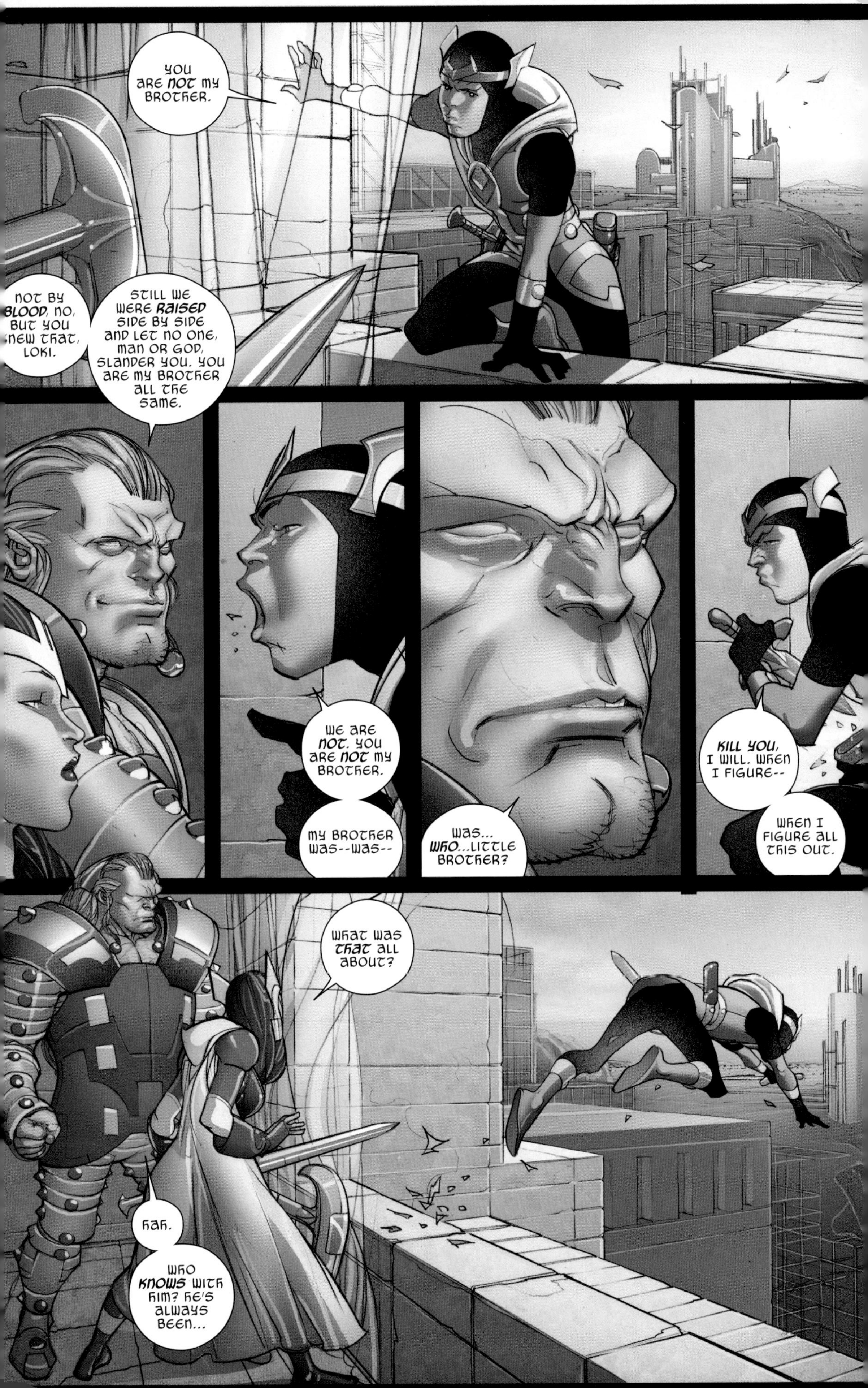
YOU ARE NOT MY BROTHER.
NOT BY BLOOD, NO, BUT YOU KNEW THAT, LOKI.
STILL WE WERE RAISED SIDE BY SIDE AND LET NO ONE, MAN OR GOD, SLANDER YOU. YOU ARE MY BROTHER ALL THE SAME.
WE ARE NOT. YOU ARE NOT MY BROTHER.
MY BROTHER WAS--WAS--
WAS... WHO...LITTLE BROTHER?
KILL YOU, I WILL. WHEN I FIGURE--
WHEN I FIGURE ALL THIS OUT.
WHAT WAS THAT ALL ABOUT?
HAH.
WHO KNOWS WITH HIM? HE'S ALWAYS BEEN...

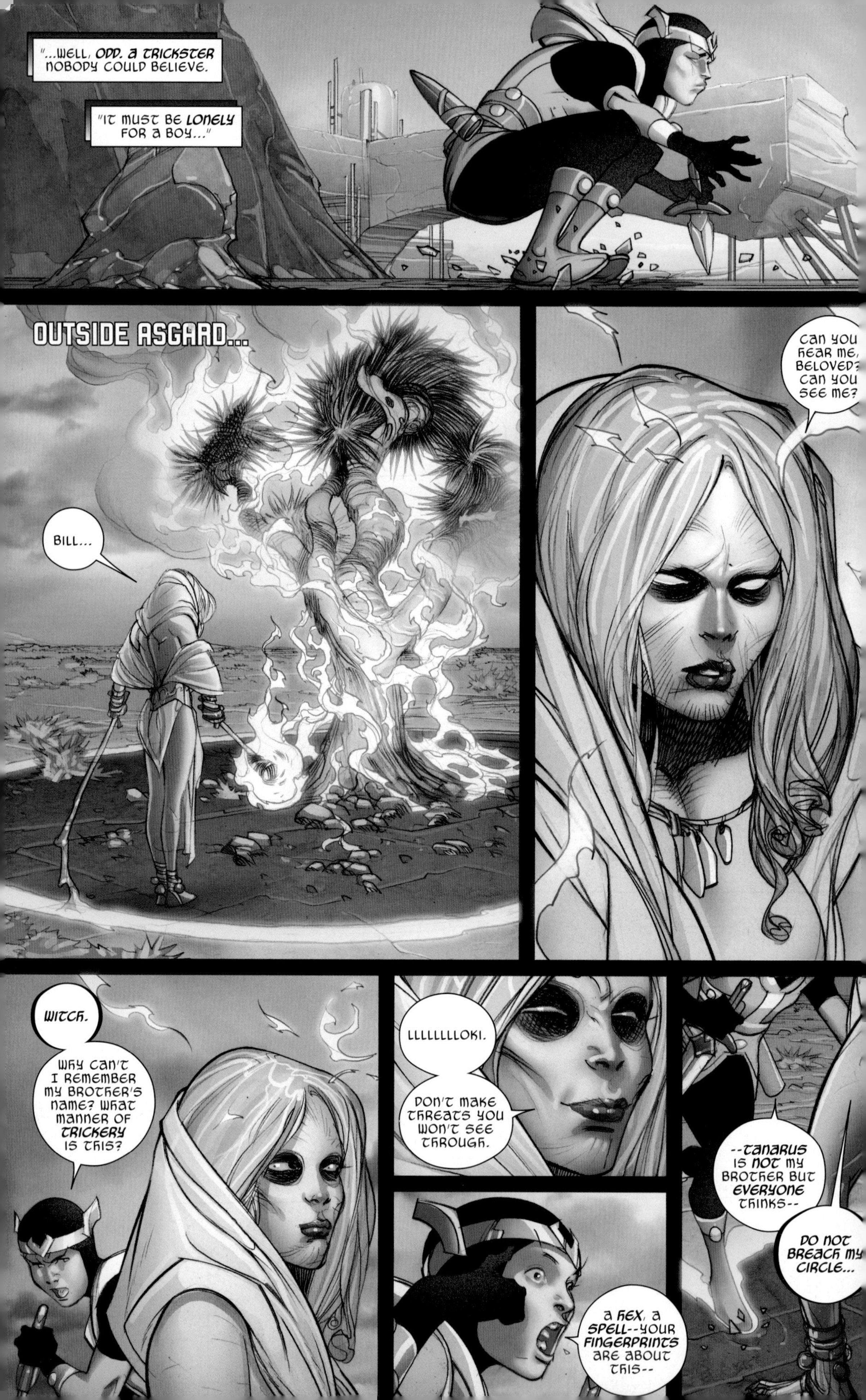

"...WELL, ODD. A TRICKSTER NOBODY COULD BELIEVE.
"IT MUST BE LONELY FOR A BOY..."
OUTSIDE ASGARD...
BILL...
CAN YOU HEAR ME, BELOVED? CAN YOU SEE ME?
WITCH.
WHY CAN'T I REMEMBER MY BROTHER'S NAME? WHAT MANNER OF TRICKERY IS THIS?
LLLLLLLLOKI.
DON'T MAKE THREATS YOU WON'T SEE THROUGH.
A HEX, A SPELL--YOUR FINGERPRINTS ARE ABOUT THIS--
--TANARUS IS NOT MY BROTHER BUT EVERYONE THINKS--
DO NOT BREACH MY CIRCLE...

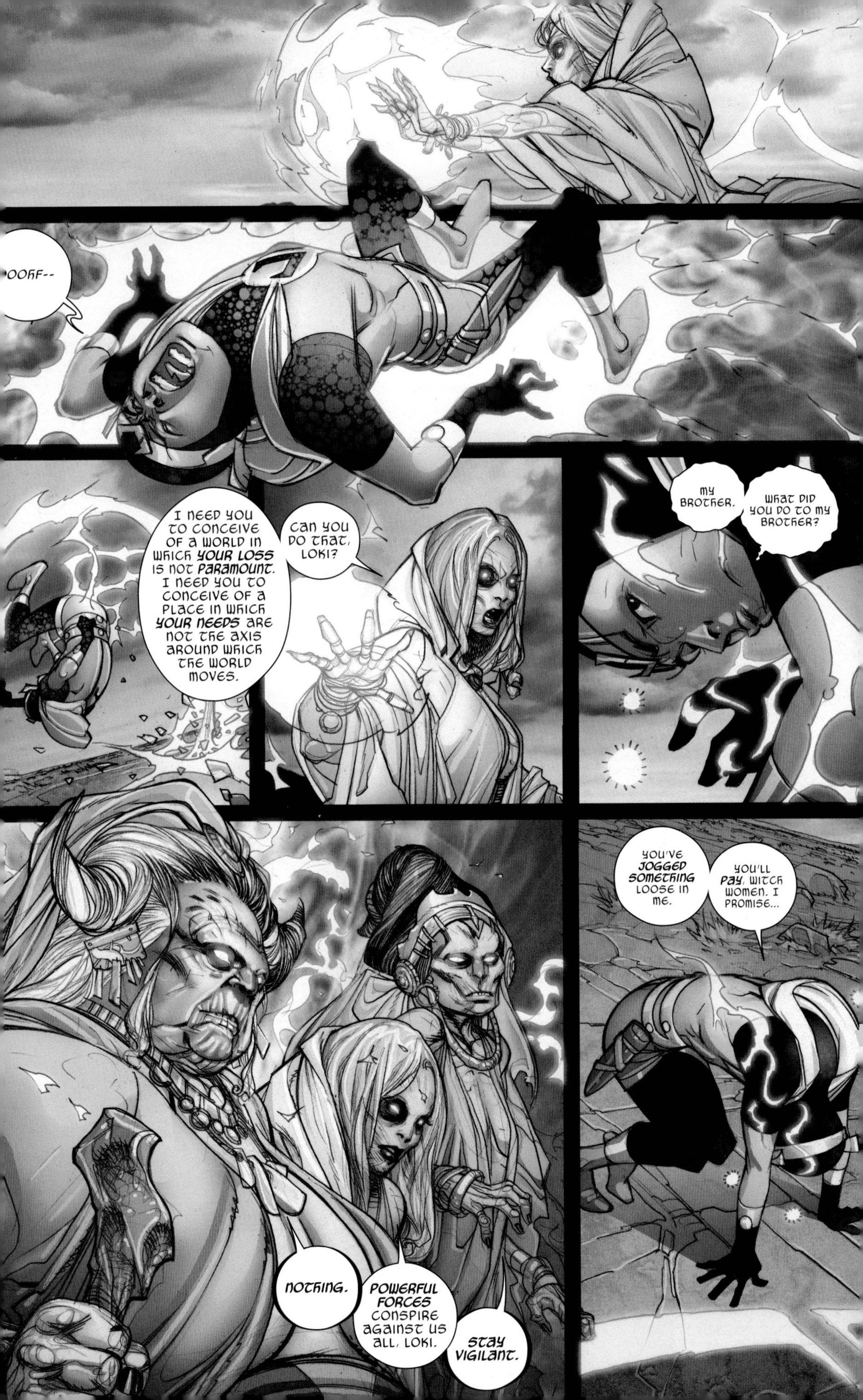
OOHF--
I NEED YOU TO CONCEIVE OF A WORLD IN WHICH YOUR LOSS IS NOT PARAMOUNT. I NEED YOU TO CONCEIVE OF A PLACE IN WHICH YOUR NEEDS ARE NOT THE AXIS AROUND WHICH THE WORLD MOVES.
CAN YOU DO THAT, LOKI?
MY BROTHER.
WHAT DID YOU DO TO MY BROTHER?
NOTHING.
POWERFUL FORCES CONSPIRE AGAINST US ALL, LOKI.
STAY VIGILANT.
YOU'VE JOGGED SOMETHING LOOSE IN ME.
YOU'LL PAY, WITCH WOMEN. I PROMISE...

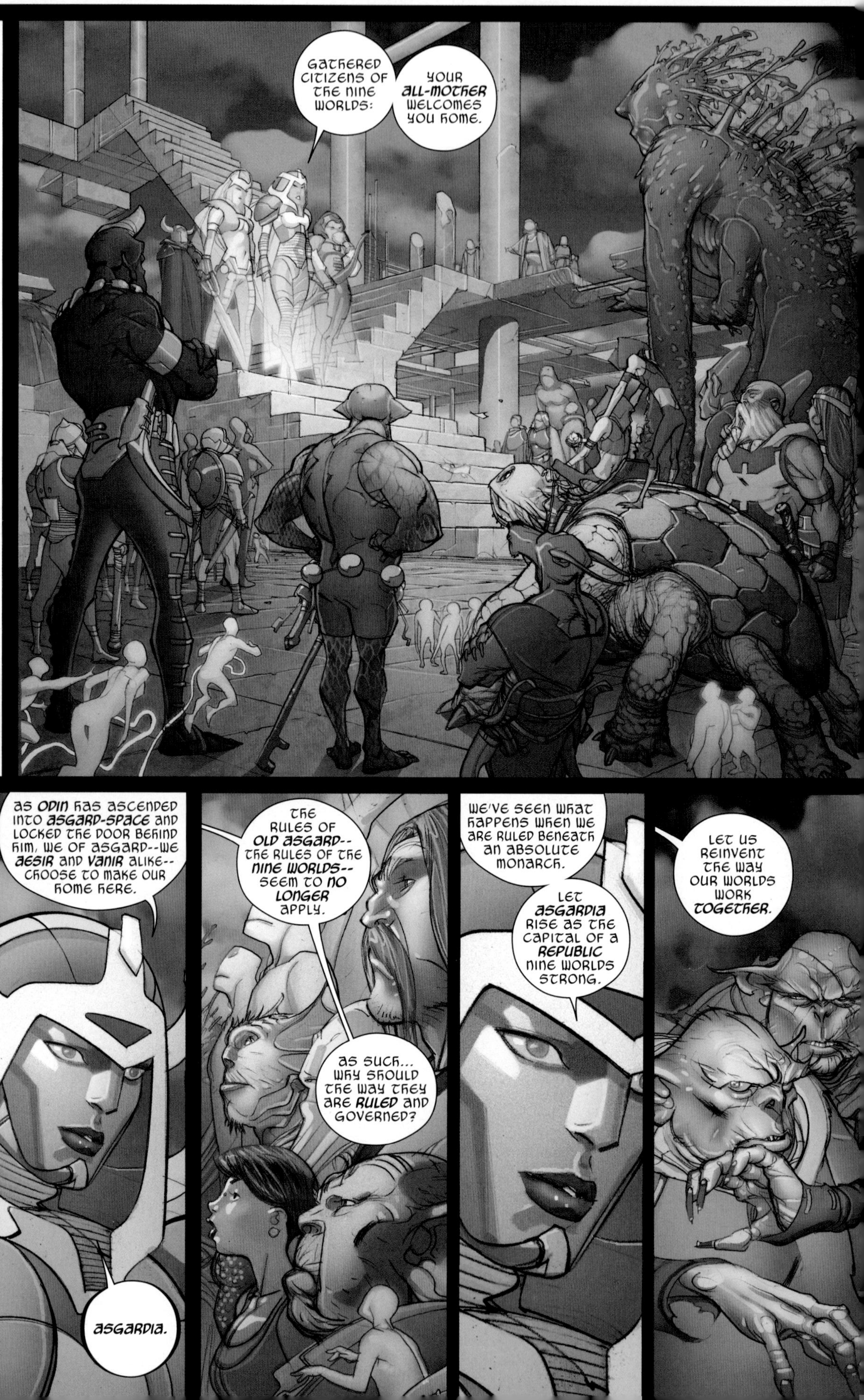
GATHERED CITIZENS OF THE NINE WORLDS:
YOUR ALL-MOTHER WELCOMES YOU HOME.
AS ODIN HAS ASCENDED INTO ASGARD-SPACE AND LOCKED THE DOOR BEHIND HIM, WE OF ASGARD--WE AESIR AND VANIR ALIKE--CHOOSE TO MAKE OUR HOME HERE.
ASGARDIA.
THE RULES OF OLD ASGARD--THE RULES OF THE NINE WORLDS--SEEM TO NO LONGER APPLY.
AS SUCH... WHY SHOULD THE WAY THEY ARE RULED AND GOVERNED?
WE'VE SEEN WHAT HAPPENS WHEN WE ARE RULED BENEATH AN ABSOLUTE MONARCH.
LET ASGARDIA RISE AS THE CAPITAL OF A REPUBLIC NINE WORLDS STRONG.
LET US REINVENT THE WAY OUR WORLDS WORK TOGETHER.

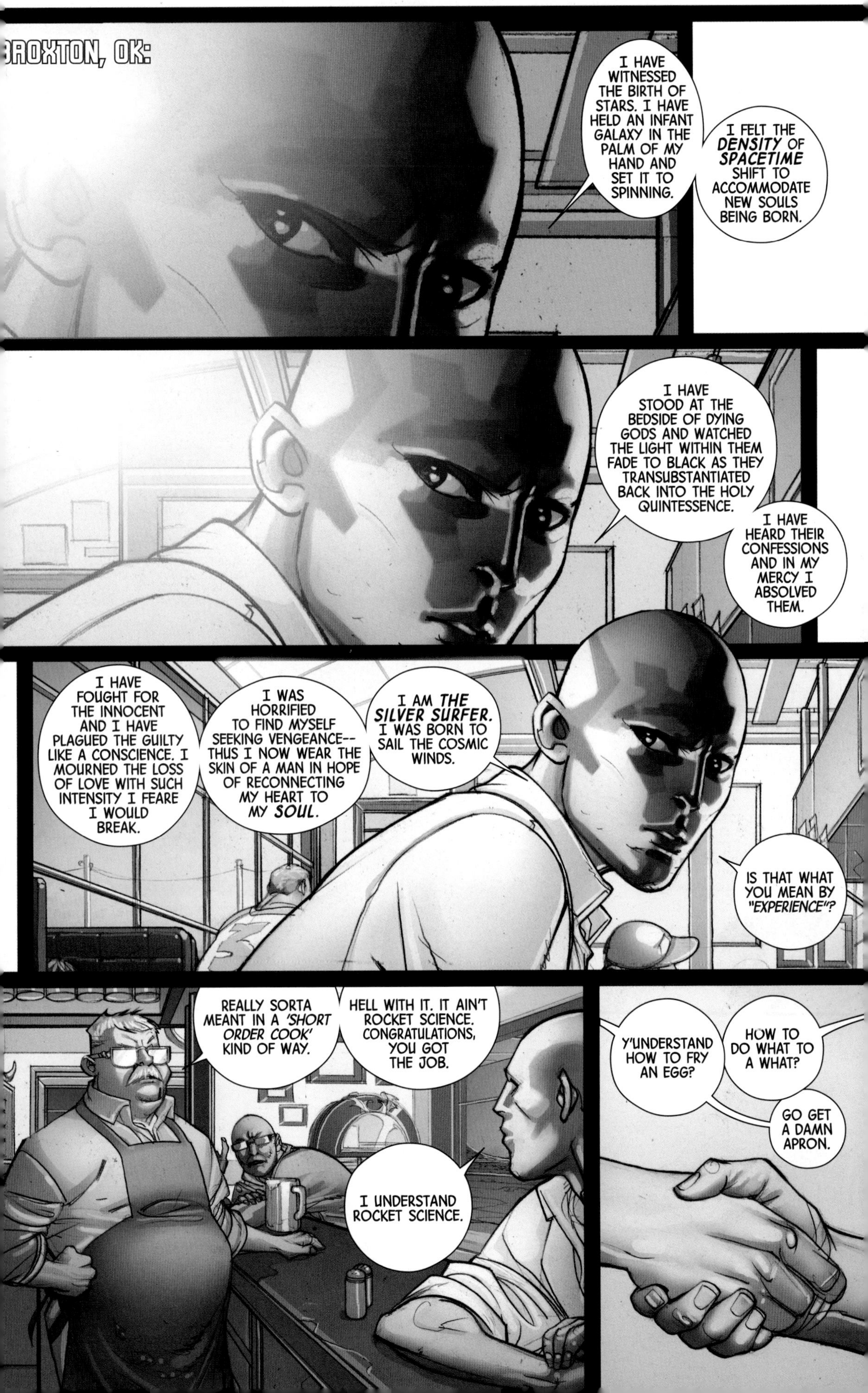
BROXTON, OK:
I HAVE WITNESSED THE BIRTH OF STARS. I HAVE HELD AN INFANT GALAXY IN THE PALM OF MY HAND AND SET IT TO SPINNING.
I FELT THE DENSITY OF SPACETIME SHIFT TO ACCOMMODATE NEW SOULS BEING BORN.
I HAVE STOOD AT THE BEDSIDE OF DYING GODS AND WATCHED THE LIGHT WITHIN THEM FADE TO BLACK AS THEY TRANSUBSTANTIATED BACK INTO THE HOLY QUINTESSENCE.
I HAVE HEARD THEIR CONFESSIONS AND IN MY MERCY I ABSOLVED THEM.
I HAVE FOUGHT FOR THE INNOCENT AND I HAVE PLAGUED THE GUILTY LIKE A CONSCIENCE. I MOURNED THE LOSS OF LOVE WITH SUCH INTENSITY I FEARE I WOULD BREAK.
I WAS HORRIFIED TO FIND MYSELF SEEKING VENGEANCE-- THUS I NOW WEAR THE SKIN OF A MAN IN HOPE OF RECONNECTING MY HEART TO MY SOUL.
I AM THE SILVER SURFER. I WAS BORN TO SAIL THE COSMIC WINDS.
IS THAT WHAT YOU MEAN BY "EXPERIENCE"?
REALLY SORTA MEANT IN A 'SHORT ORDER COOK' KIND OF WAY.
HELL WITH IT. IT AIN'T ROCKET SCIENCE. CONGRATULATIONS, YOU GOT THE JOB.
I UNDERSTAND ROCKET SCIENCE.
Y'UNDERSTAND HOW TO FRY AN EGG?
HOW TO DO WHAT TO A WHAT?
GO GET A DAMN APRON.

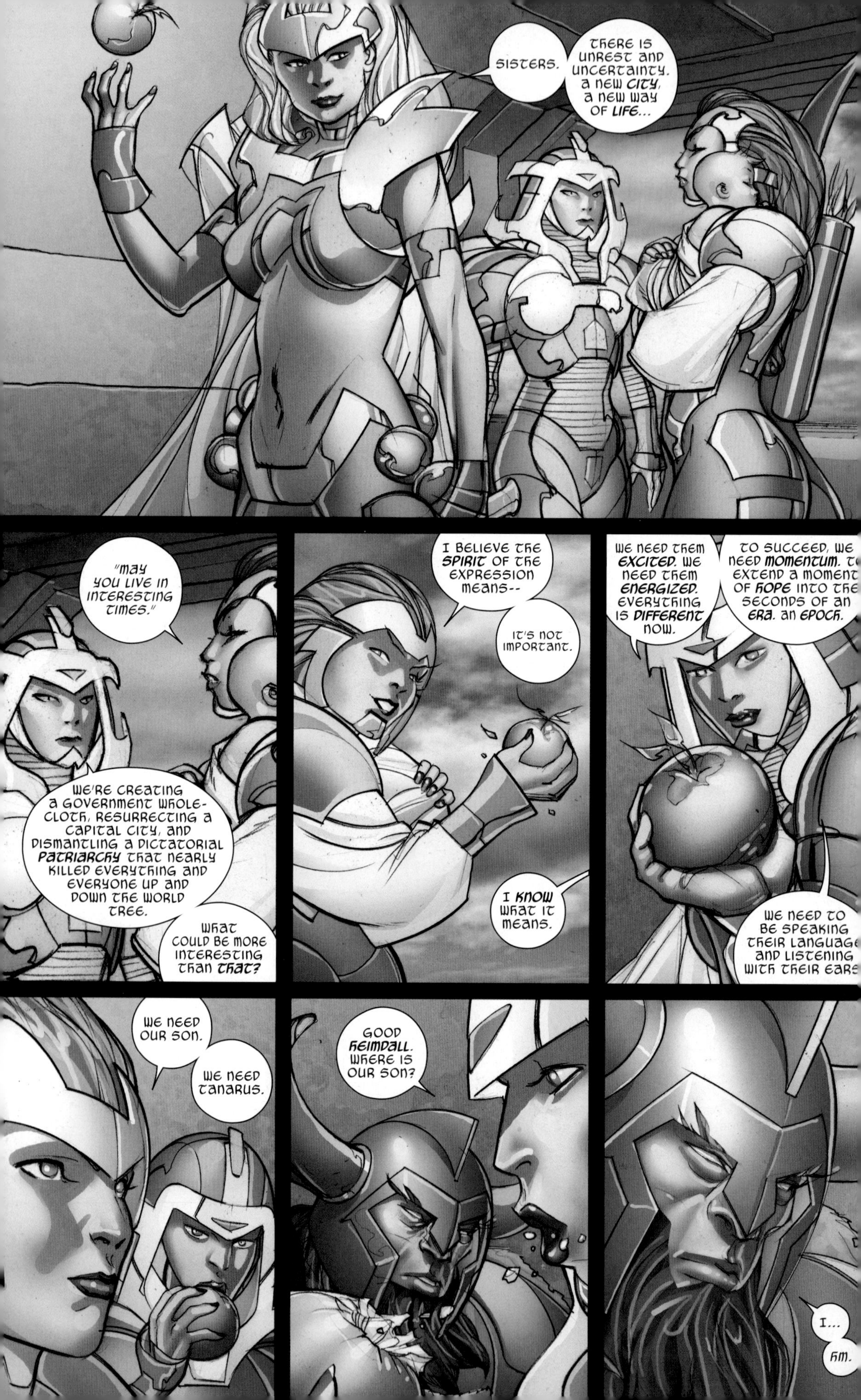
SISTERS.
THERE IS UNREST AND UNCERTAINTY. A NEW CITY, A NEW WAY OF LIFE...
"MAY YOU LIVE IN INTERESTING TIMES."
WE'RE CREATING A GOVERNMENT WHOLE-CLOTH, RESURRECTING A CAPITAL CITY, AND DISMANTLING A DICTATORIAL PATRIARCHY THAT NEARLY KILLED EVERYTHING AND EVERYONE UP AND DOWN THE WORLD TREE.
WHAT COULD BE MORE INTERESTING THAN THAT?
I BELIEVE THE SPIRIT OF THE EXPRESSION MEANS--
IT'S NOT IMPORTANT.
I KNOW WHAT IT MEANS.
WE NEED THEM EXCITED. WE NEED THEM ENERGIZED. EVERYTHING IS DIFFERENT NOW.
TO SUCCEED, WE NEED MOMENTUM. TO EXTEND A MOMENT OF HOPE INTO THE SECONDS OF AN ERA. AN EPOCH.
WE NEED TO BE SPEAKING THEIR LANGUAGE AND LISTENING WITH THEIR EARS
WE NEED OUR SON.
WE NEED TANARUS.
GOOD HEIMDALL. WHERE IS OUR SON?
I...
HM.

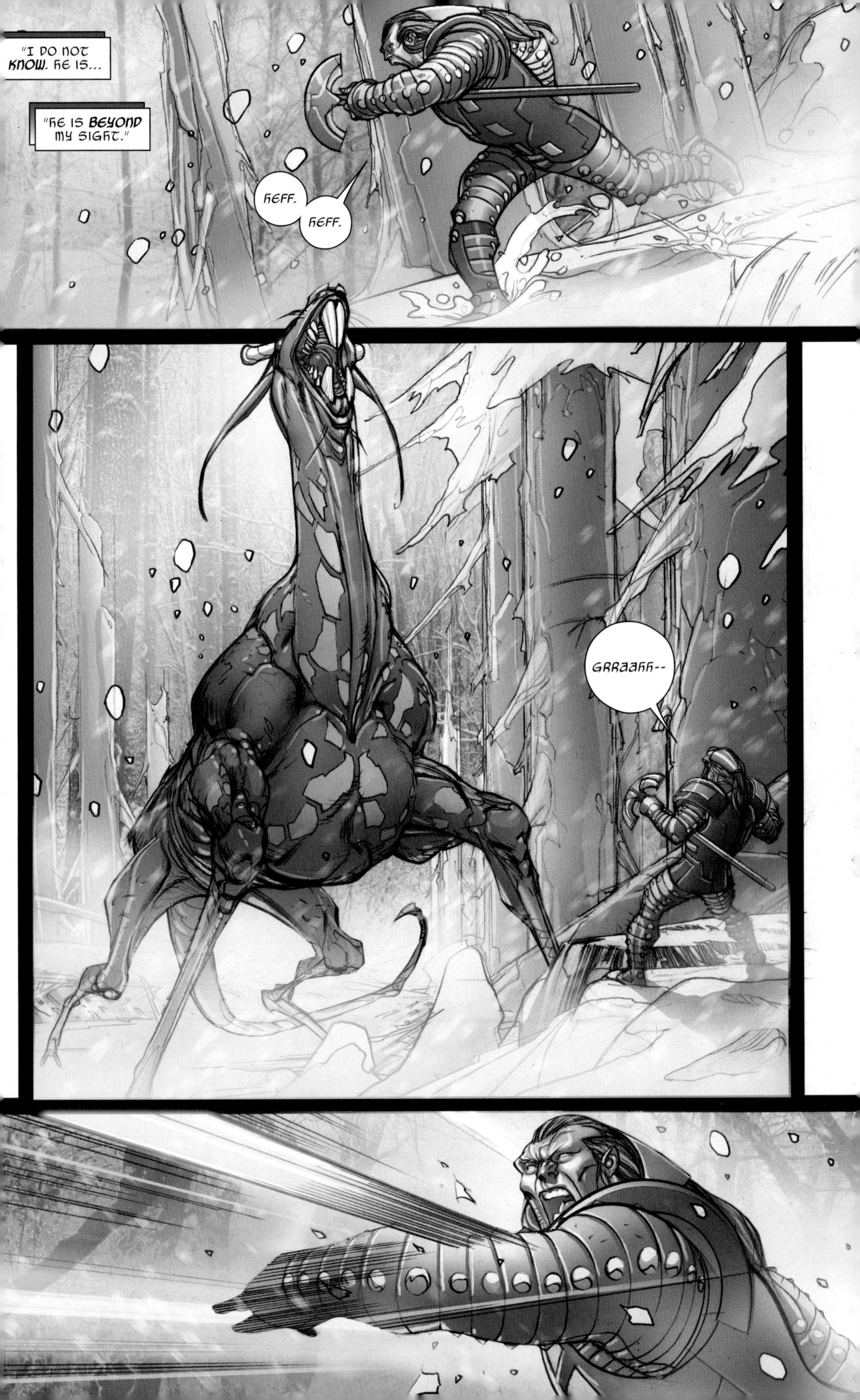
"I DO NOT KNOW. HE IS...
"HE IS BEYOND MY SIGHT."
HEFF.
HEFF.
GRRAAHH--

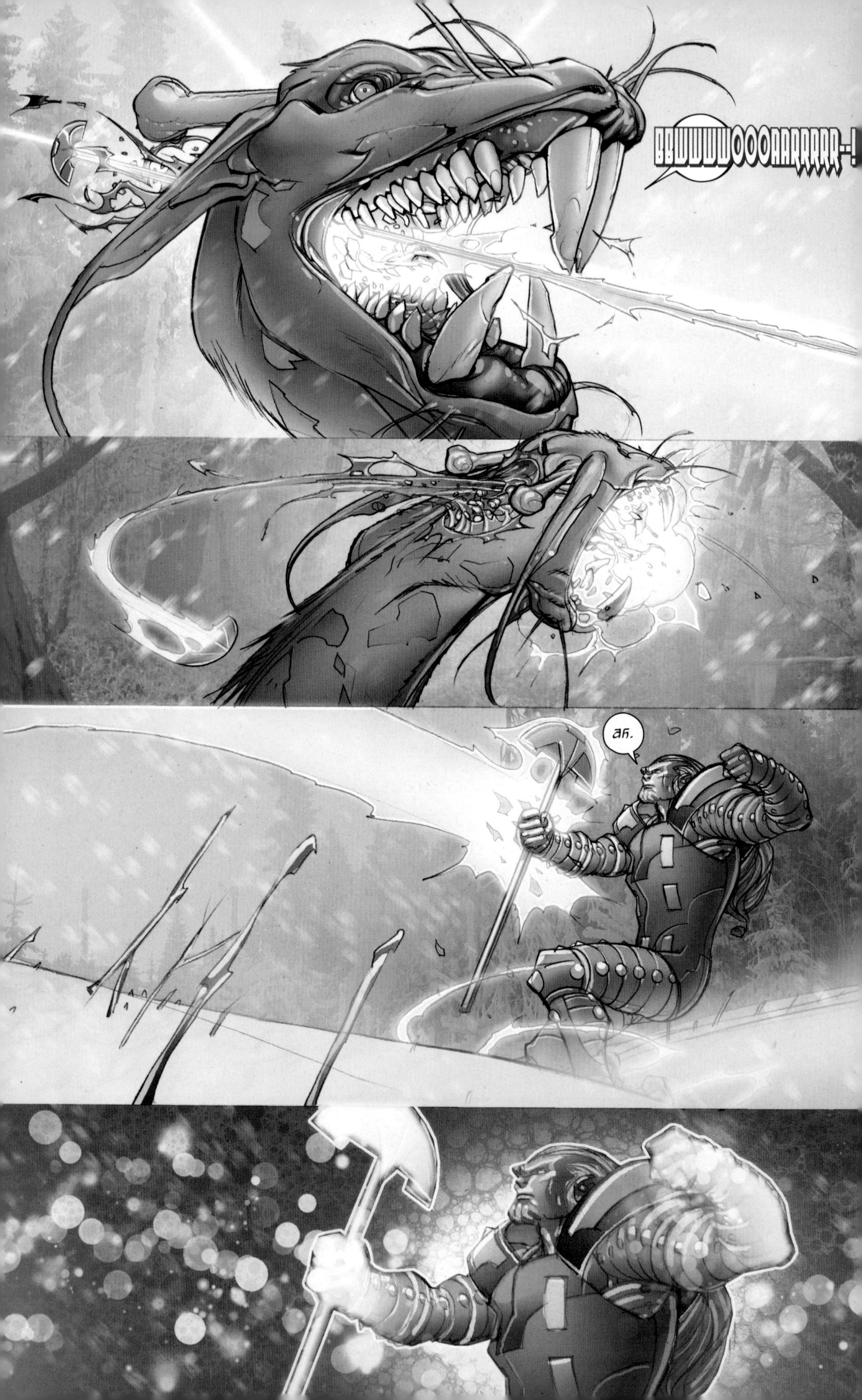
BBWWWWOOOAARRRRR--!
AH.

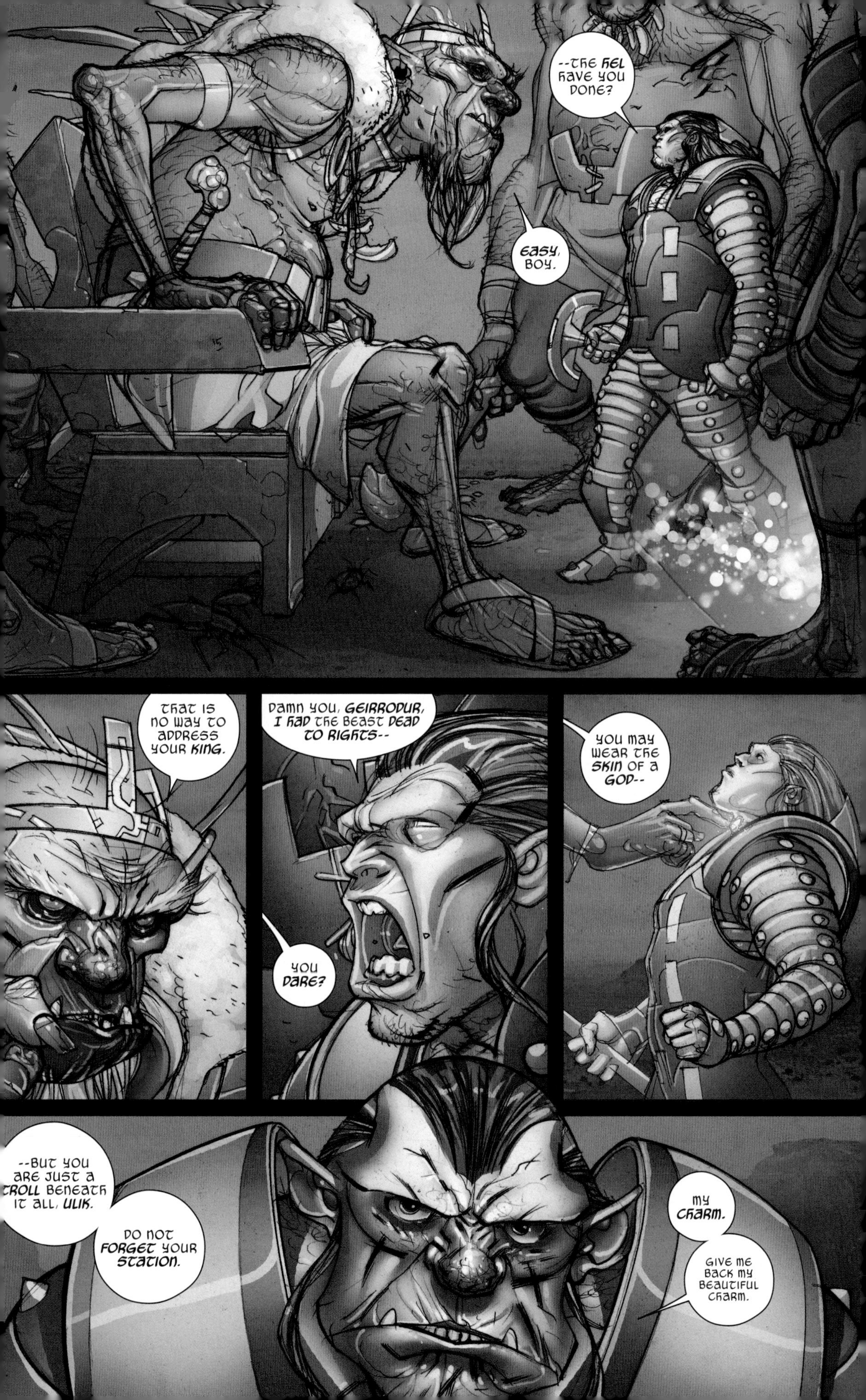
--THE HEL HAVE YOU DONE?
EASY, BOY.
THAT IS NO WAY TO ADDRESS YOUR KING.
DAMN YOU, GEIRRODUR, I HAD THE BEAST DEAD TO RIGHTS--
YOU DARE?
YOU MAY WEAR THE SKIN OF A GOD--
--BUT YOU ARE JUST A TROLL BENEATH IT ALL, ULIK.
DO NOT FORGET YOUR STATION.
MY CHARM.
GIVE ME BACK MY BEAUTIFUL CHARM.

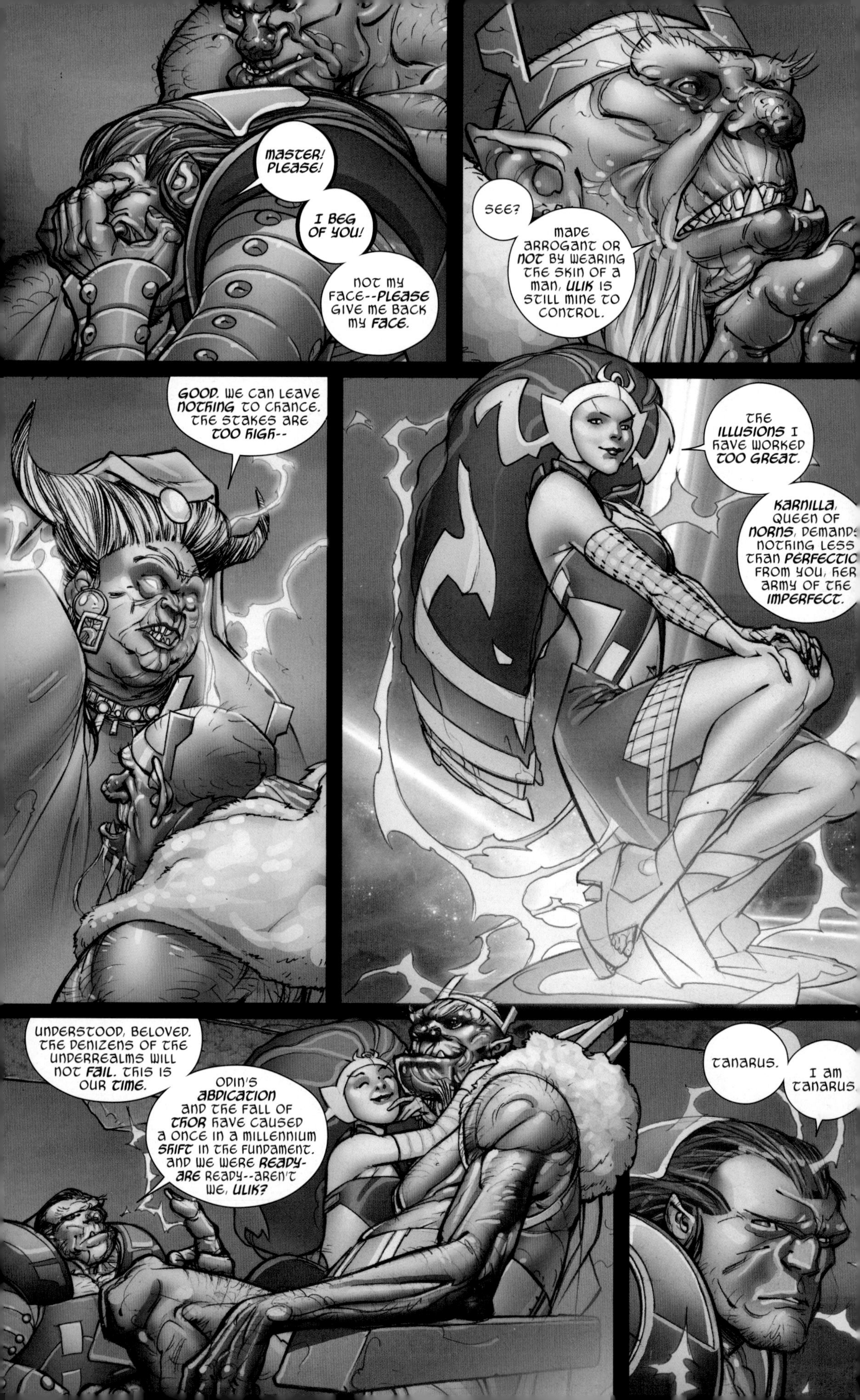
MASTER! PLEASE!
I BEG OF YOU!
NOT MY FACE--PLEASE GIVE ME BACK MY FACE.
SEE?
MADE ARROGANT OR NOT BY WEARING THE SKIN OF A MAN, ULIK IS STILL MINE TO CONTROL.
GOOD. WE CAN LEAVE NOTHING TO CHANCE. THE STAKES ARE TOO HIGH--
THE ILLUSIONS I HAVE WORKED TOO GREAT.
KARNILLA, QUEEN OF NORNS, DEMANDS NOTHING LESS THAN PERFECTIO FROM YOU, HER ARMY OF THE IMPERFECT.
UNDERSTOOD, BELOVED. THE DENIZENS OF THE UNDERREALMS WILL NOT FAIL. THIS IS OUR TIME.
ODIN'S ABDICATION AND THE FALL OF THOR HAVE CAUSED A ONCE IN A MILLENNIUM SHIFT IN THE FUNDAMENT. AND WE WERE READY-ARE READY--AREN'T WE, ULIK?
TANARUS.
I AM TANARUS.

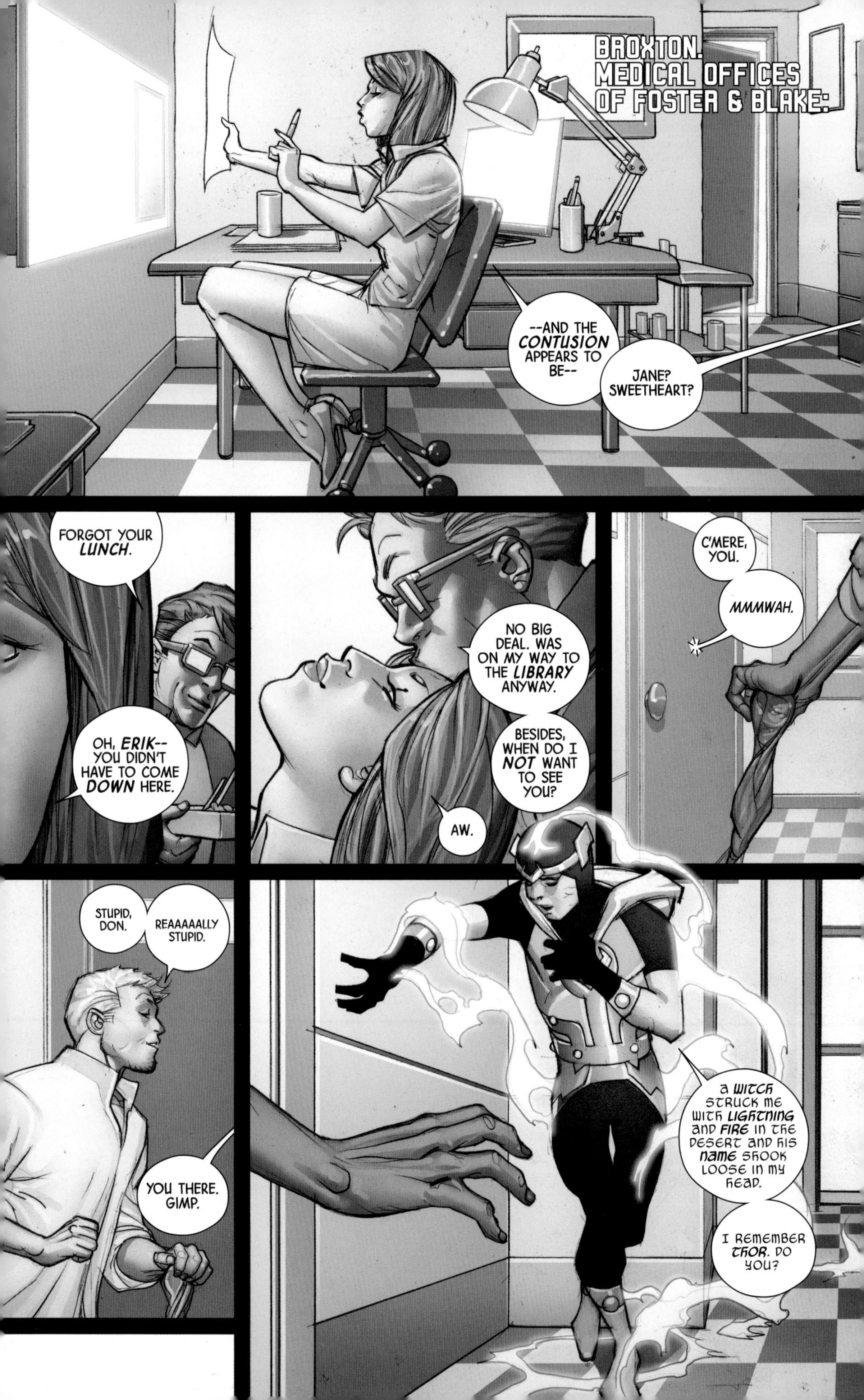
BROXTON. MEDICAL OFFICES OF FOSTER & BLAKE:
--AND THE CONTUSION APPEARS TO BE--
JANE? SWEETHEART?
FORGOT YOUR LUNCH.
OH, ERIK-- YOU DIDN'T HAVE TO COME DOWN HERE.
NO BIG DEAL. WAS ON MY WAY TO THE LIBRARY ANYWAY.
BESIDES, WHEN DO I NOT WANT TO SEE YOU?
AW.
C'MERE, YOU.
MMMWAH.
STUPID, DON.
REAAAAALLY STUPID.
YOU THERE. GIMP.
A WITCH STRUCK ME WITH LIGHTNING AND FIRE IN THE DESERT AND HIS NAME SHOOK LOOSE IN MY HEAD.
I REMEMBER THOR. DO YOU?

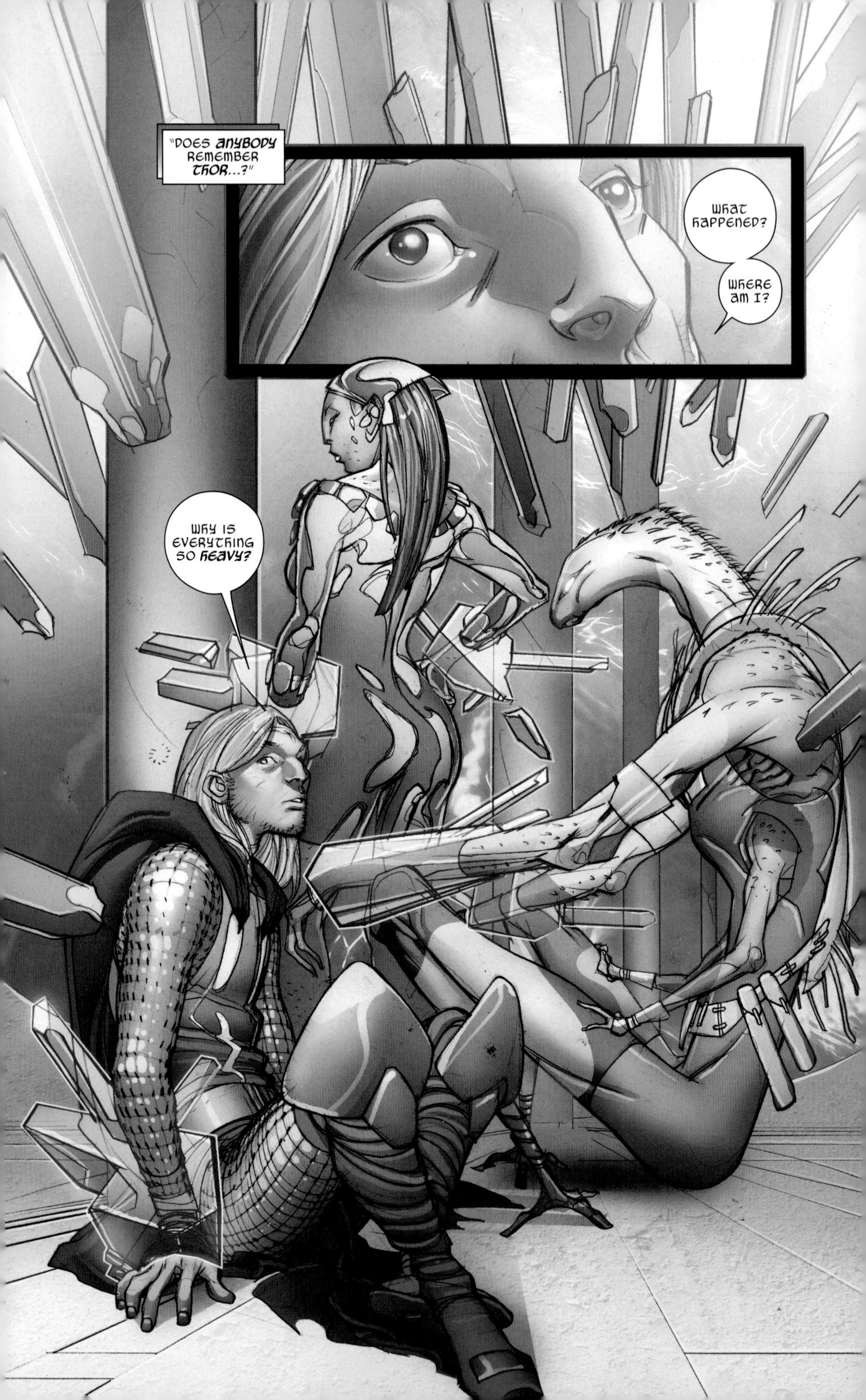
"DOES ANYBODY REMEMBER THOR...?"
WHAT HAPPENED?
WHERE AM I?
WHY IS EVERYTHING SO HEAVY?

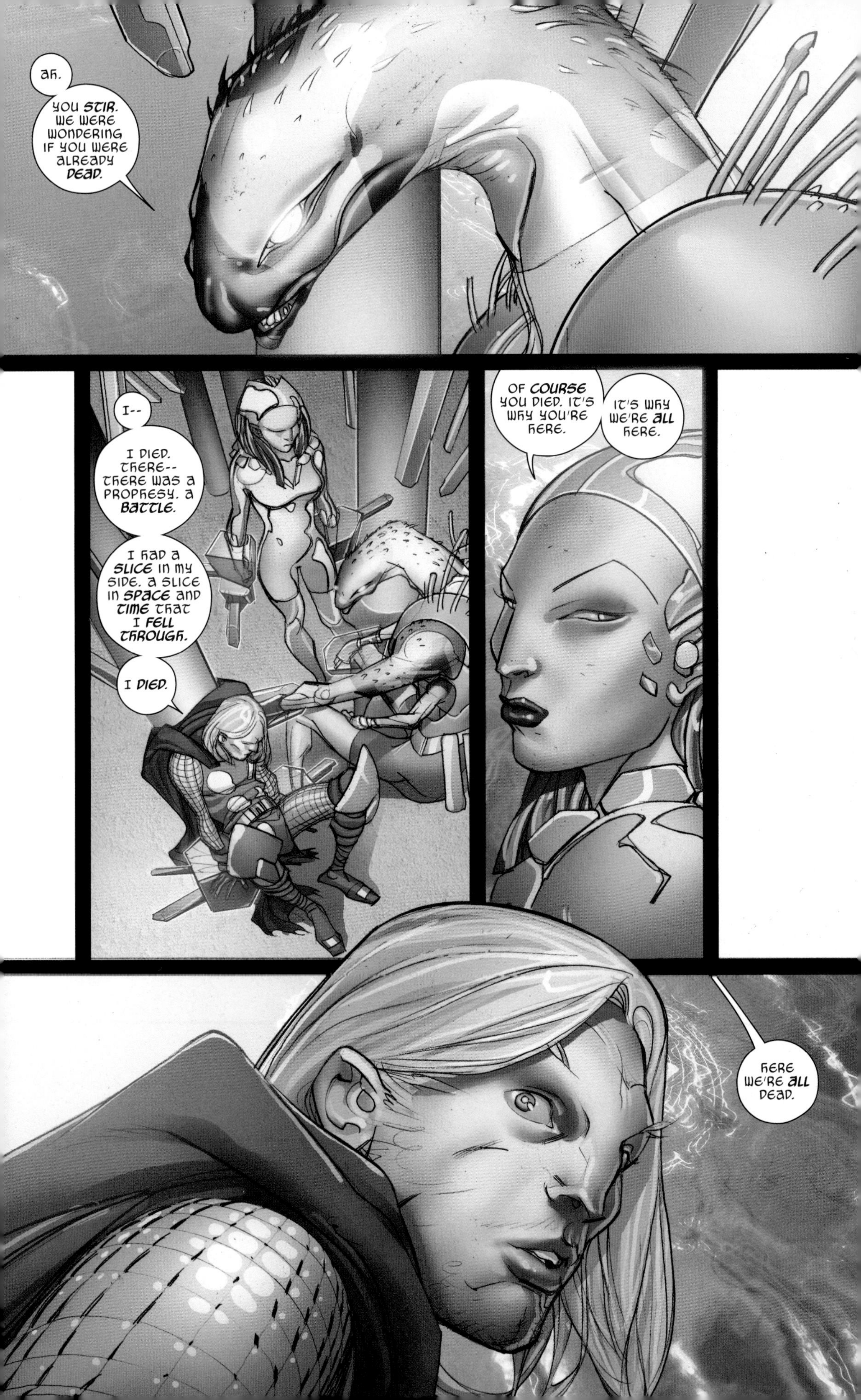
AH.
YOU STIR. WE WERE WONDERING IF YOU WERE ALREADY DEAD.
I--
I DIED. THERE--THERE WAS A PROPHESY. A BATTLE.
I HAD A SLICE IN MY SIDE. A SLICE IN SPACE AND TIME THAT I FELL THROUGH.
I DIED.
OF COURSE YOU DIED. IT'S WHY YOU'RE HERE.
IT'S WHY WE'RE ALL HERE.
HERE WE'RE ALL DEAD.

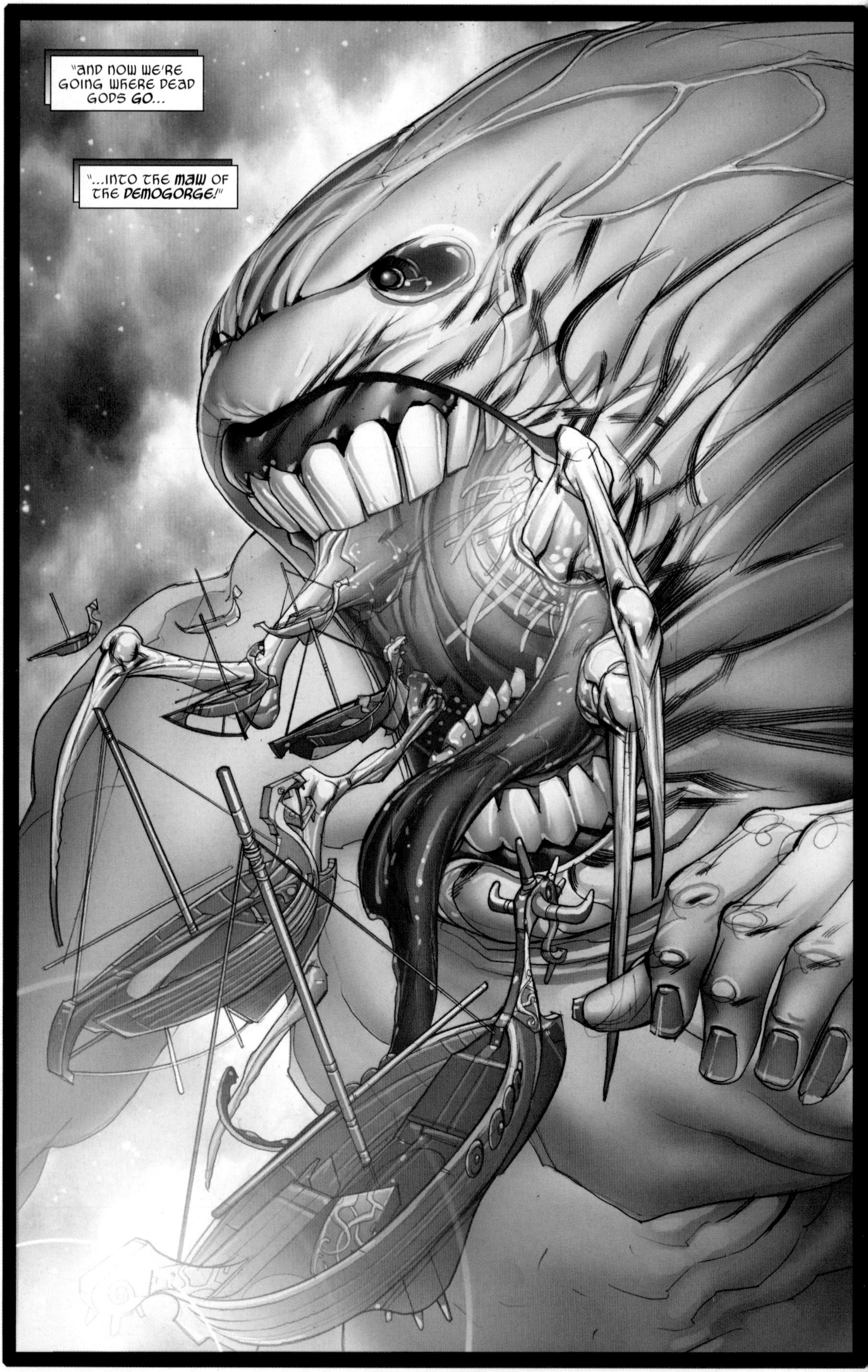
"AND NOW WE'RE GOING WHERE DEAD GODS GO...
"...INTO THE MAW OF THE DEMOGORGE!"

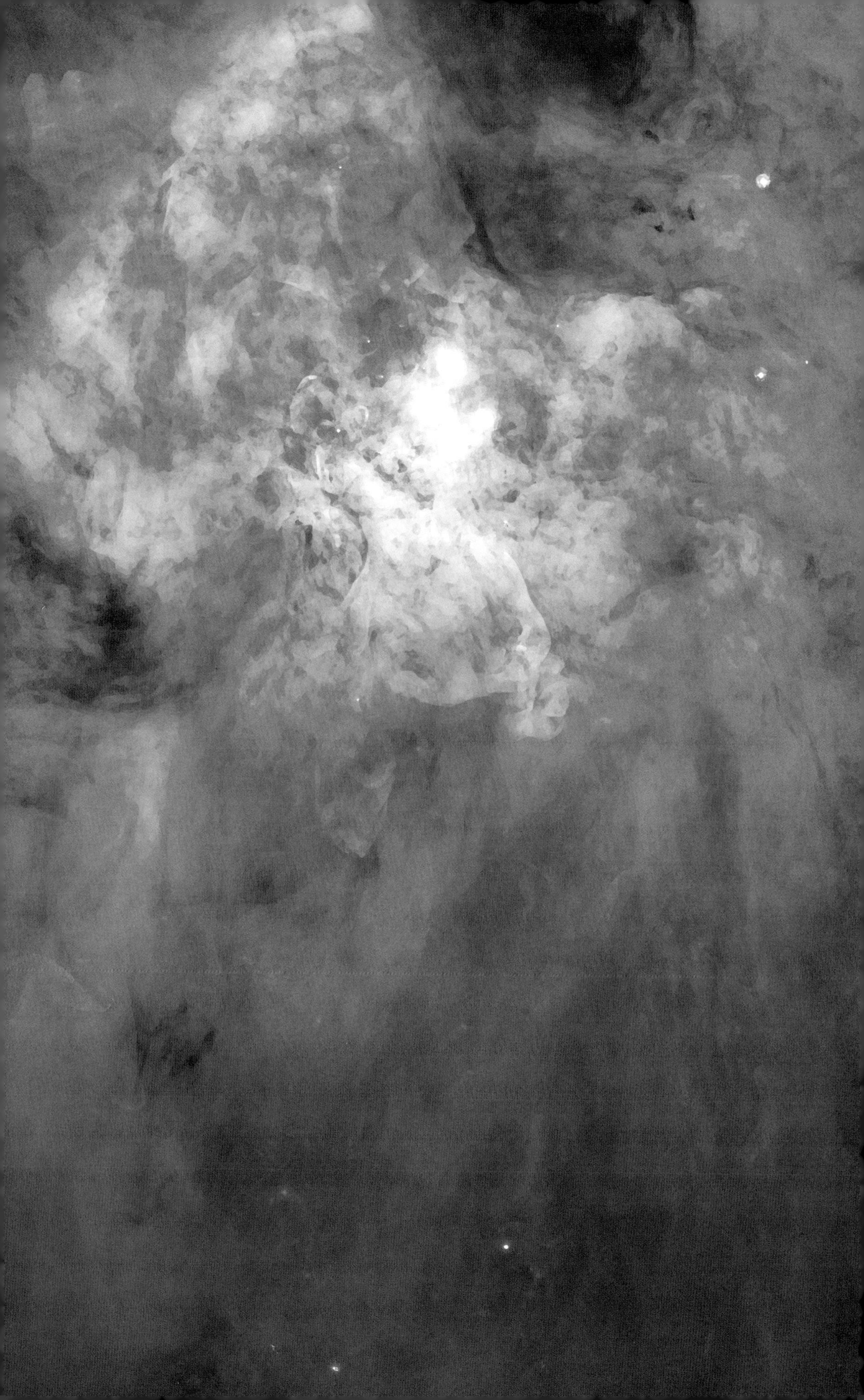

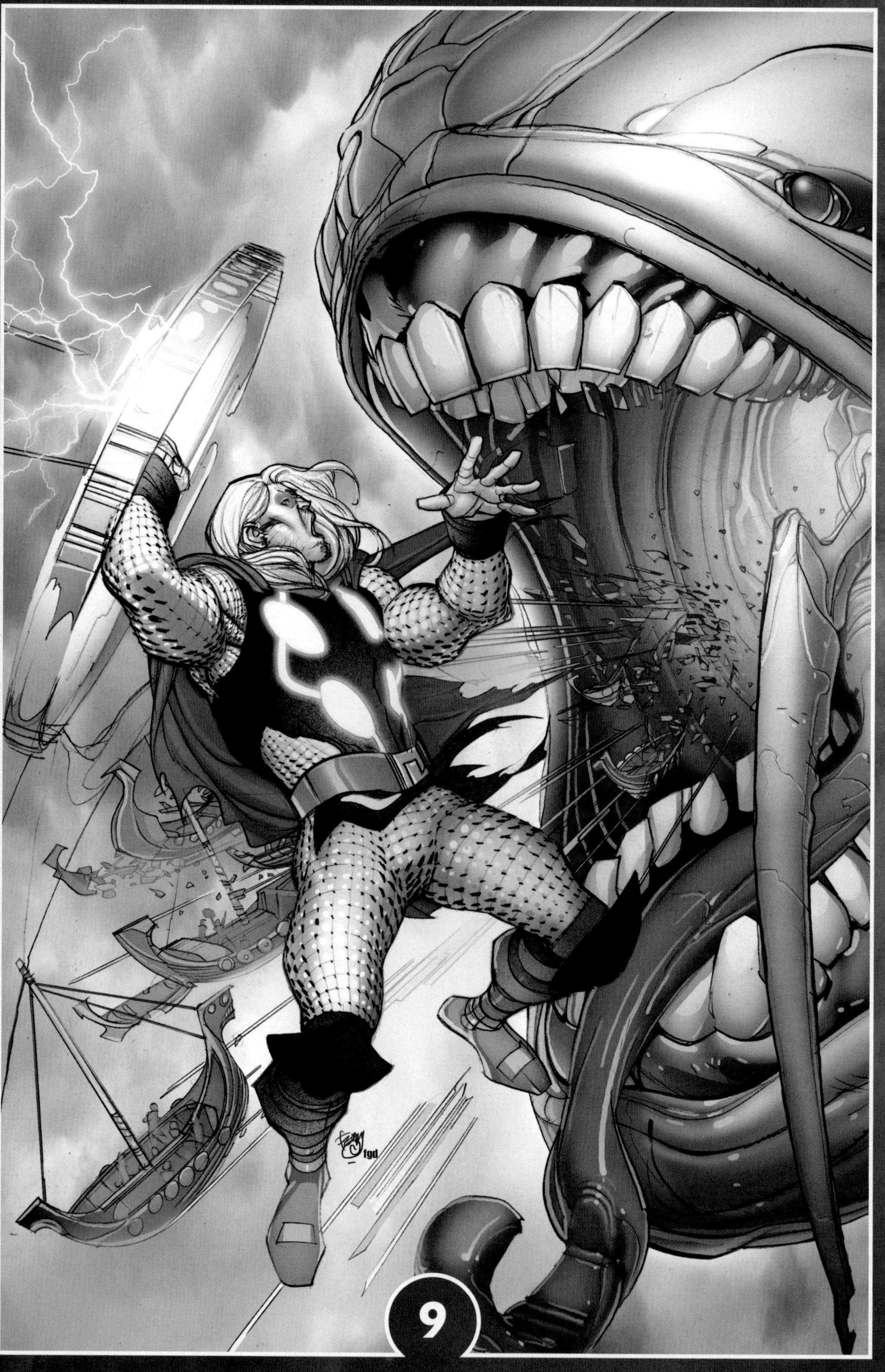

9

THE MIGHTY TANARUS 2: THE WALK

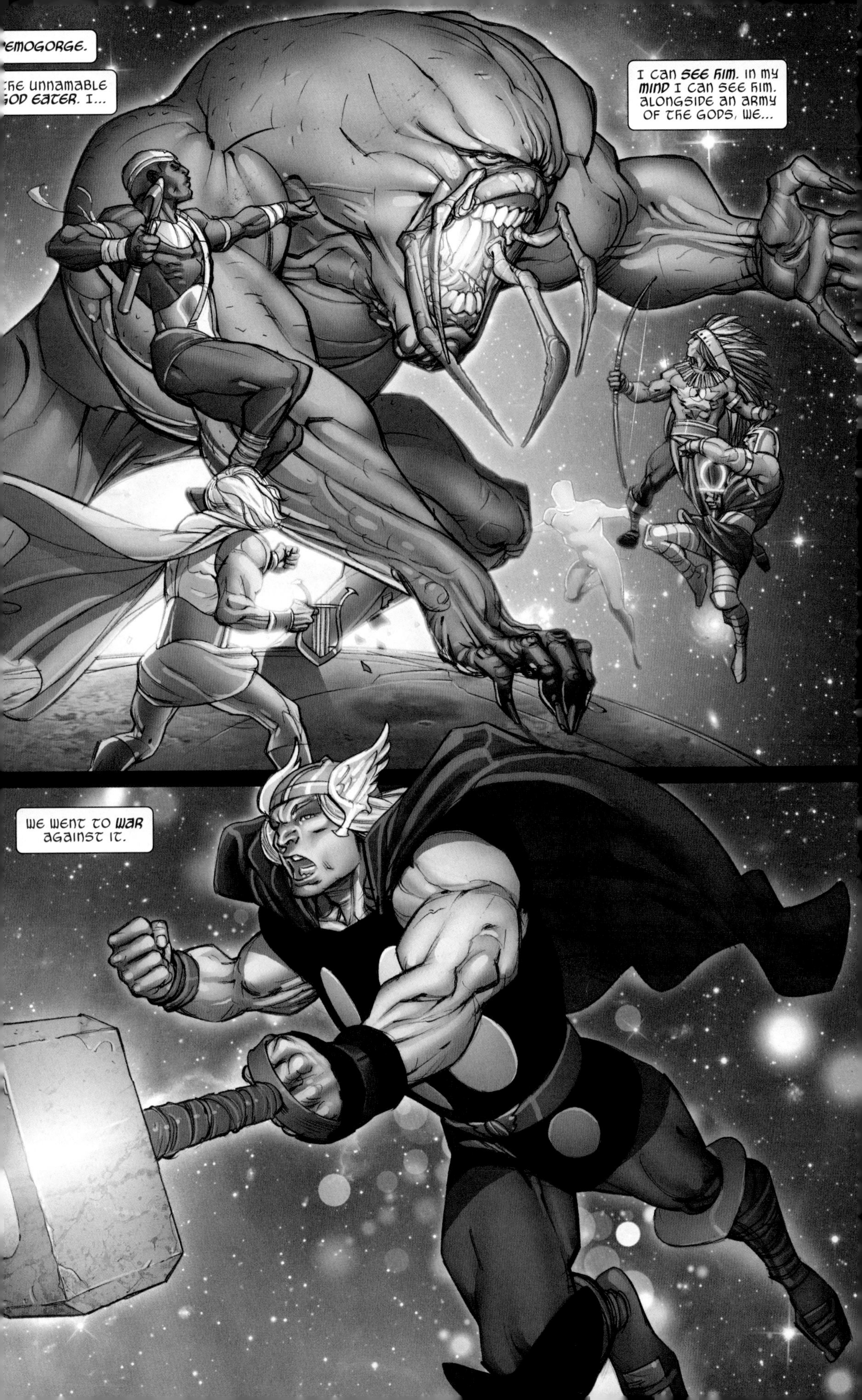
EMOGORGE.
THE UNNAMABLE GOD EATER. I...
I CAN SEE HIM. IN MY MIND I CAN SEE HIM. ALONGSIDE AN ARMY OF THE GODS, WE...
WE WENT TO WAR AGAINST IT.

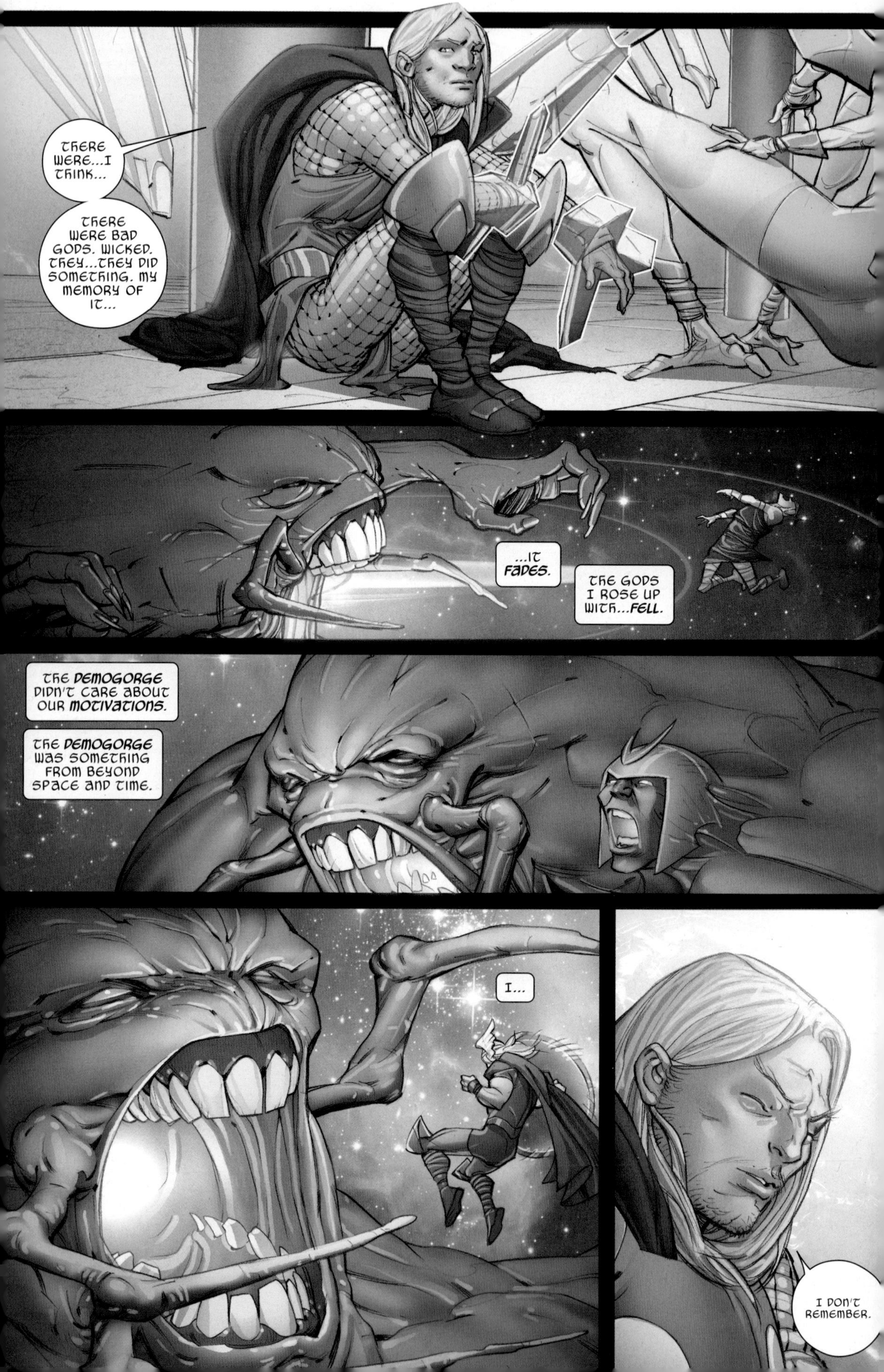
THERE WERE...I THINK...
THERE WERE BAD GODS. WICKED. THEY...THEY DID SOMETHING. MY MEMORY OF IT...
...IT FADES.
THE GODS I ROSE UP WITH...FELL.
THE DEMOGORGE DIDN'T CARE ABOUT OUR MOTIVATIONS.
THE DEMOGORGE WAS SOMETHING FROM BEYOND SPACE AND TIME.
I...
I DON'T REMEMBER.

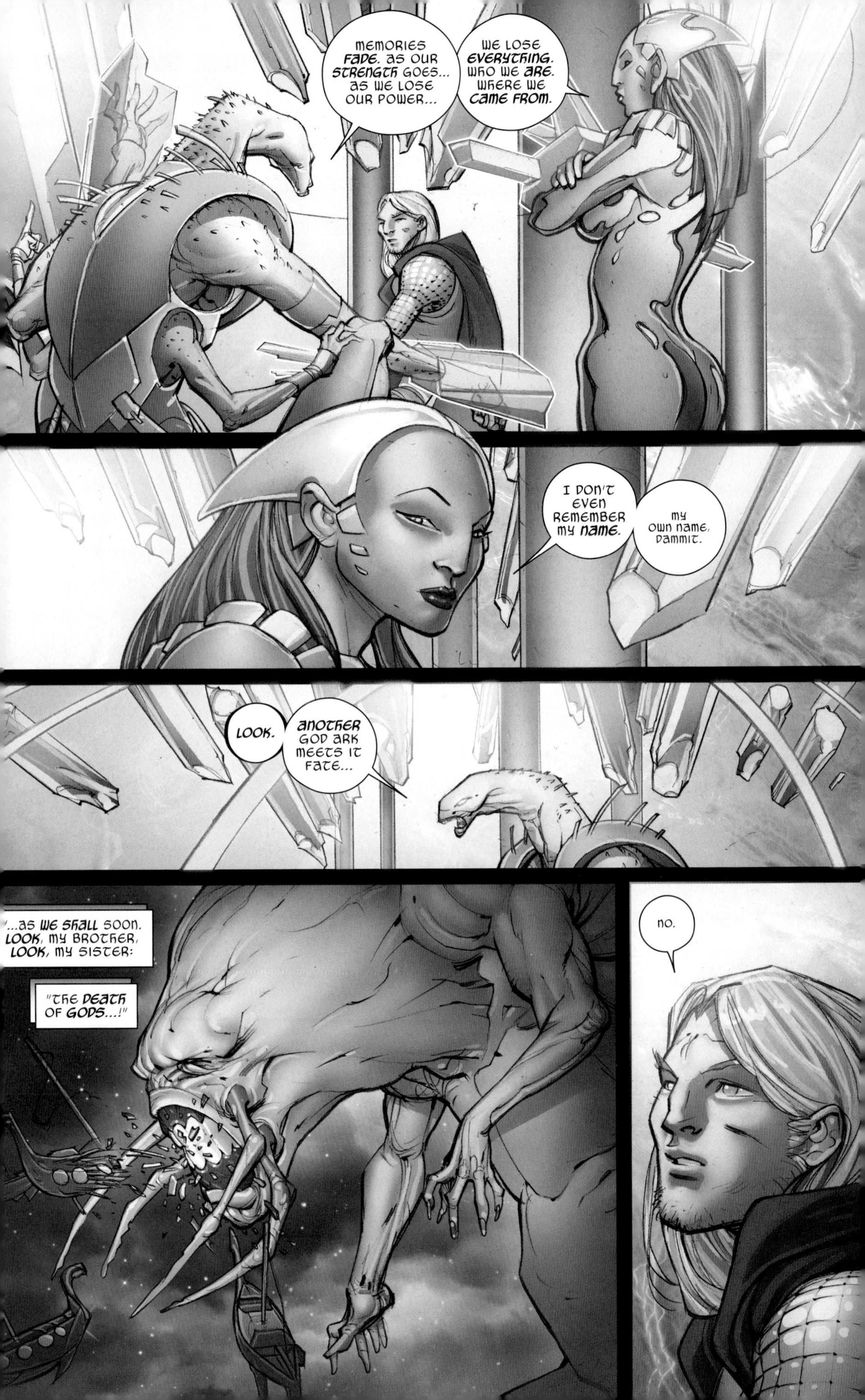
MEMORIES FADE, AS OUR STRENGTH GOES... AS WE LOSE OUR POWER...
WE LOSE EVERYTHING. WHO WE ARE. WHERE WE CAME FROM.
I DON'T EVEN REMEMBER MY NAME.
MY OWN NAME, DAMMIT.
LOOK.
ANOTHER GOD ARK MEETS IT FATE...
...AS WE SHALL SOON. LOOK, MY BROTHER, LOOK, MY SISTER:
"THE DEATH OF GODS...!"
NO.

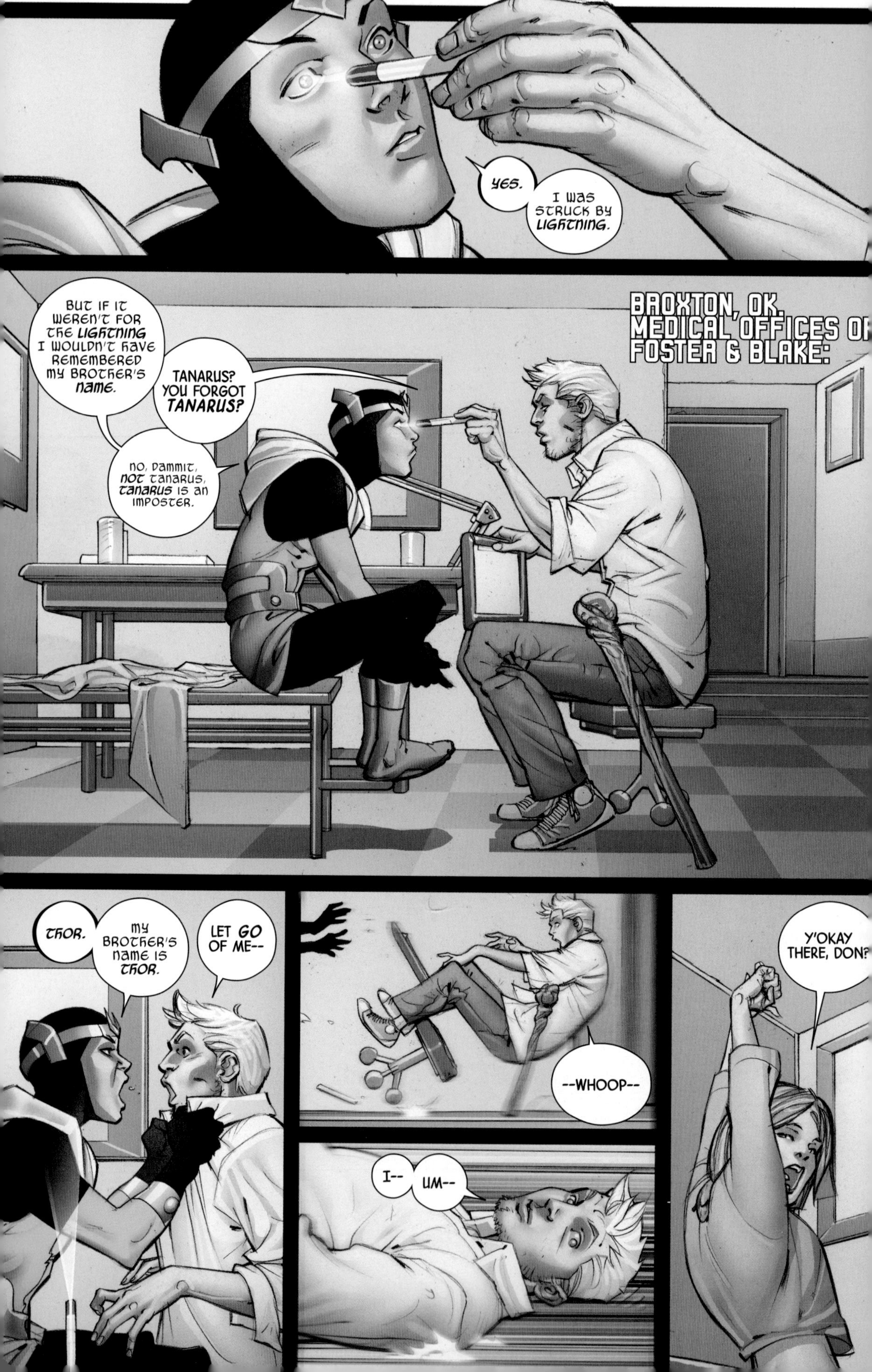
YES.
I WAS STRUCK BY LIGHTNING.
BROXTON, OK. MEDICAL OFFICES OF FOSTER & BLAKE:
BUT IF IT WEREN'T FOR THE LIGHTNING I WOULDN'T HAVE REMEMBERED MY BROTHER'S NAME.
TANARUS? YOU FORGOT TANARUS?
NO, DAMMIT, NOT TANARUS. TANARUS IS AN IMPOSTER.
THOR.
MY BROTHER'S NAME IS THOR.
LET GO OF ME--
--WHOOP--
I--
UM--
Y'OKAY THERE, DON?

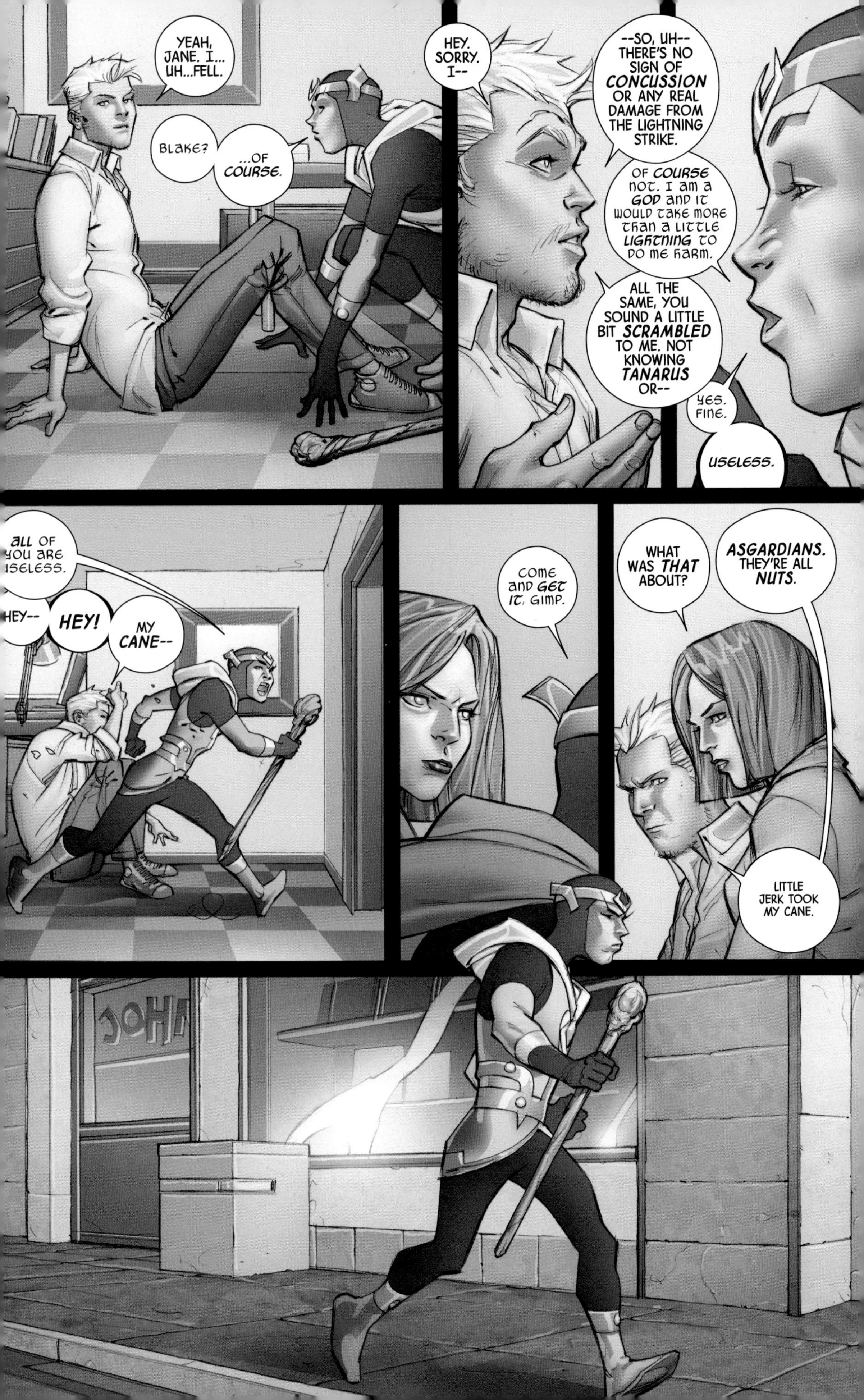
YEAH, JANE. I... UH...FELL.
BLAKE?
...OF COURSE.
HEY. SORRY. I--
--SO, UH-- THERE'S NO SIGN OF CONCUSSION OR ANY REAL DAMAGE FROM THE LIGHTNING STRIKE.
OF COURSE NOT. I AM A GOD AND IT WOULD TAKE MORE THAN A LITTLE LIGHTNING TO DO ME HARM.
ALL THE SAME, YOU SOUND A LITTLE BIT SCRAMBLED TO ME. NOT KNOWING TANARUS OR--
YES. FINE.
USELESS.
ALL OF YOU ARE USELESS.
HEY--
HEY!
MY CANE--
COME AND GET IT, GIMP.
WHAT WAS THAT ABOUT?
ASGARDIANS. THEY'RE ALL NUTS.
LITTLE JERK TOOK MY CANE.

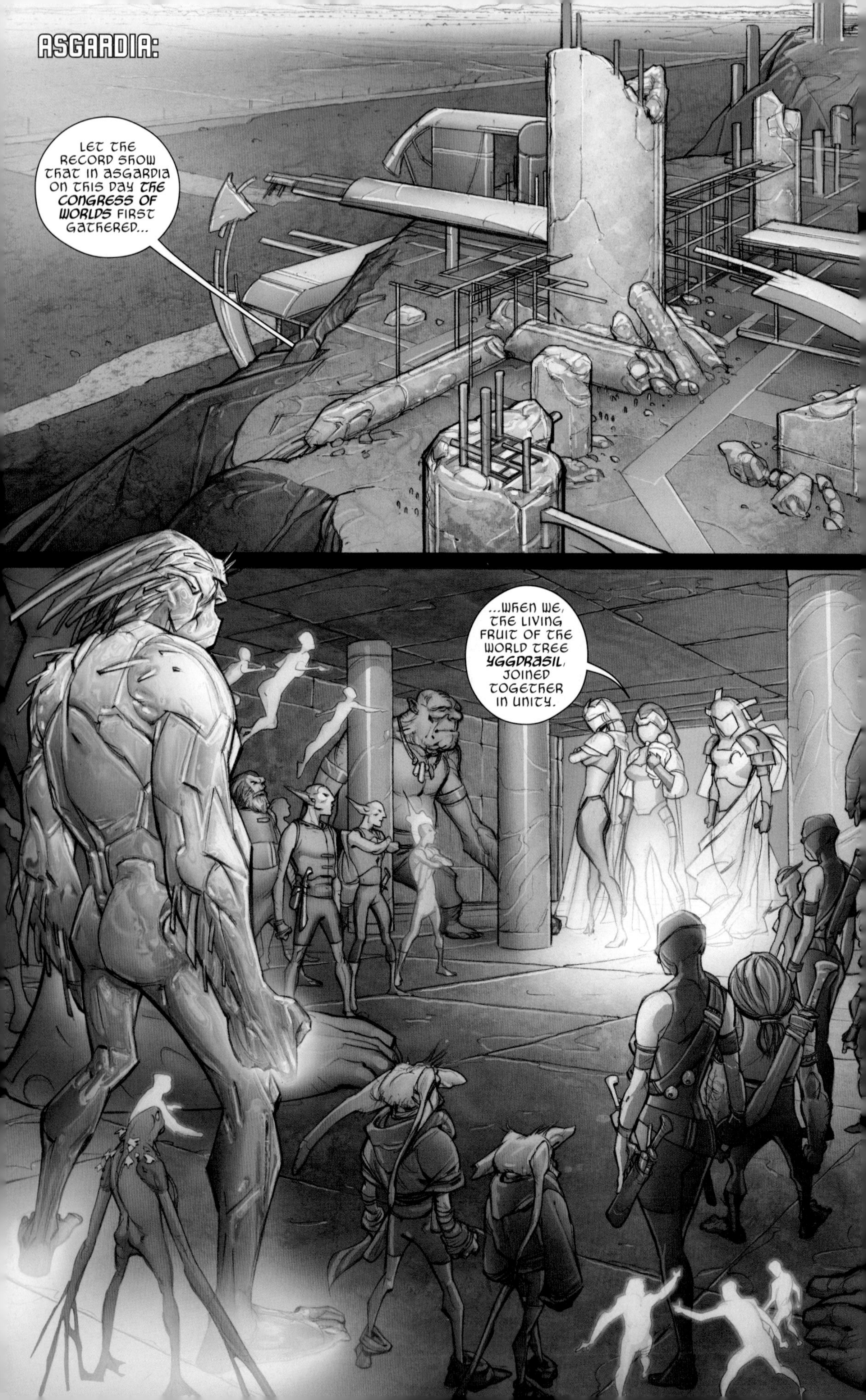
ASGARDIA:
LET THE RECORD SHOW THAT IN ASGARDIA ON THIS DAY THE CONGRESS OF WORLDS FIRST GATHERED...
...WHEN WE, THE LIVING FRUIT OF THE WORLD TREE YGGDRASIL, JOINED TOGETHER IN UNITY.

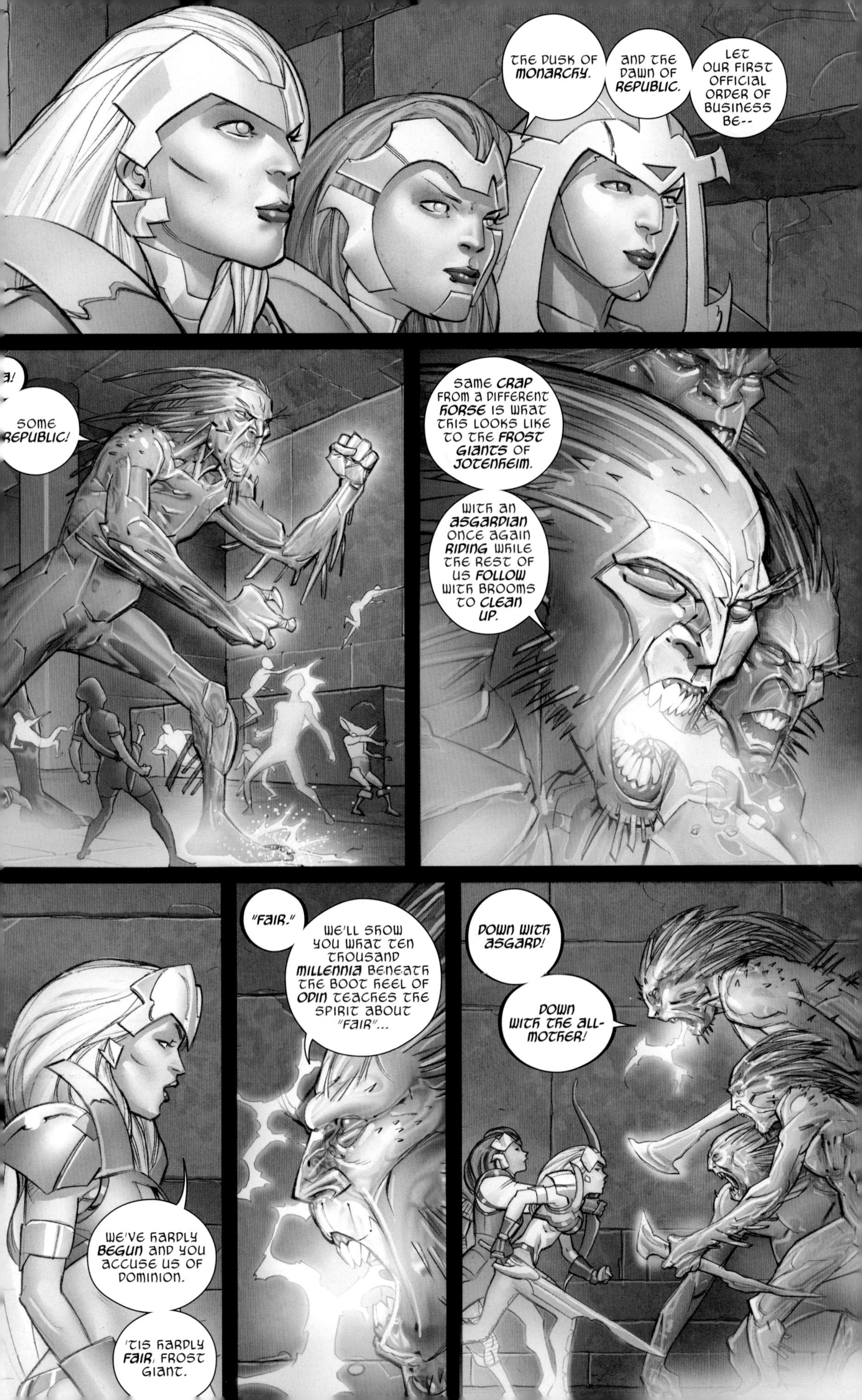
THE DUSK OF MONARCHY.
AND THE DAWN OF REPUBLIC.
LET OUR FIRST OFFICIAL ORDER OF BUSINESS BE--
SOME REPUBLIC!
SAME CRAP FROM A DIFFERENT HORSE IS WHAT THIS LOOKS LIKE TO THE FROST GIANTS OF JOTENHEIM.
WITH AN ASGARDIAN ONCE AGAIN RIDING WHILE THE REST OF US FOLLOW WITH BROOMS TO CLEAN UP.
WE'VE HARDLY BEGUN AND YOU ACCUSE US OF DOMINION.
'TIS HARDLY FAIR, FROST GIANT.
"FAIR."
WE'LL SHOW YOU WHAT TEN THOUSAND MILLENNIA BENEATH THE BOOT HEEL OF ODIN TEACHES THE SPIRIT ABOUT "FAIR"...
DOWN WITH ASGARD!
DOWN WITH THE ALL-MOTHER!

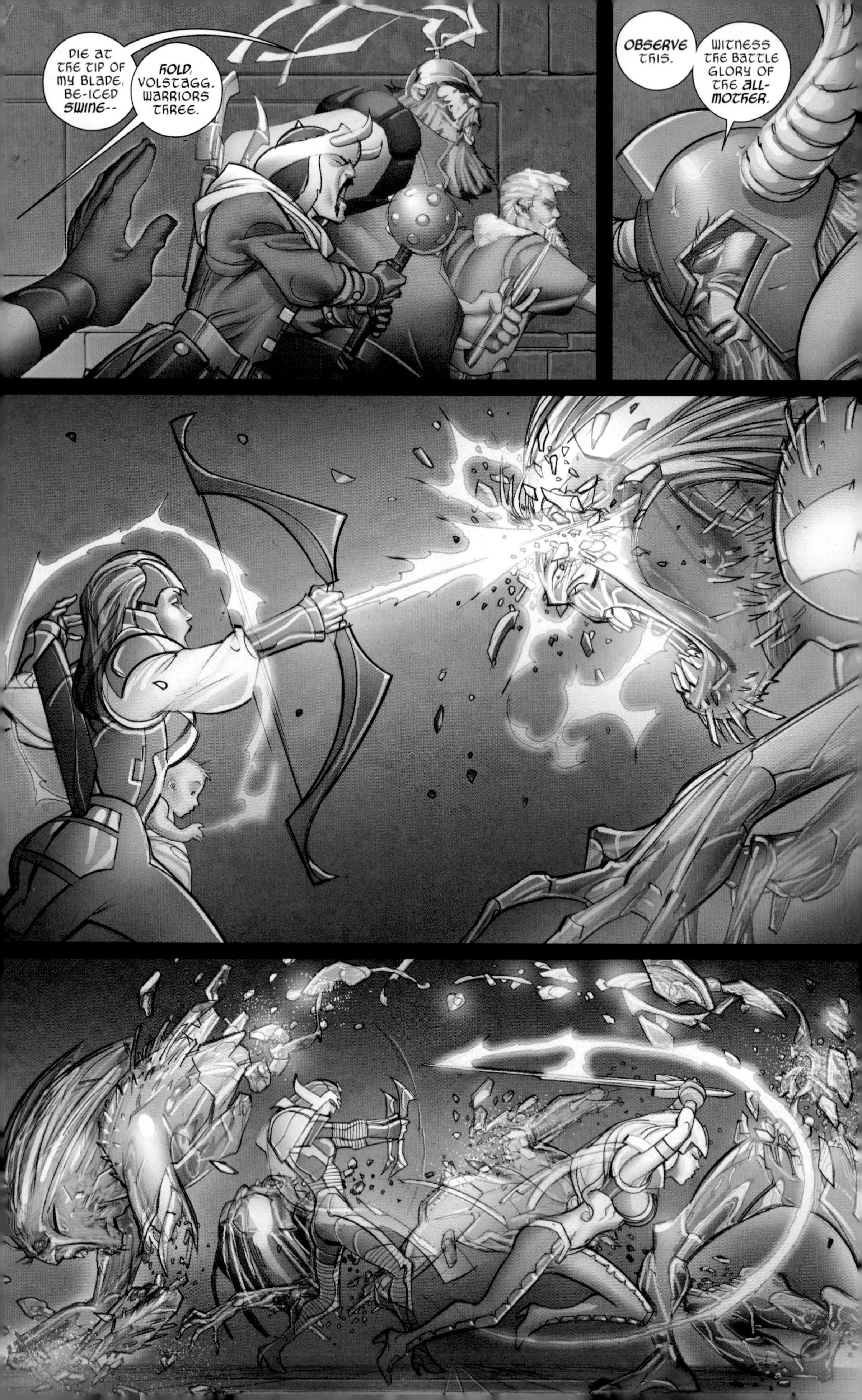
DIE AT THE TIP OF MY BLADE, BE-ICED SWINE--
HOLD, VOLSTAGG. WARRIORS THREE.
OBSERVE THIS.
WITNESS THE BATTLE GLORY OF THE ALL-MOTHER.

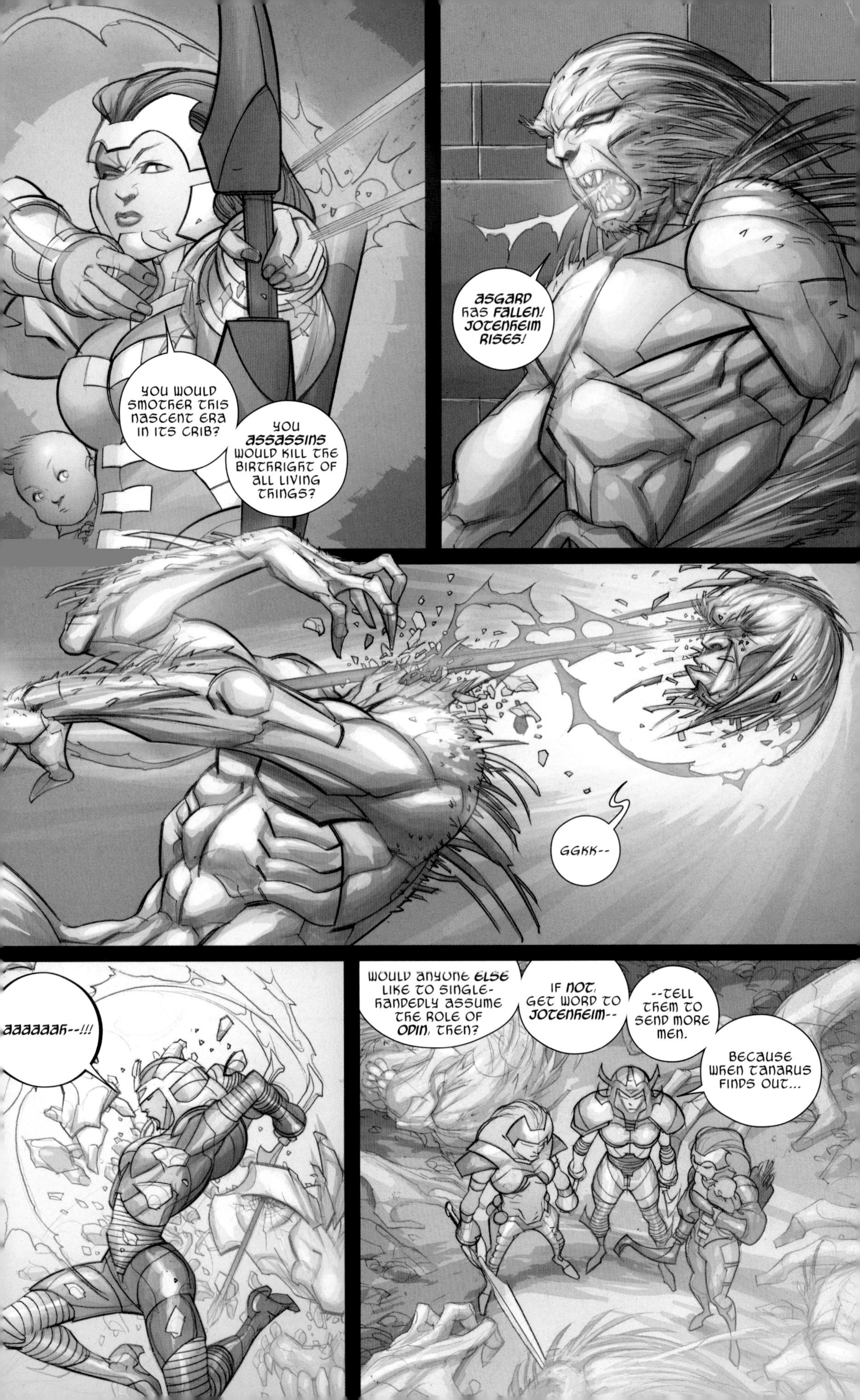
YOU WOULD SMOTHER THIS NASCENT ERA IN ITS CRIB?
YOU ASSASSINS WOULD KILL THE BIRTHRIGHT OF ALL LIVING THINGS?
ASGARD HAS FALLEN! JOTENHEIM RISES!
GGKK--
AAAAAAH--!!!
WOULD ANYONE ELSE LIKE TO SINGLE-HANDEDLY ASSUME THE ROLE OF ODIN, THEN?
IF NOT, GET WORD TO JOTENHEIM--
--TELL THEM TO SEND MORE MEN.
BECAUSE WHEN TANARUS FINDS OUT...

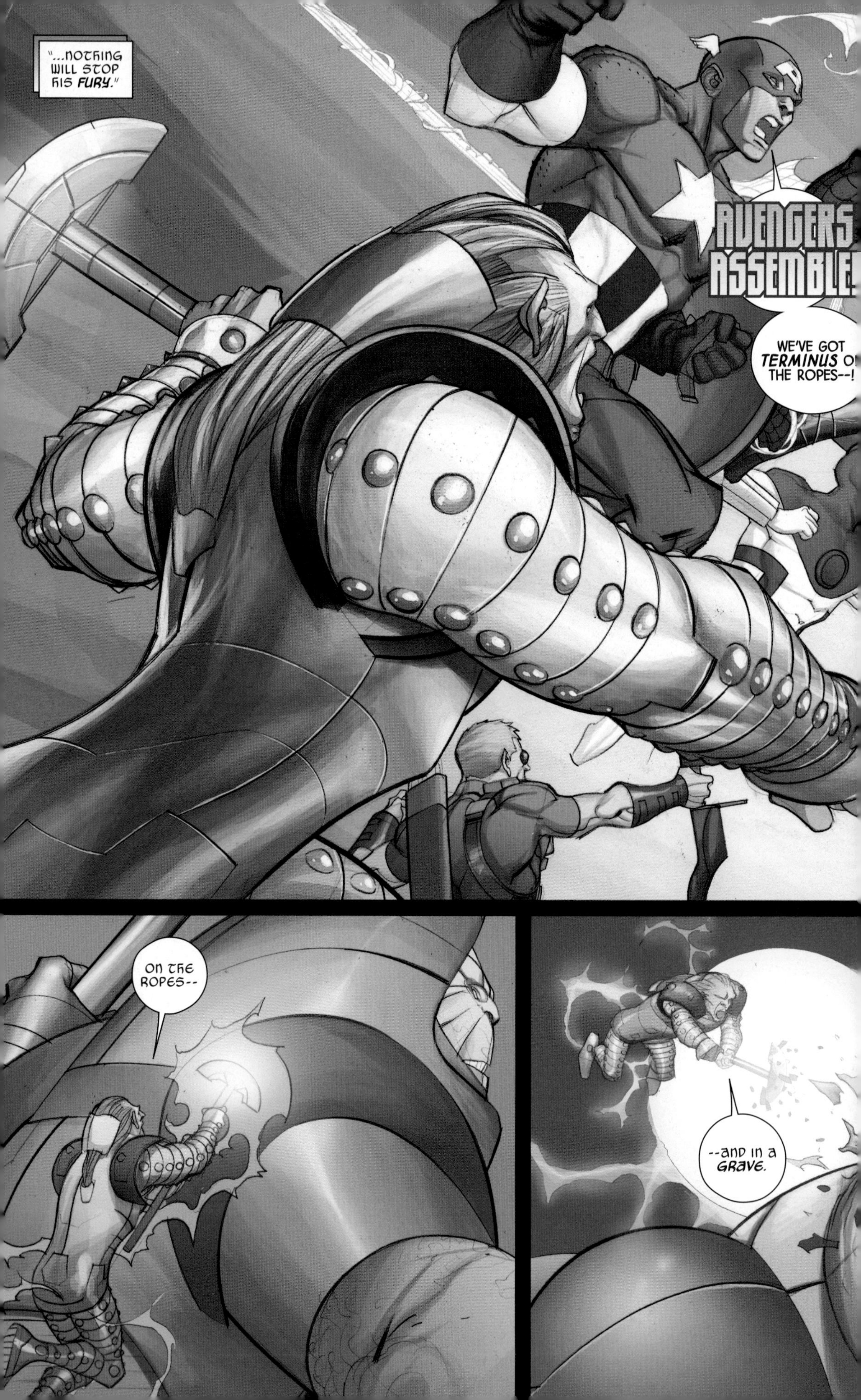
"...NOTHING WILL STOP HIS *FURY*."
AVENGERS ASSEMBLE!
WE'VE GOT *TERMINUS* O THE ROPES--!
ON THE ROPES--
--AND IN A *GRAVE*.

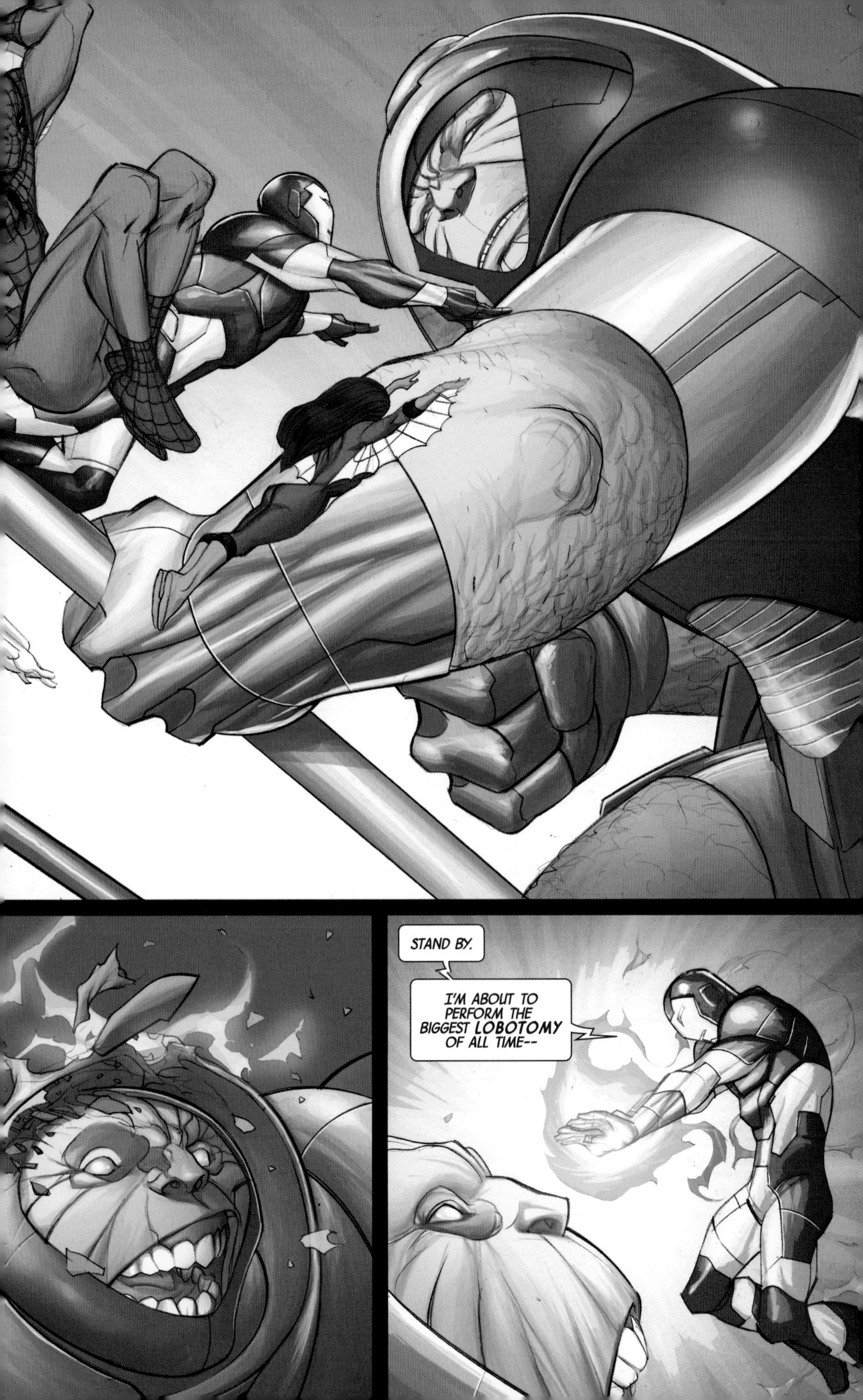
STAND BY.
I'M ABOUT TO PERFORM THE BIGGEST LOBOTOMY OF ALL TIME--

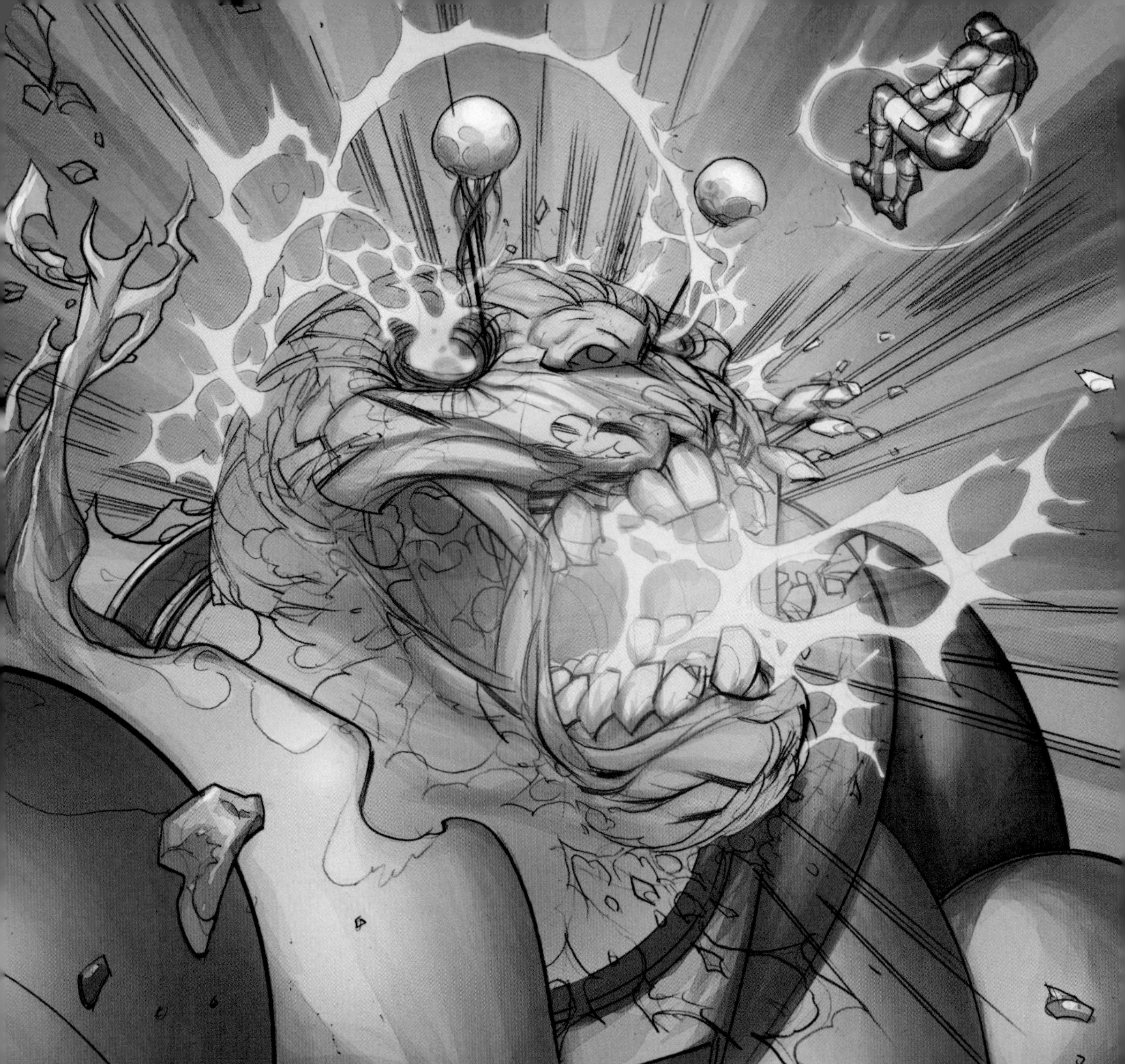

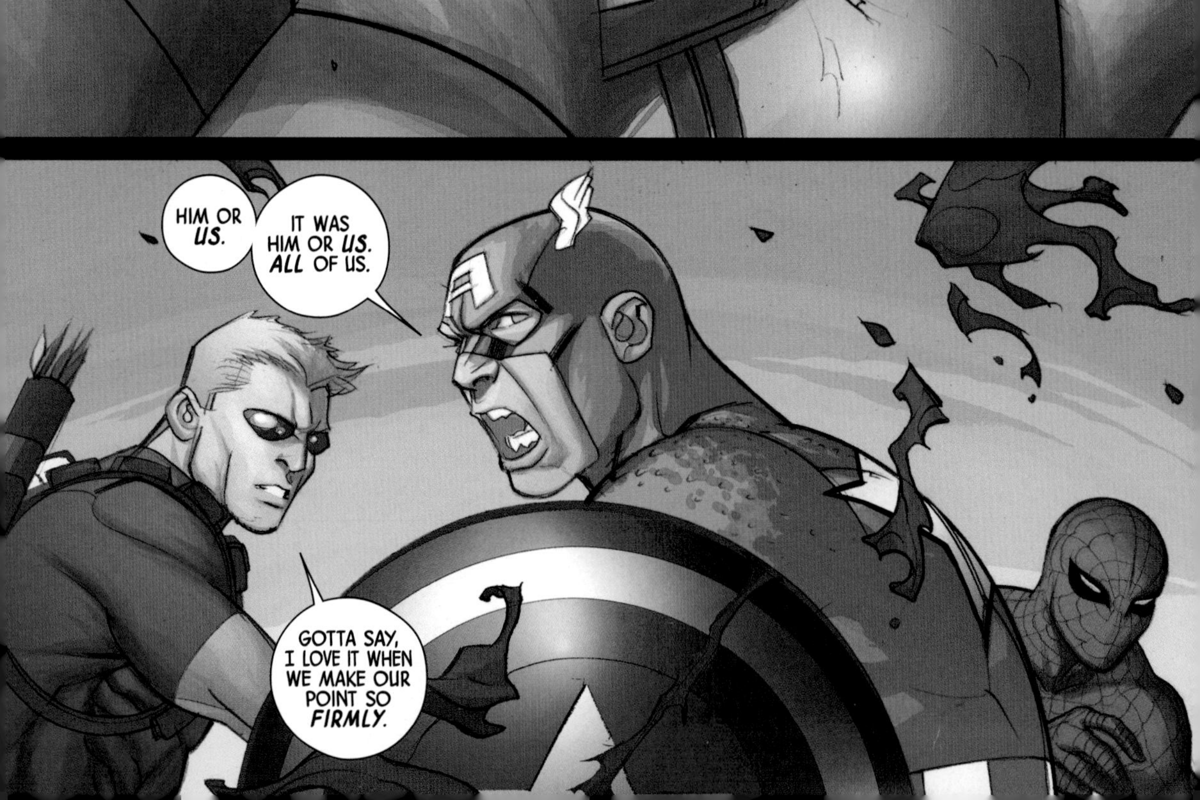
HIM OR US.
IT WAS HIM OR US. ALL OF US.
GOTTA SAY, I LOVE IT WHEN WE MAKE OUR POINT SO FIRMLY.

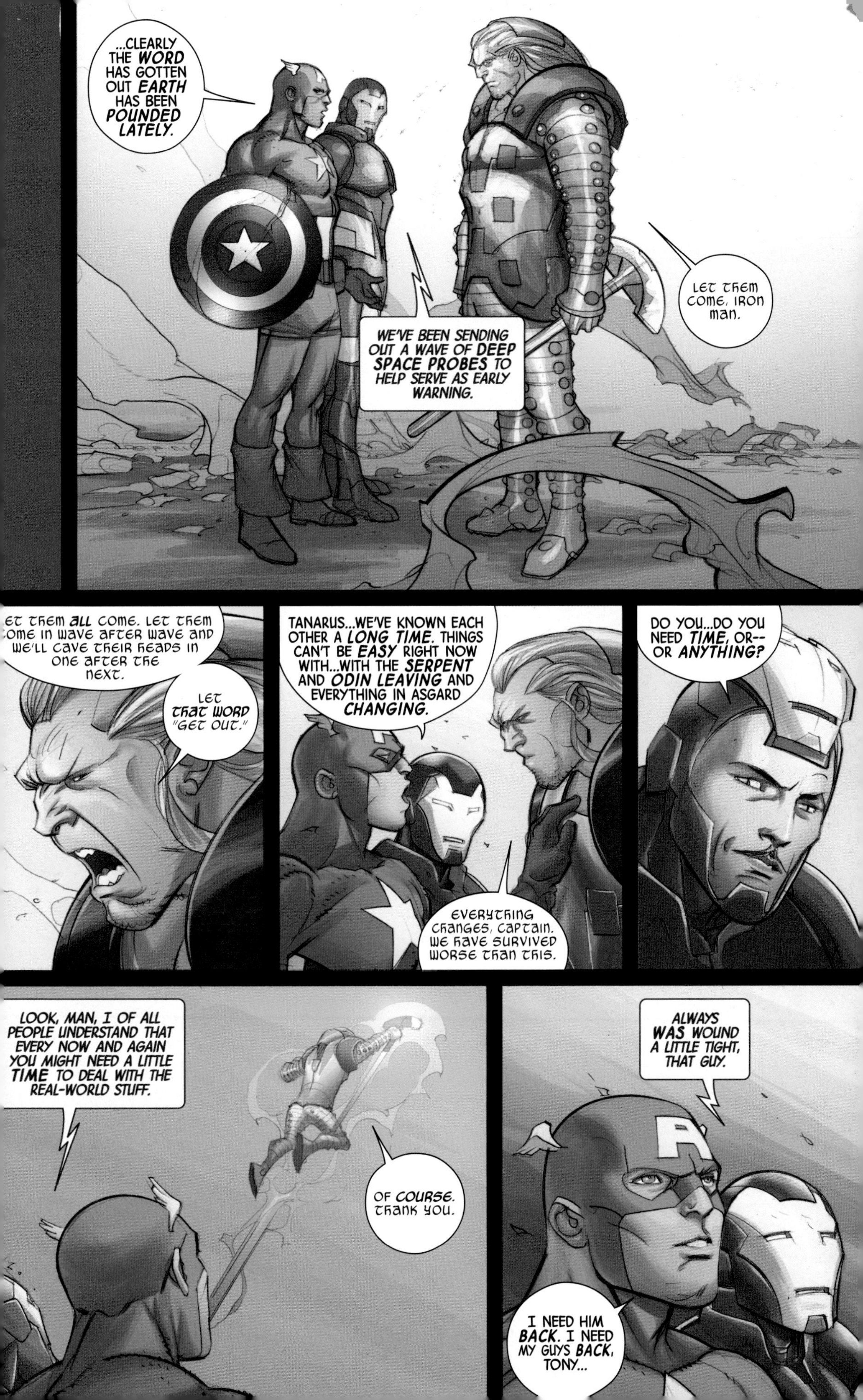
...CLEARLY THE WORD HAS GOTTEN OUT EARTH HAS BEEN POUNDED LATELY.
WE'VE BEEN SENDING OUT A WAVE OF DEEP SPACE PROBES TO HELP SERVE AS EARLY WARNING.
LET THEM COME, IRON MAN.
LET THEM ALL COME. LET THEM COME IN WAVE AFTER WAVE AND WE'LL CAVE THEIR HEADS IN ONE AFTER THE NEXT.
LET THAT WORD "GET OUT."
TANARUS...WE'VE KNOWN EACH OTHER A LONG TIME. THINGS CAN'T BE EASY RIGHT NOW WITH...WITH THE SERPENT AND ODIN LEAVING AND EVERYTHING IN ASGARD CHANGING.
EVERYTHING CHANGES, CAPTAIN. WE HAVE SURVIVED WORSE THAN THIS.
DO YOU...DO YOU NEED TIME, OR-- OR ANYTHING?
LOOK, MAN, I OF ALL PEOPLE UNDERSTAND THAT EVERY NOW AND AGAIN YOU MIGHT NEED A LITTLE TIME TO DEAL WITH THE REAL-WORLD STUFF.
OF COURSE. THANK YOU.
ALWAYS WAS WOUND A LITTLE TIGHT, THAT GUY.
I NEED HIM BACK. I NEED MY GUYS BACK, TONY...

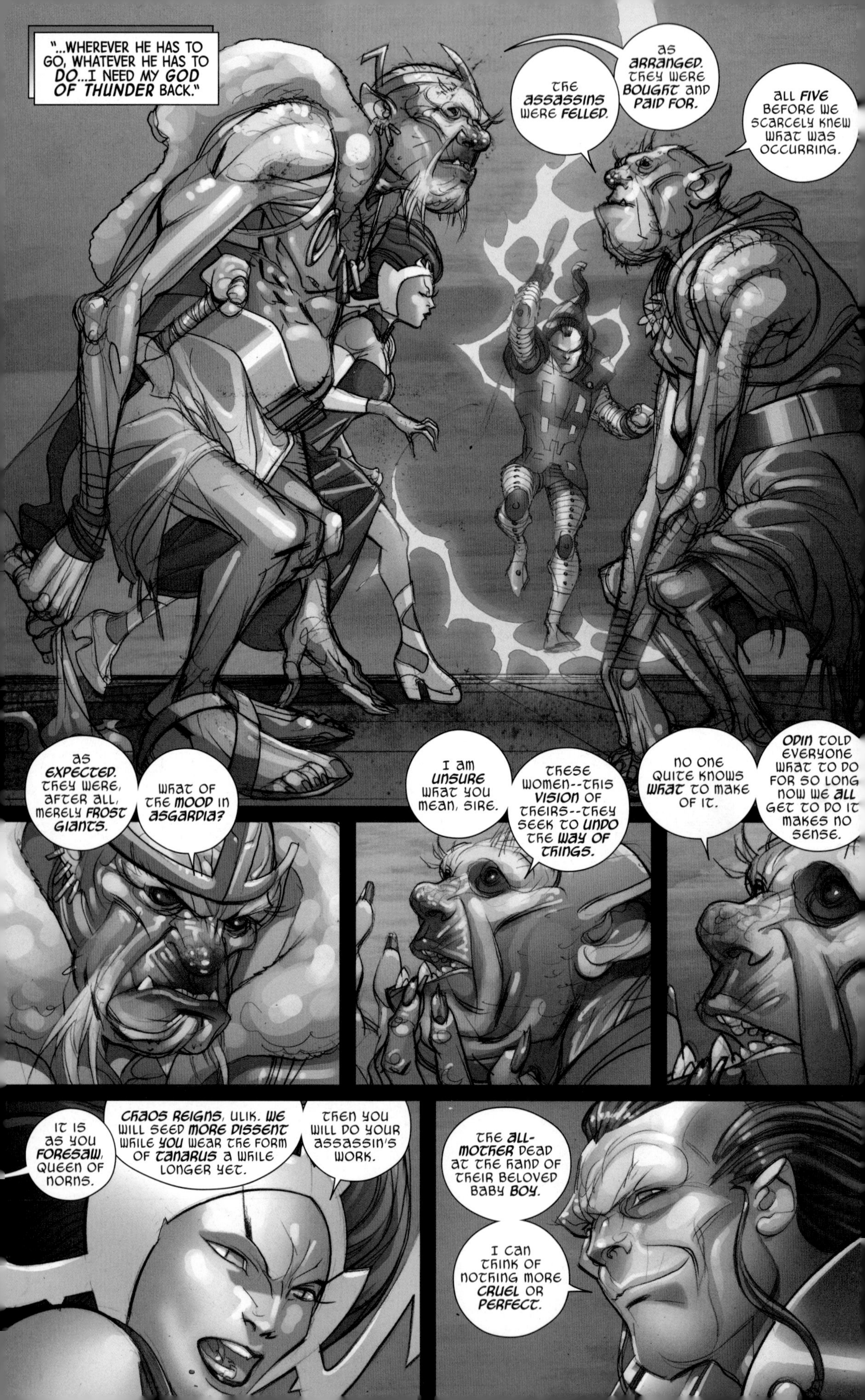
"...WHEREVER HE HAS TO GO, WHATEVER HE HAS TO DO...I NEED MY GOD OF THUNDER BACK."
THE ASSASSINS WERE FELLED.
AS ARRANGED. THEY WERE BOUGHT AND PAID FOR.
ALL FIVE BEFORE WE SCARCELY KNEW WHAT WAS OCCURRING.
AS EXPECTED. THEY WERE, AFTER ALL, MERELY FROST GIANTS.
WHAT OF THE MOOD IN ASGARDIA?
I AM UNSURE WHAT YOU MEAN, SIRE.
THESE WOMEN--THIS VISION OF THEIRS--THEY SEEK TO UNDO THE WAY OF THINGS.
NO ONE QUITE KNOWS WHAT TO MAKE OF IT.
ODIN TOLD EVERYONE WHAT TO DO FOR SO LONG NOW WE ALL GET TO DO IT MAKES NO SENSE.
IT IS AS YOU FORESAW, QUEEN OF NORNS.
CHAOS REIGNS, ULIK. WE WILL SEED MORE DISSENT WHILE YOU WEAR THE FORM OF TANARUS A WHILE LONGER YET.
THEN YOU WILL DO YOUR ASSASSIN'S WORK.
THE ALL-MOTHER DEAD AT THE HAND OF THEIR BELOVED BABY BOY.
I CAN THINK OF NOTHING MORE CRUEL OR PERFECT.

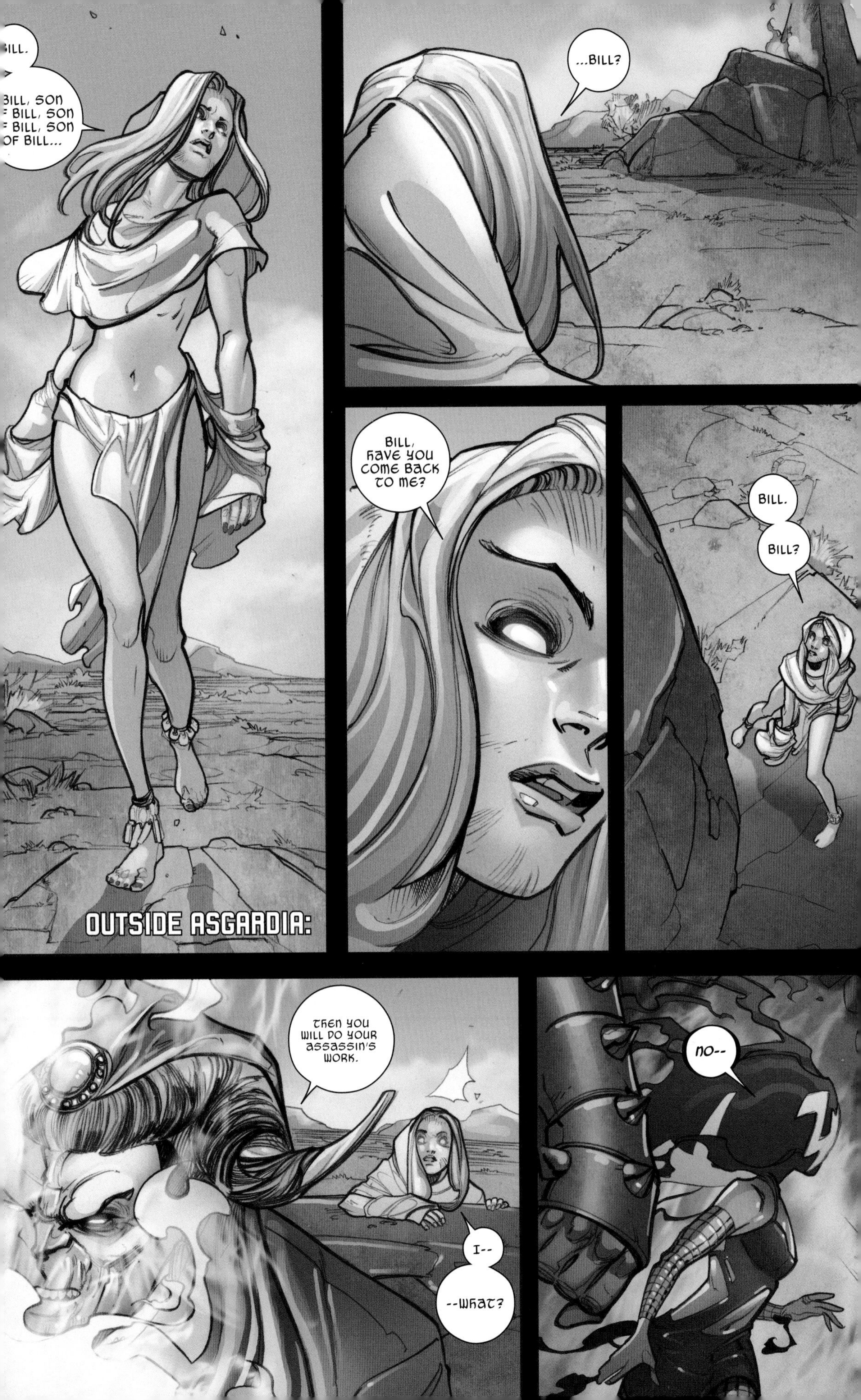
BILL.
BILL, SON OF BILL, SON OF BILL, SON OF BILL...
OUTSIDE ASGARDIA:
...BILL?
BILL, HAVE YOU COME BACK TO ME?
BILL.
BILL?
THEN YOU WILL DO YOUR ASSASSIN'S WORK.
I--
--WHAT?
NO--

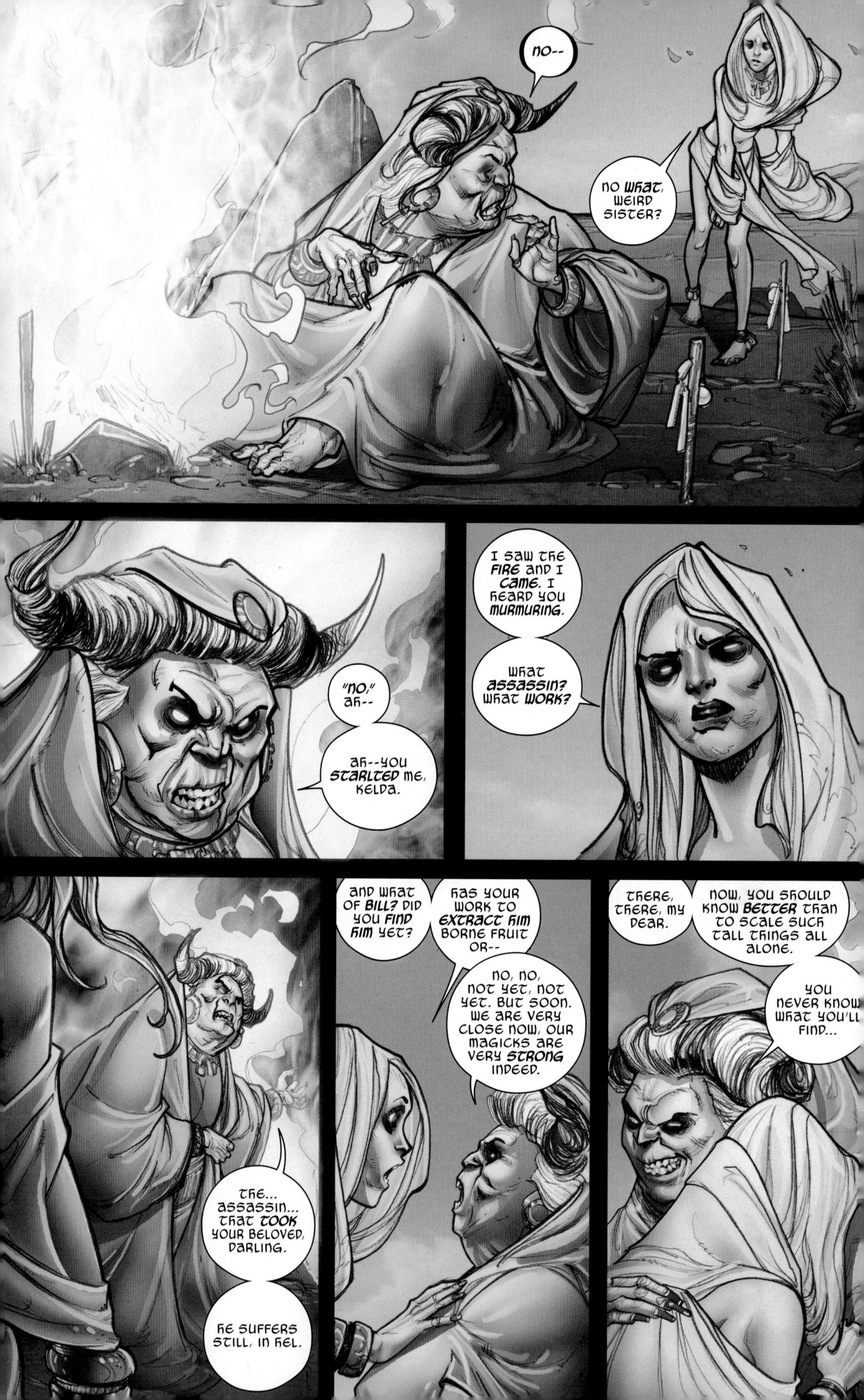
NO--
NO WHAT, WEIRD SISTER?
"NO," AH--
AH--YOU STARLTED ME, KELDA.
I SAW THE FIRE AND I CAME. I HEARD YOU MURMURING.
WHAT ASSASSIN? WHAT WORK?
THE... ASSASSIN... THAT TOOK YOUR BELOVED, DARLING.
HE SUFFERS STILL, IN HEL.
AND WHAT OF BILL? DID YOU FIND HIM YET?
HAS YOUR WORK TO EXTRACT HIM BORNE FRUIT OR--
NO, NO, NOT YET, NOT YET. BUT SOON. WE ARE VERY CLOSE NOW, OUR MAGICKS ARE VERY STRONG INDEED.
THERE, THERE, MY DEAR.
NOW, YOU SHOULD KNOW BETTER THAN TO SCALE SUCH TALL THINGS ALL ALONE.
YOU NEVER KNOW WHAT YOU'LL FIND...

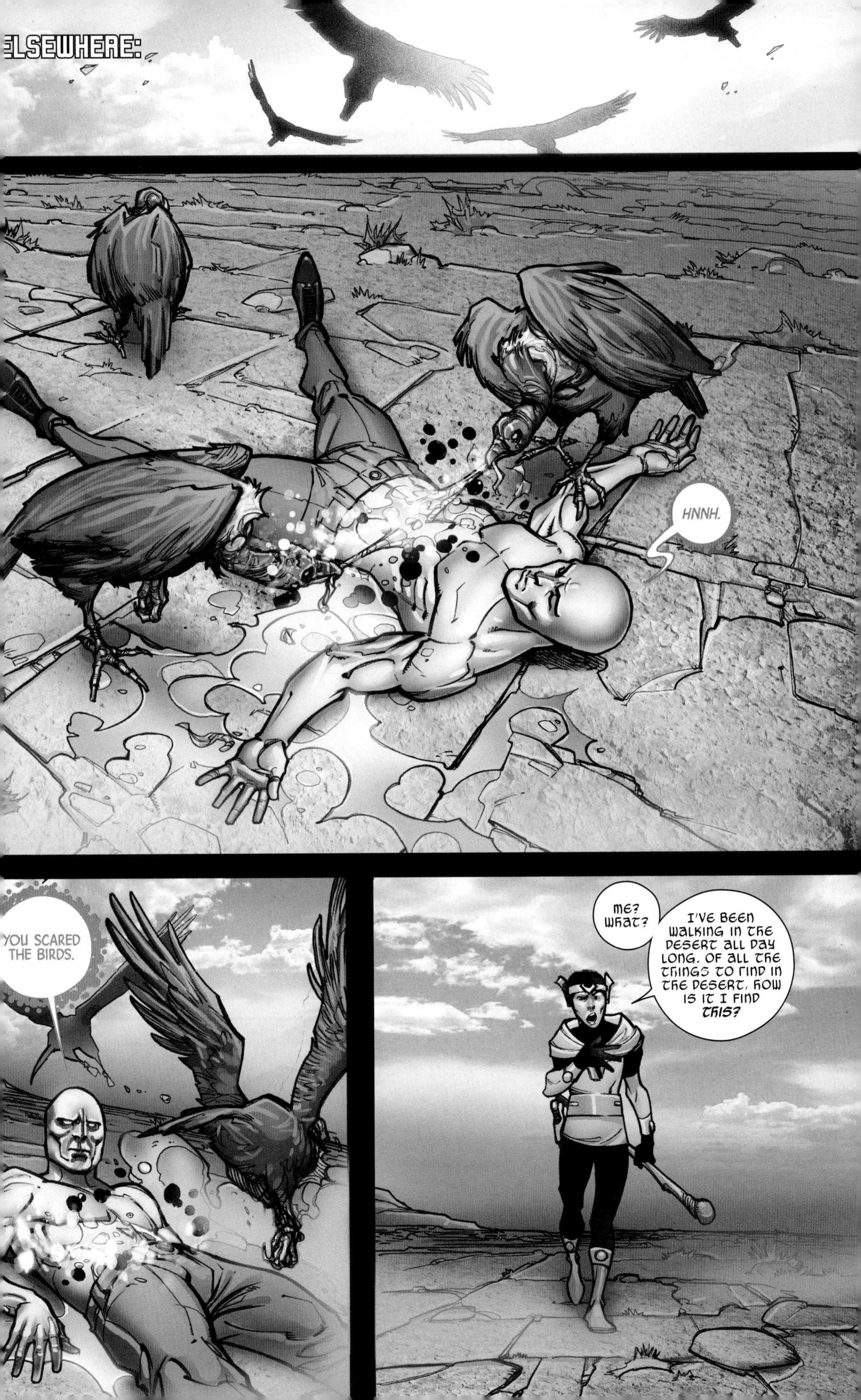
ELSEWHERE:
HNNH.
YOU SCARED THE BIRDS.
ME? WHAT?
I'VE BEEN WALKING IN THE DESERT ALL DAY LONG. OF ALL THE THINGS TO FIND IN THE DESERT, HOW IS IT I FIND *THIS?*

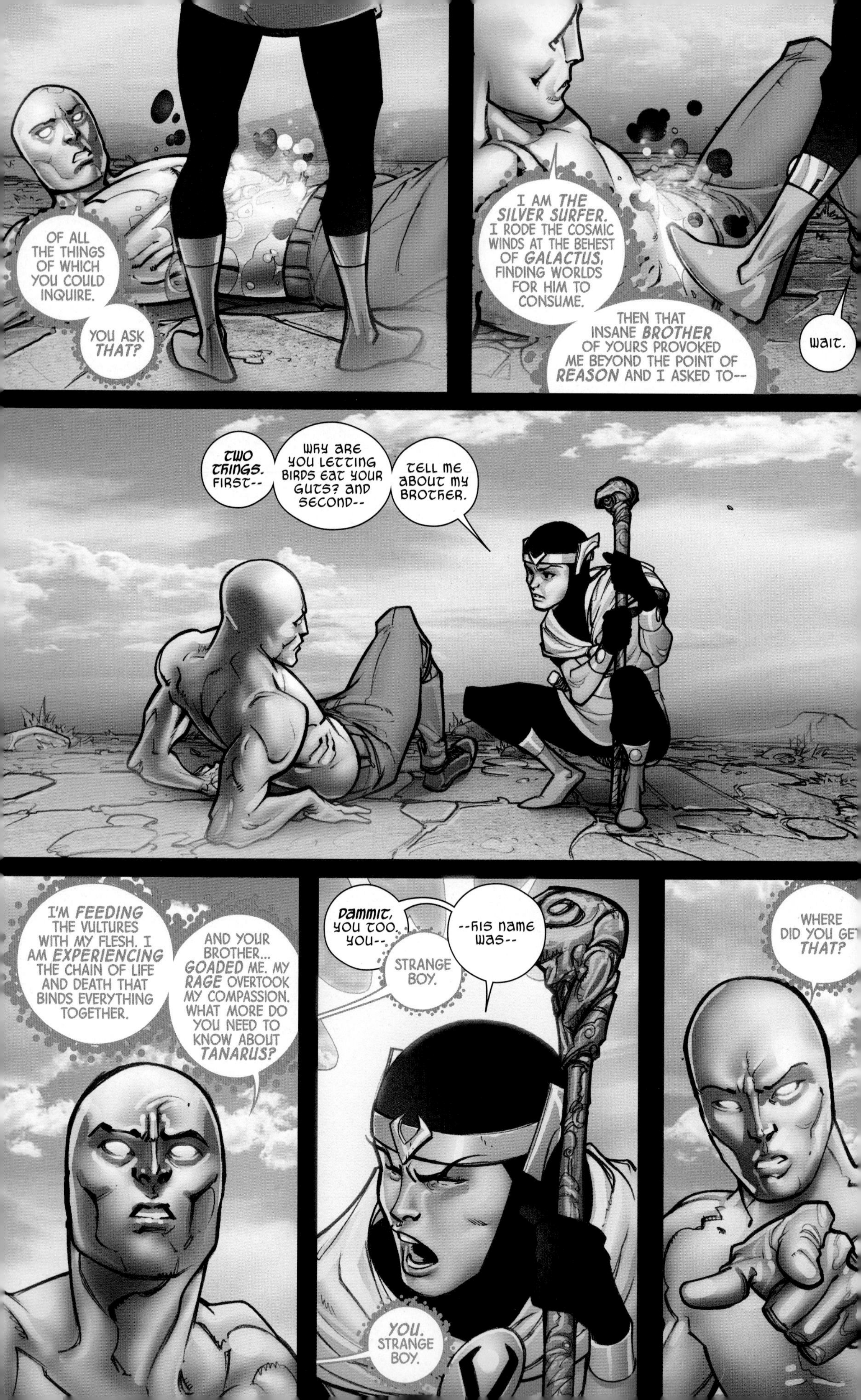
OF ALL THE THINGS OF WHICH YOU COULD INQUIRE.
YOU ASK THAT?
I AM THE SILVER SURFER. I RODE THE COSMIC WINDS AT THE BEHEST OF GALACTUS, FINDING WORLDS FOR HIM TO CONSUME.
THEN THAT INSANE BROTHER OF YOURS PROVOKED ME BEYOND THE POINT OF REASON AND I ASKED TO--
WAIT.
TWO THINGS. FIRST--
WHY ARE YOU LETTING BIRDS EAT YOUR GUTS? AND SECOND--
TELL ME ABOUT MY BROTHER.
I'M FEEDING THE VULTURES WITH MY FLESH. I AM EXPERIENCING THE CHAIN OF LIFE AND DEATH THAT BINDS EVERYTHING TOGETHER.
AND YOUR BROTHER... GOADED ME. MY RAGE OVERTOOK MY COMPASSION. WHAT MORE DO YOU NEED TO KNOW ABOUT TANARUS?
DAMMIT, YOU TOO. YOU--
STRANGE BOY.
--HIS NAME WAS--
YOU. STRANGE BOY.
WHERE DID YOU GET THAT?

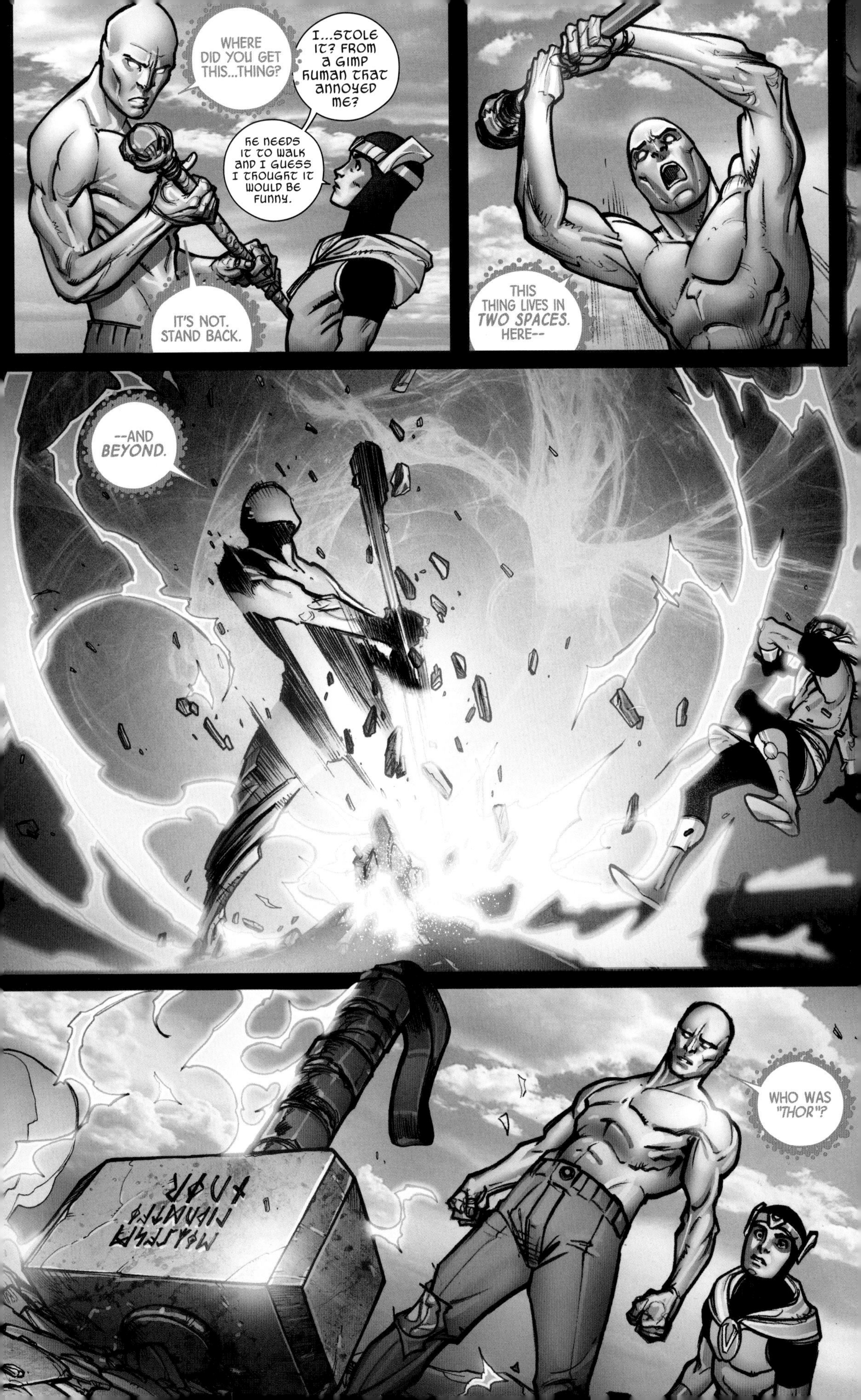
WHERE DID YOU GET THIS...THING?
I...STOLE IT? FROM A GIMP HUMAN THAT ANNOYED ME?
HE NEEDS IT TO WALK AND I GUESS I THOUGHT IT WOULD BE FUNNY.
IT'S NOT. STAND BACK.
THIS THING LIVES IN TWO SPACES. HERE--
--AND BEYOND.
WHO WAS "THOR"?

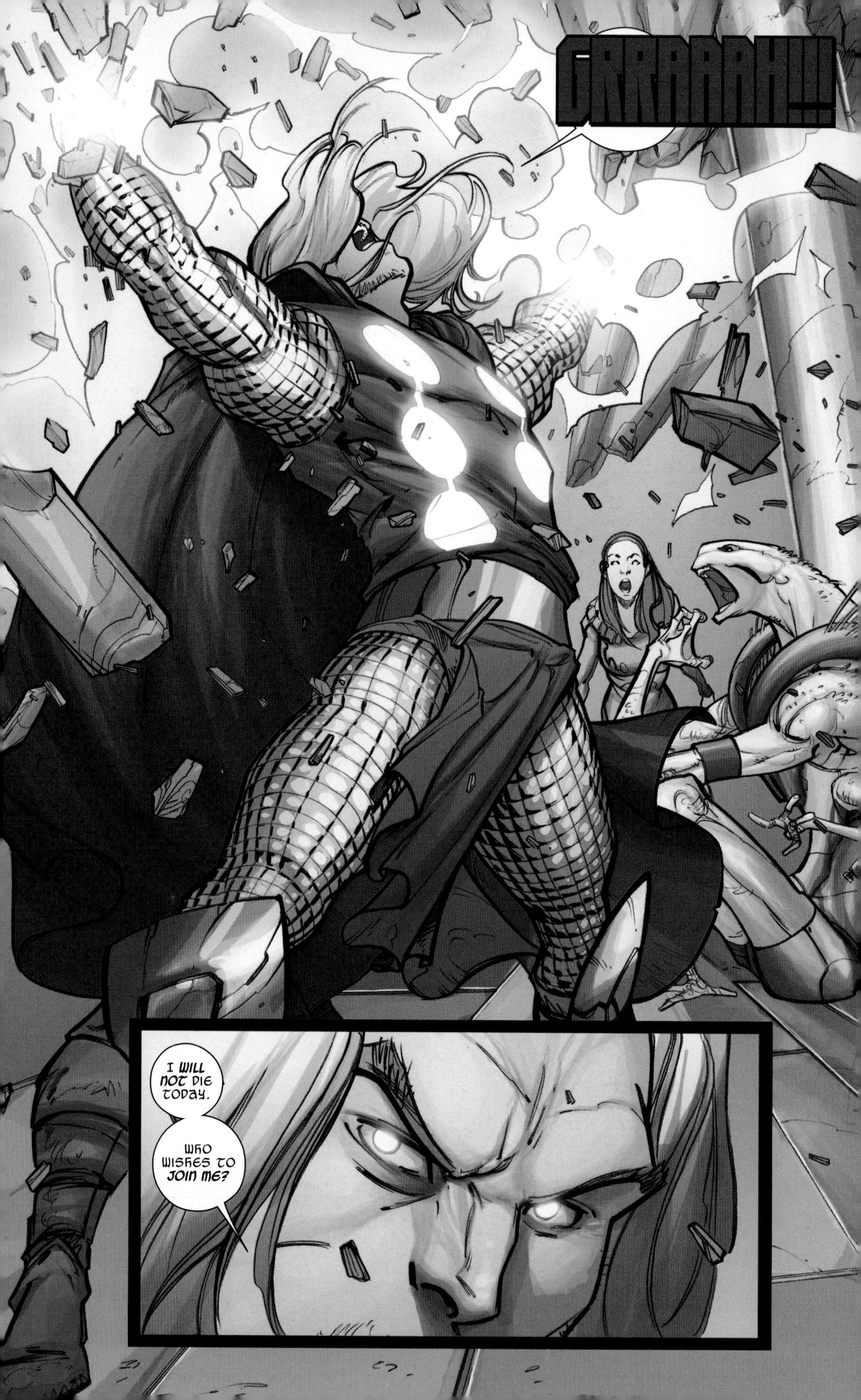
GRRAAAH!!!
I WILL NOT DIE TODAY.
WHO WISHES TO JOIN ME?

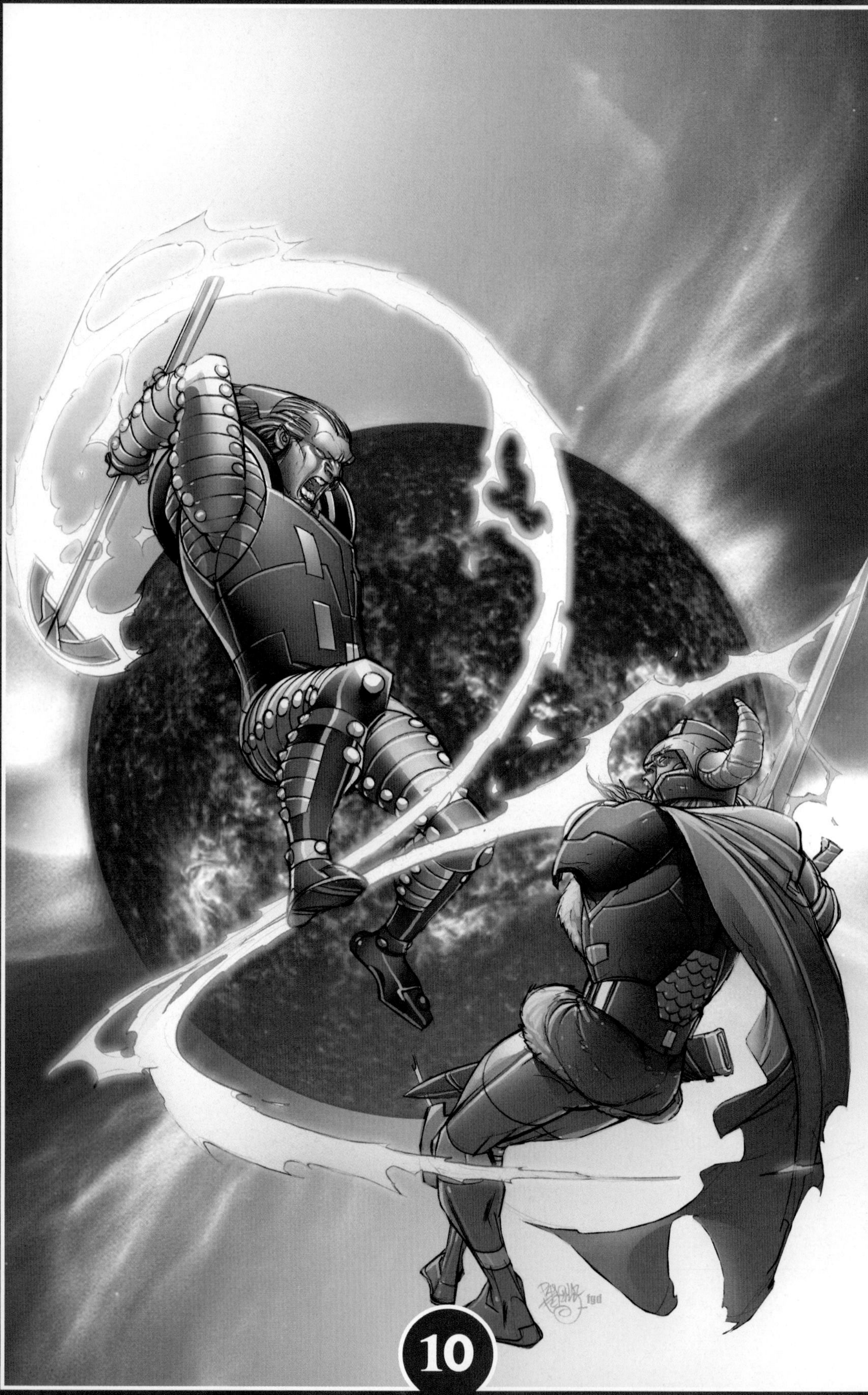

10

THE MIGHTY TANARUS 3: DOOMED

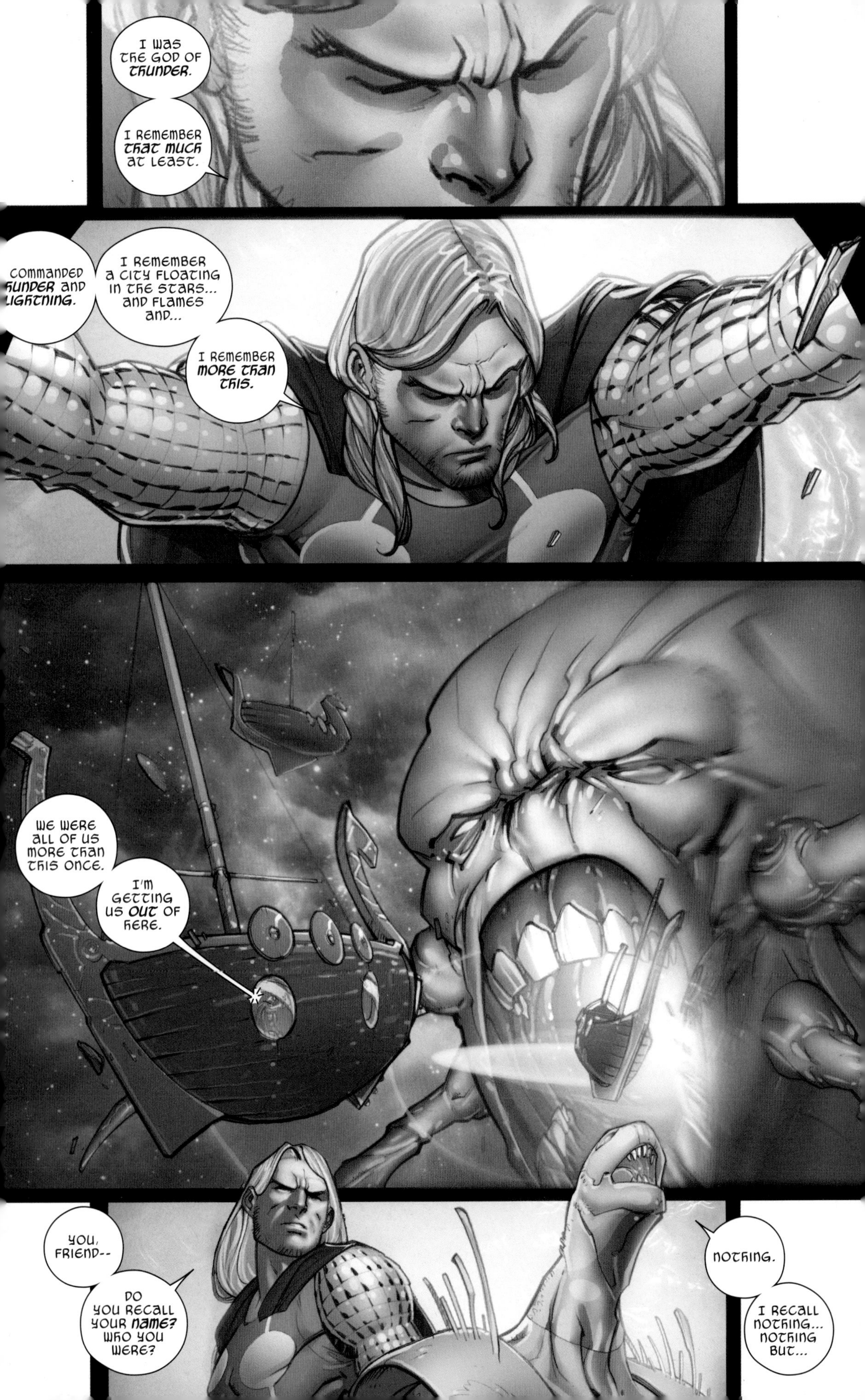

I WAS THE GOD OF THUNDER.
I REMEMBER THAT MUCH AT LEAST.
COMMANDED THUNDER AND LIGHTNING.
I REMEMBER A CITY FLOATING IN THE STARS... AND FLAMES AND...
I REMEMBER MORE THAN THIS.
WE WERE ALL OF US MORE THAN THIS ONCE.
I'M GETTING US OUT OF HERE.
YOU, FRIEND--
DO YOU RECALL YOUR NAME? WHO YOU WERE?
NOTHING.
I RECALL NOTHING... NOTHING BUT...

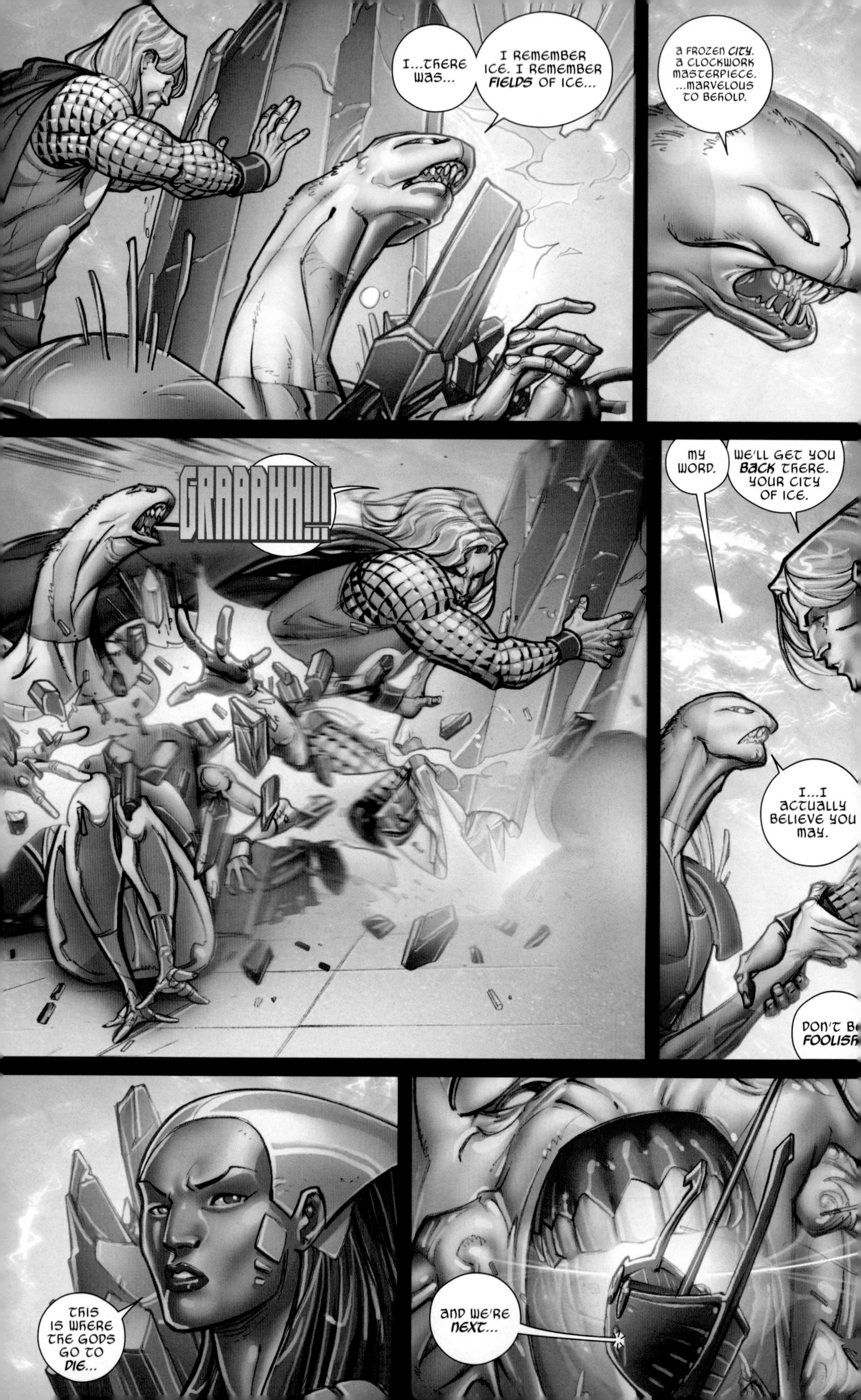

I...THERE WAS...
I REMEMBER ICE. I REMEMBER FIELDS OF ICE...
A FROZEN CITY. A CLOCKWORK MASTERPIECE. ...MARVELOUS TO BEHOLD.
GRAAAHH!!!
MY WORD.
WE'LL GET YOU BACK THERE. YOUR CITY OF ICE.
I...I ACTUALLY BELIEVE YOU MAY.
DON'T BE FOOLISH
THIS IS WHERE THE GODS GO TO DIE...
AND WE'RE NEXT...

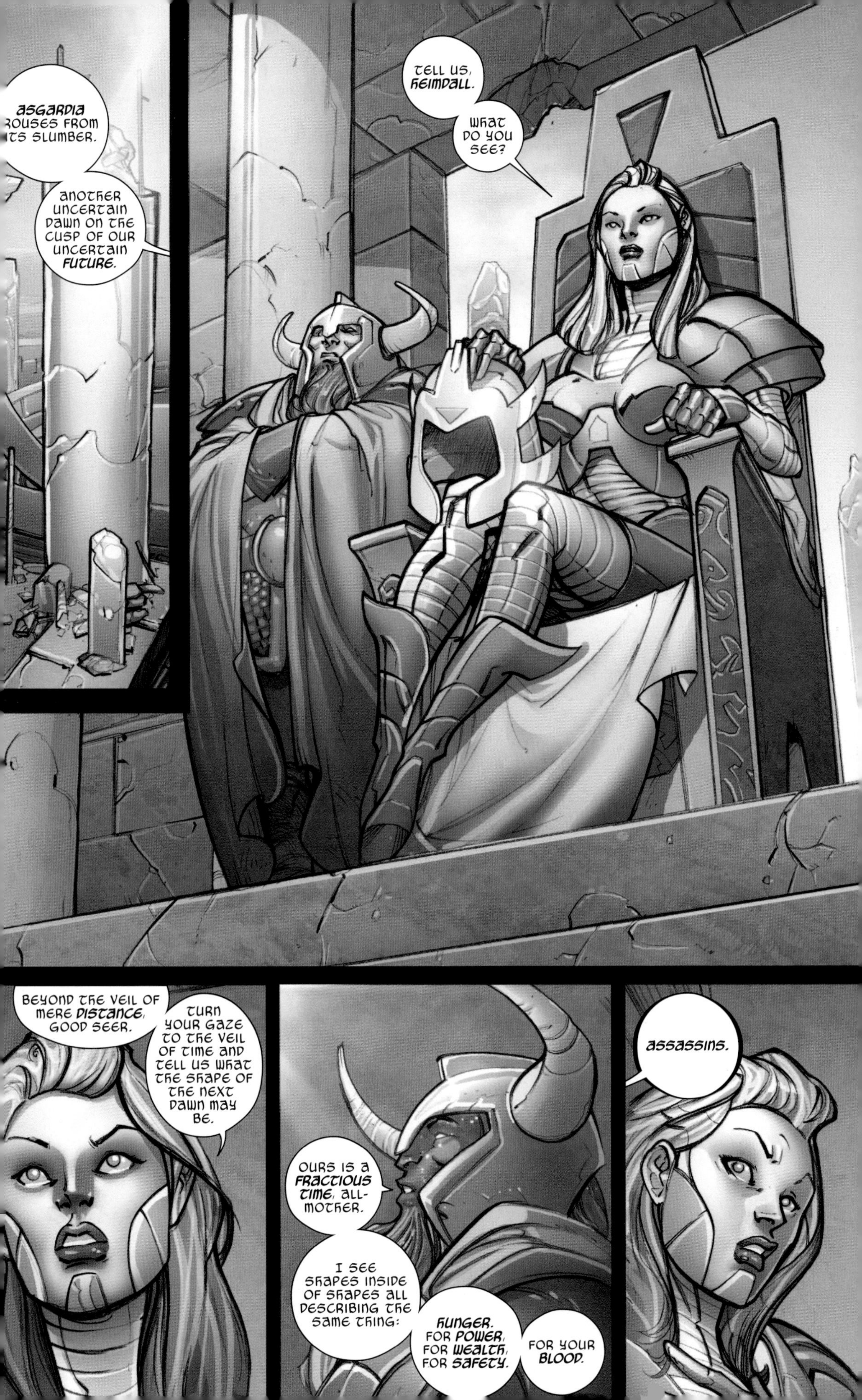

ASGARDIA ROUSES FROM ITS SLUMBER.
ANOTHER UNCERTAIN DAWN ON THE CUSP OF OUR UNCERTAIN FUTURE.
TELL US, HEIMDALL.
WHAT DO YOU SEE?
BEYOND THE VEIL OF MERE DISTANCE, GOOD SEER.
TURN YOUR GAZE TO THE VEIL OF TIME AND TELL US WHAT THE SHAPE OF THE NEXT DAWN MAY BE.
OURS IS A FRACTIOUS TIME, ALL-MOTHER.
I SEE SHAPES INSIDE OF SHAPES ALL DESCRIBING THE SAME THING:
HUNGER. FOR POWER, FOR WEALTH, FOR SAFETY.
FOR YOUR BLOOD.
ASSASSINS.

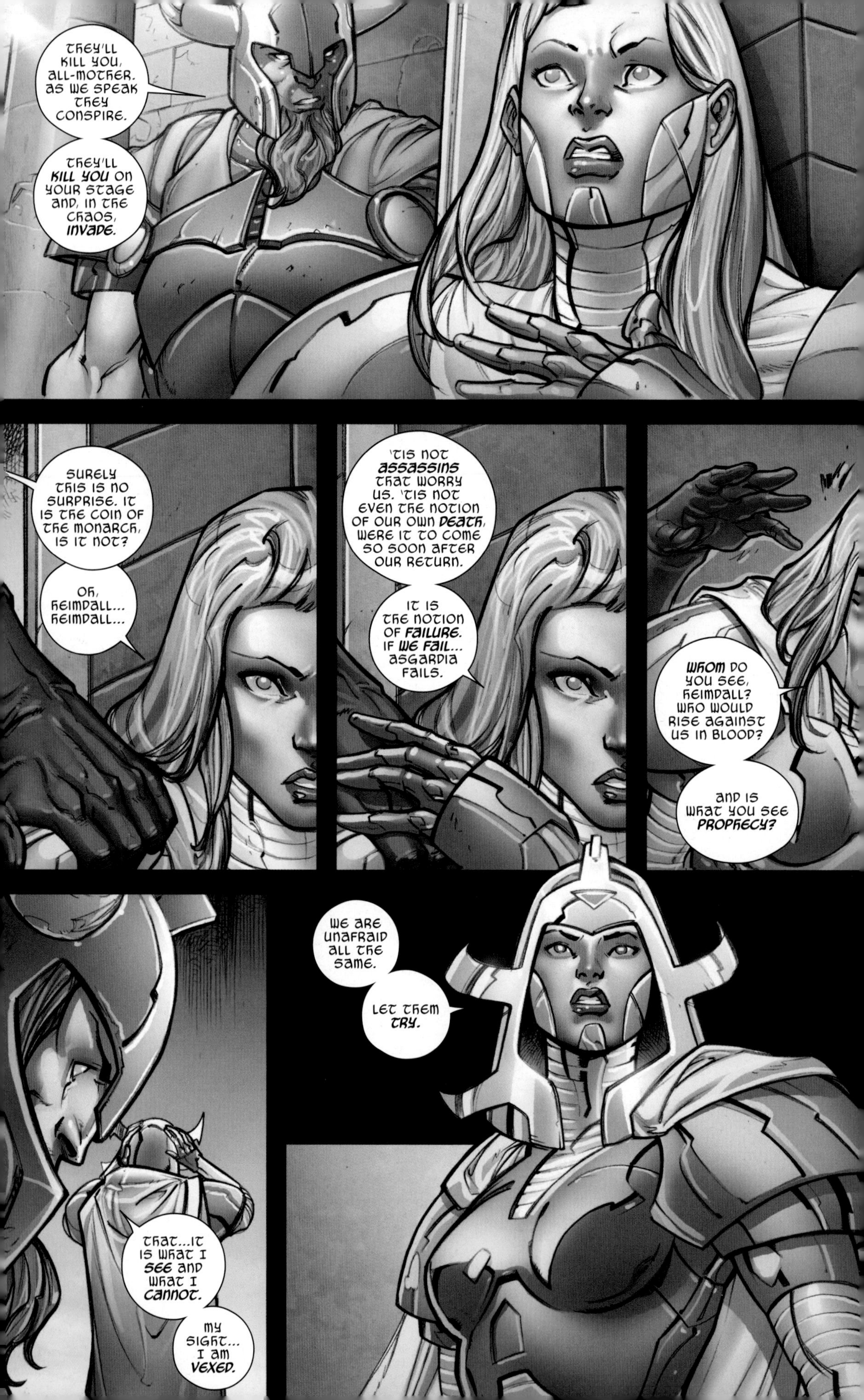
THEY'LL KILL YOU, ALL-MOTHER. AS WE SPEAK THEY CONSPIRE.
THEY'LL KILL YOU ON YOUR STAGE AND, IN THE CHAOS, INVADE.
SURELY THIS IS NO SURPRISE. IT IS THE COIN OF THE MONARCH, IS IT NOT?
OH, HEIMDALL... HEIMDALL...
'TIS NOT ASSASSINS THAT WORRY US. 'TIS NOT EVEN THE NOTION OF OUR OWN DEATH, WERE IT TO COME SO SOON AFTER OUR RETURN.
IT IS THE NOTION OF FAILURE. IF WE FAIL... ASGARDIA FAILS.
WHOM DO YOU SEE, HEIMDALL? WHO WOULD RISE AGAINST US IN BLOOD?
AND IS WHAT YOU SEE PROPHECY?
THAT...IT IS WHAT I SEE AND WHAT I CANNOT.
MY SIGHT... I AM VEXED.
WE ARE UNAFRAID ALL THE SAME.
LET THEM TRY.

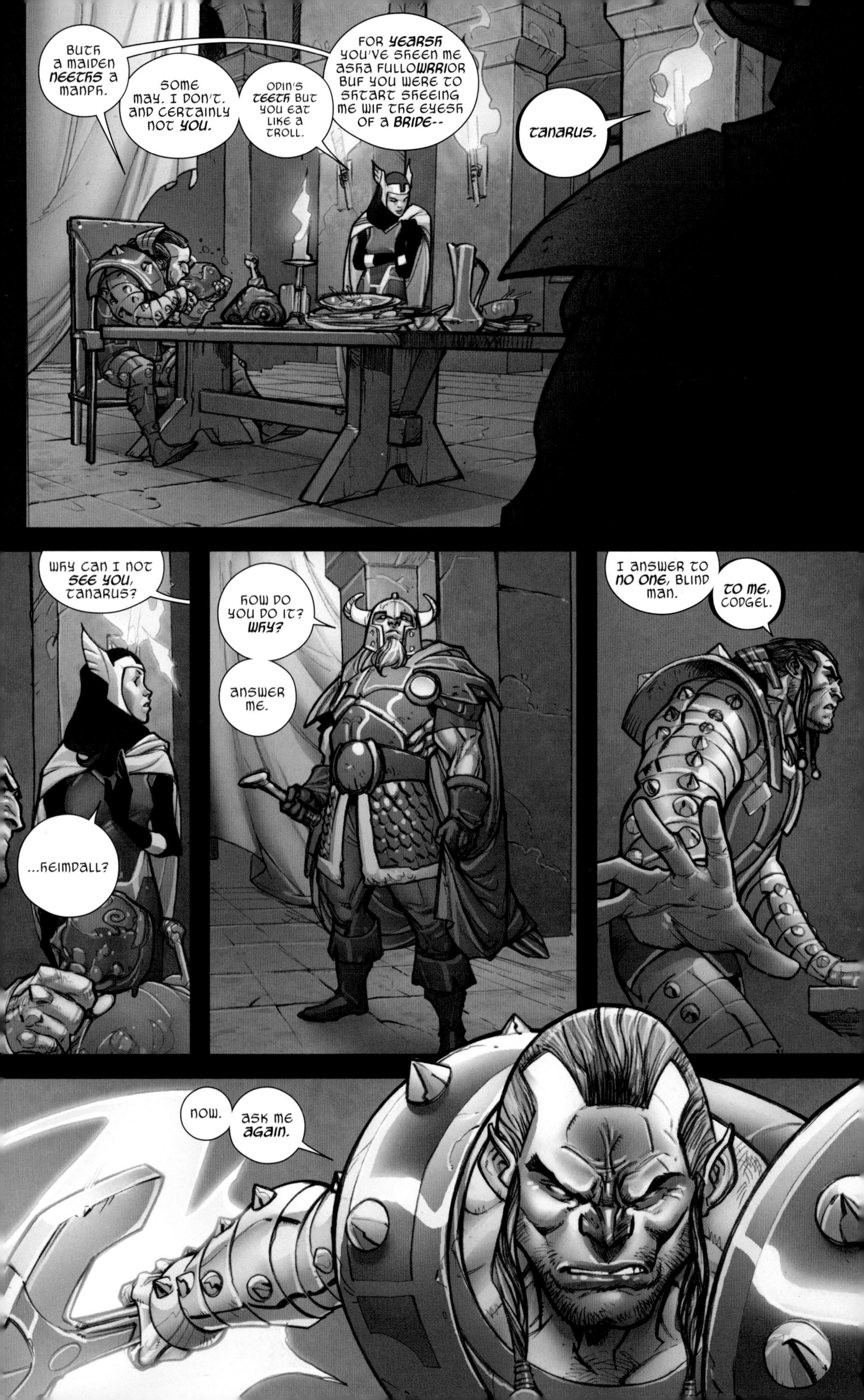
BUTH A MAIDEN NEETHS A MANPH.
SOME MAY. I DON'T. AND CERTAINLY NOT YOU.
ODIN'S TEETH BUT YOU EAT LIKE A TROLL.
FOR YEARSH YOU'VE SHEEN ME ASHA FULLOWRRIOR BUF YOU WERE TO SHTART SHEEING ME WIF THE EYESH OF A BRIDE--
TANARUS.
WHY CAN I NOT SEE YOU, TANARUS?
...HEIMDALL?
HOW DO YOU DO IT? WHY?
ANSWER ME.
I ANSWER TO NO ONE, BLIND MAN.
TO ME, CODGEL.
NOW.
ASK ME AGAIN.

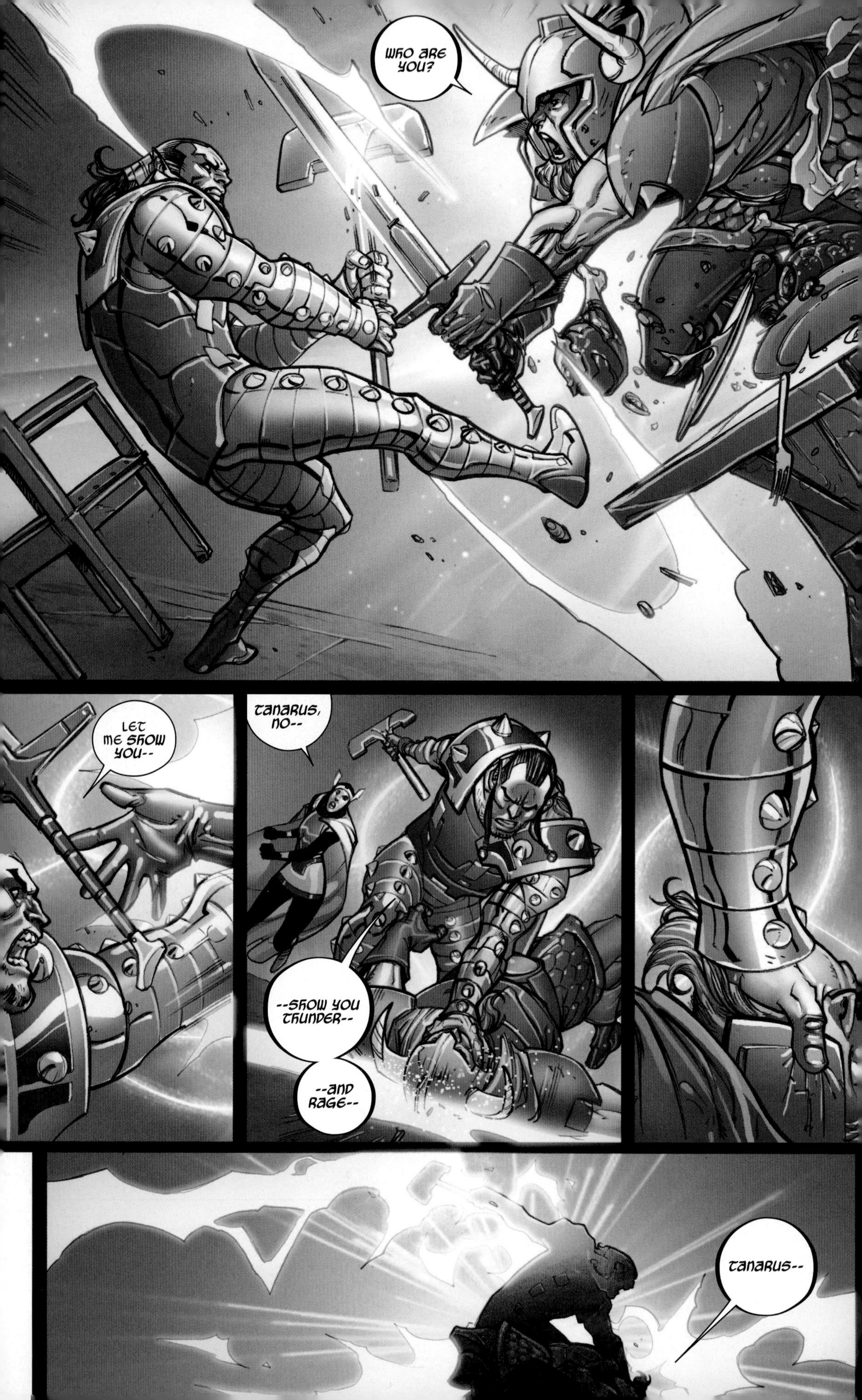
WHO ARE YOU?
LET ME SHOW YOU--
TANARUS, NO--
--SHOW YOU THUNDER--
--AND RAGE--
TANARUS--

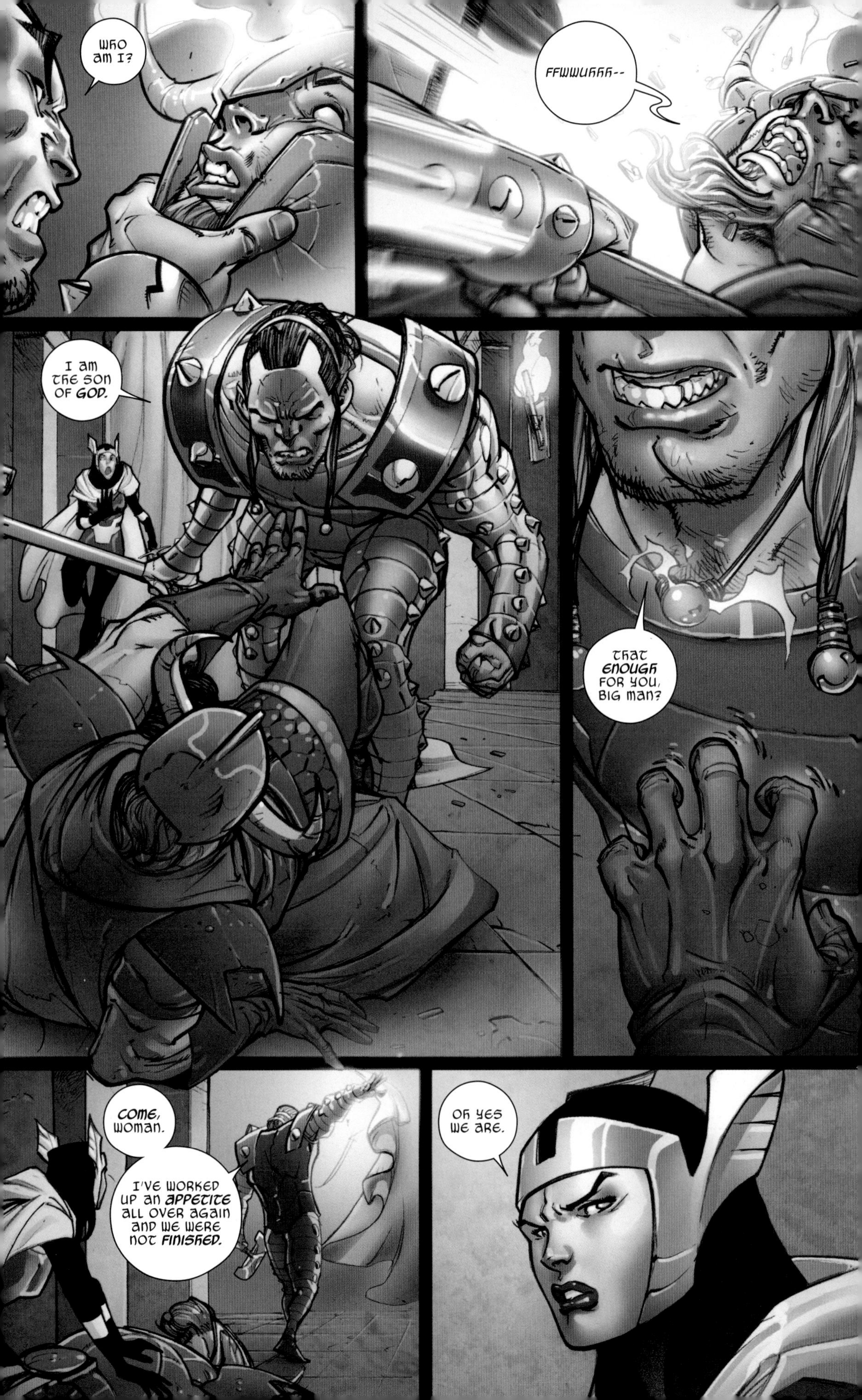
WHO AM I?
FFWWUHHH--
I AM THE SON OF GOD.
THAT ENOUGH FOR YOU, BIG MAN?
COME, WOMAN.
I'VE WORKED UP AN APPETITE ALL OVER AGAIN AND WE WERE NOT FINISHED.
OH YES WE ARE.

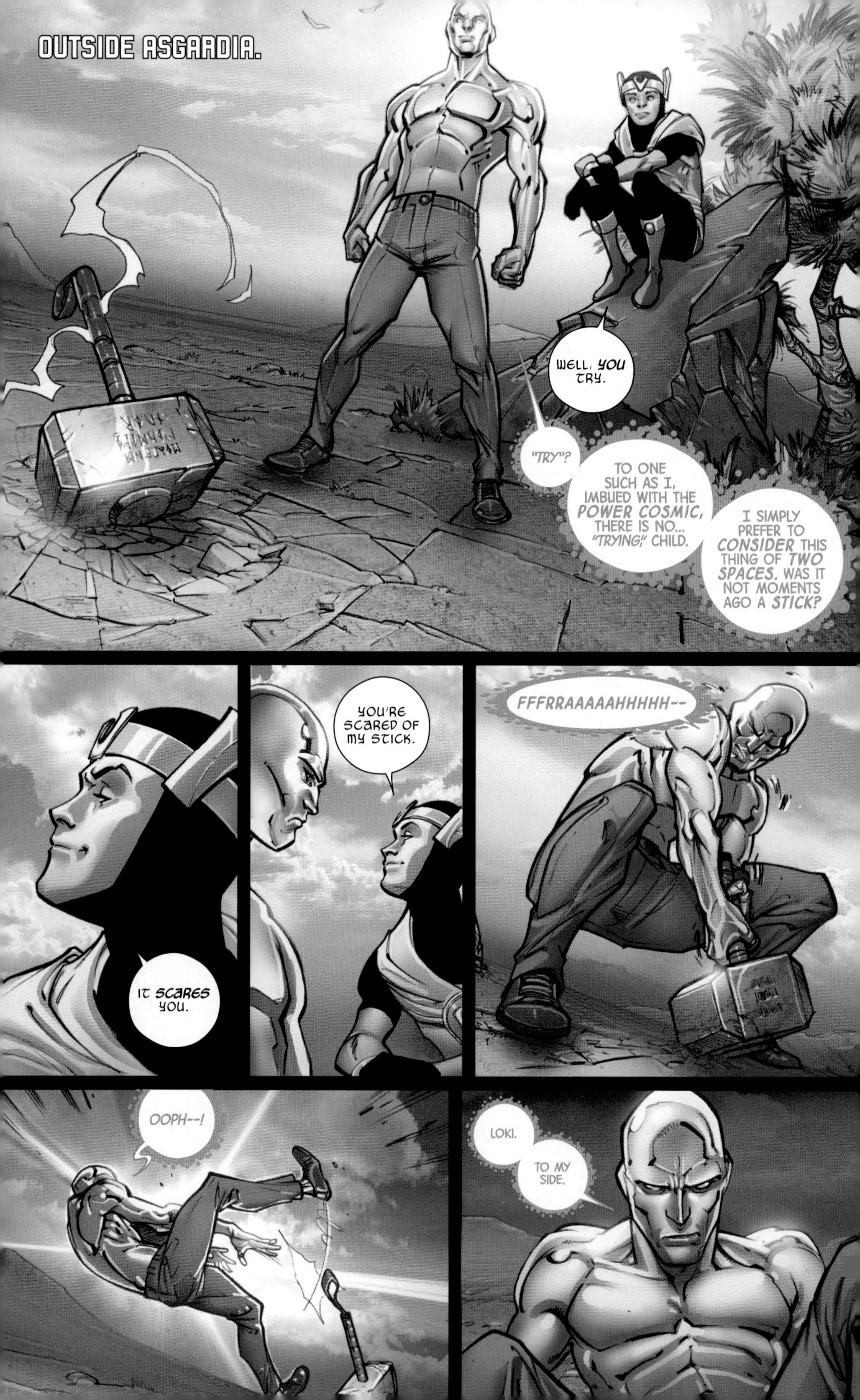

OUTSIDE ASGARDIA.
WELL, YOU TRY.
"TRY"?
TO ONE SUCH AS I, IMBUED WITH THE POWER COSMIC, THERE IS NO... "TRYING," CHILD.
I SIMPLY PREFER TO CONSIDER THIS THING OF TWO SPACES. WAS IT NOT MOMENTS AGO A STICK?
IT SCARES YOU.
YOU'RE SCARED OF MY STICK.
FFFRRAAAAAHHHHH--
OOPH--!
LOKI.
TO MY SIDE.

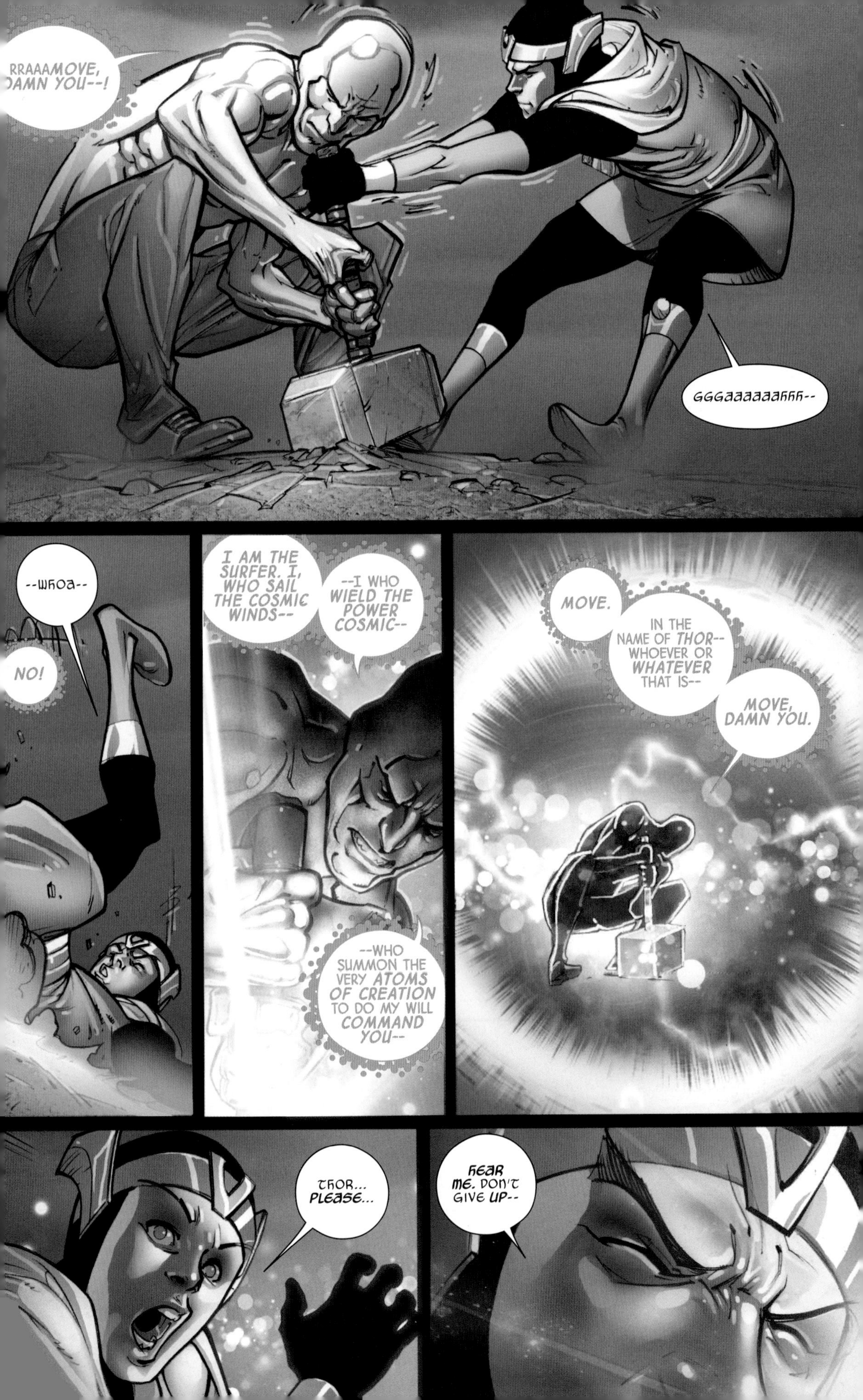
RRAAAMOVE,
DAMN YOU--!
GGGAAAAAAHHH--
--WHOA--
NO!
I AM THE SURFER. I, WHO SAIL THE COSMIC WINDS--
--I WHO WIELD THE POWER COSMIC--
--WHO SUMMON THE VERY ATOMS OF CREATION TO DO MY WILL COMMAND YOU--
MOVE.
IN THE NAME OF THOR-- WHOEVER OR WHATEVER THAT IS--
MOVE, DAMN YOU.
THOR... PLEASE...
HEAR ME. DON'T GIVE UP--

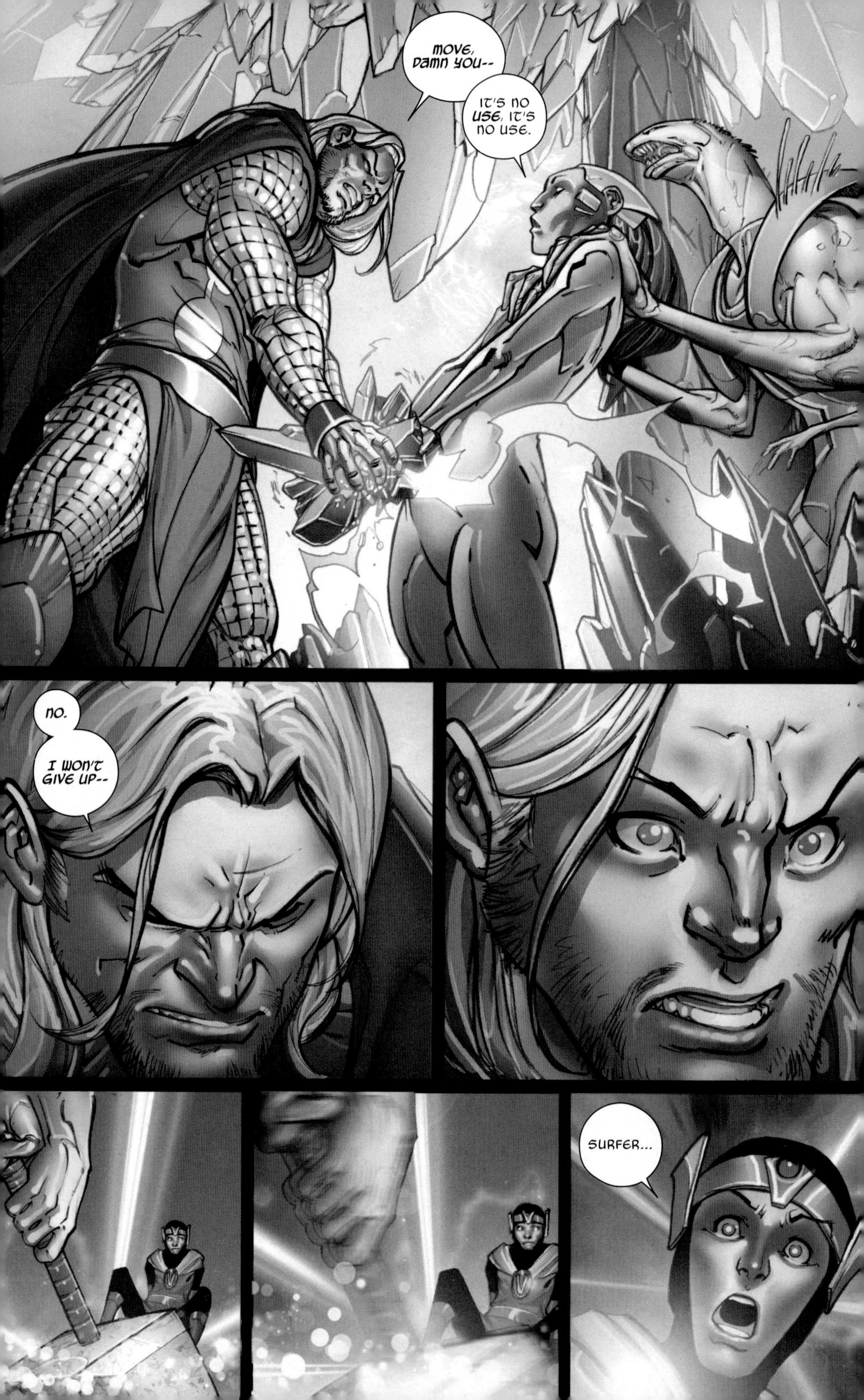
MOVE, DAMN YOU--
IT'S NO USE, IT'S NO USE.
NO.
I WON'T GIVE UP--
SURFER...

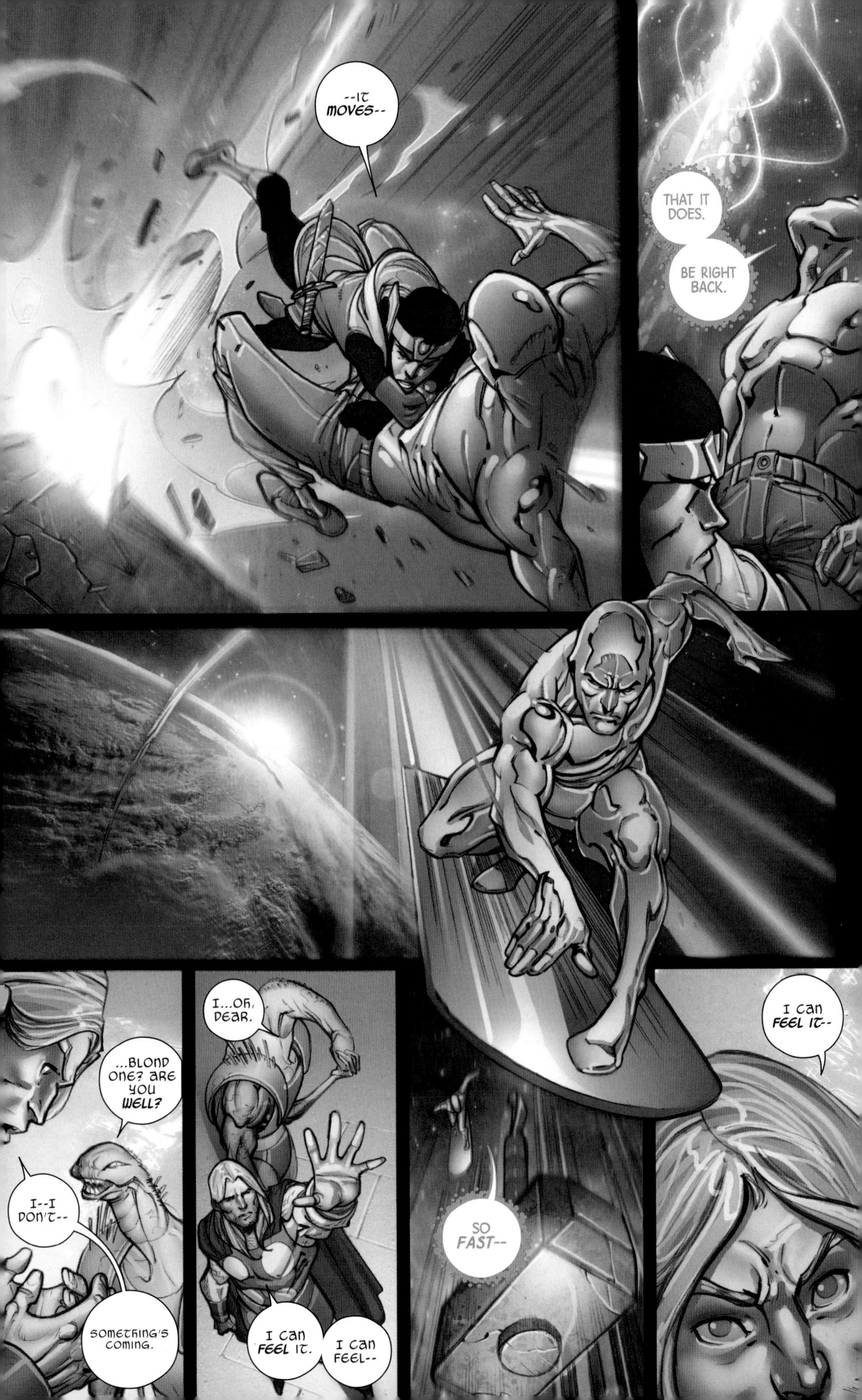
--IT MOVES--
THAT IT DOES.
BE RIGHT BACK.
...BLOND ONE? ARE YOU WELL?
I--I DON'T--
SOMETHING'S COMING.
I...OH, DEAR.
I CAN FEEL IT.
I CAN FEEL--
SO FAST--
I CAN FEEL IT--

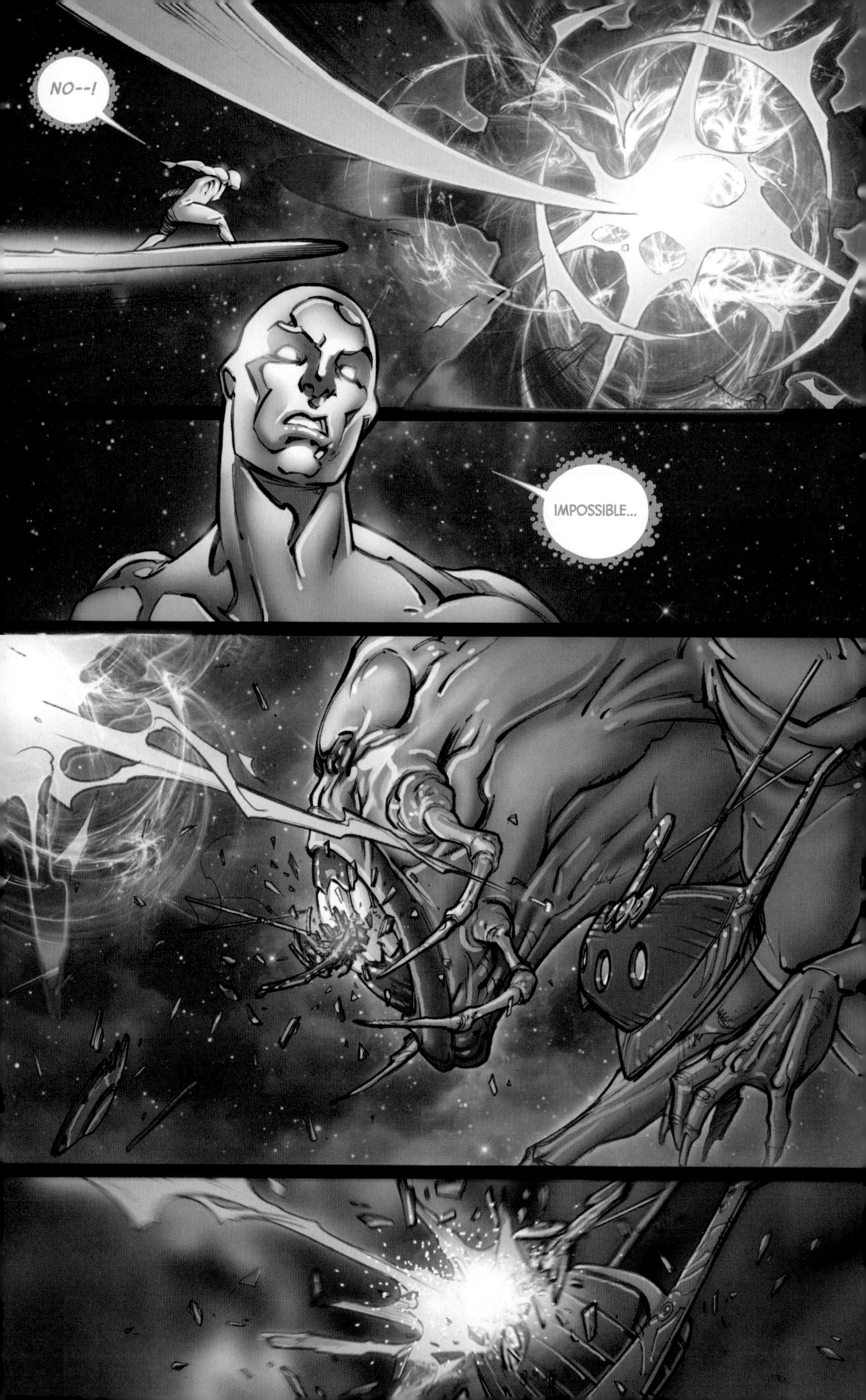
NO--!
IMPOSSIBLE...

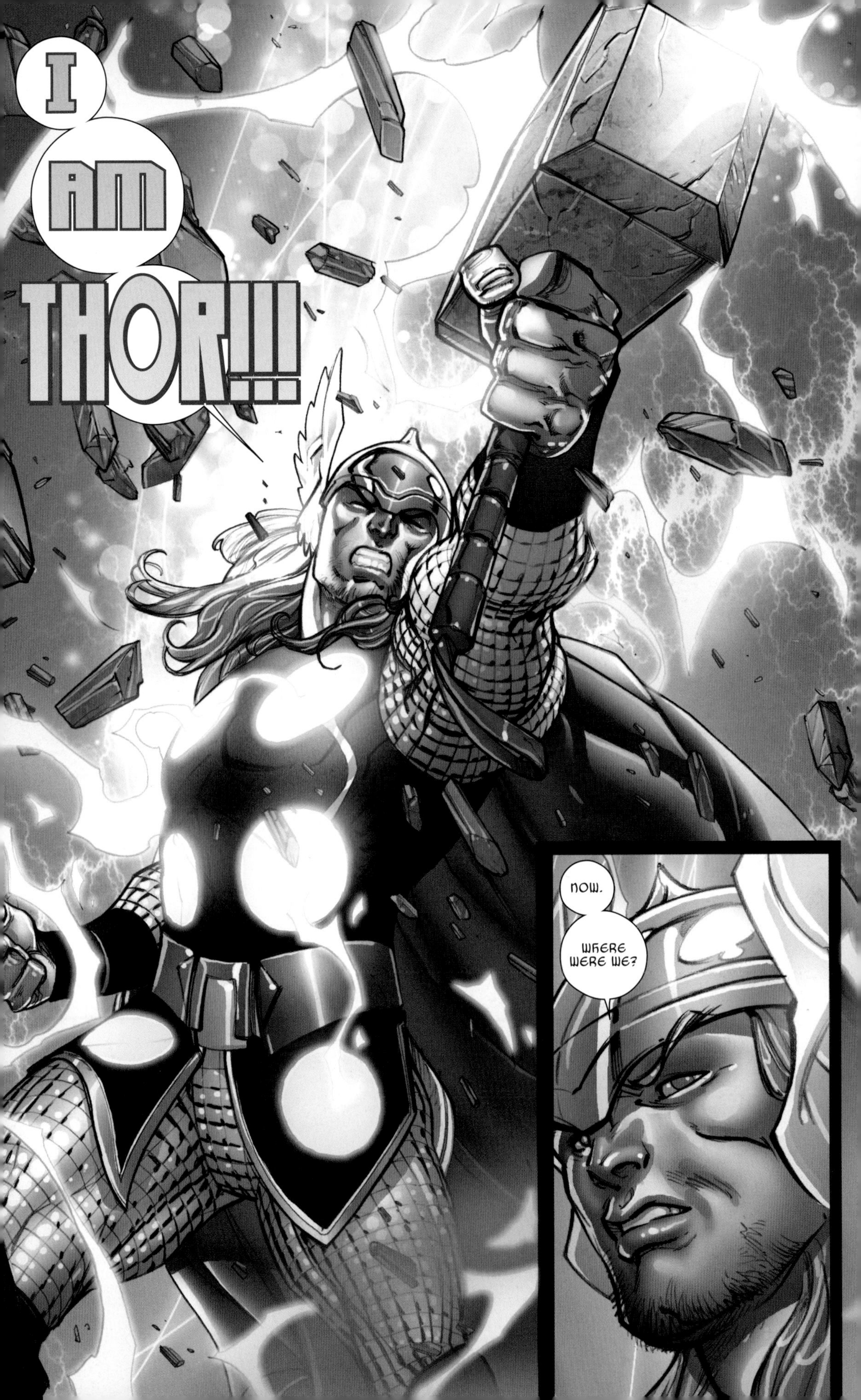
I
AM
THOR!!!
NOW.
WHERE WERE WE?

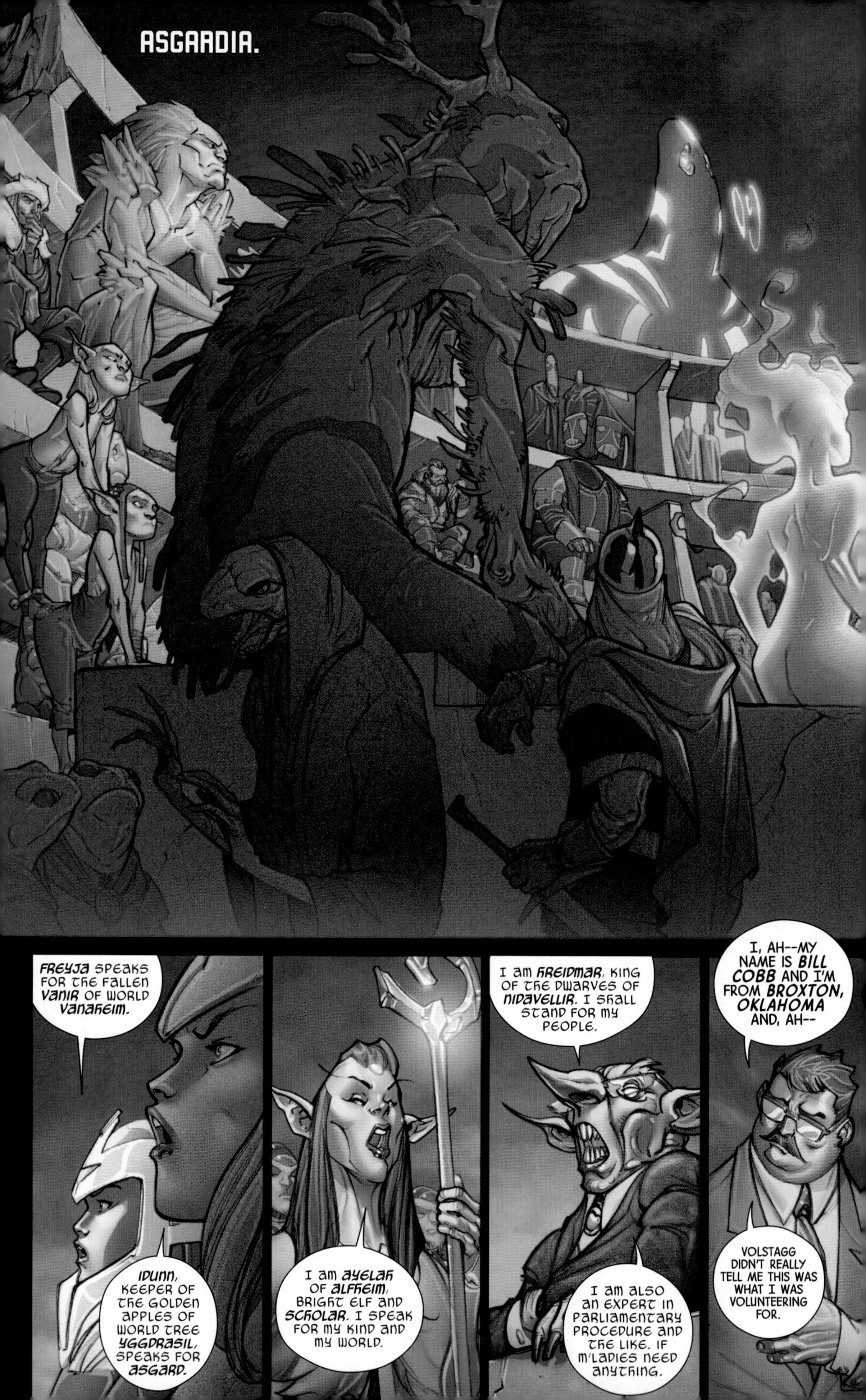
ASGARDIA.
FREYJA SPEAKS FOR THE FALLEN VANIR OF WORLD VANAHEIM.
IDUNN, KEEPER OF THE GOLDEN APPLES OF WORLD TREE YGGDRASIL, SPEAKS FOR ASGARD.
I AM AYELAH OF ALFHEIM, BRIGHT ELF AND SCHOLAR. I SPEAK FOR MY KIND AND MY WORLD.
I AM HREIDMAR, KING OF THE DWARVES OF NIDAVELLIR. I SHALL STAND FOR MY PEOPLE.
I AM ALSO AN EXPERT IN PARLIAMENTARY PROCEDURE AND THE LIKE. IF M'LADIES NEED ANYTHING.
I, AH--MY NAME IS BILL COBB AND I'M FROM BROXTON, OKLAHOMA AND, AH--
VOLSTAGG DIDN'T REALLY TELL ME THIS WAS WHAT I WAS VOLUNTEERING FOR.

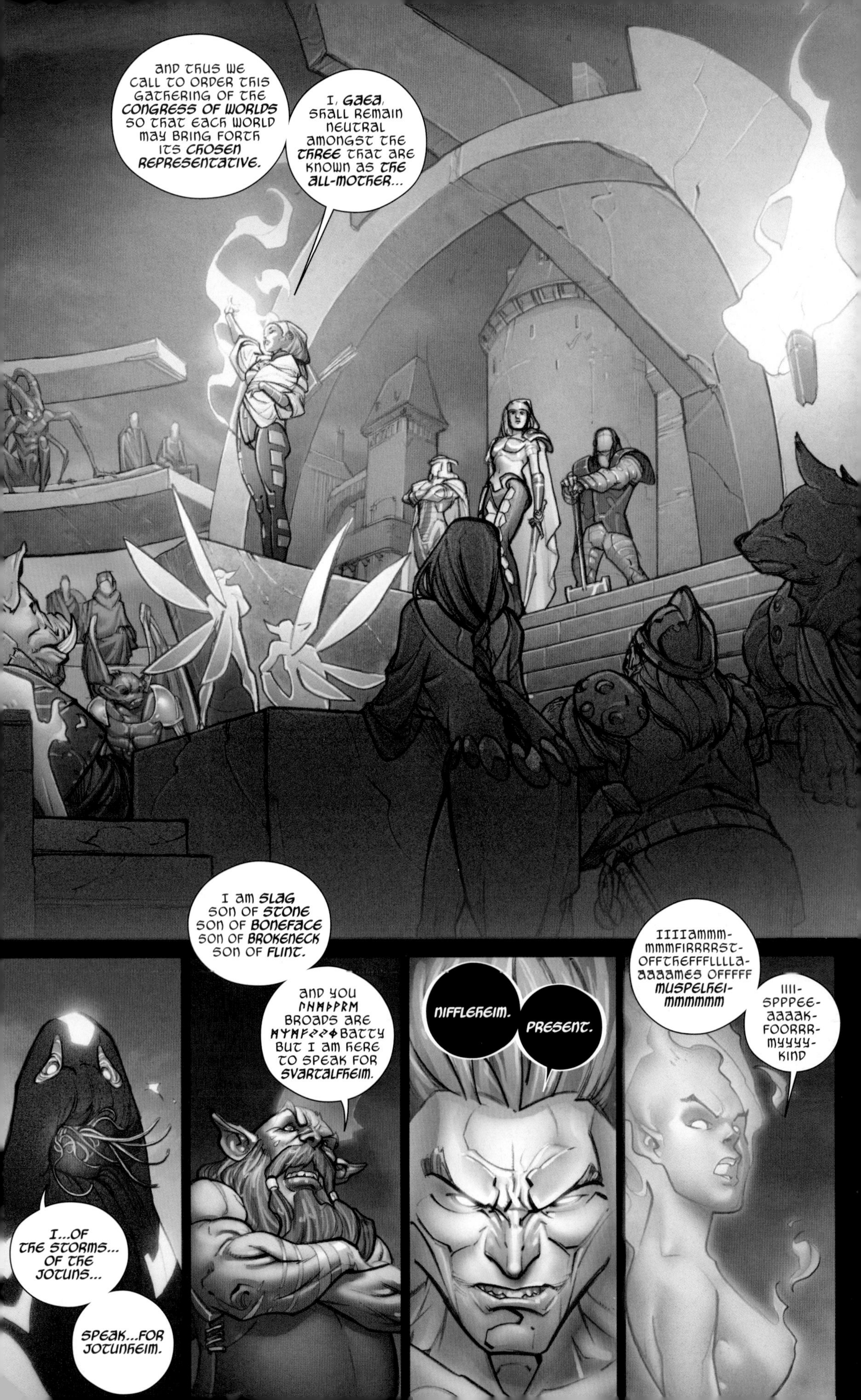
AND THUS WE CALL TO ORDER THIS GATHERING OF THE CONGRESS OF WORLDS SO THAT EACH WORLD MAY BRING FORTH ITS CHOSEN REPRESENTATIVE.
I, GAEA, SHALL REMAIN NEUTRAL AMONGST THE THREE THAT ARE KNOWN AS THE ALL-MOTHER...
I...OF THE STORMS... OF THE JOTUNS...
SPEAK...FOR JOTUNHEIM.
I AM SLAG SON OF STONE SON OF BONEFACE SON OF BROKENECK SON OF FLINT.
AND YOU ᛚᚺᛗᚦᚹᚱᛖ BROADS ARE ᛗᛉᛖᚠ⇐⇐Φ BATTY BUT I AM HERE TO SPEAK FOR SVARTALFHEIM.
NIFFLEHEIM.
PRESENT.
IIIIAMMM-MMMFIRRRRST-OFFTHEFFFLLLLA-AAAAMES OFFFFF MUSPELHEI-MMMMMM
IIII-SPPPEE-AAAAK-FOORRR-MYYYY-KIND

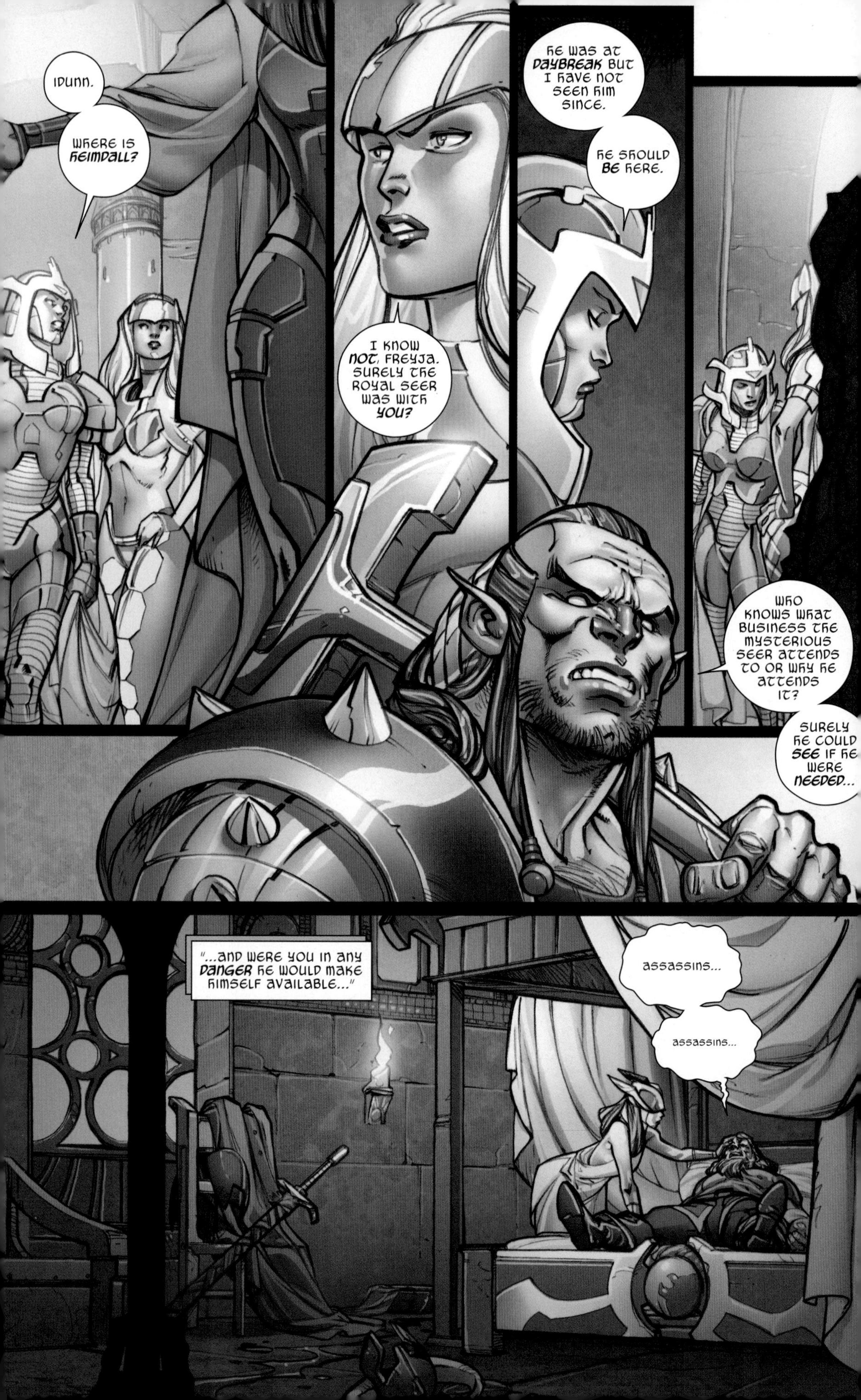
IDUNN.
WHERE IS HEIMDALL?
I KNOW NOT, FREYJA. SURELY THE ROYAL SEER WAS WITH YOU?
HE WAS AT DAYBREAK BUT I HAVE NOT SEEN HIM SINCE.
HE SHOULD BE HERE.
WHO KNOWS WHAT BUSINESS THE MYSTERIOUS SEER ATTENDS TO OR WHY HE ATTENDS IT?
SURELY HE COULD SEE IF HE WERE NEEDED...
"...AND WERE YOU IN ANY DANGER HE WOULD MAKE HIMSELF AVAILABLE..."
assassins...
assassins...

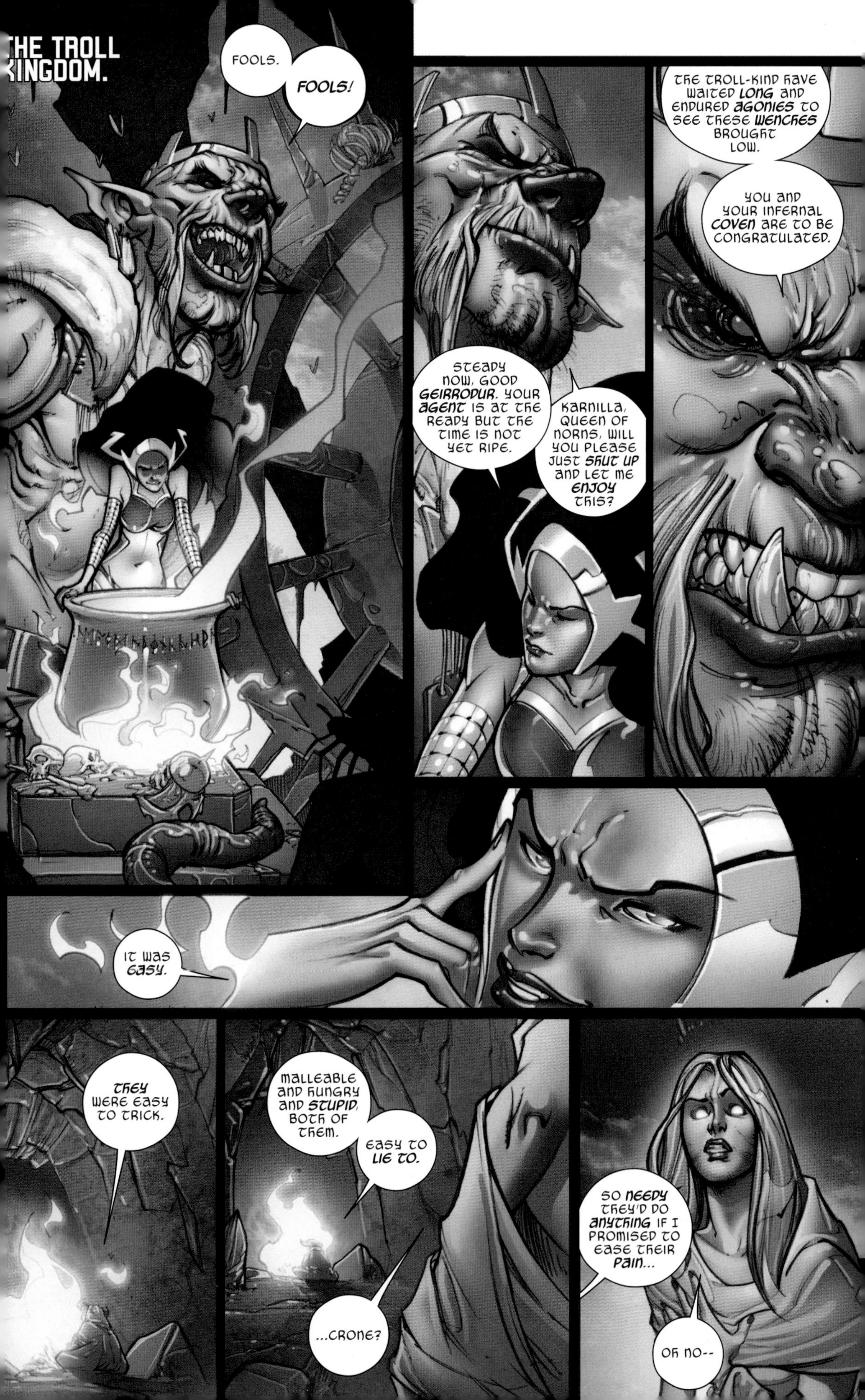
THE TROLL KINGDOM.
FOOLS.
FOOLS!
THE TROLL-KIND HAVE WAITED LONG AND ENDURED AGONIES TO SEE THESE WENCHES BROUGHT LOW.
YOU AND YOUR INFERNAL COVEN ARE TO BE CONGRATULATED.
STEADY NOW, GOOD GEIRRODUR. YOUR AGENT IS AT THE READY BUT THE TIME IS NOT YET RIPE.
KARNILLA, QUEEN OF NORNS, WILL YOU PLEASE JUST SHUT UP AND LET ME ENJOY THIS?
IT WAS EASY.
THEY WERE EASY TO TRICK.
MALLEABLE AND HUNGRY AND STUPID, BOTH OF THEM.
EASY TO LIE TO.
...CRONE?
SO NEEDY THEY'D DO ANYTHING IF I PROMISED TO EASE THEIR PAIN...
OH NO--

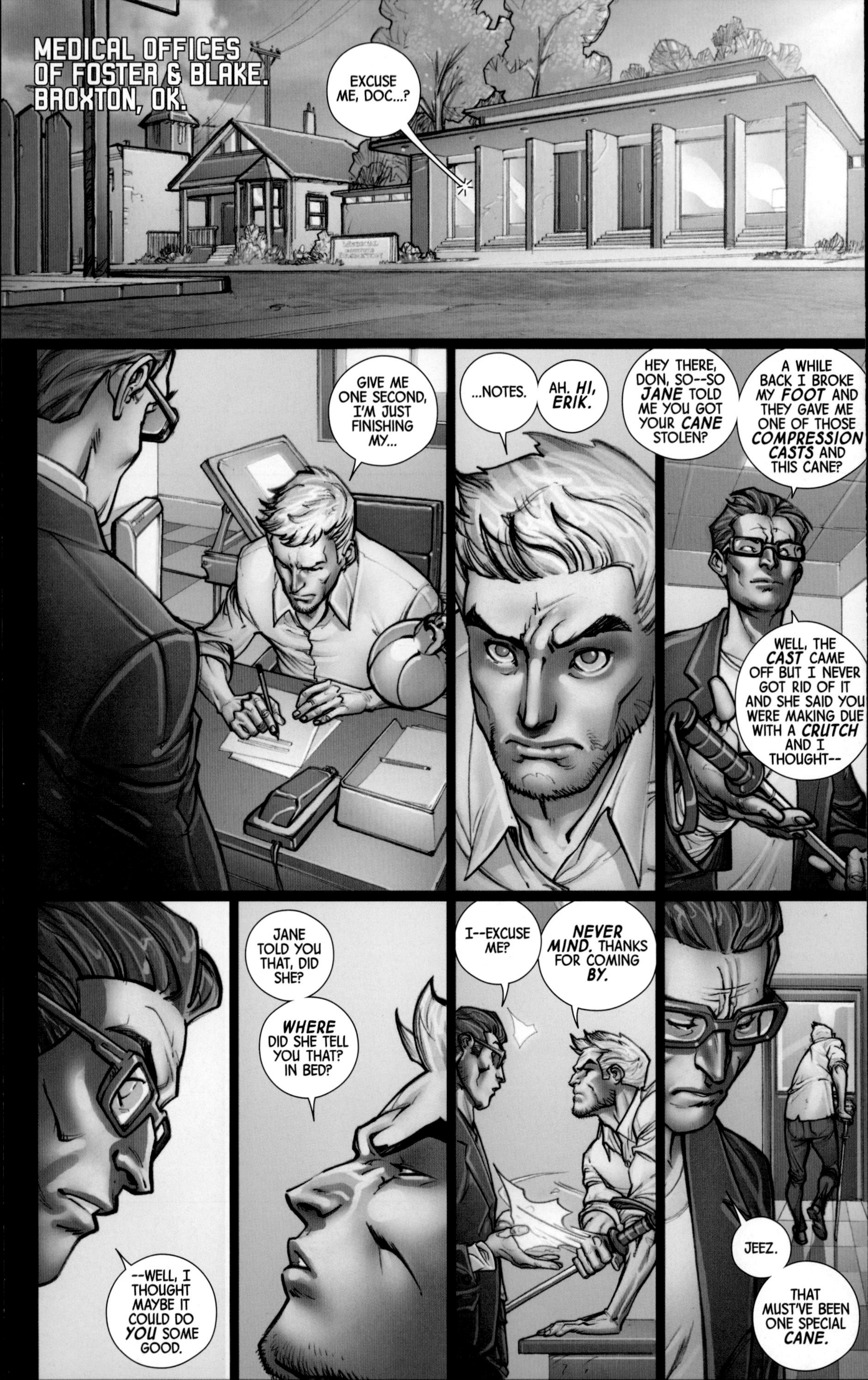
MEDICAL OFFICES OF FOSTER & BLAKE. BROXTON, OK.
EXCUSE ME, DOC...?
GIVE ME ONE SECOND, I'M JUST FINISHING MY...
...NOTES.
AH. HI, ERIK.
HEY THERE, DON, SO--SO JANE TOLD ME YOU GOT YOUR CANE STOLEN?
A WHILE BACK I BROKE MY FOOT AND THEY GAVE ME ONE OF THOSE COMPRESSION CASTS AND THIS CANE?
WELL, THE CAST CAME OFF BUT I NEVER GOT RID OF IT AND SHE SAID YOU WERE MAKING DUE WITH A CRUTCH AND I THOUGHT--
--WELL, I THOUGHT MAYBE IT COULD DO YOU SOME GOOD.
JANE TOLD YOU THAT, DID SHE?
WHERE DID SHE TELL YOU THAT? IN BED?
I--EXCUSE ME?
NEVER MIND. THANKS FOR COMING BY.
JEEZ.
THAT MUST'VE BEEN ONE SPECIAL CANE.

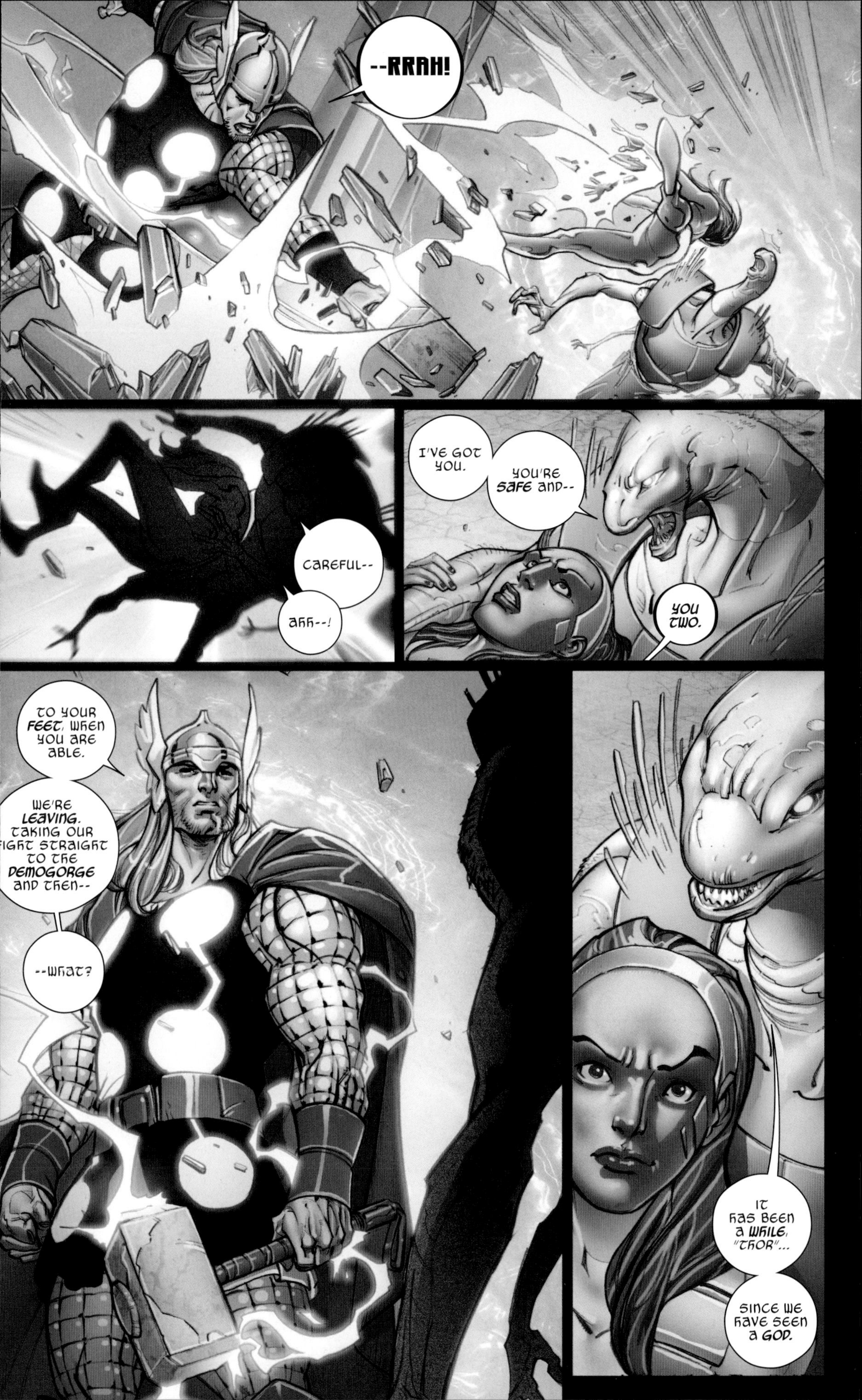
--RRAH!
CAREFUL--
AHH--!
I'VE GOT YOU.
YOU'RE SAFE AND--
YOU TWO.
TO YOUR FEET, WHEN YOU ARE ABLE.
WE'RE LEAVING. TAKING OUR FIGHT STRAIGHT TO THE DEMOGORGE AND THEN--
--WHAT?
IT HAS BEEN A WHILE, "THOR"...
SINCE WE HAVE SEEN A GOD.

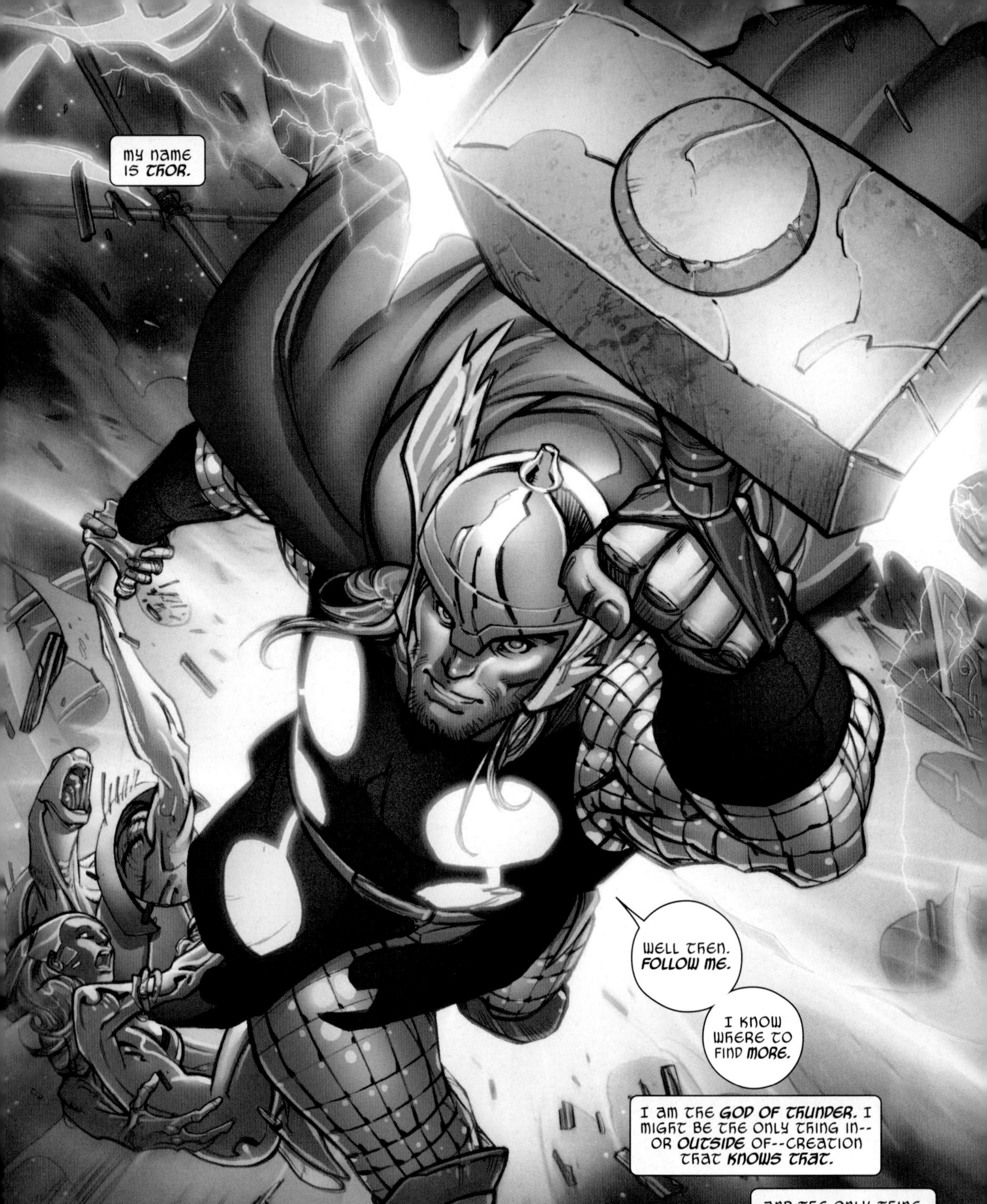
MY NAME IS THOR.
WELL THEN. FOLLOW ME.
I KNOW WHERE TO FIND MORE.
I AM THE GOD OF THUNDER. I MIGHT BE THE ONLY THING IN--OR OUTSIDE OF--CREATION THAT KNOWS THAT.
AND THE ONLY THING STANDING BETWEEN ME AND GOING HOME...

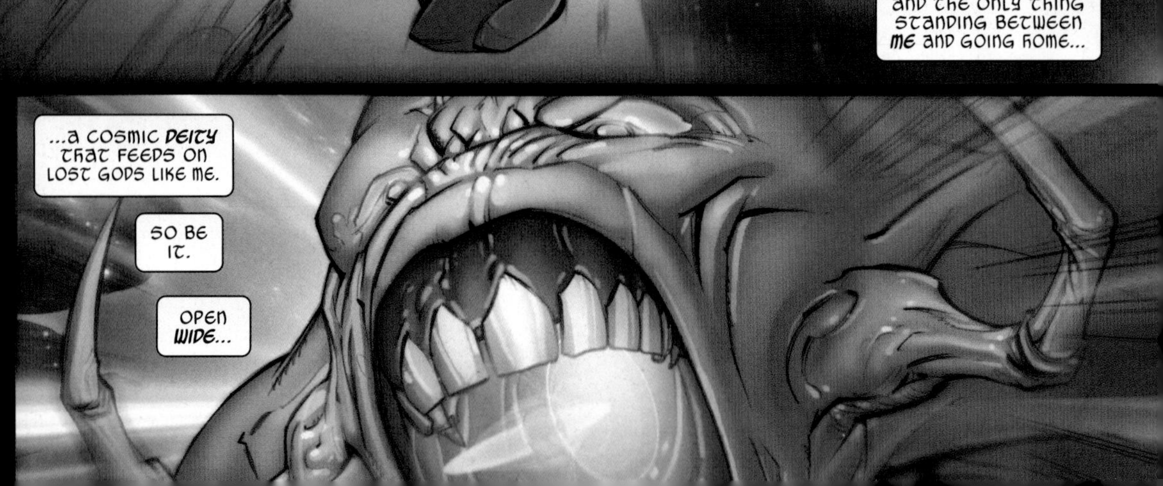
...A COSMIC DEITY THAT FEEDS ON LOST GODS LIKE ME.
SO BE IT.
OPEN WIDE...

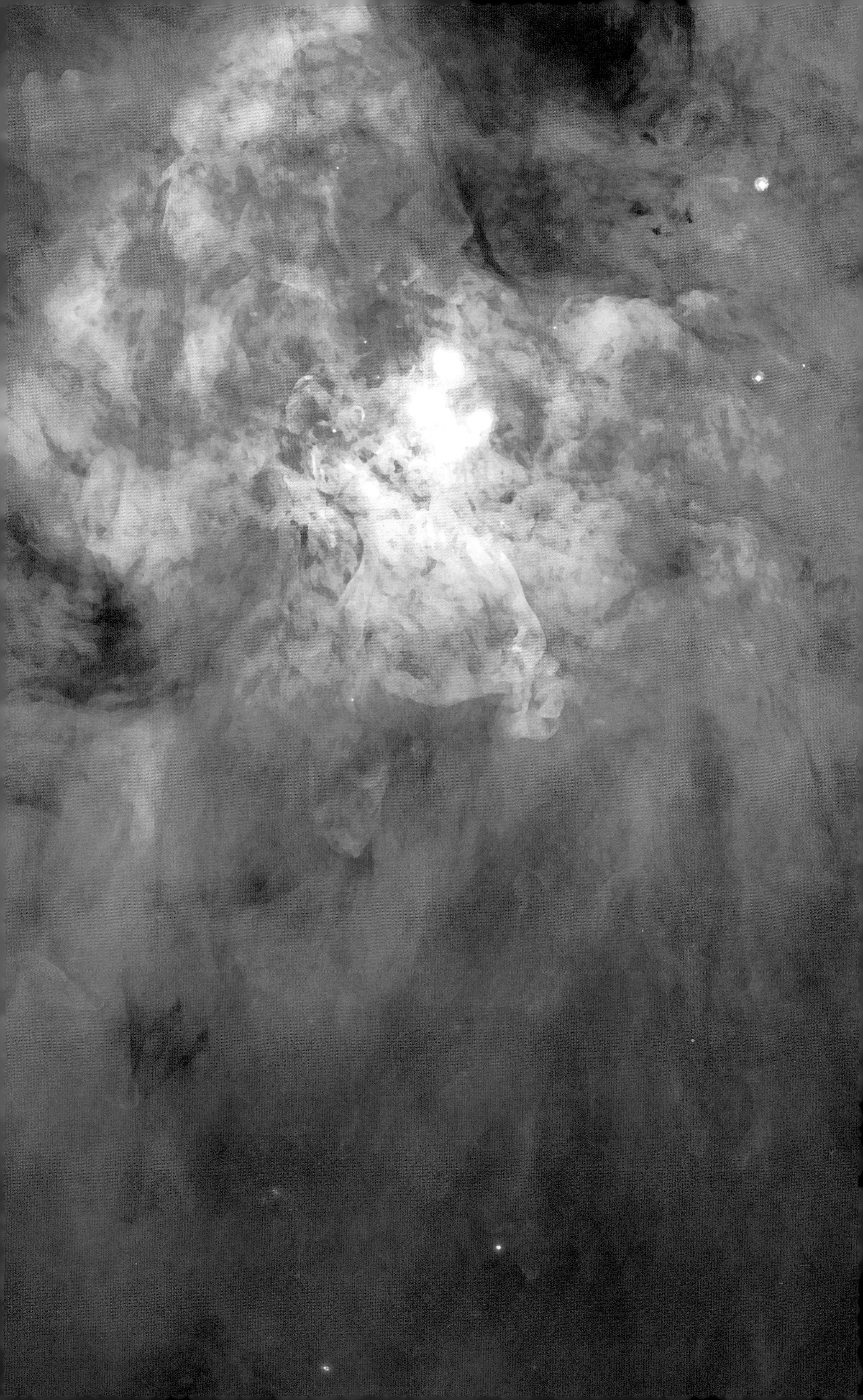

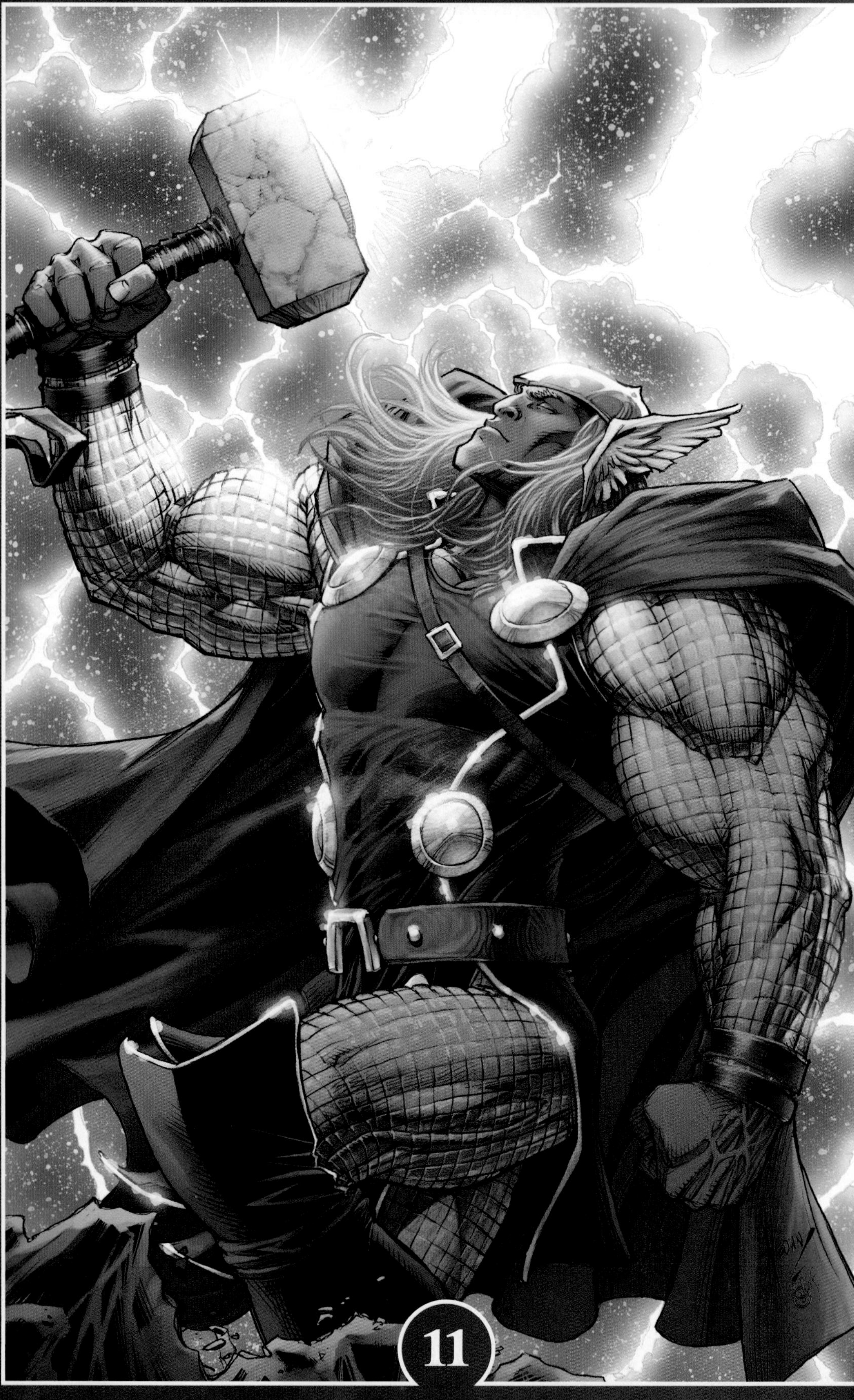

THE MIGHTY TANARUS 4: THE ASGARDIAN

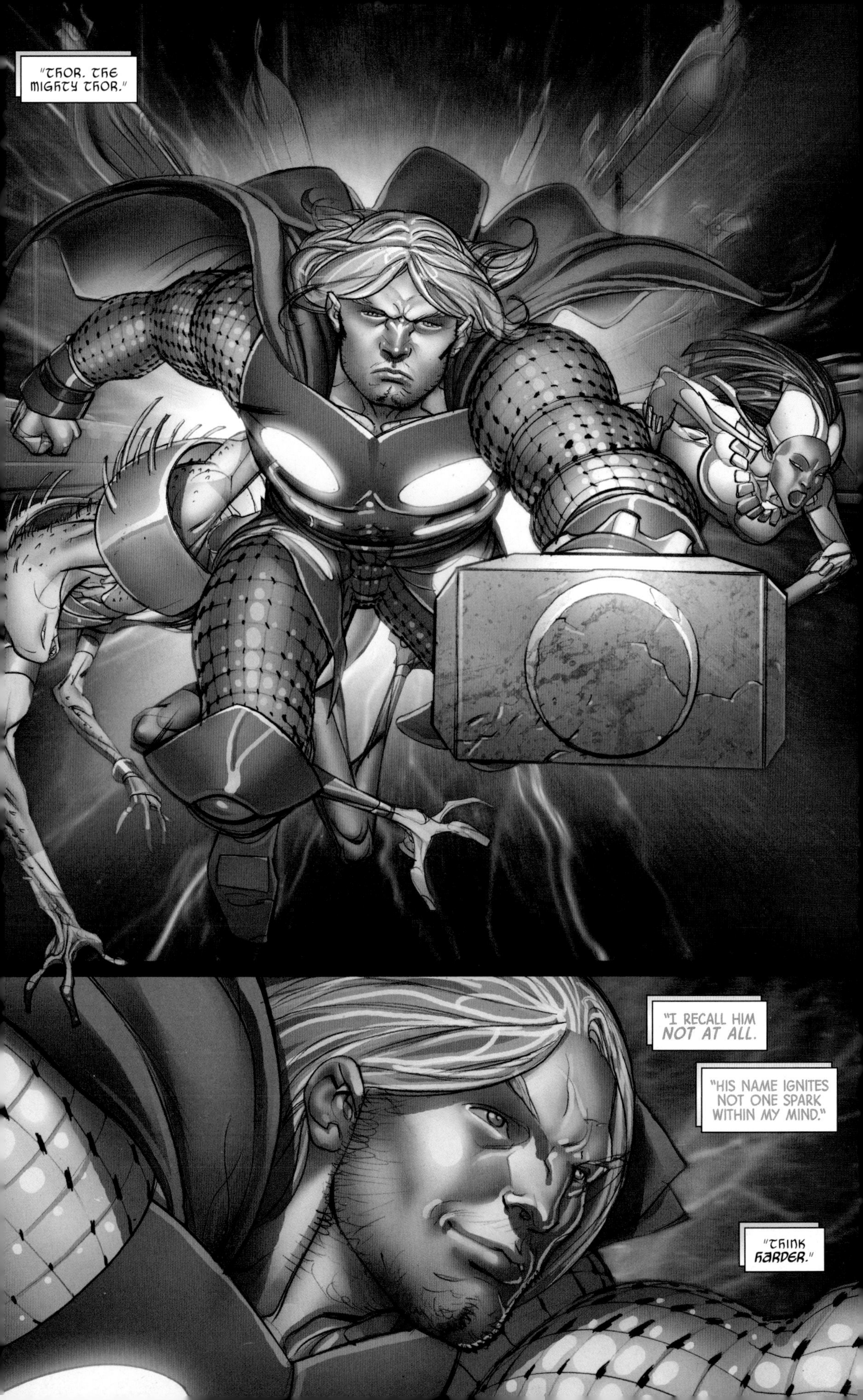
"THOR. THE MIGHTY THOR."
"I RECALL HIM NOT AT ALL.
"HIS NAME IGNITES NOT ONE SPARK WITHIN MY MIND."
"THINK HARDER."

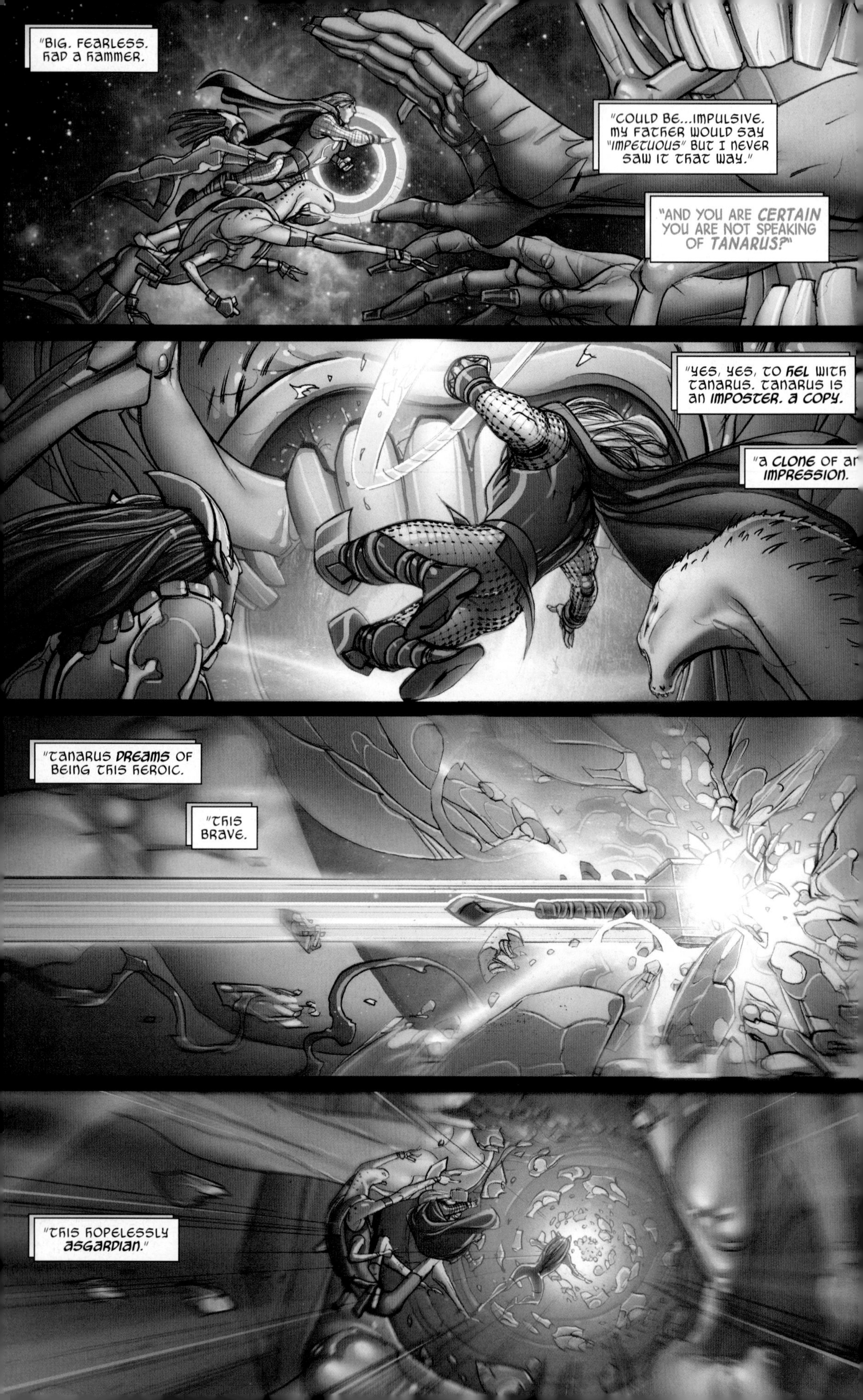
"BIG. FEARLESS. HAD A HAMMER.
"COULD BE...IMPULSIVE. MY FATHER WOULD SAY "IMPETUOUS" BUT I NEVER SAW IT THAT WAY."
"AND YOU ARE CERTAIN YOU ARE NOT SPEAKING OF TANARUS?"
"YES, YES, TO HEL WITH TANARUS. TANARUS IS AN IMPOSTER. A COPY.
"A CLONE OF A
IMPRESSION.
"TANARUS DREAMS OF BEING THIS HEROIC.
"THIS BRAVE.
"THIS HOPELESSLY ASGARDIAN."

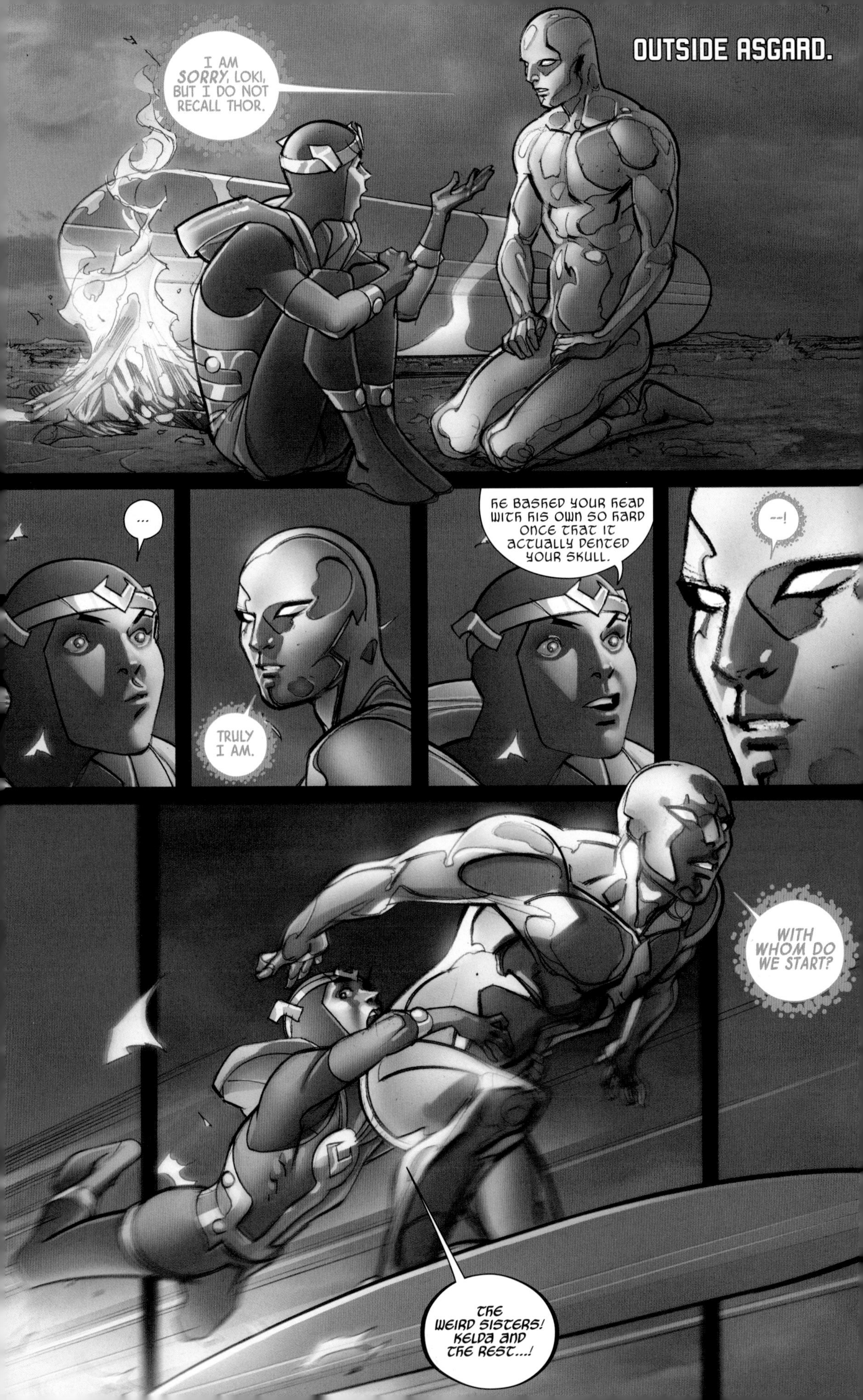
OUTSIDE ASGARD.
I AM SORRY, LOKI, BUT I DO NOT RECALL THOR.
...
TRULY I AM.
HE BASHED YOUR HEAD WITH HIS OWN SO HARD ONCE THAT IT ACTUALLY DENTED YOUR SKULL.
--!
WITH WHOM DO WE START?
THE WEIRD SISTERS! KELDA AND THE REST...!

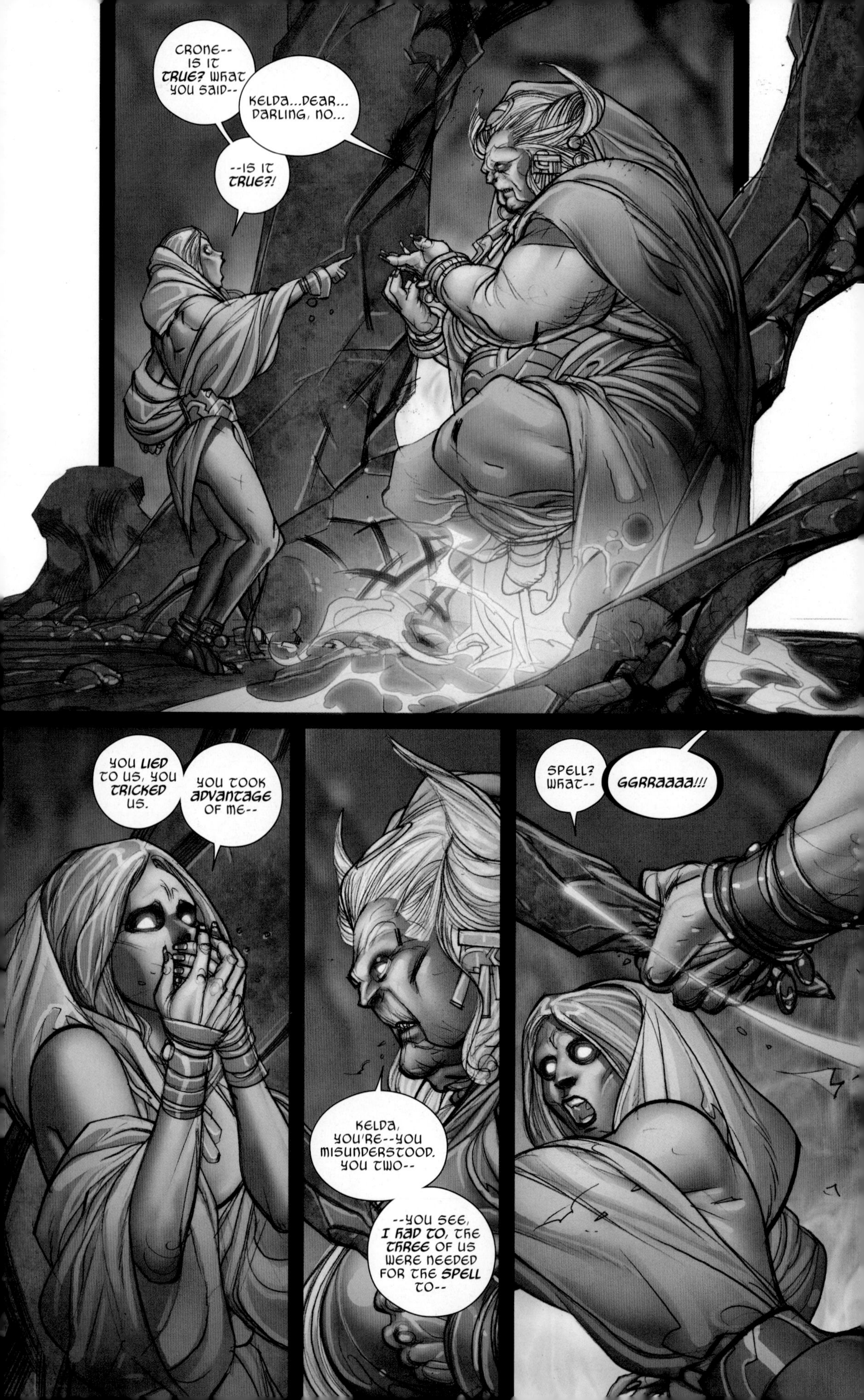
CRONE--
IS IT TRUE? WHAT YOU SAID--
KELDA...DEAR... DARLING, NO...
--IS IT TRUE?!
YOU LIED TO US, YOU TRICKED US.
YOU TOOK ADVANTAGE OF ME--
KELDA, YOU'RE--YOU MISUNDERSTOOD. YOU TWO--
--YOU SEE, I HAD TO, THE THREE OF US WERE NEEDED FOR THE SPELL TO--
SPELL? WHAT--
GGRRAAAA!!!

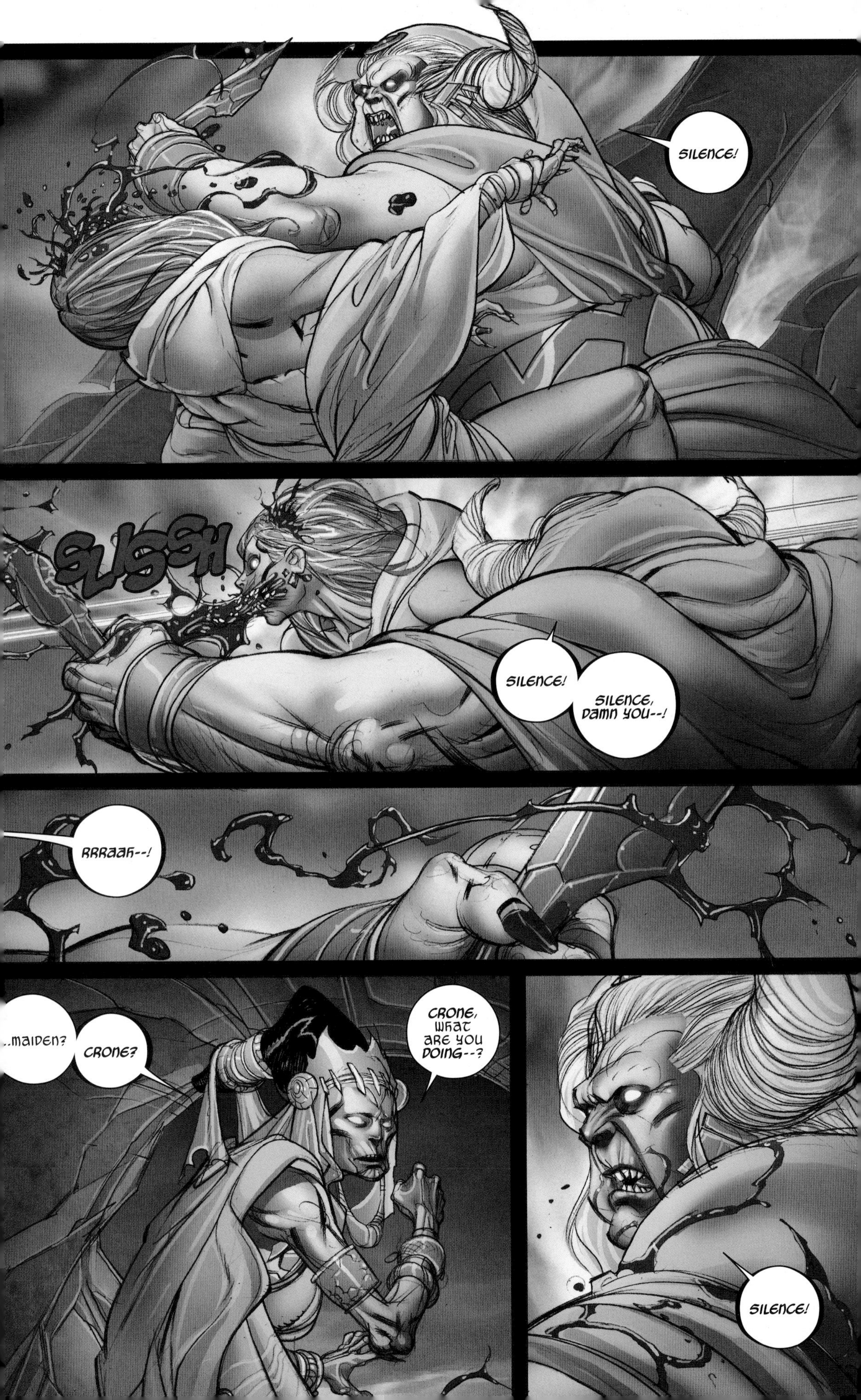
SILENCE!
SLISSH
SILENCE!
SILENCE, DAMN YOU--!
RRRAAH--!
...MAIDEN?
CRONE?
CRONE, WHAT ARE YOU DOING--?
SILENCE!

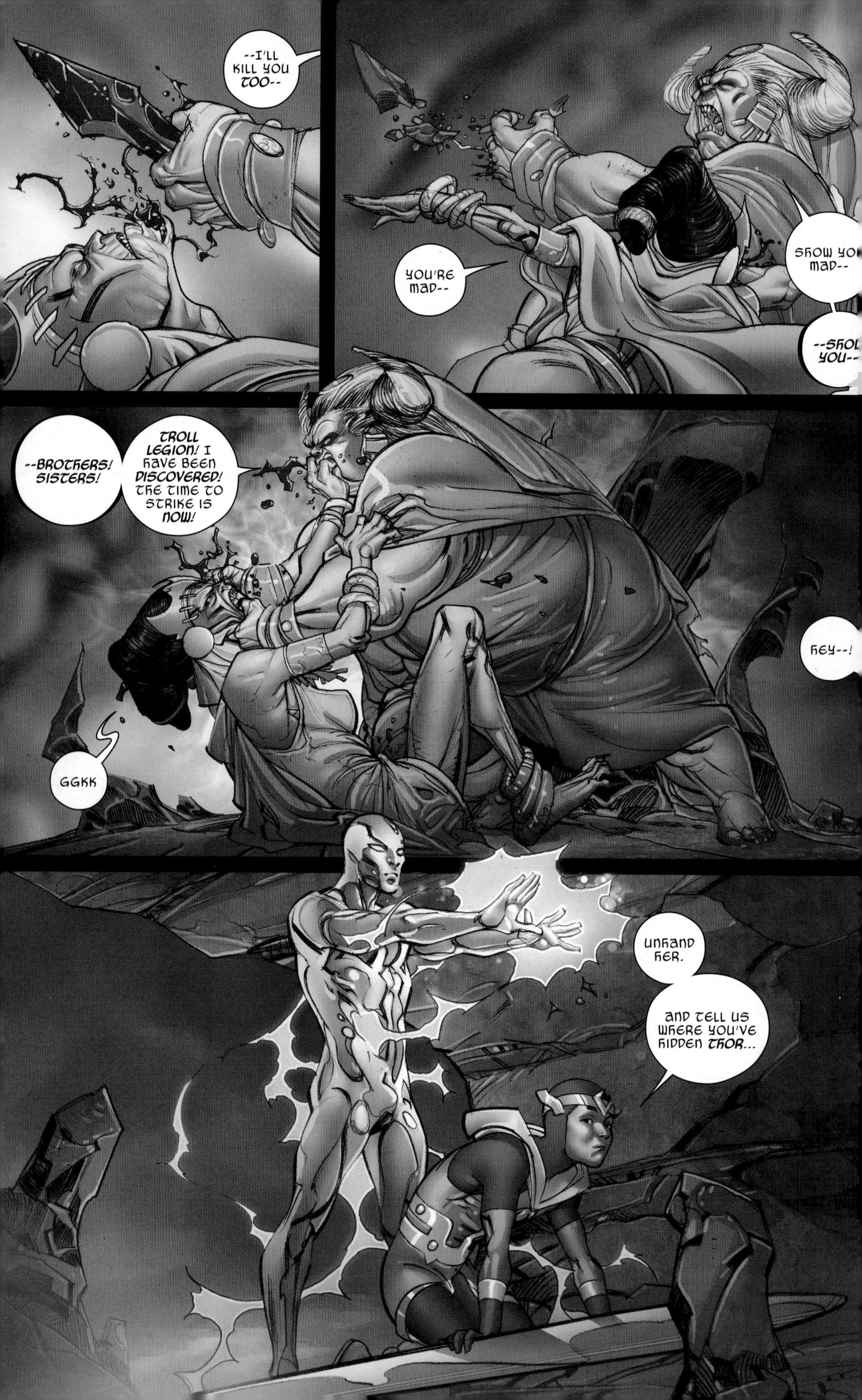
--I'LL KILL YOU TOO--
YOU'RE MAD--
SHOW YO MAD--
--SHO YOU--
--BROTHERS! SISTERS!
TROLL LEGION! I HAVE BEEN DISCOVERED! THE TIME TO STRIKE IS NOW!
HEY--!
GGKK
UNHAND HER.
AND TELL US WHERE YOU'VE HIDDEN THOR...

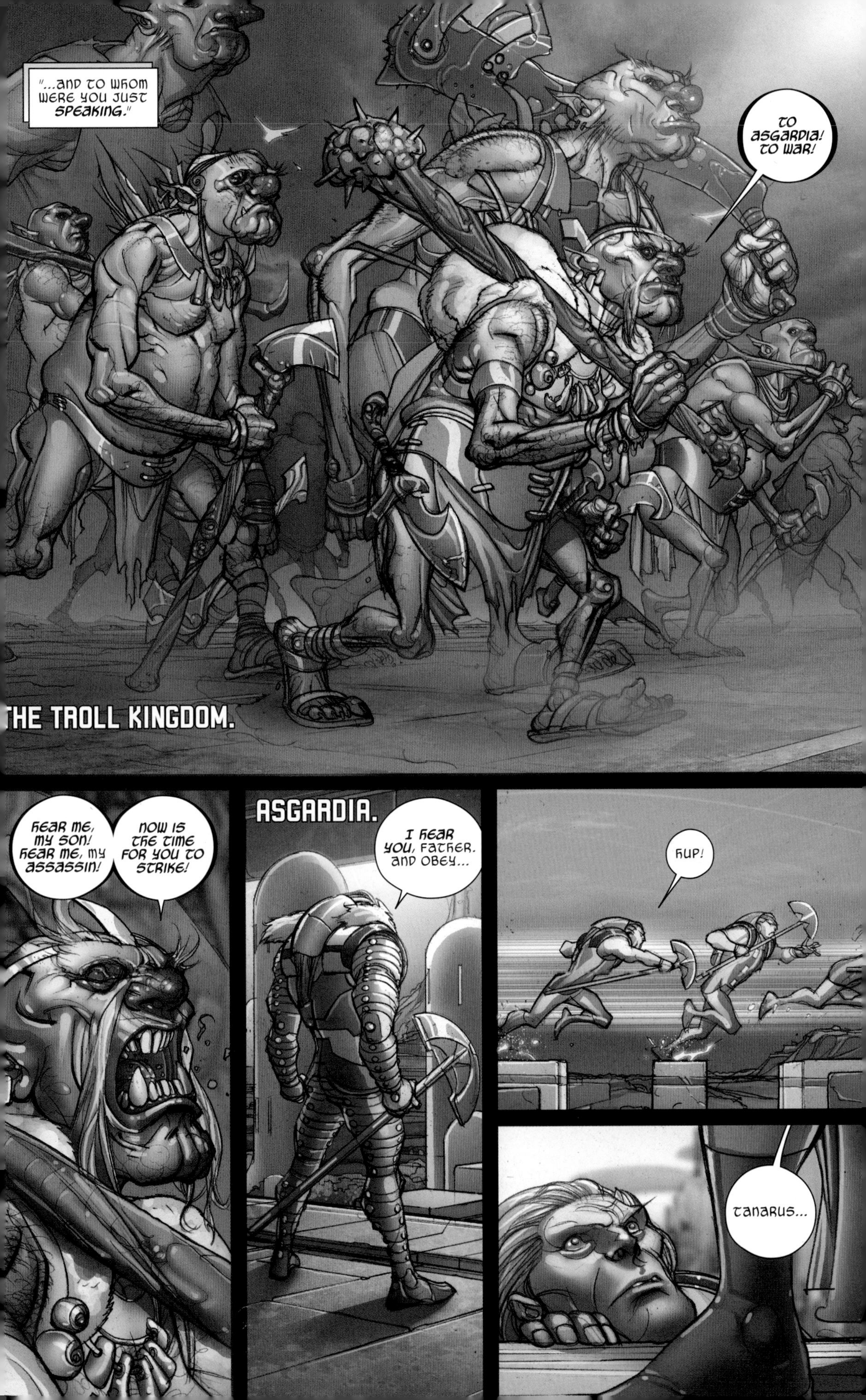
"...AND TO WHOM WERE YOU JUST SPEAKING."
TO ASGARDIA! TO WAR!
THE TROLL KINGDOM.
HEAR ME, MY SON! HEAR ME, MY ASSASSIN!
NOW IS THE TIME FOR YOU TO STRIKE!
ASGARDIA.
I HEAR YOU, FATHER. AND OBEY...
HUP!
TANARUS...

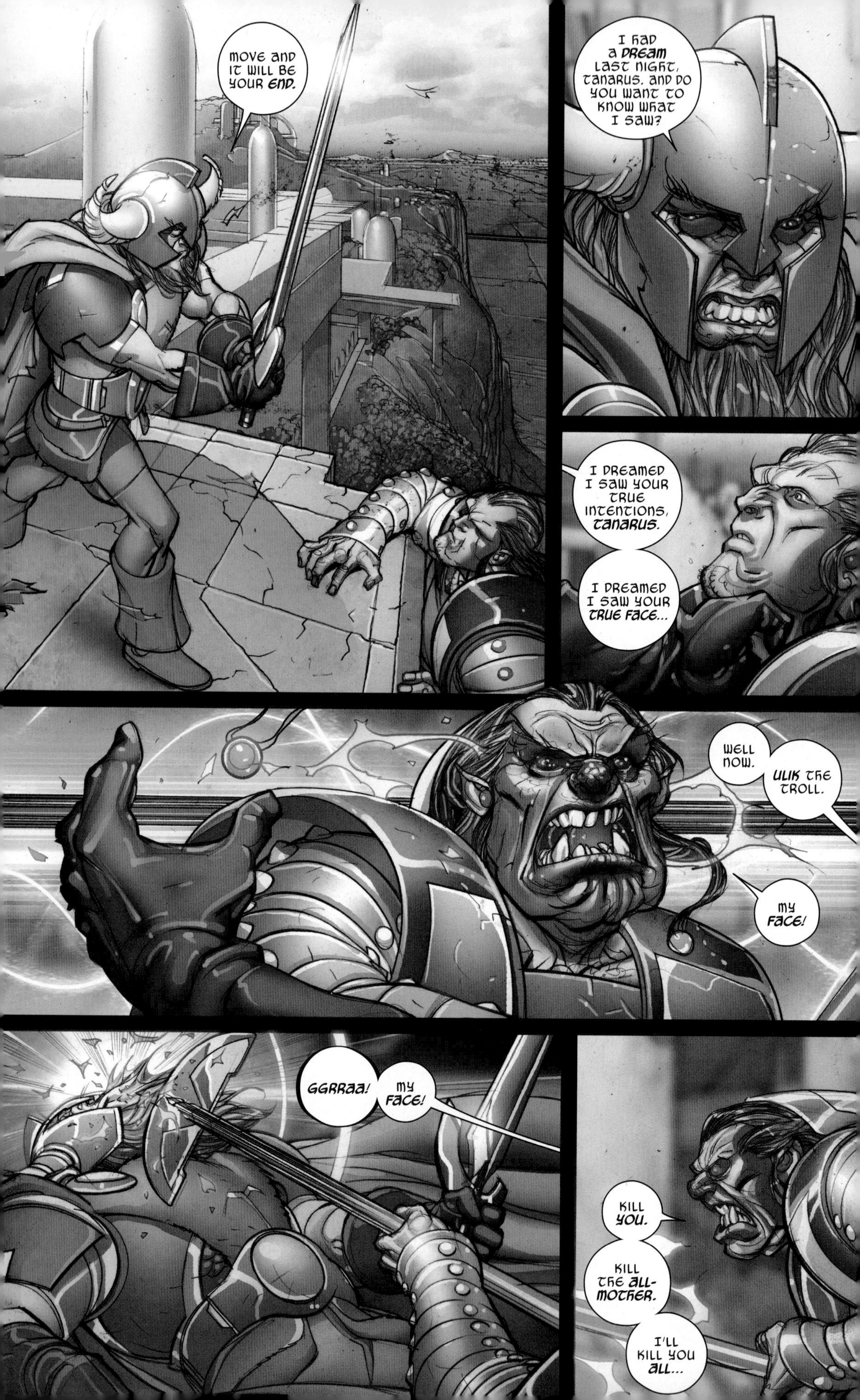
MOVE AND IT WILL BE YOUR END.
I HAD A DREAM LAST NIGHT, TANARUS. AND DO YOU WANT TO KNOW WHAT I SAW?
I DREAMED I SAW YOUR TRUE INTENTIONS, TANARUS.
I DREAMED I SAW YOUR TRUE FACE...
WELL NOW.
ULIK THE TROLL.
MY FACE!
GGRRAA!
MY FACE!
KILL YOU.
KILL THE ALL-MOTHER.
I'LL KILL YOU ALL...

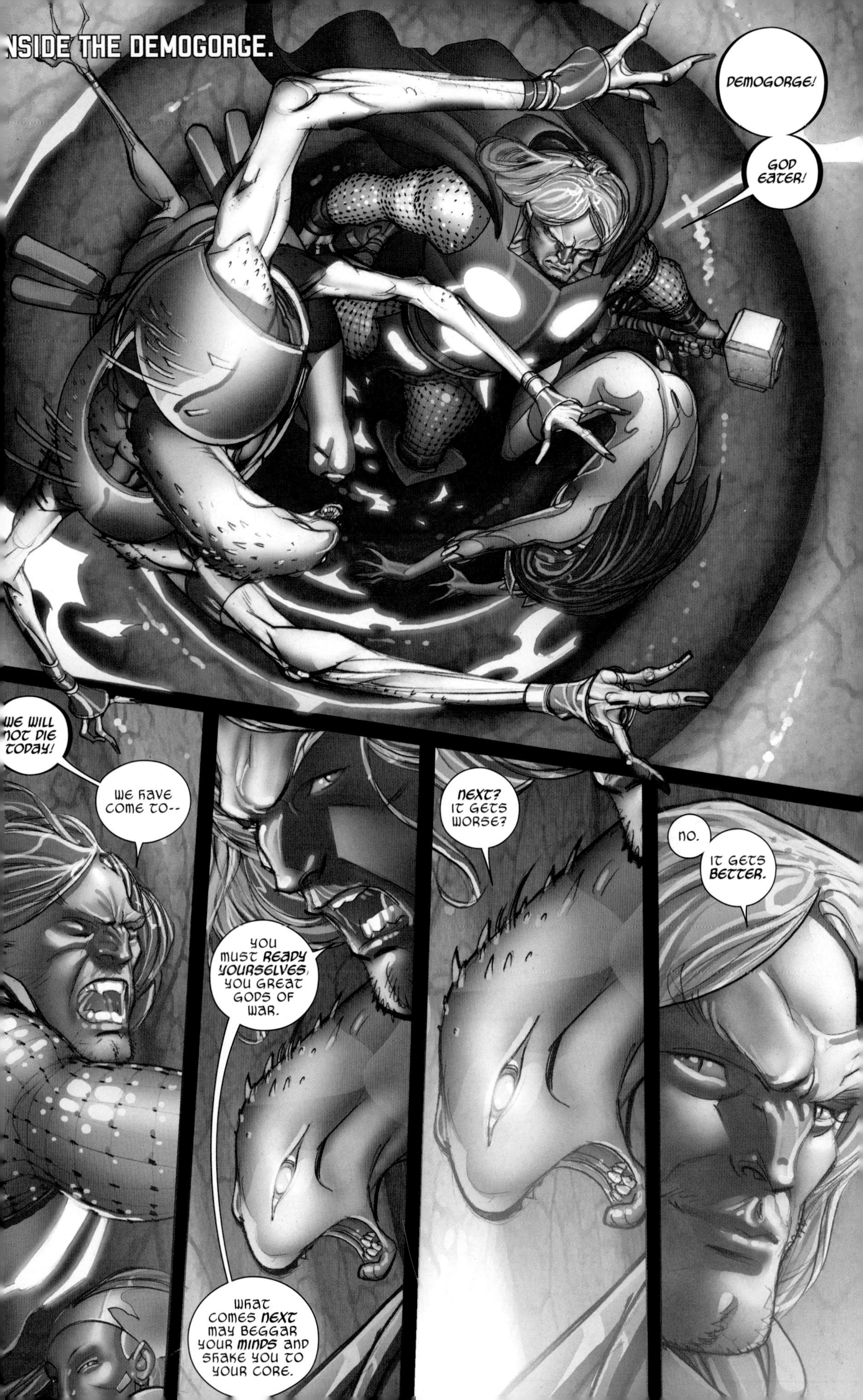

NSIDE THE DEMOGORGE.
DEMOGORGE!
GOD EATER!
WE WILL NOT DIE TODAY!
WE HAVE COME TO--
YOU MUST READY YOURSELVES, YOU GREAT GODS OF WAR.
WHAT COMES NEXT MAY BEGGAR YOUR MINDS AND SHAKE YOU TO YOUR CORE.
NEXT? IT GETS WORSE?
NO.
IT GETS BETTER.

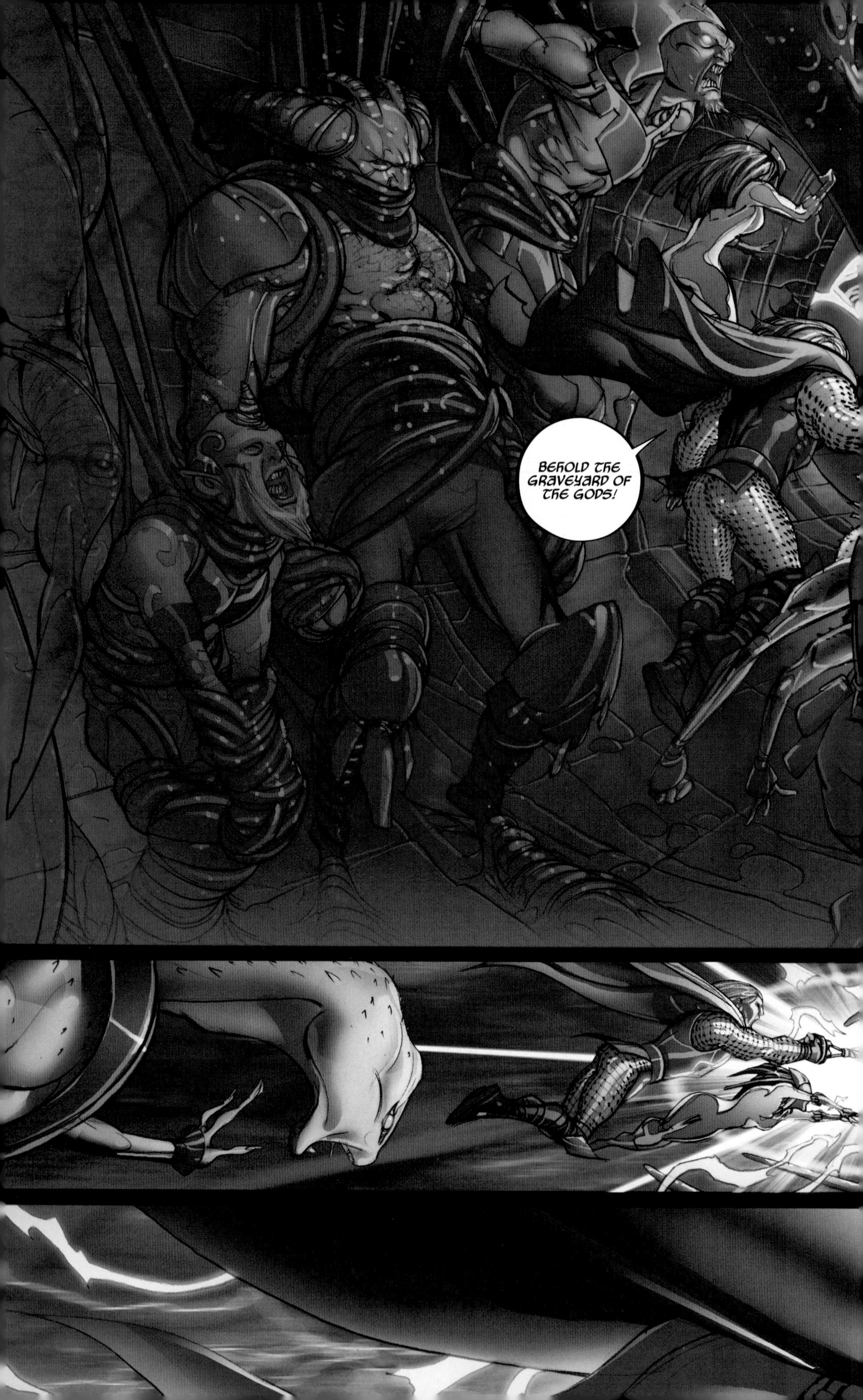
BEHOLD THE GRAVEYARD OF THE GODS!

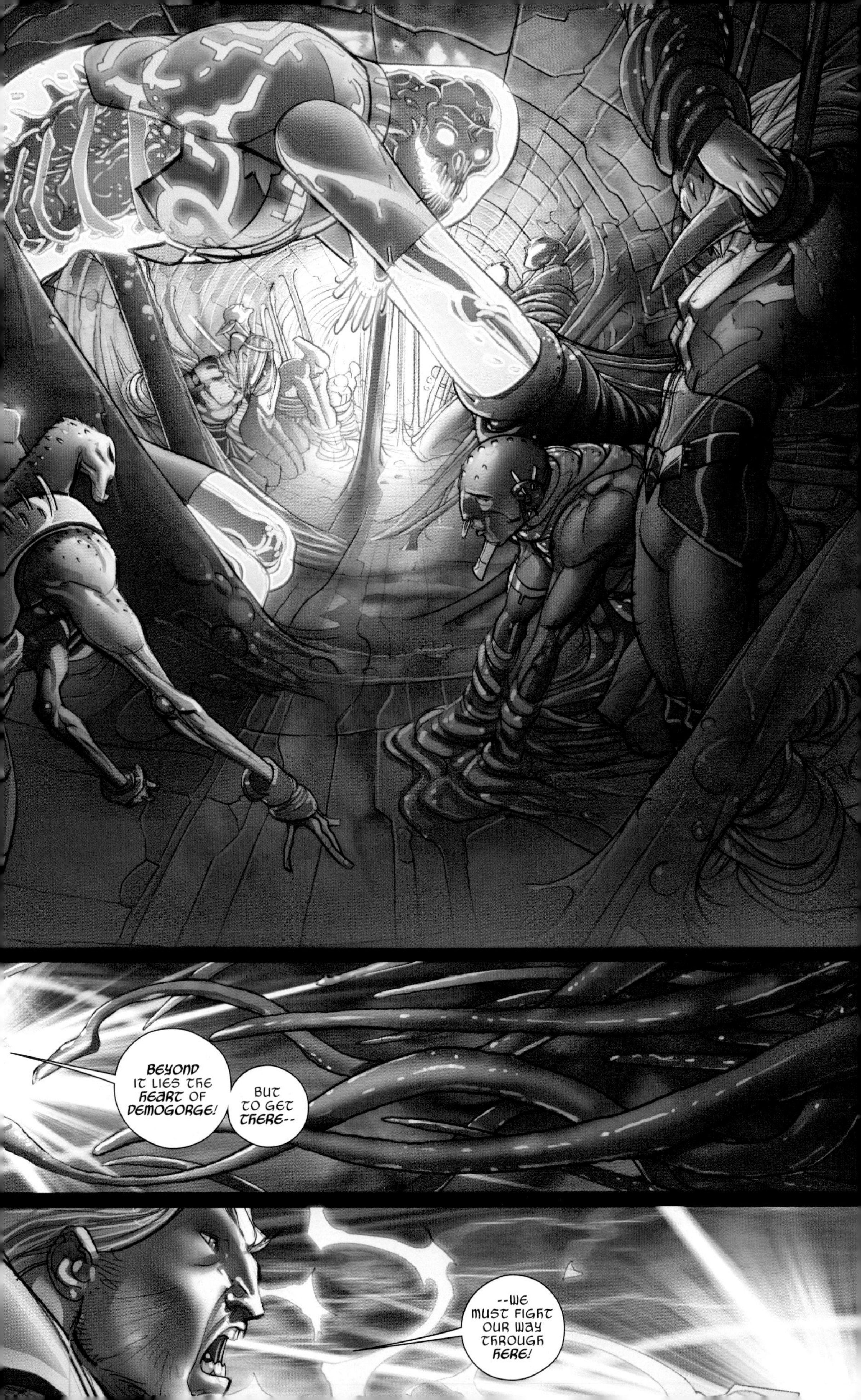
BEYOND IT LIES THE HEART OF DEMOGORGE!
BUT TO GET THERE--
--WE MUST FIGHT OUR WAY THROUGH HERE!

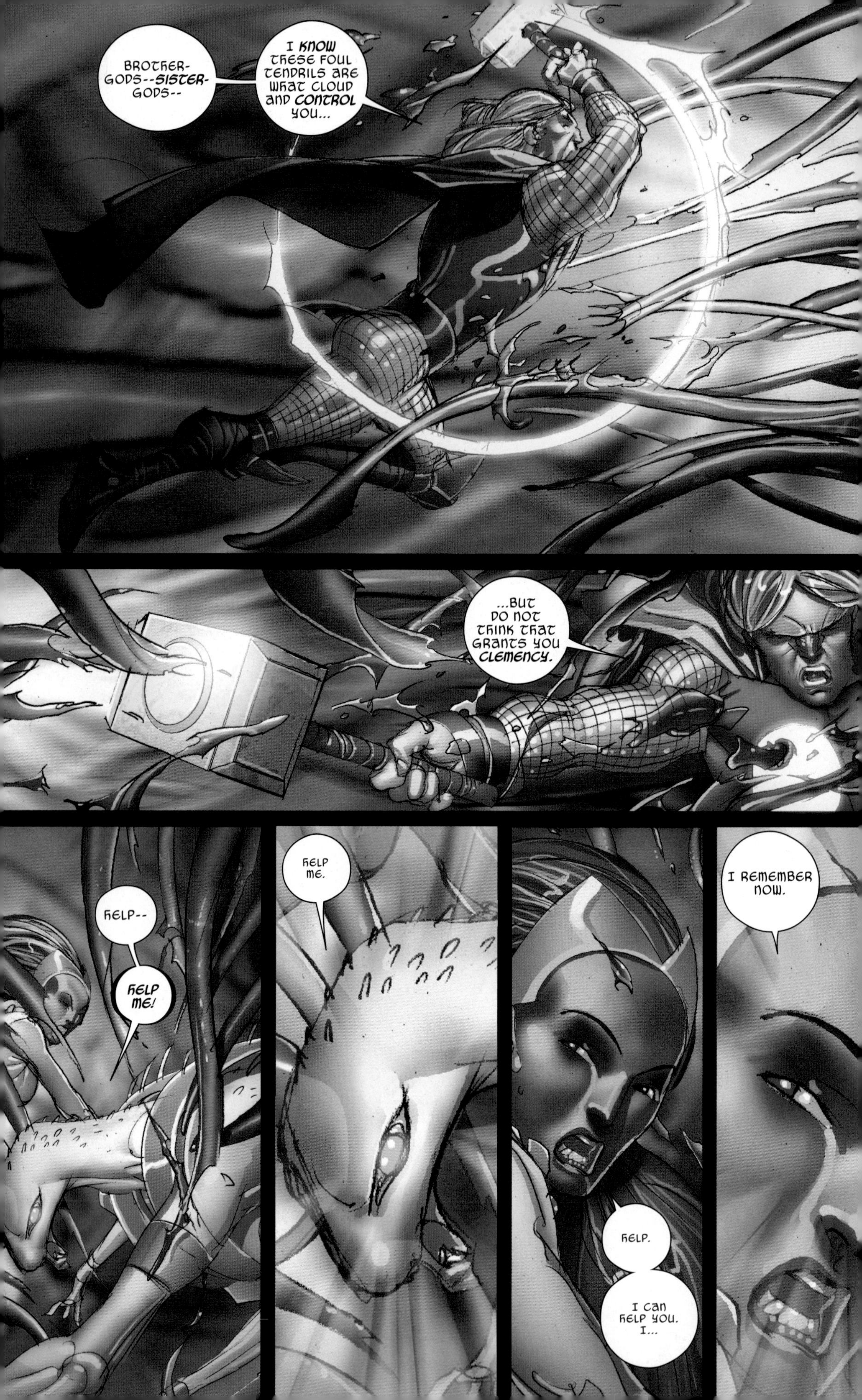
BROTHER-GODS--SISTER-GODS--
I KNOW THESE FOUL TENDRILS ARE WHAT CLOUD AND CONTROL YOU...
...BUT DO NOT THINK THAT GRANTS YOU CLEMENCY.
HELP--
HELP ME!
HELP ME.
HELP.
I CAN HELP YOU. I...
I REMEMBER NOW.

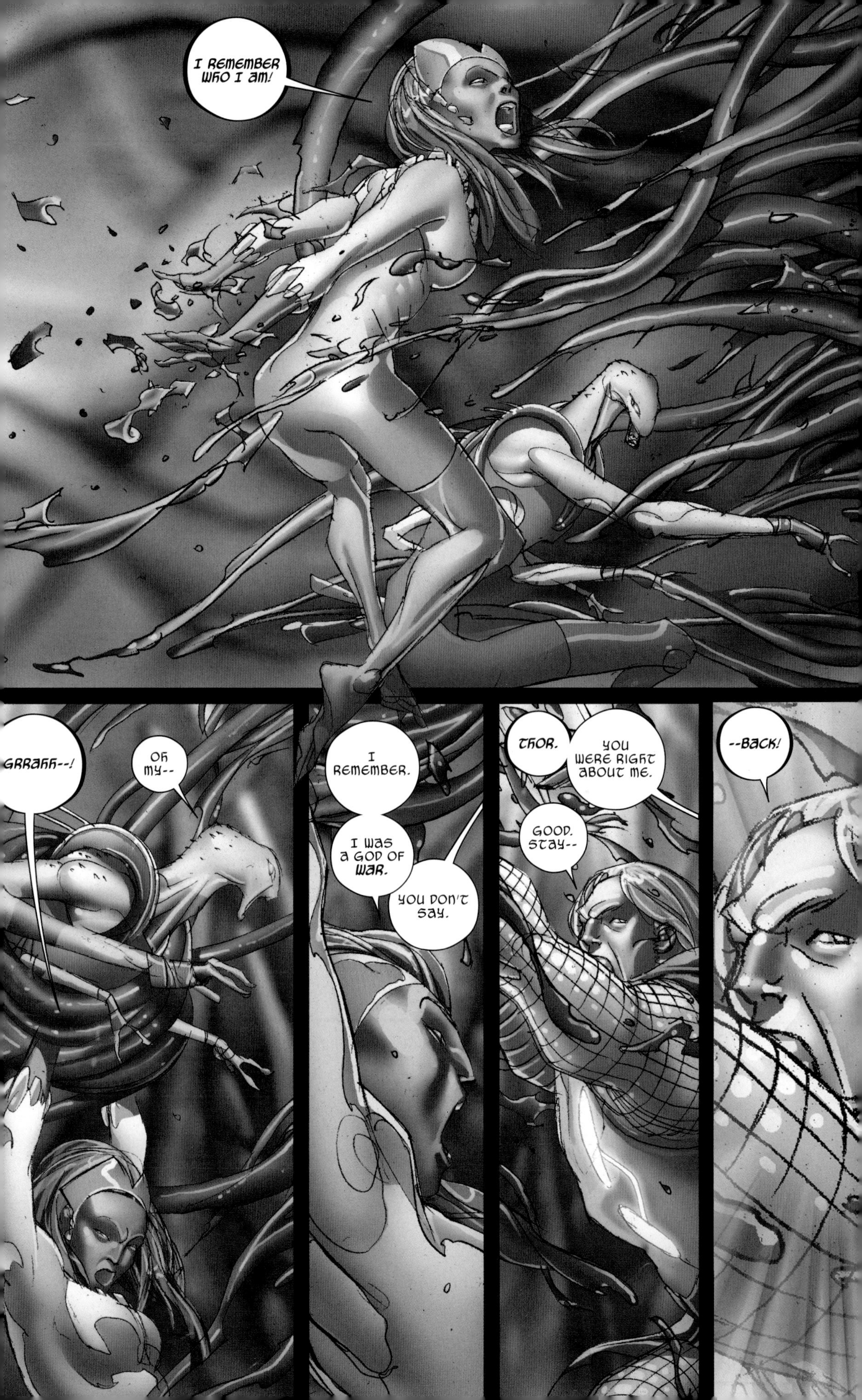
I REMEMBER WHO I AM!
GRRAHH--!
OH MY--
I REMEMBER.
I WAS A GOD OF WAR.
YOU DON'T SAY.
THOR.
YOU WERE RIGHT ABOUT ME.
GOOD. STAY--
--BACK!

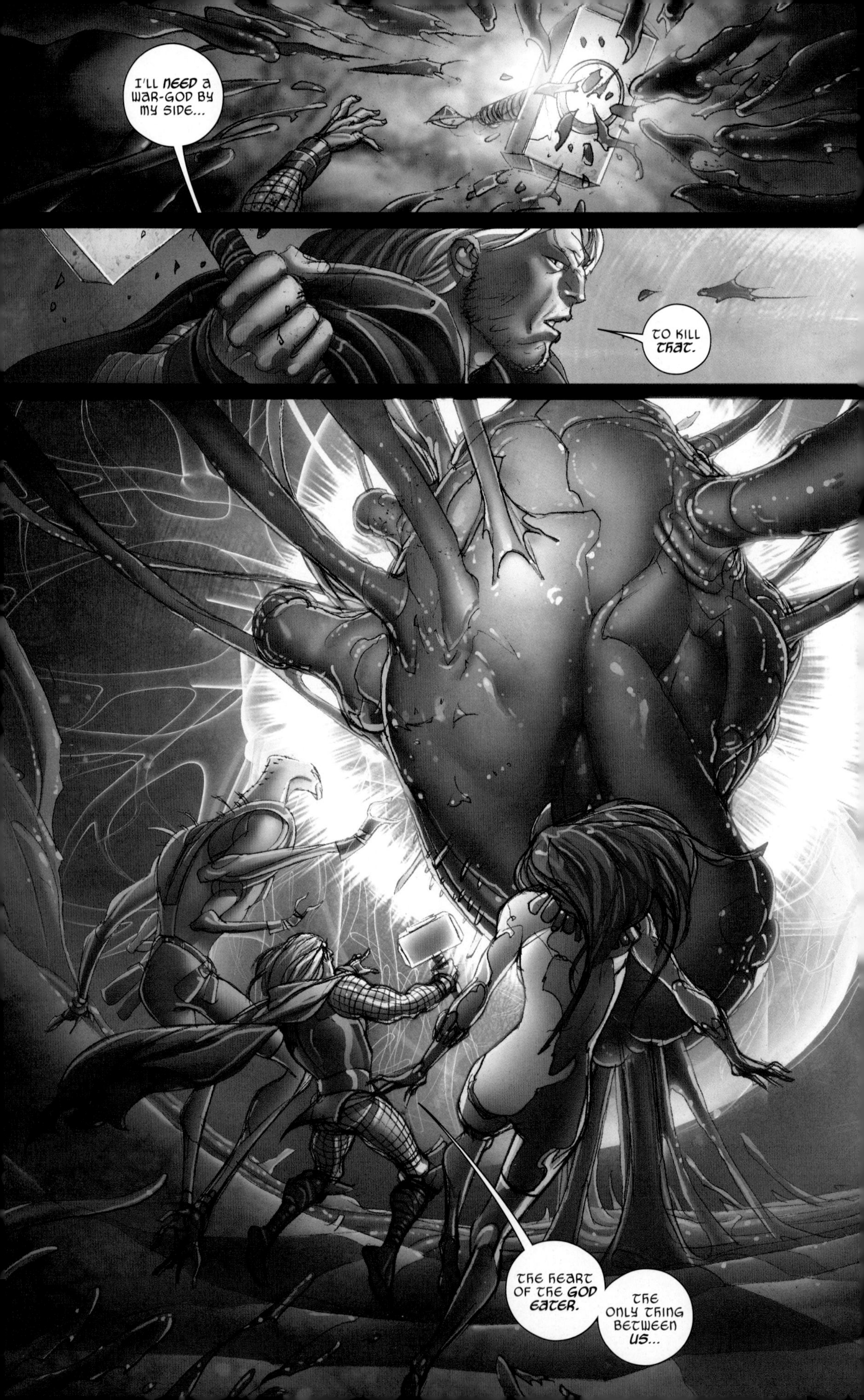
I'LL NEED A WAR-GOD BY MY SIDE...
TO KILL THAT.
THE HEART OF THE GOD EATER.
THE ONLY THING BETWEEN US...

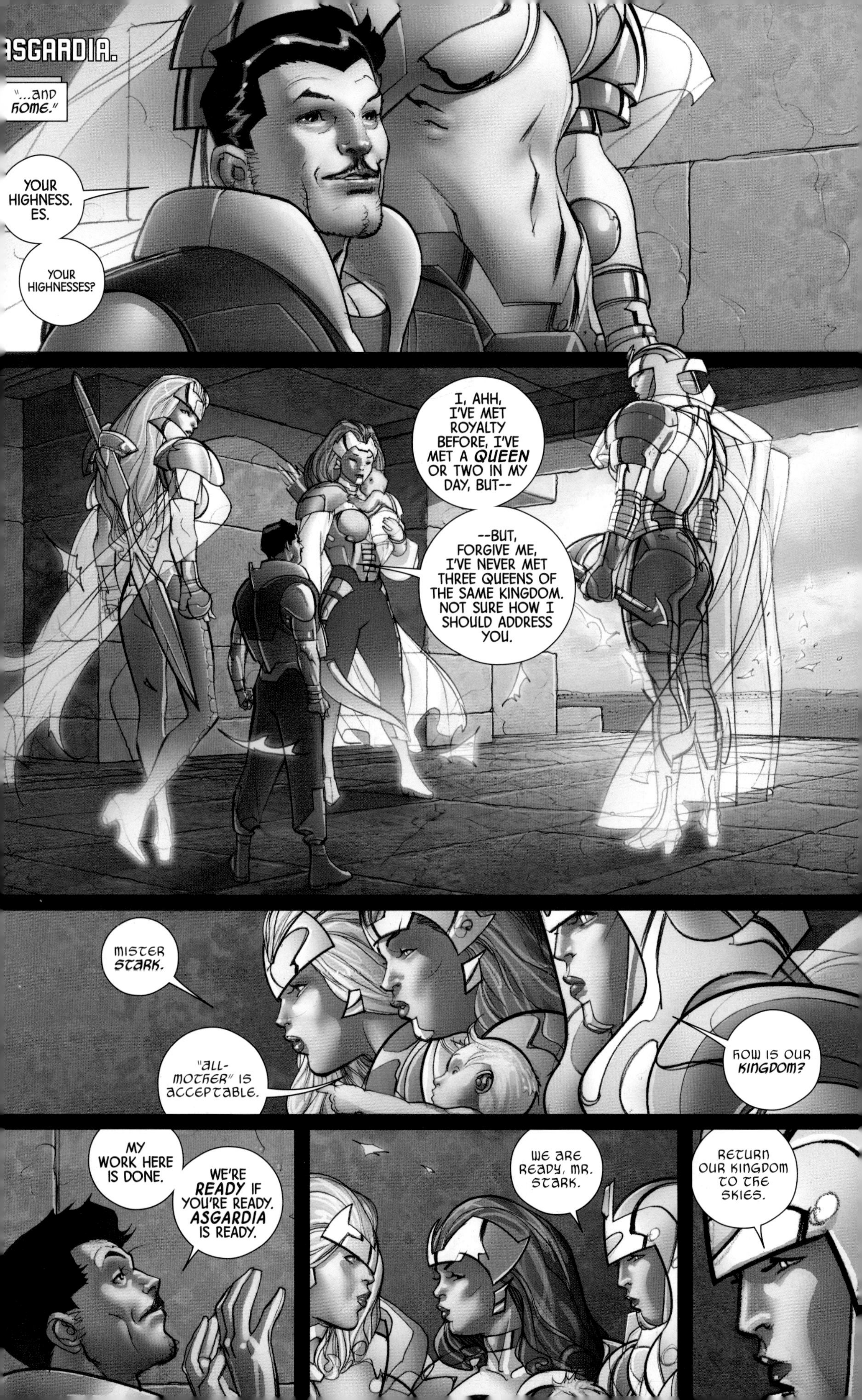
ASGARDIA.
"...AND HOME."
YOUR HIGHNESS. ES.
YOUR HIGHNESSES?
I, AHH, I'VE MET ROYALTY BEFORE, I'VE MET A *QUEEN* OR TWO IN MY DAY, BUT--
--BUT, FORGIVE ME, I'VE NEVER MET THREE QUEENS OF THE SAME KINGDOM. NOT SURE HOW I SHOULD ADDRESS YOU.
MISTER *STARK.*
"ALL-MOTHER" IS ACCEPTABLE.
HOW IS OUR *KINGDOM?*
MY WORK HERE IS DONE.
WE'RE *READY* IF YOU'RE READY. *ASGARDIA* IS READY.
WE ARE READY, MR. STARK.
RETURN OUR KINGDOM TO THE SKIES.

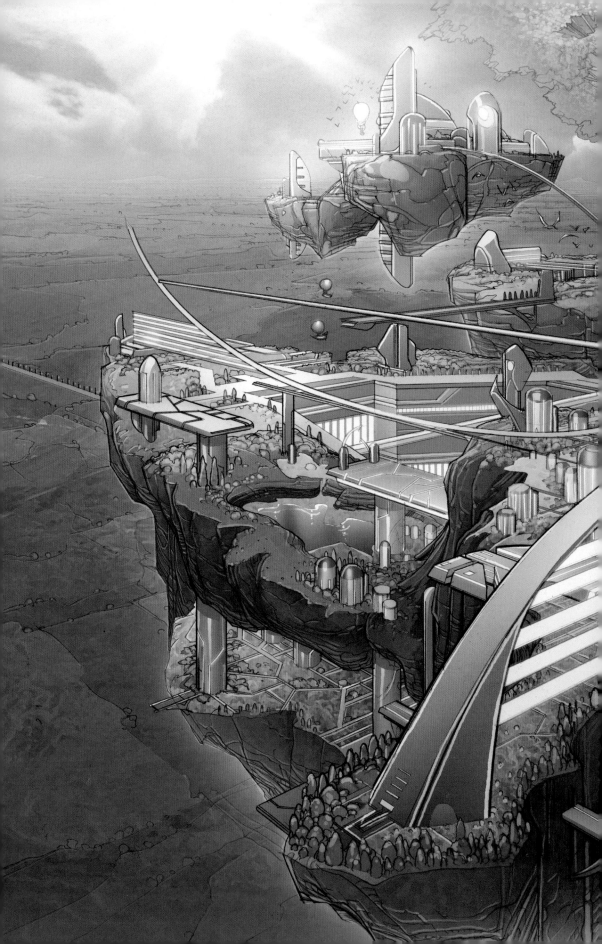

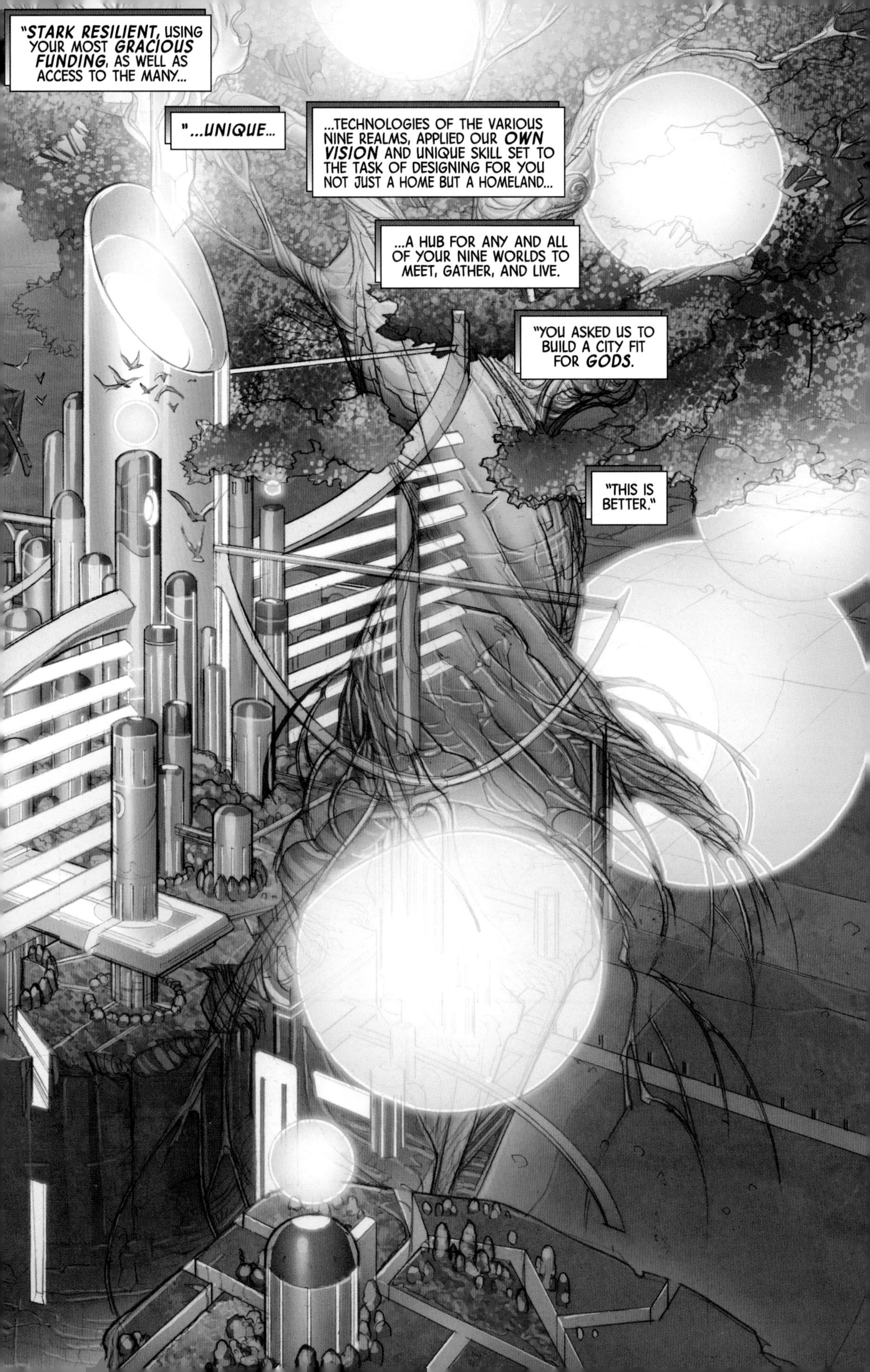
"STARK RESILIENT, USING YOUR MOST GRACIOUS FUNDING, AS WELL AS ACCESS TO THE MANY...
"...UNIQUE...
...TECHNOLOGIES OF THE VARIOUS NINE REALMS, APPLIED OUR OWN VISION AND UNIQUE SKILL SET TO THE TASK OF DESIGNING FOR YOU NOT JUST A HOME BUT A HOMELAND...
...A HUB FOR ANY AND ALL OF YOUR NINE WORLDS TO MEET, GATHER, AND LIVE.
"YOU ASKED US TO BUILD A CITY FIT FOR GODS.
"THIS IS BETTER."

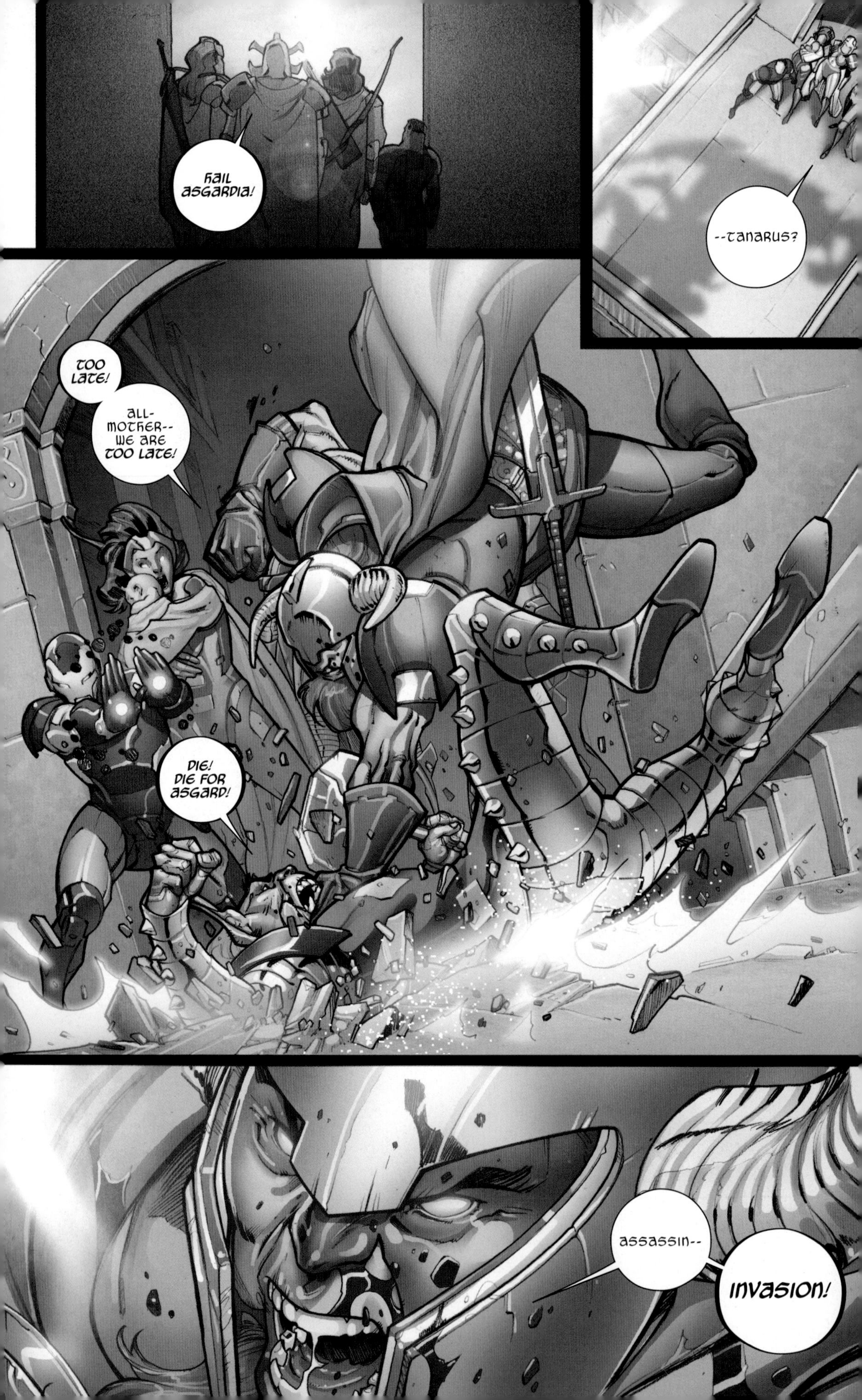
HAIL ASGARDIA!
--TANARUS?
TOO LATE!
ALL-MOTHER-- WE ARE TOO LATE!
DIE! DIE FOR ASGARD!
ASSASSIN--
INVASION!

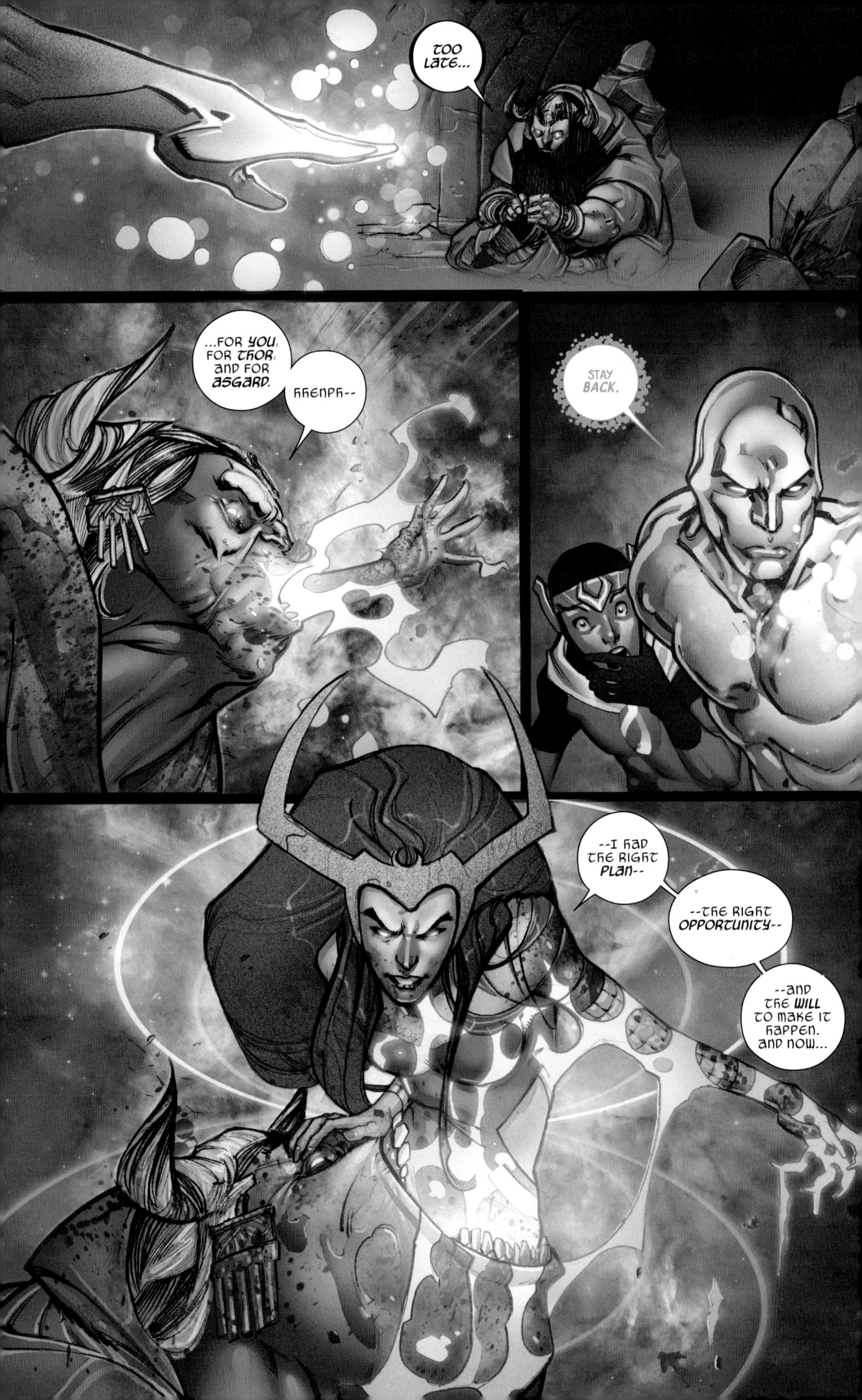
TOO LATE...
...FOR YOU, FOR THOR, AND FOR ASGARD.
HHENPH--
STAY BACK.
--I HAD THE RIGHT PLAN--
--THE RIGHT OPPORTUNITY--
--AND THE WILL TO MAKE IT HAPPEN. AND NOW...

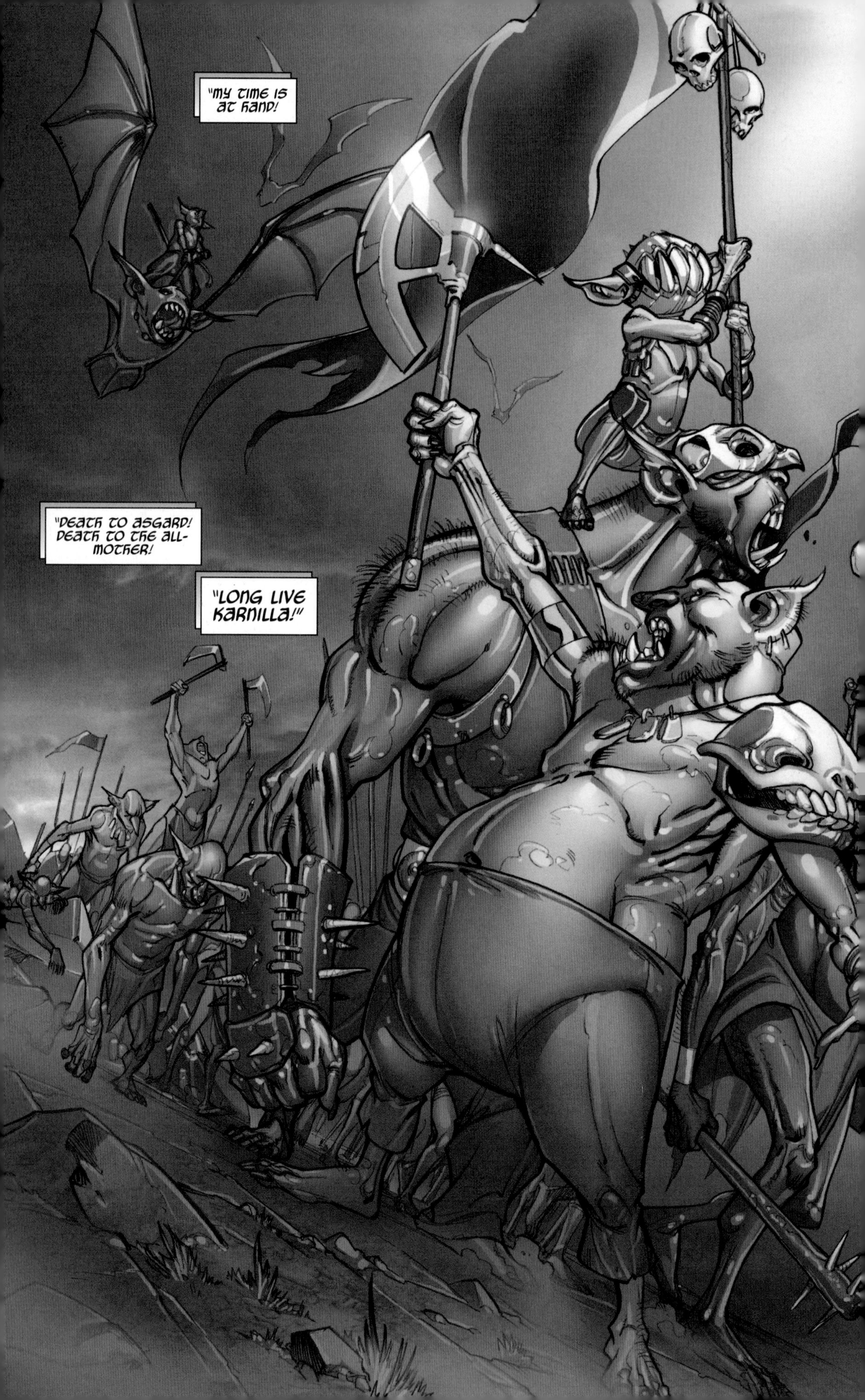
"MY TIME IS AT HAND!
"DEATH TO ASGARD! DEATH TO THE ALL-MOTHER!
"LONG LIVE KARNILLA!"

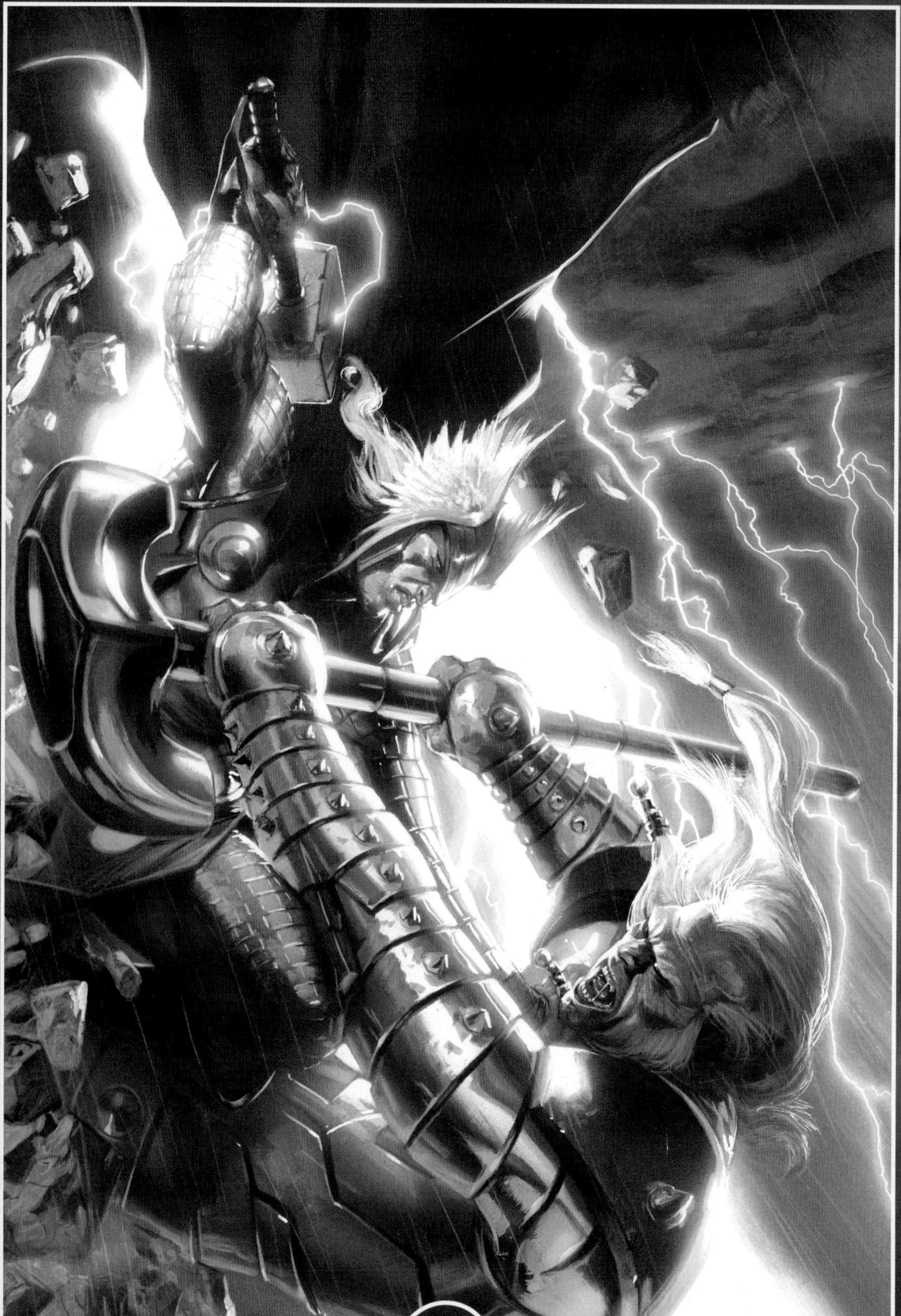
12

THE MIGHTY TANARUS 5: THE RETURN

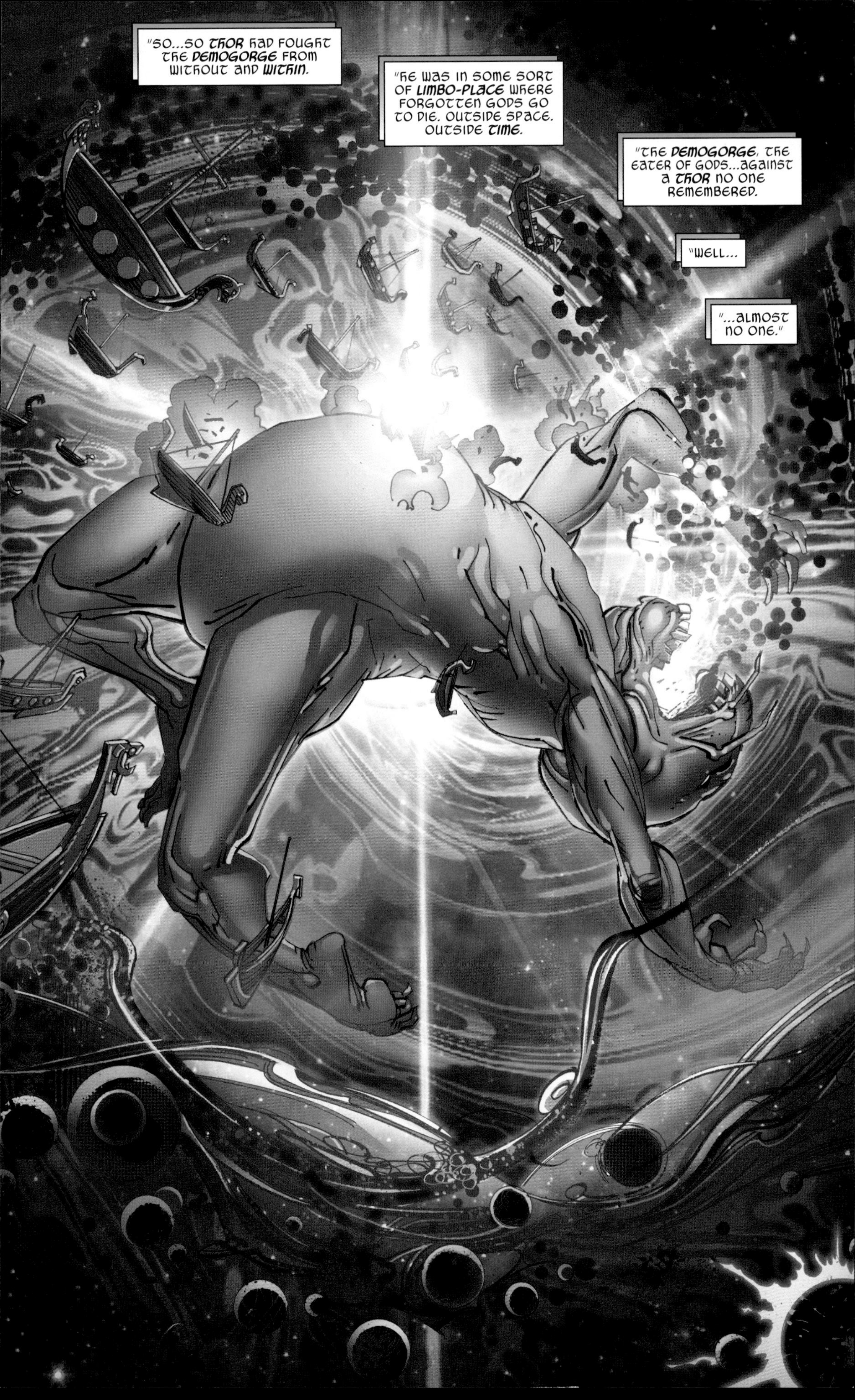
"SO...SO THOR HAD FOUGHT THE DEMOGORGE FROM WITHOUT AND WITHIN.
"HE WAS IN SOME SORT OF LIMBO-PLACE WHERE FORGOTTEN GODS GO TO DIE. OUTSIDE SPACE. OUTSIDE TIME.
"THE DEMOGORGE, THE EATER OF GODS...AGAINST A THOR NO ONE REMEMBERED.
"WELL...
"...ALMOST NO ONE."

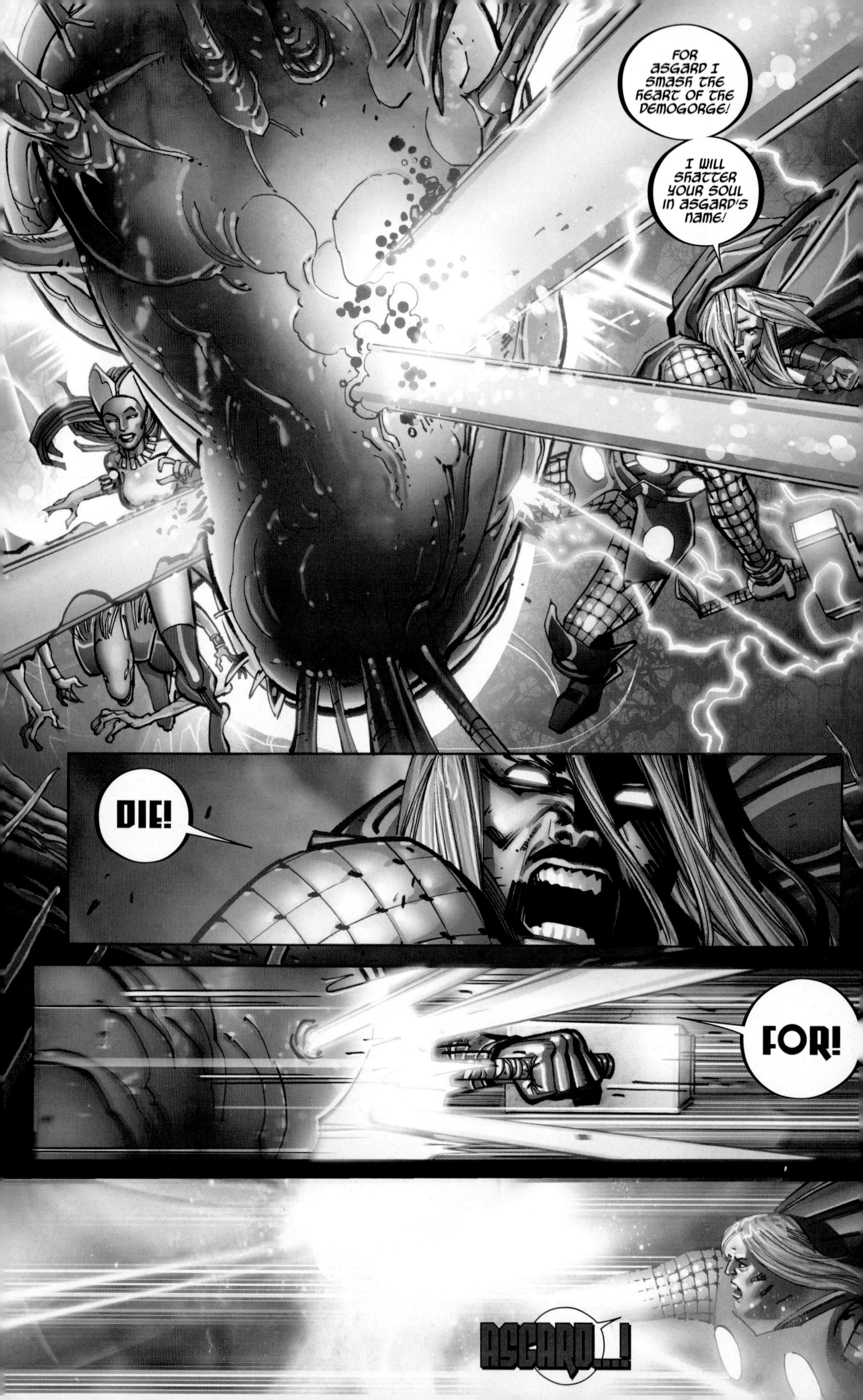
FOR ASGARD I SMASH THE HEART OF THE DEMOGORGE!
I WILL SHATTER YOUR SOUL IN ASGARD'S NAME!
DIE!
FOR!
ASGARD...!

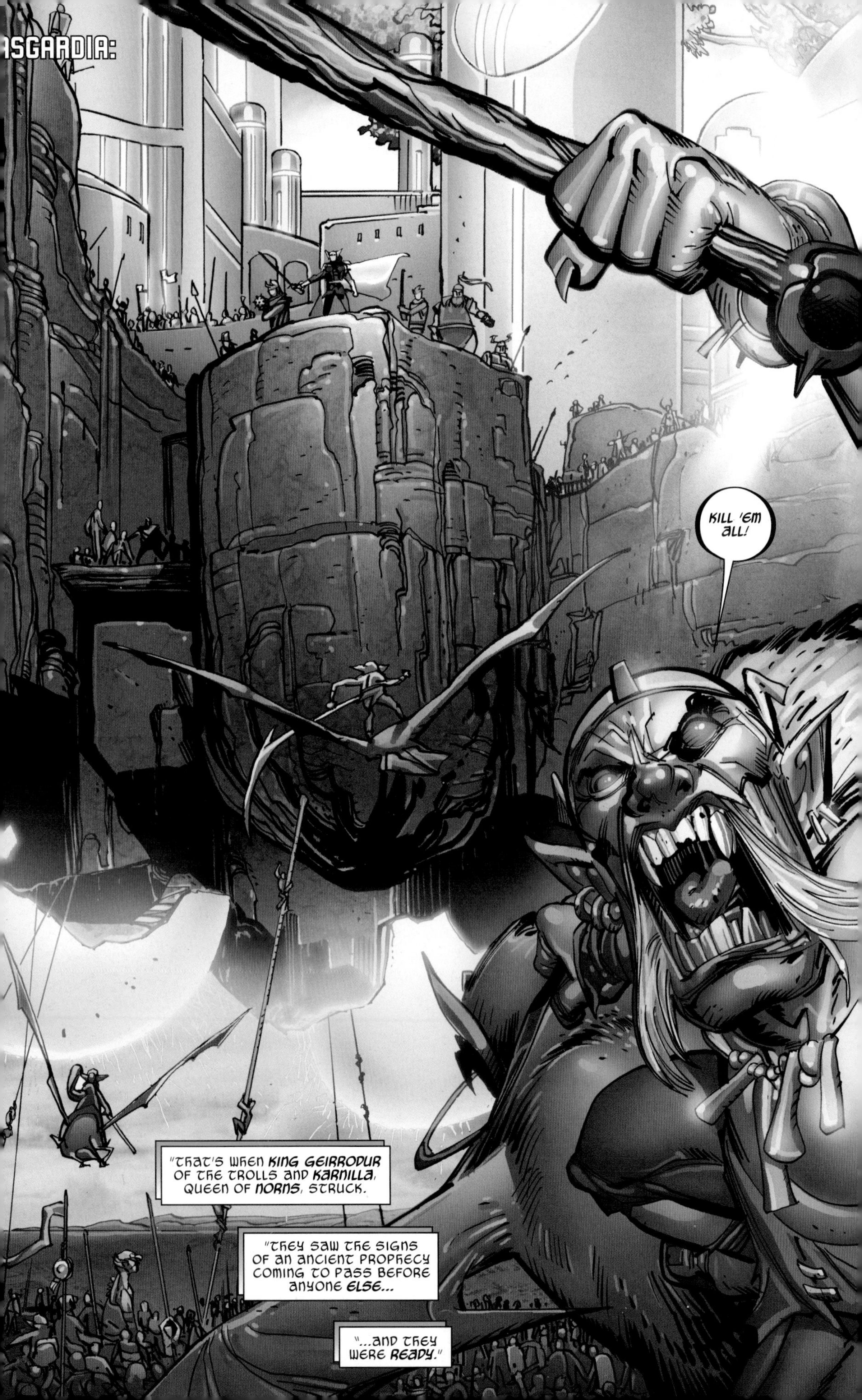
ASGARDIA:
KILL 'EM ALL!
"THAT'S WHEN KING GEIRRODUR OF THE TROLLS AND KARNILLA, QUEEN OF NORNS, STRUCK.
"THEY SAW THE SIGNS OF AN ANCIENT PROPHECY COMING TO PASS BEFORE ANYONE ELSE...
"...AND THEY WERE READY."

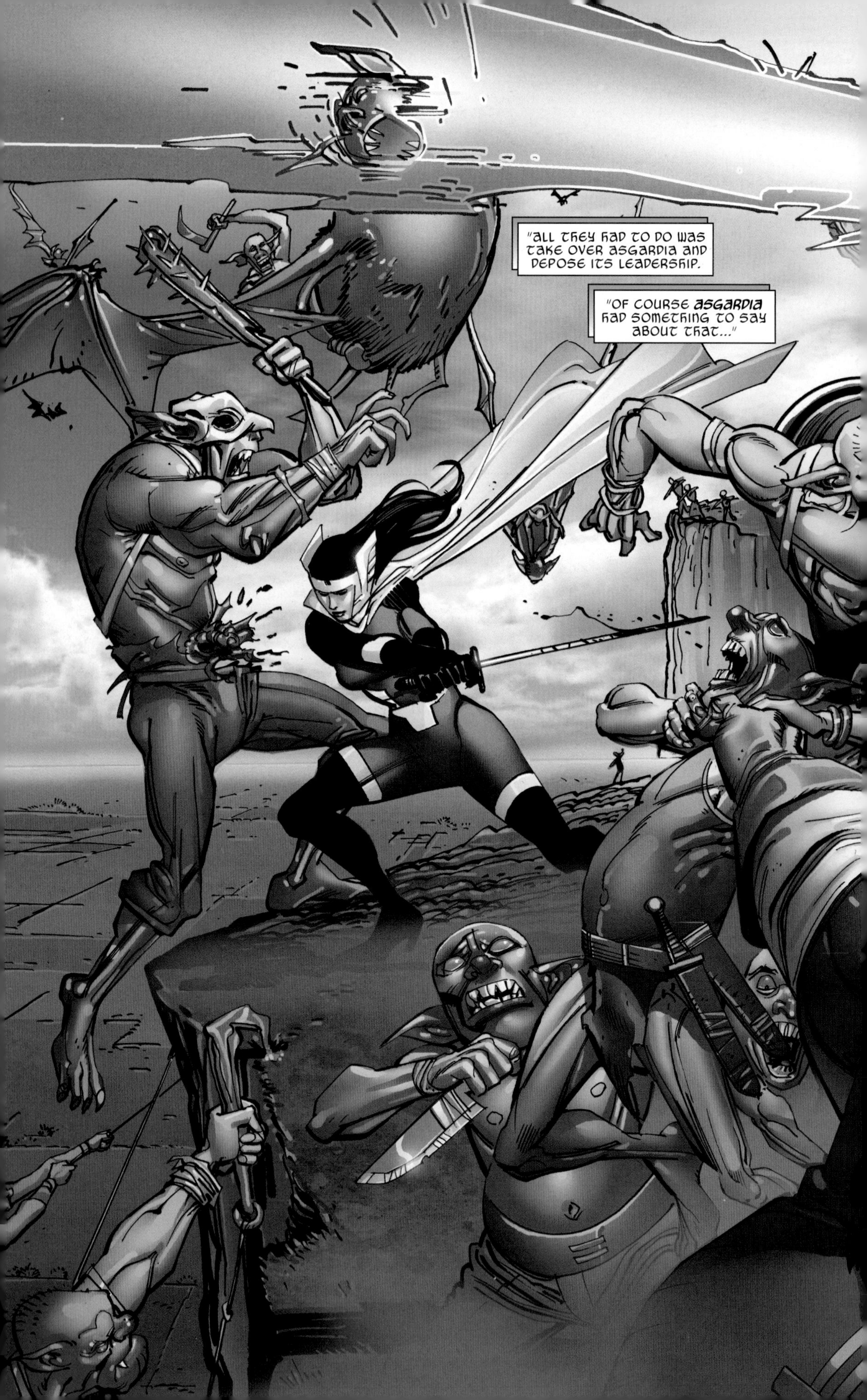
"ALL THEY HAD TO DO WAS TAKE OVER ASGARDIA AND DEPOSE ITS LEADERSHIP.
"OF COURSE ASGARDIA HAD SOMETHING TO SAY ABOUT THAT..."

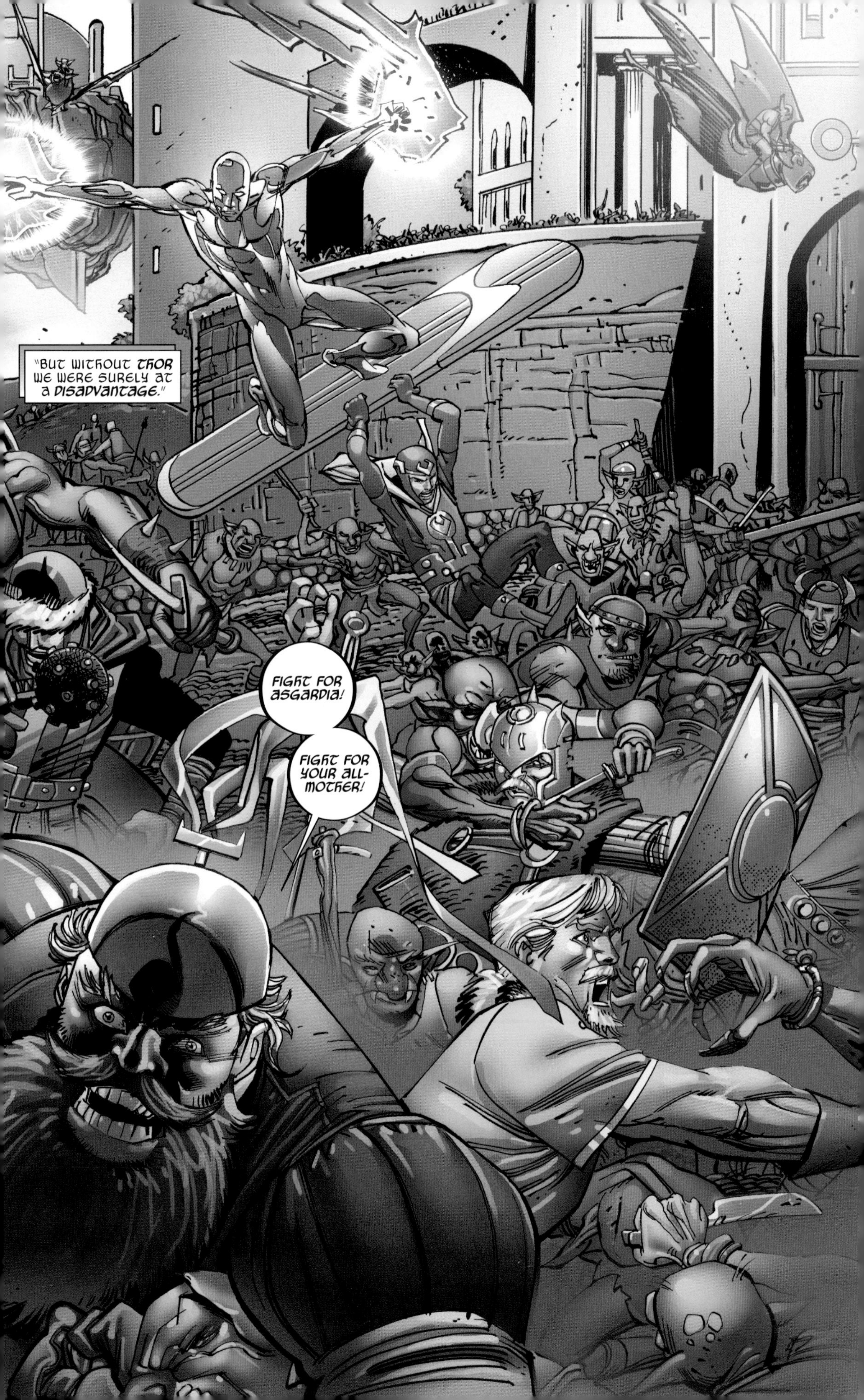
"BUT WITHOUT THOR WE WERE SURELY AT A DISADVANTAGE."
FIGHT FOR ASGARDIA!
FIGHT FOR YOUR ALL-MOTHER!

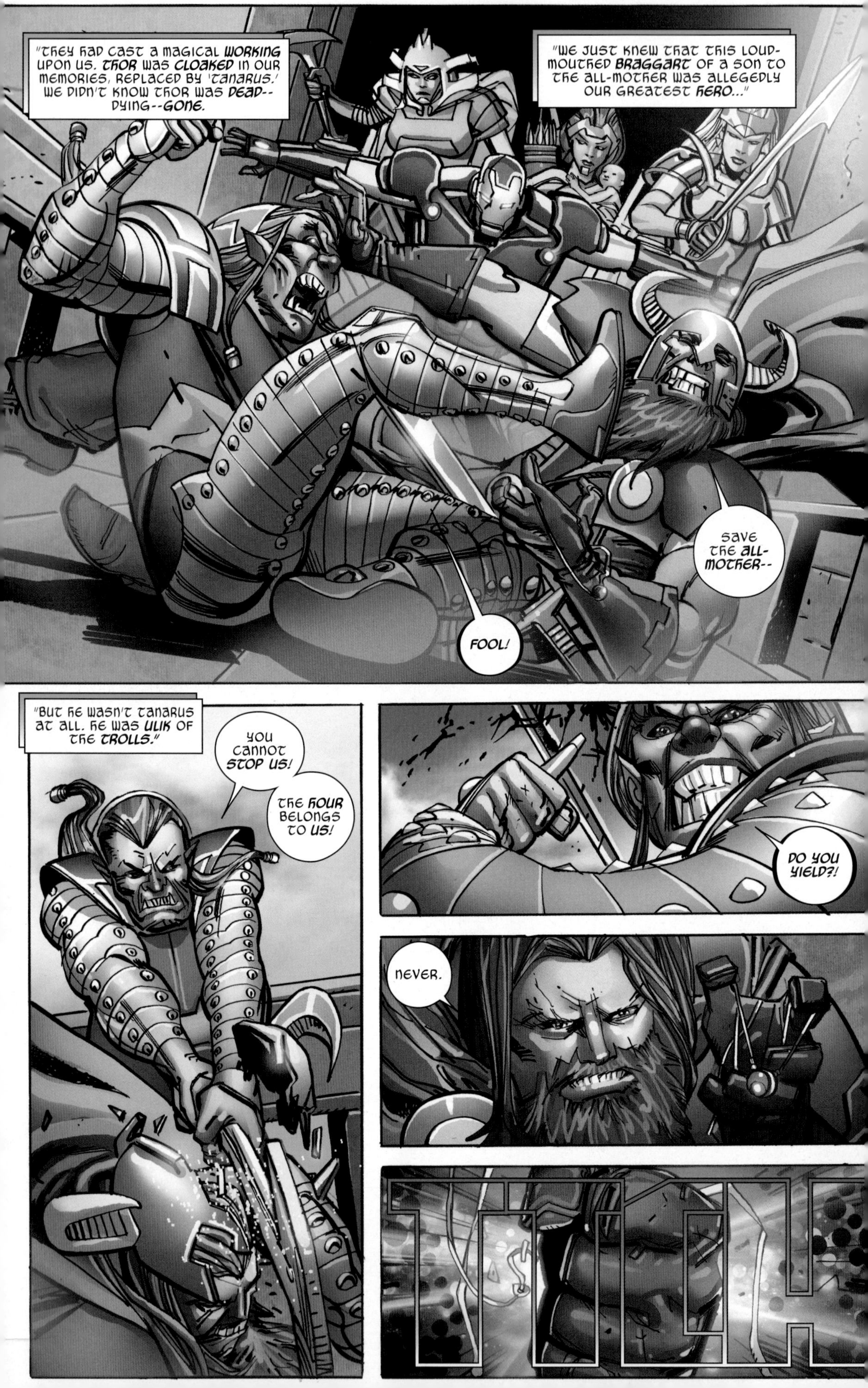
"THEY HAD CAST A MAGICAL WORKING UPON US. THOR WAS CLOAKED IN OUR MEMORIES, REPLACED BY 'TANARUS.' WE DIDN'T KNOW THOR WAS DEAD--DYING--GONE.
"WE JUST KNEW THAT THIS LOUD-MOUTHED BRAGGART OF A SON TO THE ALL-MOTHER WAS ALLEGEDLY OUR GREATEST HERO..."
SAVE THE ALL-MOTHER--
FOOL!
"BUT HE WASN'T TANARUS AT ALL. HE WAS ULIK OF THE TROLLS."
YOU CANNOT STOP US!
THE HOUR BELONGS TO US!
DO YOU YIELD?!
NEVER.

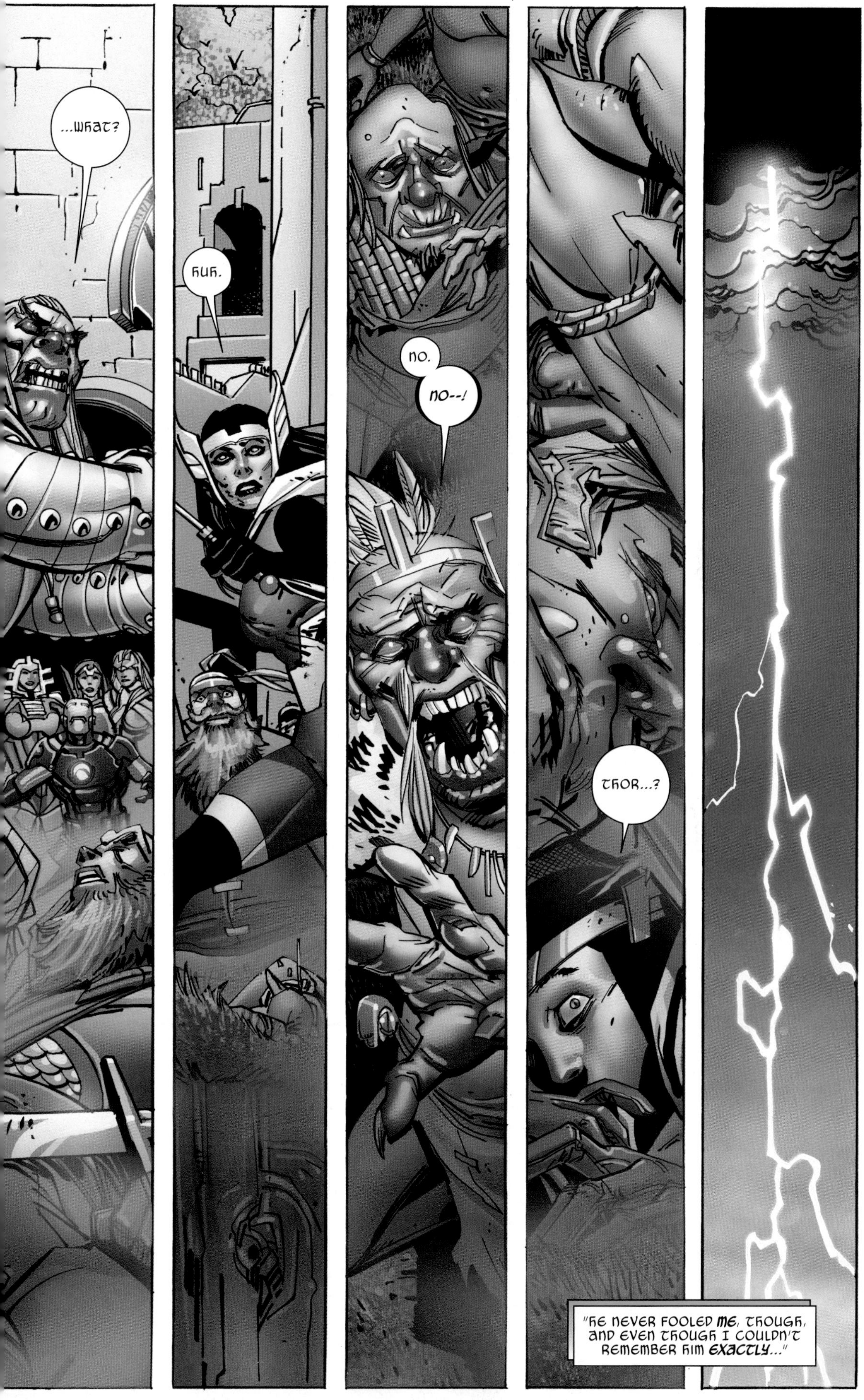
...WHAT?
HUH.
NO.
NO--!
THOR...?
"HE NEVER FOOLED ME, THOUGH, AND EVEN THOUGH I COULDN'T REMEMBER HIM EXACTLY..."

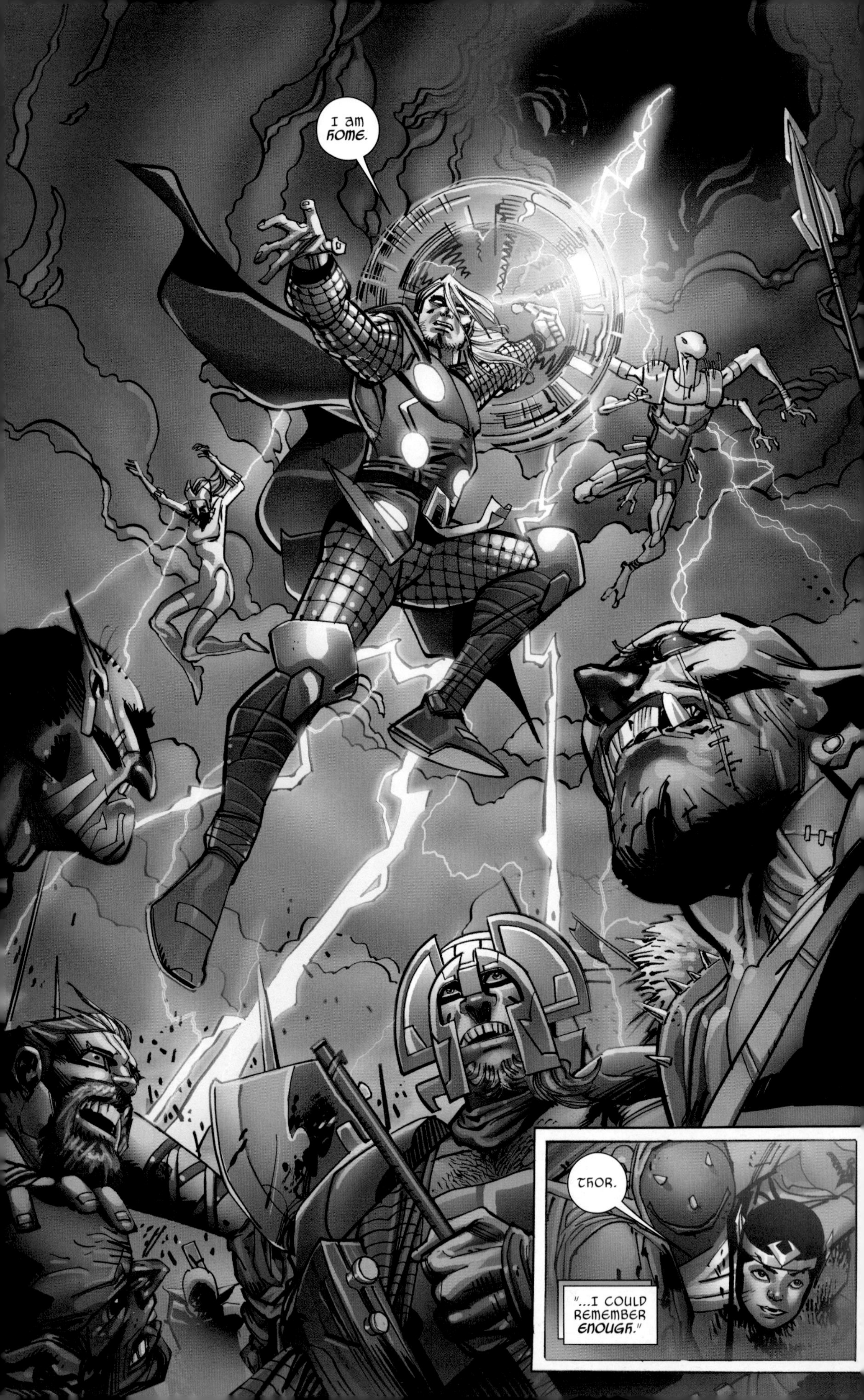
I am HOME.
THOR.
"...I COULD REMEMBER ENOUGH."

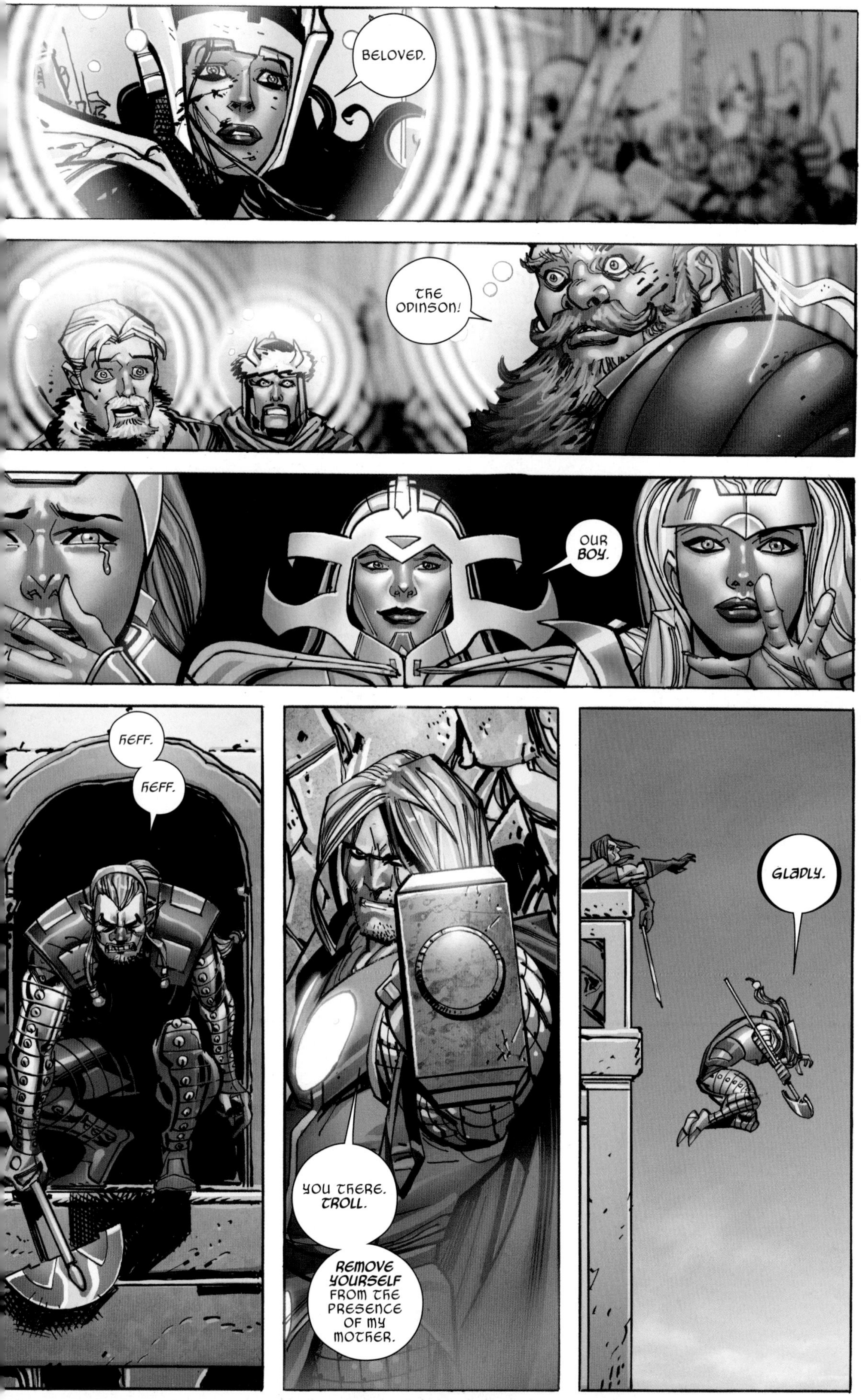
BELOVED.
THE ODINSON!
OUR BOY.
HEFF.
HEFF.
YOU THERE. TROLL.
REMOVE YOURSELF FROM THE PRESENCE OF MY MOTHER.
GLADLY.

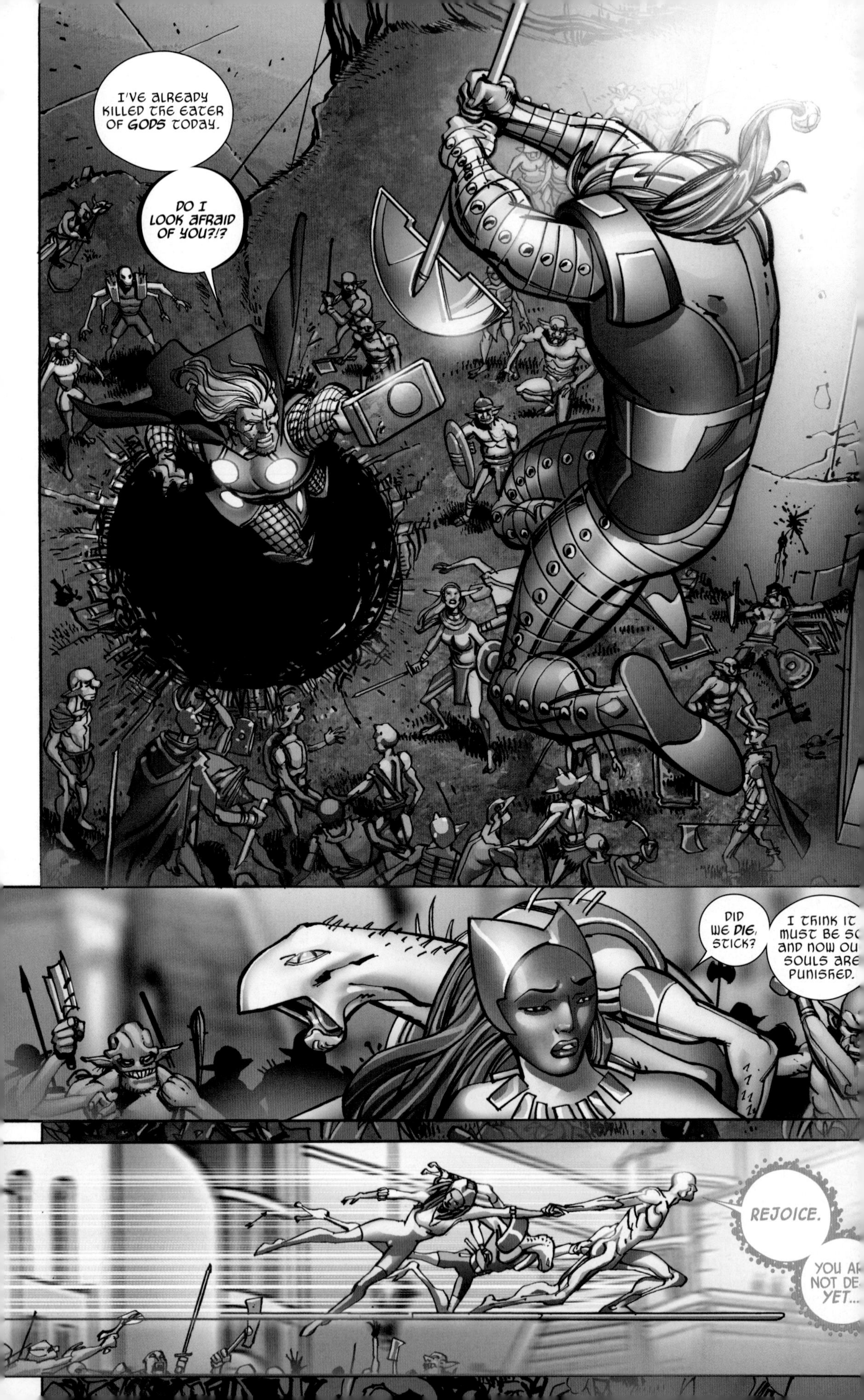
I'VE ALREADY KILLED THE EATER OF GODS TODAY.
DO I LOOK AFRAID OF YOU?!?
DID WE DIE, STICK?
I THINK IT MUST BE SO AND NOW OU SOULS ARE PUNISHED.
REJOICE.
YOU AR NOT DE YET...

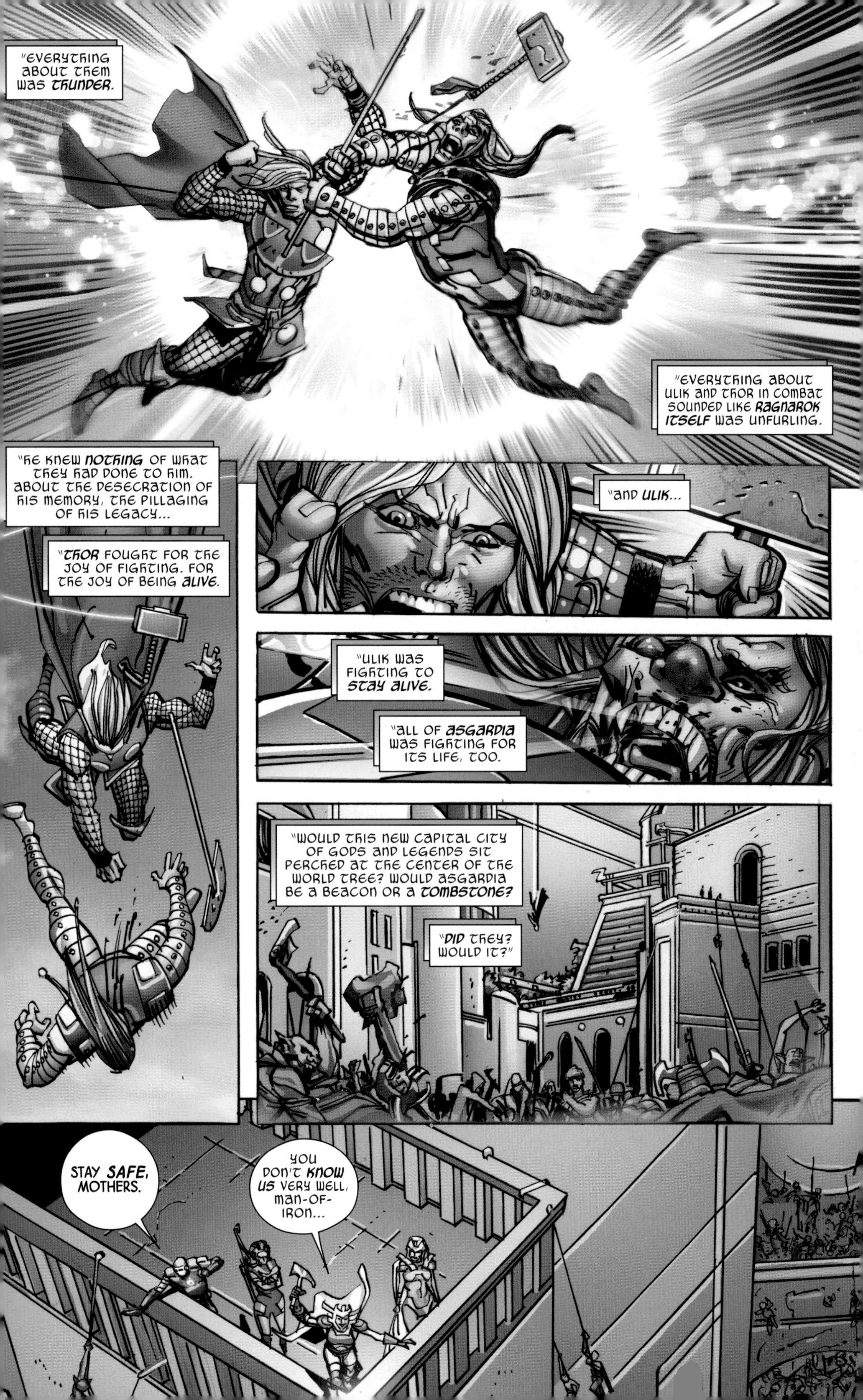
"EVERYTHING ABOUT THEM WAS THUNDER.
"EVERYTHING ABOUT ULIK AND THOR IN COMBAT SOUNDED LIKE RAGNAROK ITSELF WAS UNFURLING.
"HE KNEW NOTHING OF WHAT THEY HAD DONE TO HIM. ABOUT THE DESECRATION OF HIS MEMORY, THE PILLAGING OF HIS LEGACY...
"THOR FOUGHT FOR THE JOY OF FIGHTING. FOR THE JOY OF BEING ALIVE.
"AND ULIK...
"ULIK WAS FIGHTING TO STAY ALIVE.
"ALL OF ASGARDIA WAS FIGHTING FOR ITS LIFE, TOO.
"WOULD THIS NEW CAPITAL CITY OF GODS AND LEGENDS SIT PERCHED AT THE CENTER OF THE WORLD TREE? WOULD ASGARDIA BE A BEACON OR A TOMBSTONE?
"DID THEY? WOULD IT?"
STAY SAFE, MOTHERS.
YOU DON'T KNOW US VERY WELL, MAN-OF-IRON...

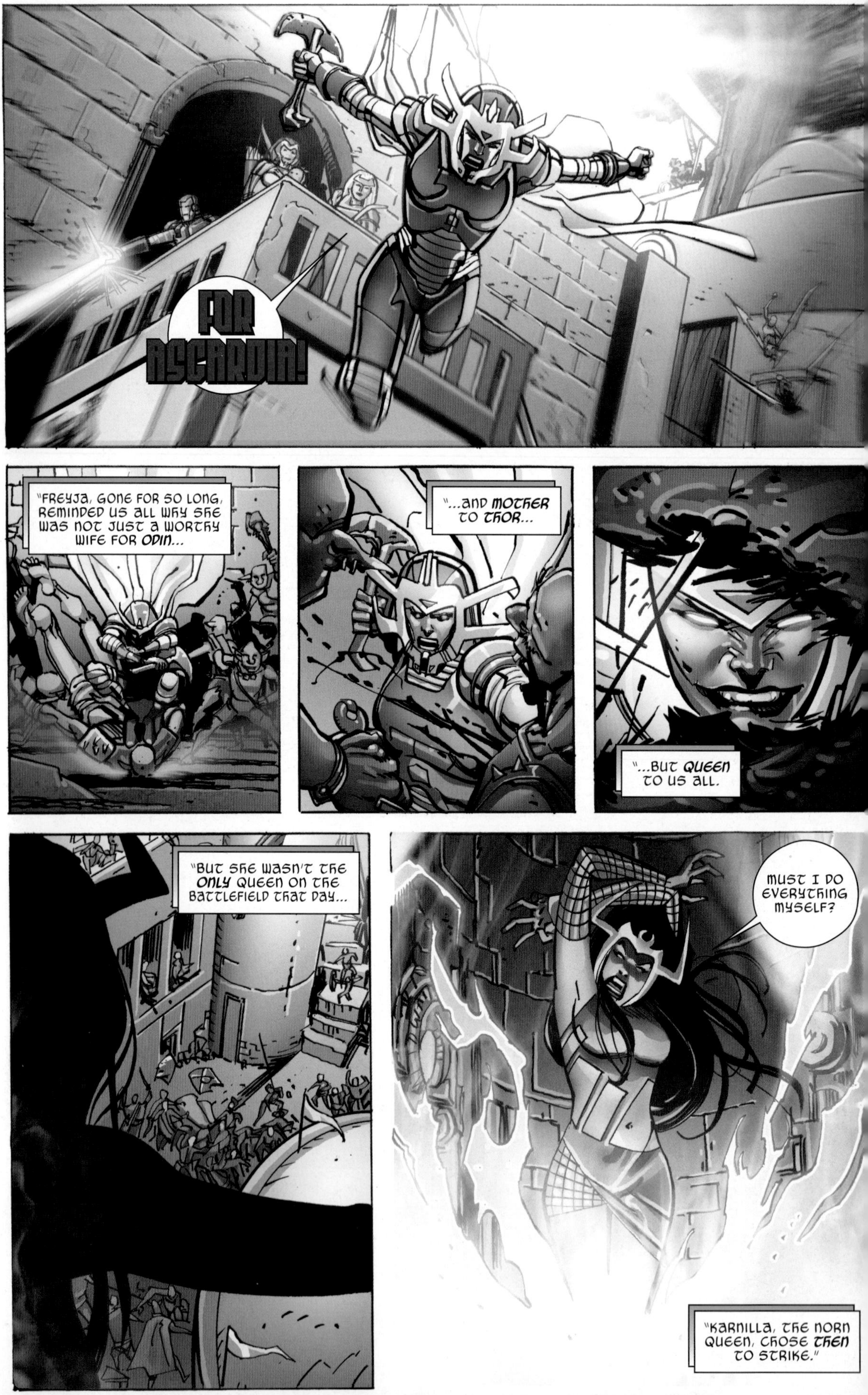
FOR ASGARDIA!
"FREYJA, GONE FOR SO LONG, REMINDED US ALL WHY SHE WAS NOT JUST A WORTHY WIFE FOR ODIN...
"...AND MOTHER TO THOR...
"...BUT QUEEN TO US ALL.
"BUT SHE WASN'T THE ONLY QUEEN ON THE BATTLEFIELD THAT DAY...
MUST I DO EVERYTHING MYSELF?
"KARNILLA, THE NORN QUEEN, CHOSE THEN TO STRIKE."

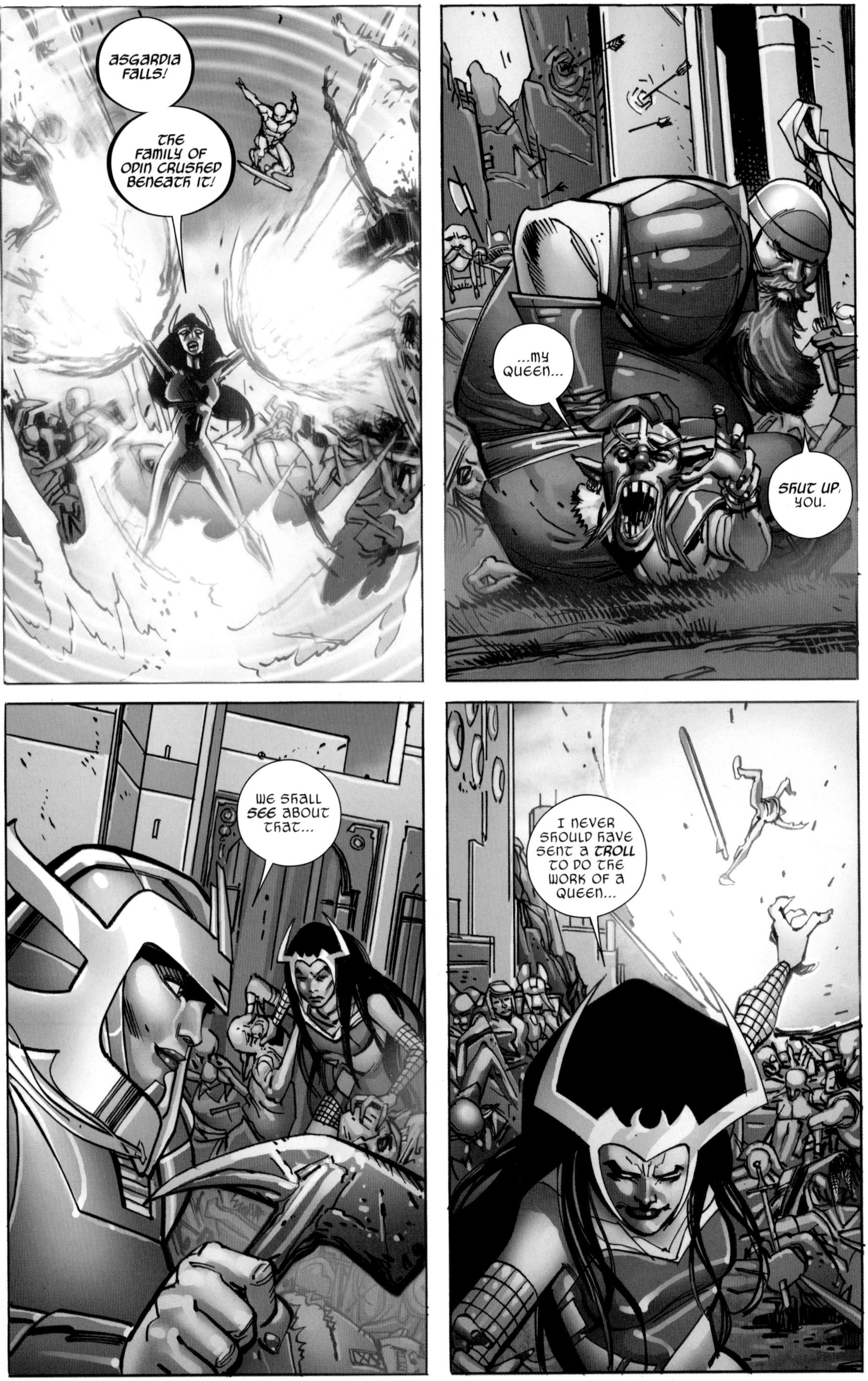
ASGARDIA FALLS!
THE FAMILY OF ODIN CRUSHED BENEATH IT!
...MY QUEEN...
SHUT UP, YOU.
WE SHALL SEE ABOUT THAT...
I NEVER SHOULD HAVE SENT A TROLL TO DO THE WORK OF A QUEEN...

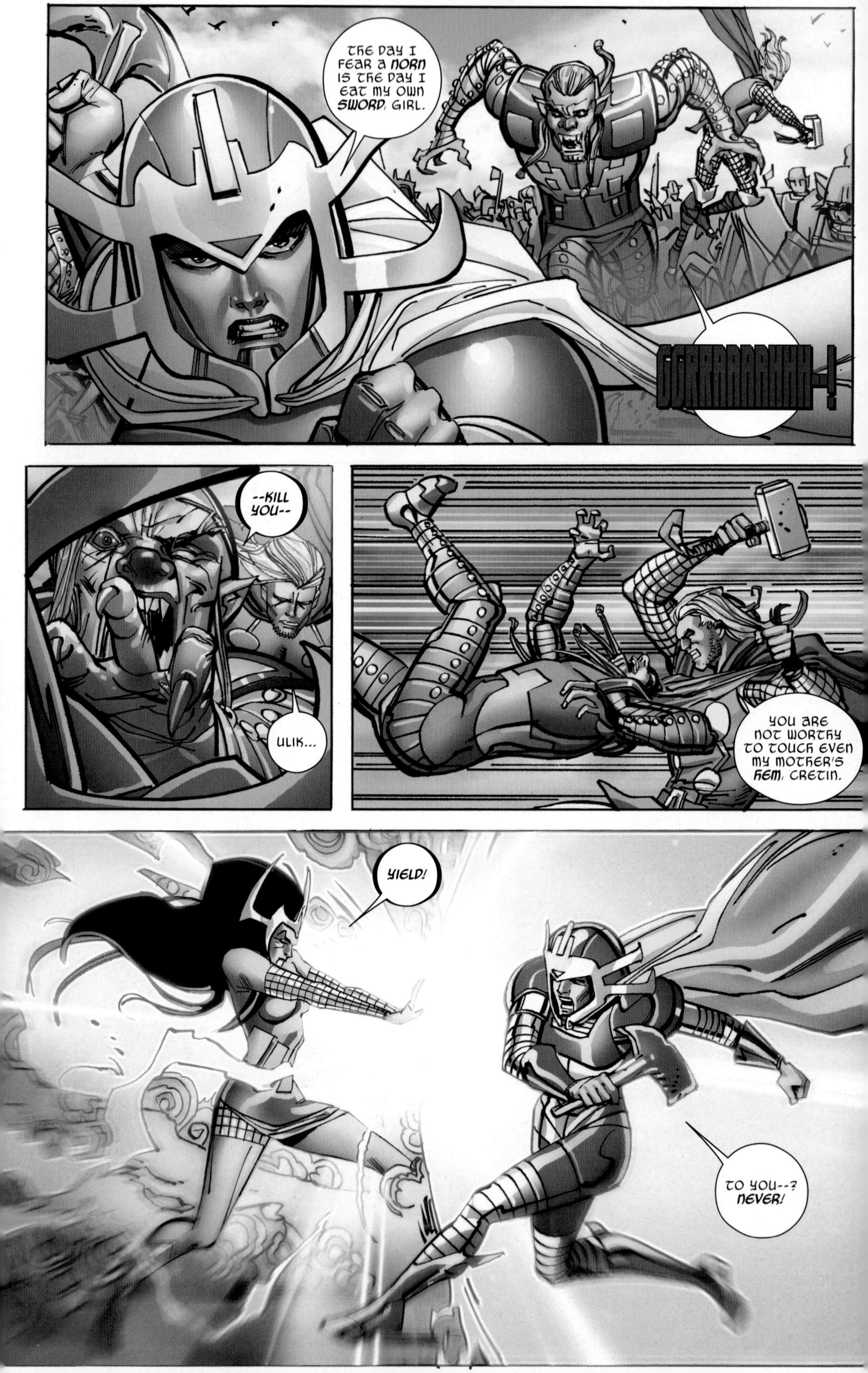
THE DAY I FEAR A NORN IS THE DAY I EAT MY OWN SWORD, GIRL.
GGRRAAAAHHH--!
--KILL YOU--
ULIK...
YOU ARE NOT WORTHY TO TOUCH EVEN MY MOTHER'S HEM, CRETIN.
YIELD!
TO YOU--? NEVER!

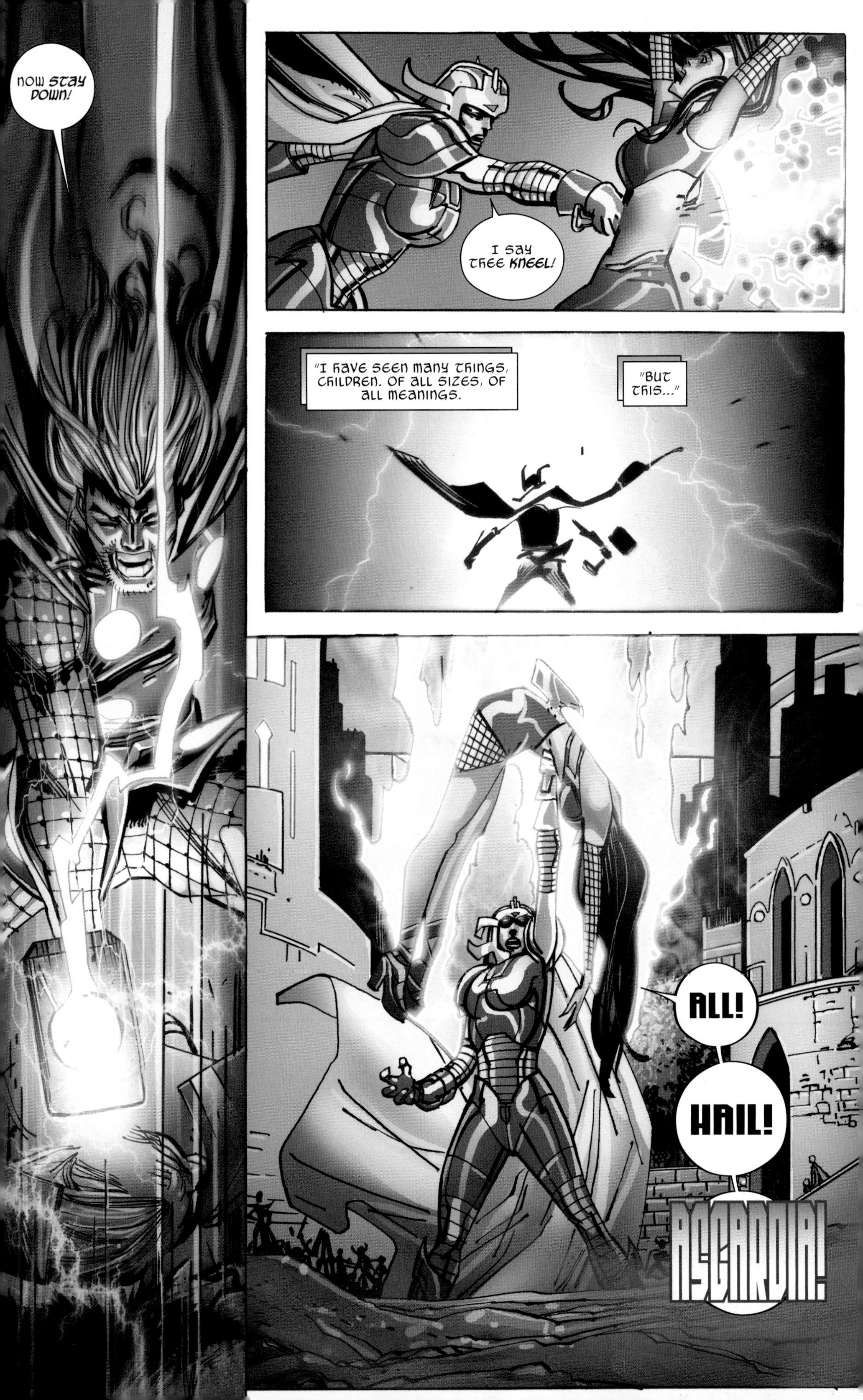
NOW STAY DOWN!
I SAY THEE KNEEL!
"I HAVE SEEN MANY THINGS, CHILDREN. OF ALL SIZES, OF ALL MEANINGS.
"BUT THIS..."
ALL!
HAIL!
ASGARDIA!

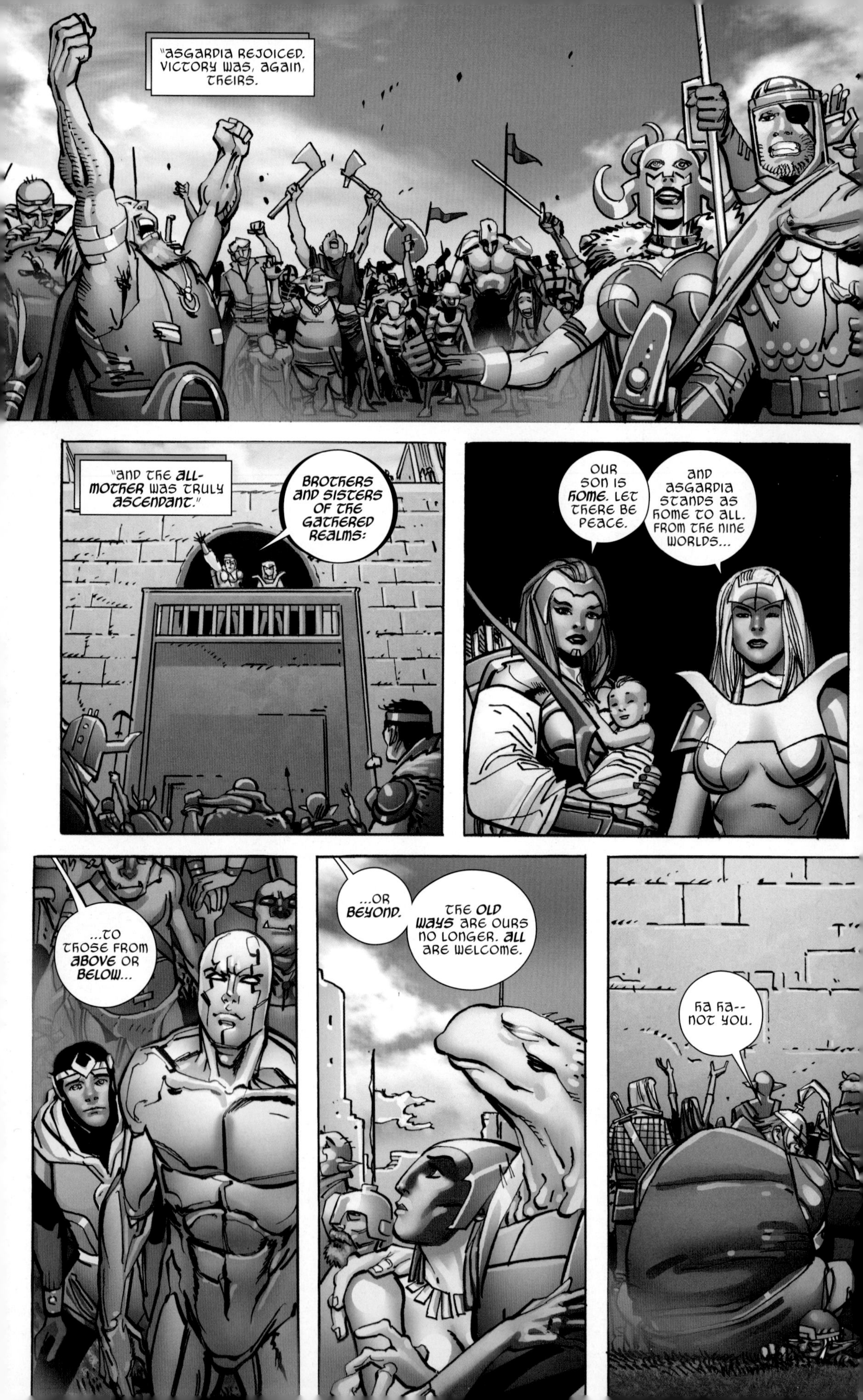
"ASGARDIA REJOICED. VICTORY WAS, AGAIN, THEIRS.
"AND THE ALL-MOTHER WAS TRULY ASCENDANT."
BROTHERS AND SISTERS OF THE GATHERED REALMS:
OUR SON IS HOME. LET THERE BE PEACE.
AND ASGARDIA STANDS AS HOME TO ALL. FROM THE NINE WORLDS...
...TO THOSE FROM ABOVE OR BELOW...
...OR BEYOND.
THE OLD WAYS ARE OURS NO LONGER. ALL ARE WELCOME.
HA HA--NOT YOU.

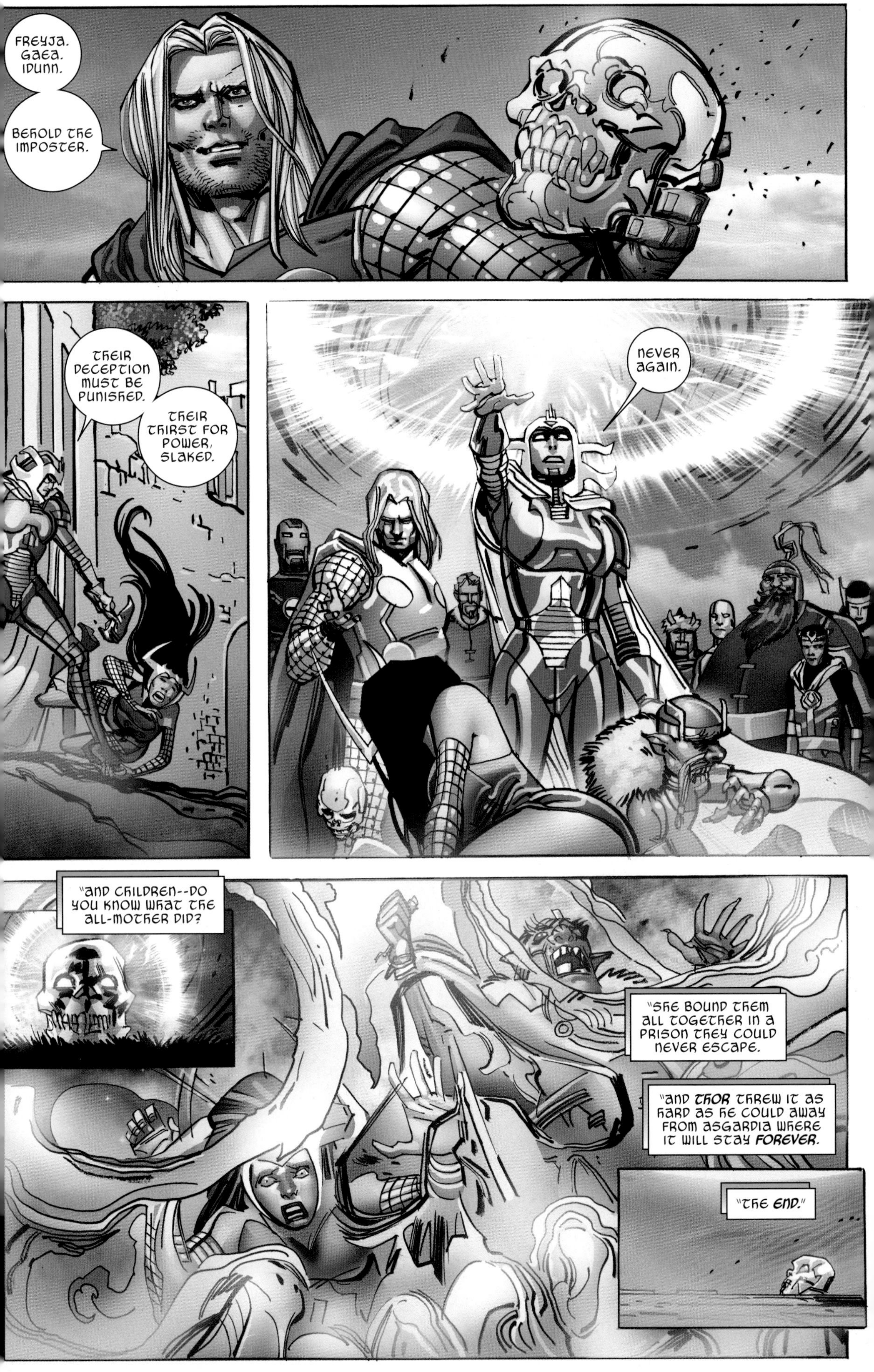
FREYJA. GAEA. IDUNN.
BEHOLD THE IMPOSTER.
THEIR DECEPTION MUST BE PUNISHED.
THEIR THIRST FOR POWER, SLAKED.
NEVER AGAIN.
"AND CHILDREN--DO YOU KNOW WHAT THE ALL-MOTHER DID?
"SHE BOUND THEM ALL TOGETHER IN A PRISON THEY COULD NEVER ESCAPE.
"AND THOR THREW IT AS HARD AS HE COULD AWAY FROM ASGARDIA WHERE IT WILL STAY FOREVER.
"THE END."

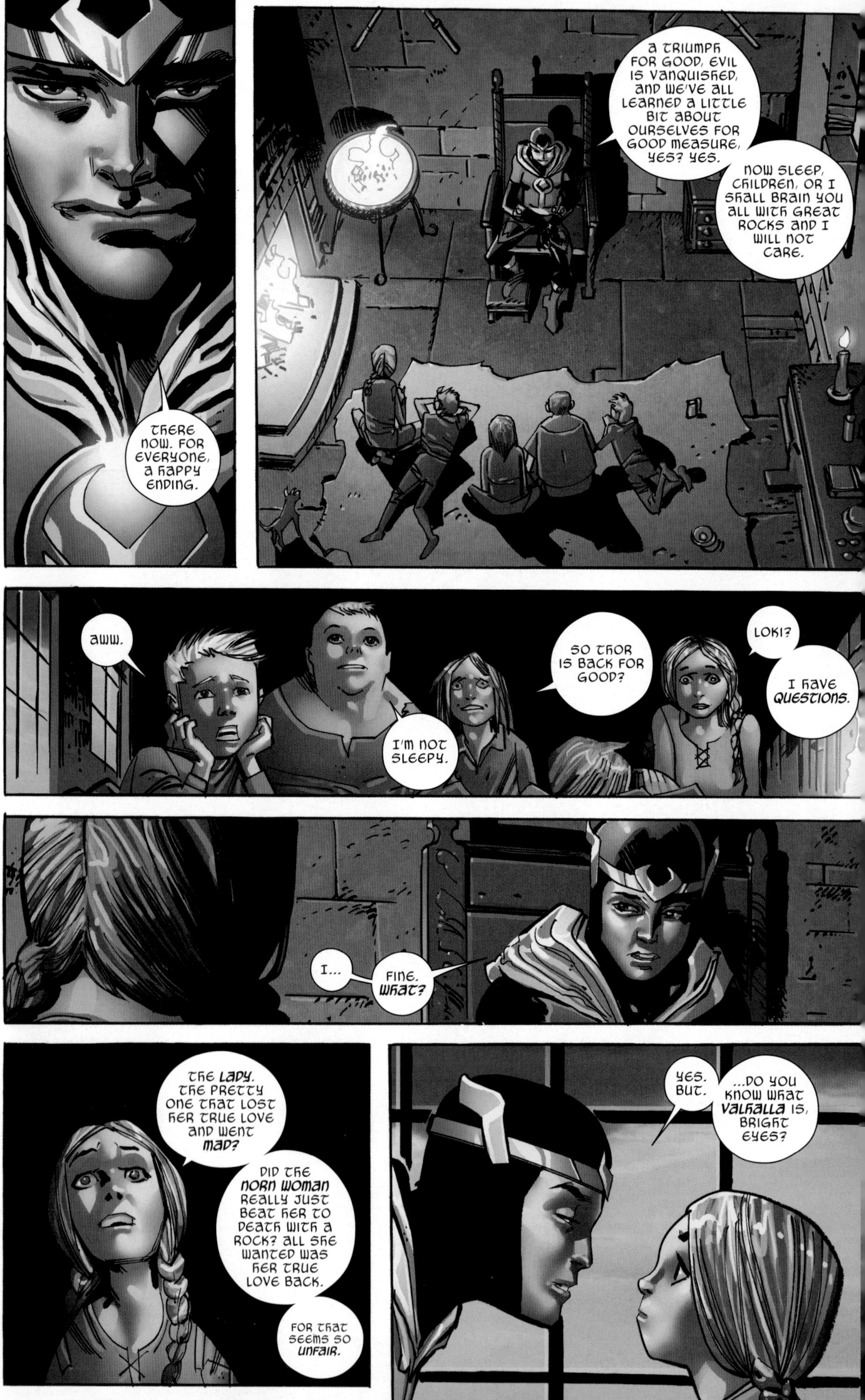
THERE NOW. FOR EVERYONE, A HAPPY ENDING.
A TRIUMPH FOR GOOD, EVIL IS VANQUISHED, AND WE'VE ALL LEARNED A LITTLE BIT ABOUT OURSELVES FOR GOOD MEASURE, YES? YES.
NOW SLEEP, CHILDREN, OR I SHALL BRAIN YOU ALL WITH GREAT ROCKS AND I WILL NOT CARE.
AWW.
I'M NOT SLEEPY.
SO THOR IS BACK FOR GOOD?
LOKI?
I HAVE QUESTIONS.
I...
FINE. WHAT?
THE LADY. THE PRETTY ONE THAT LOST HER TRUE LOVE AND WENT MAD?
DID THE NORN WOMAN REALLY JUST BEAT HER TO DEATH WITH A ROCK? ALL SHE WANTED WAS HER TRUE LOVE BACK.
FOR THAT SEEMS SO UNFAIR.
YES. BUT.
...DO YOU KNOW WHAT VALHALLA IS, BRIGHT EYES?

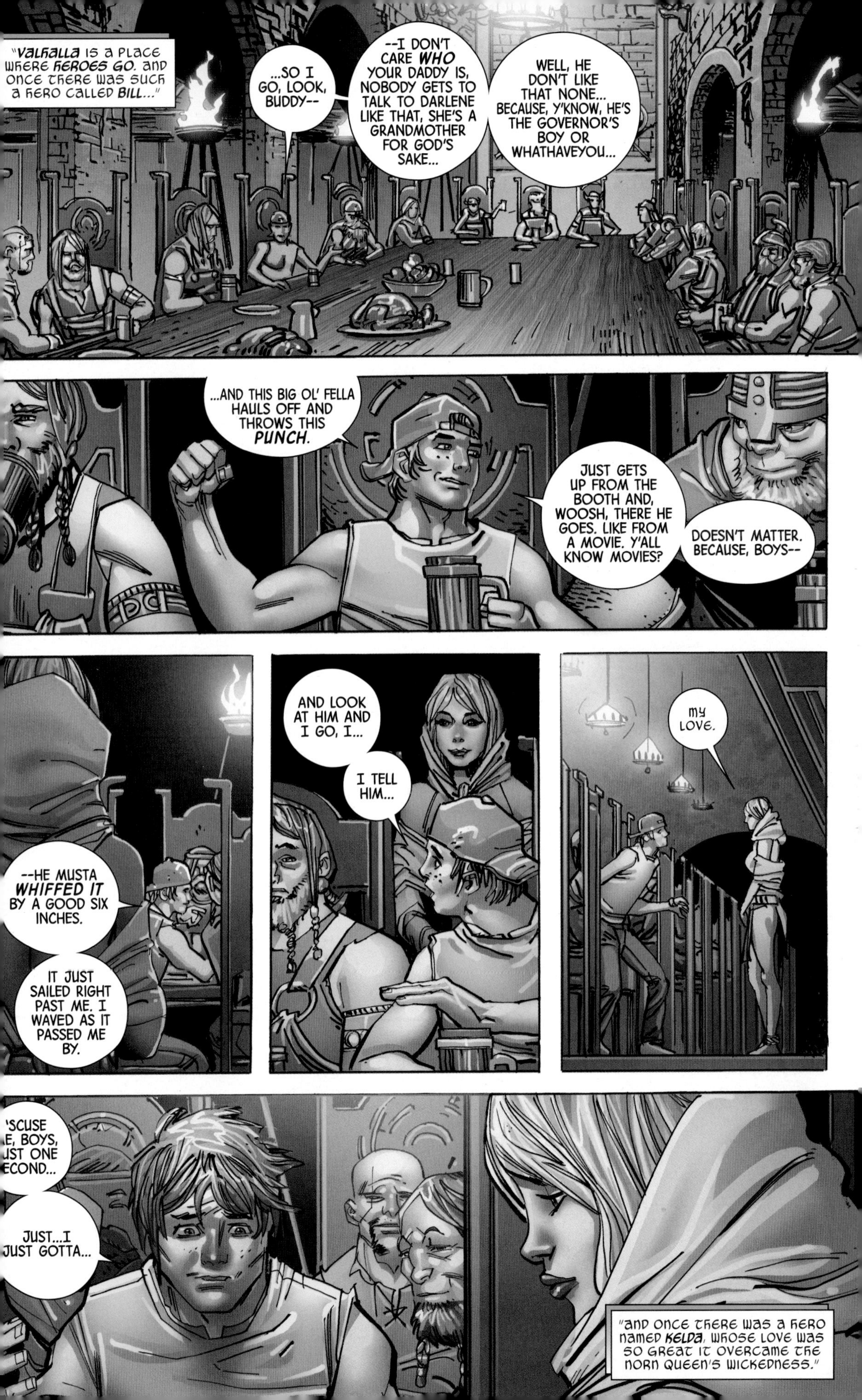
"VALHALLA IS A PLACE WHERE HEROES GO. AND ONCE THERE WAS SUCH A HERO CALLED BILL..."
...SO I GO, LOOK, BUDDY--
--I DON'T CARE WHO YOUR DADDY IS, NOBODY GETS TO TALK TO DARLENE LIKE THAT, SHE'S A GRANDMOTHER FOR GOD'S SAKE...
WELL, HE DON'T LIKE THAT NONE... BECAUSE, Y'KNOW, HE'S THE GOVERNOR'S BOY OR WHATHAVEYOU...
...AND THIS BIG OL' FELLA HAULS OFF AND THROWS THIS PUNCH.
JUST GETS UP FROM THE BOOTH AND, WOOSH, THERE HE GOES. LIKE FROM A MOVIE. Y'ALL KNOW MOVIES?
DOESN'T MATTER. BECAUSE, BOYS--
--HE MUSTA WHIFFED IT BY A GOOD SIX INCHES.
IT JUST SAILED RIGHT PAST ME. I WAVED AS IT PASSED ME BY.
AND LOOK AT HIM AND I GO, I...
I TELL HIM...
MY LOVE.
'SCUSE E, BOYS, UST ONE ECOND...
JUST...I JUST GOTTA...
"AND ONCE THERE WAS A HERO NAMED KELDA, WHOSE LOVE WAS SO GREAT IT OVERCAME THE NORN QUEEN'S WICKEDNESS."

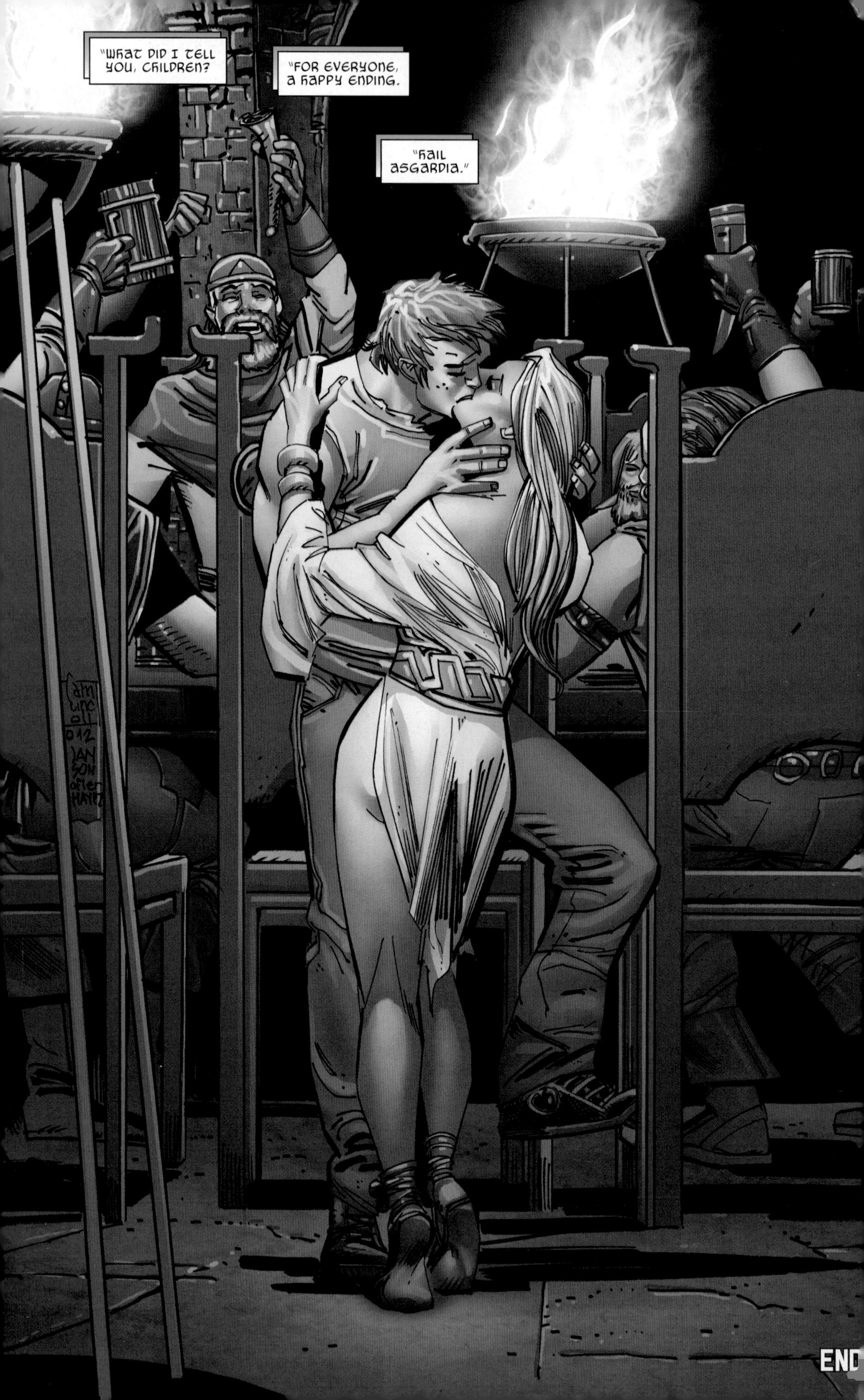
"WHAT DID I TELL YOU, CHILDREN?
"FOR EVERYONE, A HAPPY ENDING.
"HAIL ASGARDIA."
END

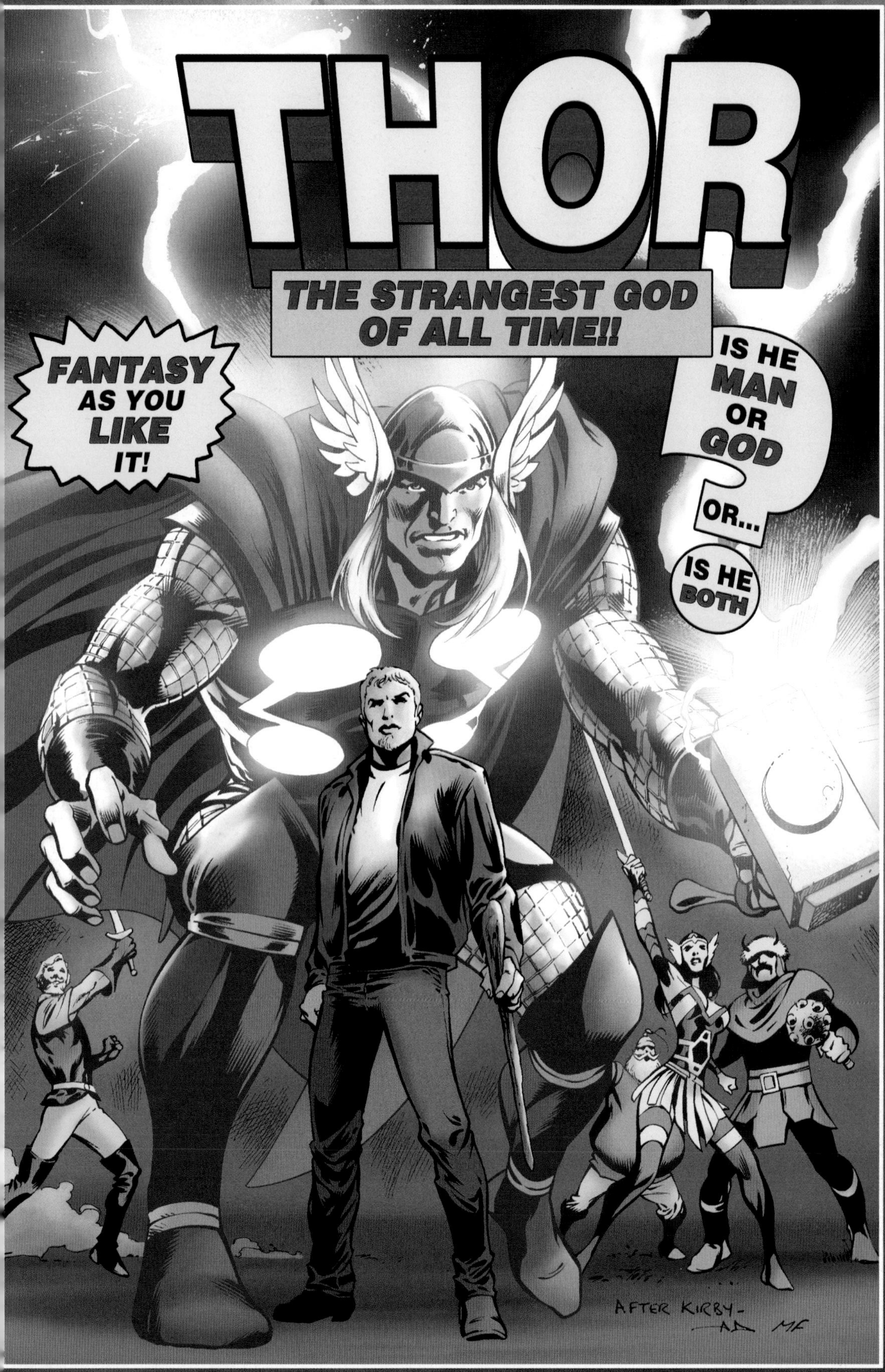
THOR
THE STRANGEST GOD OF ALL TIME!!
FANTASY AS YOU LIKE IT!
IS HE MAN OR GOD
OR...
IS HE BOTH
AFTER KIRBY- AD MF

#7 MARVEL 50TH ANNIVERSARY VARIANT
BY ALAN DAVIS, MARK FARMER & JAVIER RODRIGUEZ

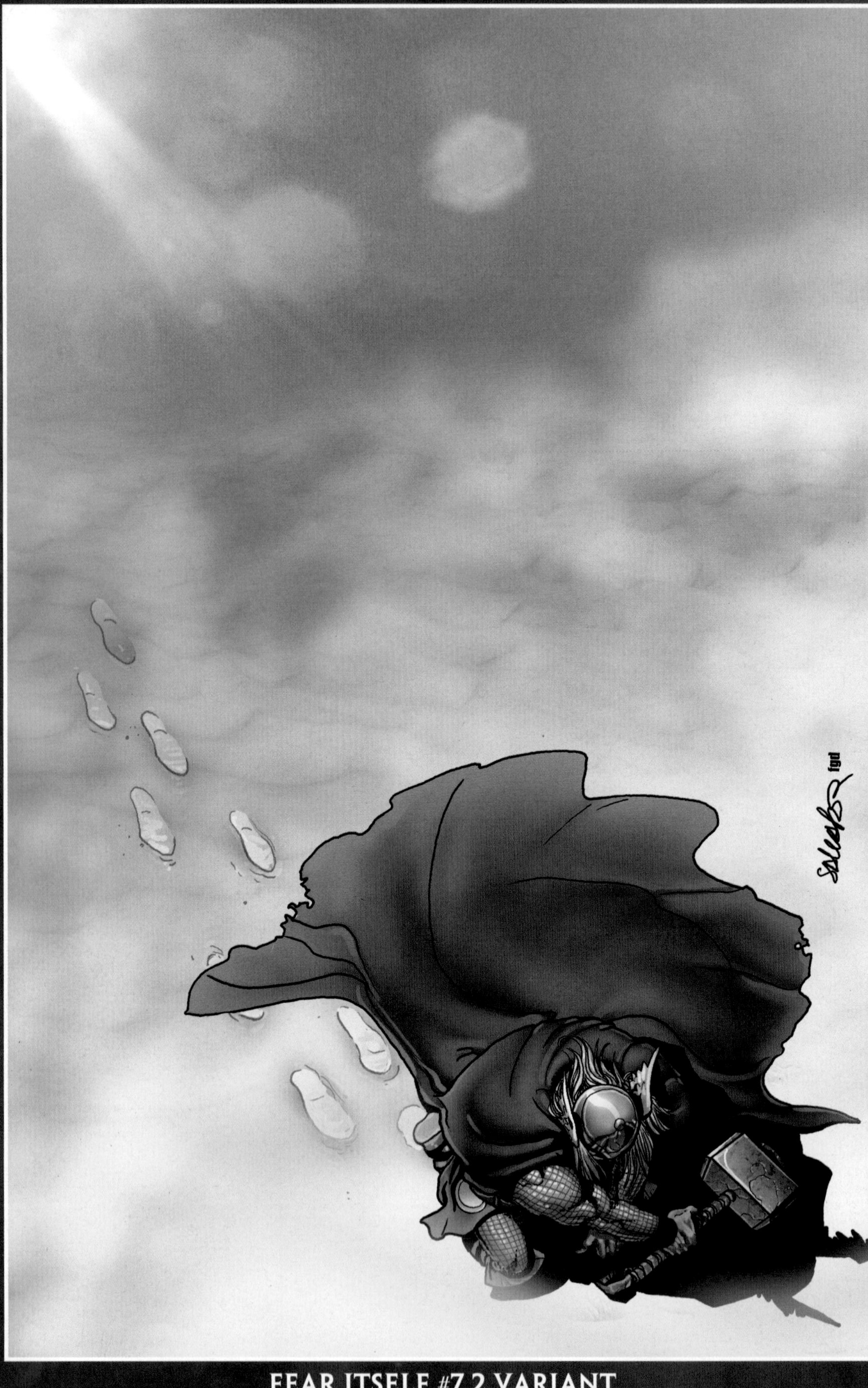

FEAR ITSELF #7.2 VARIANT
BY SALVADOR LARROCA & FRANK D'ARMATA

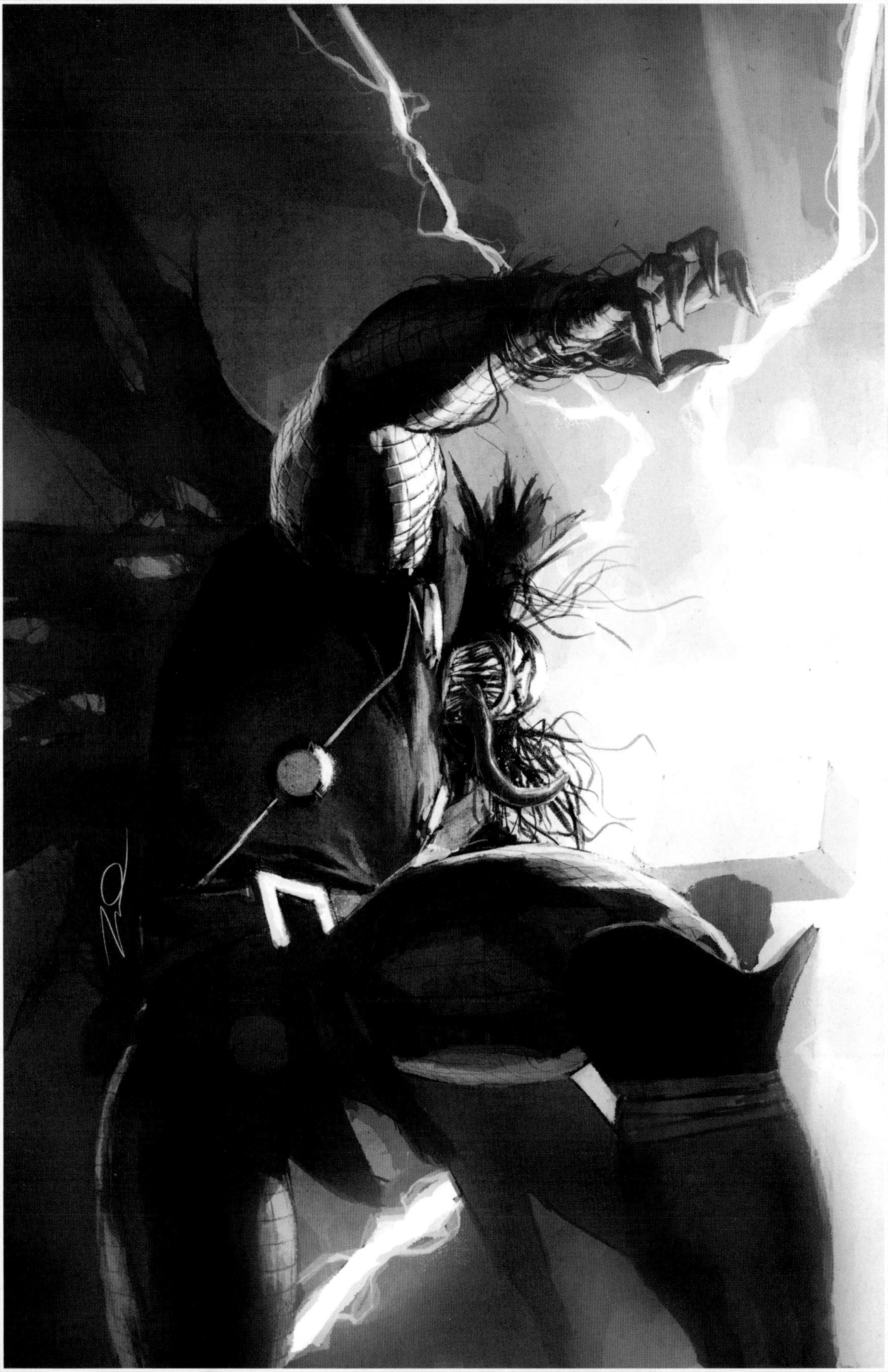

#10 VENOM VARIANT BY **GERALD PAREL**